国际法双语教学试用教材

本教材的出版受"推进上海自贸区建设的国际法律问题研究"项目（项目编号：B-6001-15-00602）资助。

国际税法

（第二版）

张泽平 主　编
李　泳　李　娜 副主编

北京大学出版社
PEKING UNIVERSITY PRESS

图书在版编目(CIP)数据

国际税法/张泽平主编. —2 版. —北京:北京大学出版社,2016.6
（国际法双语教学试用教材）
ISBN 978-7-301-16370-2

Ⅰ. ①国… Ⅱ. ①张… Ⅲ. ①国际税法—双语教学—高等学校—教材 Ⅳ. ①D996.3

中国版本图书馆 CIP 数据核字(2016)第 126768 号

书　　　名	国际税法（第二版） GUOJI SHUIFA
著作责任者	张泽平　主编　李　泳　李　娜　副主编
责任编辑	朱梅全　尹　璐
标准书号	ISBN 978-7-301-16370-2
出版发行	北京大学出版社
地　　　址	北京市海淀区成府路 205 号　100871
网　　　址	http://www.pup.cn
电子信箱	sdyy_2005@126.com
新浪微博	@北京大学出版社
电　　　话	邮购部 62752015　发行部 62750672　编辑部 021-62071998
印　刷　者	三河市北燕印装有限公司
经　销　者	新华书店
	730 毫米×980 毫米　16 开本　25.5 印张　458 千字 2014 年 3 月第 1 版 2016 年 6 月第 2 版　2020 年 7 月第 2 次印刷
定　　　价	52.00 元

未经许可，不得以任何方式复制或抄袭本书之部分或全部内容。
版权所有，侵权必究
举报电话：010-62752024　电子信箱：fd@pup.pku.edu.cn
图书如有印装质量问题，请与出版部联系，电话：010-62756370

第二版前言

自本教材第一版面世以来,国际税收领域发生了诸多重大事件。这些事件对当今国际税收秩序的变革和走向无疑将产生重大影响,尤其是2015年10月由经合组织出台,并由二十国集团领导人背书的"税基侵蚀和利润转移行动报告",更是标志着国际税收秩序自形成近百年以来的首次重大变革取得了实质性的进展。

二十国集团领导人于2013年9月发布《圣彼得堡宣言》,委托经合组织启动《税基侵蚀和利润转移行动方案》的15项行动计划,改革现行的国际税收规则体系。二十国集团及经合组织的所有成员国均以平等身份共同参与了相关工作,发展中国家通过征询机制加入了新规则的讨论和制定过程,非洲税收管理论坛、欧洲税收管理组织、美洲税收管理组织以及联合国、国际货币基金组织、世界银行等区域性或全球性国际组织也都参与了新规则的磋商过程,这使得税基侵蚀和利润转移行动项目成为一个具有全球性影响的国际税收合作项目。2015年10月5日,经合组织发布了该项目的最终成果报告,涵盖行动方案的所有15项行动计划。虽然这些报告不具有法律强制约束力,但参与各方的共识以及二十国集团国家领导人的背书标志着重塑国际税收治理体系的努力已得到国际政治层面的广泛认同。

近年来,我国在落实税收协定、完善税收法制方面步伐加快。我国政府还致力于加强多边和双边的国际税收合作,批准加入了《多边税收征管互助公约》,积极寻求"税基侵蚀和利润转移行动报告"在国内的落实,打造国际税收升级版。

可见,当前是国际税收秩序飞速发展的阶段,也是变革的关键阶段,为体现发展和变革的最新成果和动态,借编写第二版之际,我们对相关内容进行了更新。当然,由于内容较新,有些发展趋势还不够明朗,理论研究也还不够成熟,加之编者水平限制,第二版中难免还存在一些错误和疏漏之处,恳请读者予以指正。

编者
2016年4月

目　　录

第一章　绪论 ………………………………………………… 1
　　第一节　国际税法概述 …………………………………… 1
　　第二节　国际税法的产生与发展 ………………………… 14
　　本章阅读材料 ……………………………………………… 22

第二章　国际税收管辖权 …………………………………… 43
　　第一节　国际税收管辖权概述 …………………………… 43
　　第二节　居民税收管辖权的行使 ………………………… 46
　　第三节　收入来源地税收管辖权的行使 ………………… 51
　　第四节　公民税收管辖权的行使 ………………………… 56
　　第五节　电子商务对传统税收管辖权制度的挑战 ……… 61
　　本章阅读材料 ……………………………………………… 65

第三章　国际双重征税 ……………………………………… 75
　　第一节　国际双重征税概述 ……………………………… 75
　　第二节　法律性国际双重征税的解决方法 ……………… 77
　　第三节　经济性国际双重征税的解决方法 ……………… 82
　　第四节　税收饶让抵免 …………………………………… 85
　　本章阅读材料 ……………………………………………… 88

第四章　不同类型跨国所得的征税规则 …………………… 103
　　第一节　对跨国营业利润的征税 ………………………… 103
　　第二节　对跨国个人劳务所得的征税 …………………… 117
　　第三节　对跨国投资所得的征税 ………………………… 131
　　第四节　对跨国财产收益和其他所得的征税 …………… 144
　　本章阅读材料 ……………………………………………… 148

第五章　国际避税与反避税 ………………………………… 166
　　第一节　国际避税与反避税概述 ………………………… 166
　　第二节　滥用税收协定 …………………………………… 170
　　第三节　资本弱化 ………………………………………… 176

第四节　受控外国公司 …………………………………… 181
　　第五节　税基侵蚀和利润转移 …………………………… 185
　　本章阅读材料 ……………………………………………… 195

第六章　转让定价的法律制度 ………………………………… 228
　　第一节　转让定价概述 …………………………………… 228
　　第二节　规制转让定价的基本原则 ……………………… 233
　　第三节　针对转让定价的调整方法 ……………………… 236
　　第四节　避免和解决转让定价争议的方法 ……………… 245
　　第五节　关于无形资产转让定价的特殊考虑 …………… 249
　　第六节　关于集团内劳务转让定价的特殊考虑 ………… 254
　　第七节　成本分摊协议 …………………………………… 257
　　第八节　UN转让定价指南 ……………………………… 260
　　本章阅读材料 ……………………………………………… 262

第七章　国际税务合作的法律机制 …………………………… 308
　　第一节　国际税收竞争及其协调 ………………………… 308
　　第二节　国际税收情报交换 ……………………………… 312
　　第三节　税款协助征收与文书送达 ……………………… 323
　　第四节　国际税收争端的解决 …………………………… 328
　　本章阅读材料 ……………………………………………… 339

附录一　联合国税收协定范本（2011年版本）……………… 346

附录二　经合组织税收协定范本（2014年版本）…………… 378

第一章 绪 论

第一节 国际税法概述

一、国际税法的定义

国际税法是调整国际税收关系的法律规范的总和。由于对国际税法的内涵和外延认识不一致,目前关于国际税法的具体定义存有"广义论""狭义论""新国际税法论"等学说。从不同学说的具体阐述看,分歧的实质在于对国际税收的不同认识,即对国际税收理解的不一致是导致对作为调整国际税收关系的法律规范总和的国际税法理解不一致的直接和主要原因。因此,在探讨国际税法的定义之前,必须先对国际税收加以界定,并在此基础上厘清国际税收与国际税法的关系。

（一）国际税收的概念和本质

何谓"国际税收",不仅国内外学者之间认识不一,国内不同学者也是各持己见。有学者认为,国际税收是两个或两个以上的主权国家或拥有相对独立税收主权的地区,在对跨国纳税人行使各自的征税权力而形成的征纳关系中,所发生的涉及国家或地区之间税收等直接利益和涉及经济发展等潜在的间接利益的分配关系,是两个或两个以上的主权国家或拥有相对独立税收主权的地区,由于对参与国际经济活动的纳税人行使税收管辖权而引起的一系列税收活动。[1] 也有学者认为,国际税收就是两个或两个以上国家的政府,在对跨国纳税人行使各自的税收权力而形成的征纳关系中所发生的国家之间的税收分配关系。我国著名学者邓子基教授则指出：国际税收就是在国际经济活动中协调国家与国家之间的税收分配关系,国际税收研究的是国际经济活动中各个国家与有关的跨国纳税人之间的税收法律规范,以及由此而产生的有关国家与国家之间的税收分配关系。[2]

从上述不同观点看,国际税收的概念存在"狭义说"和"广义说"之分。狭义的国际税收仅指两个或两个以上的国家在凭借政治权力对从事跨国活动的纳税

---

[1] 参见胡华：《浅析国际税收概念》,载《经济论坛》2004年第7期。
[2] 参见靳东升：《邓子基教授与中国国际税收研究评述》,载《涉外税务》2007年第5期。

人征税时所形成的国家与国家之间的税收利益分配关系。各国的涉外税收应属于国内税收的范畴而排除在国际税收概念之外,即国际税收不包括各国的涉外税收。广义说认为,国际税收除了指国家与国家之间的税收利益分配关系外,还应包括各国的涉外税收。

有学者对这种"狭义说"与"广义说"的区分采取了另外一种表述,认为国际税收的概念存在"分配关系论"和"两重关系论"两种。按照"分配关系论",国际税收是指两个或两个以上的国家政府,在对跨国纳税人行使各自的征税权力而形成的征纳关系中所发生的国家之间的税收分配关系。"两重关系论"则认为国际税收是各国涉外税收的延伸和扩展,没有各国的涉外税收,便没有国家之间的税收分配关系,也就不存在各国税收权益的国际协调,国际税收的概念应包括两个方面的含义:一方面是各国政府与跨国纳税人之间的征纳关系;另一方面是国家之间的税收分配关系。[1]

不难发现,不论是"广义说"和"狭义说",抑或是"分配关系论"和"两重关系论",实质上都是以国际税收是否包括各国的涉外税收为界限,主张国际税收包括各国涉外税收的为"广义说"或"两重关系论",主张国际税收不包括各国涉外税收的为"狭义说"或"分配关系论"。于是乎,涉外税收和国际税收的关系又成了学者们讨论的对象。

尽管对于国际税收是否包括涉外税收存在分歧,但国内近乎所有学者都认为国际税收与涉外税收是既有区别又有联系的两个概念,不过对于这种区别与联系的具体内容,却又是众说纷纭。

有学者指出,涉外税收是一国税收制度中有关对外国纳税人(包括外国企业和个人)征税的部分,反映的是一国政府凭借其政治权力同其管辖范围内的外国纳税人之间所发生的征纳关系;而国际税收是一种国际关系,反映的是国与国之间在税收权益分配方面所形成的关系。[2] 另有学者认为,涉外税收概念与国际税收概念在内涵上的差异性和外延上的一致性决定了两者既有密切的联系,又有显著的区别。从内涵上看,涉外税收反映的是以国家为一方主体和以涉外纳税人为另一方主体所形成的税收征纳关系。而国际税收反映的是双重关系,第一重关系反映的是以国家一方为主体和以涉外纳税人为另一方主体所形成的税收征纳关系;第二重关系反映的是以国家一方为主体和以相关国家为另一方主体所形成的国家之间的税收分配关系。从概念外延上看,涉外税收和国际税收

---

[1] 参见尹音频:《国际税收与涉外税收关系新辨》,载《财经科学》1996年第4期。
[2] 参见杨志清:《国际税收理论与实践:回顾和展望》,载《国际税收》2013年第7期。

概念是一致的,具体包括两个方面:一是对跨国流动商品的征税,二是对跨国所得和一般财产价值的课税。①

还有学者认为国际税收与涉外税收二者的联系在于:二者在内涵方面都包含了国家政府之间的税收分配关系,外延方面都包含对跨国商品、跨国所得及跨国一般财产价值课税。二者的区别在于:首先,两者的后盾不同。涉外税收是以某一国的政治权力为后盾,而国际税收则没有超国家的政治权力为后盾。其次,两者的本质不同。涉外税收的本质是税收征纳分配关系与国家之间的税收分配关系,而国际税收本质则是国际税收关系,它包含国际税收协调关系与国际税收分配关系。最后,二者的立足点不同。一国的涉外税收主要立足于国内,而国际税收则立足于国际。②

上述众说纷纭的讨论反映了学界对国际税收这一基础理论问题的重视。不过,诚如有学者指出,不同研究者从各自的理解出发,对国际税收的概念这一基础问题产生了不同认识,这种局面不利于国际税收理论和实践的发展。③ 其实,"国际税收"是从英文"International Taxation"翻译而来的,但"International Taxation"原本的含义与我国许多学者对"国际税收"的理解并不完全一致,按照国外对国际税收的传统定义,国际税收是一个国家对外国人来源于本国的收入或财富所征的税以及对本国公民、居民或企业来源于境外的收入或财富所课的税。这一定义将国际税收具体化为国家的税收制度,使之与特定国家相联系。正因为如此,有学者认为,只存在某一个国家的国际税收,而不存在国际的国际税收。④ 另外,国外的一些相关著作对国际税收与涉外税收也不加区分。例如,美国著名的国际税收专家罗伊·罗哈吉在其《国际税收基础》一书中将国际税收定义为"对在两个或两个以上国家之间进行的跨境交易行为进行征税的一系列税收规则"⑤。保罗·R.麦克丹尼尔与休·J.奥尔特合著的《美国国际税收概论》更是将国际税收和涉外税收的概念等同起来。⑥ 这些表述在一定程度上代表了西方学者对国际税收这一现象的认识,对我们理解相关概念具有重要的参考价值。

---

① 参见郑榕:《关于涉外税收和国际税收学科概念内涵和外延的再界定》,载《扬州大学税务学院学报》1999年第3期。
② 参见尹音频:《国际税收与涉外税收关系新辨》,载《财经科学》1996年第4期。
③ 参见吕鹏:《国际税收概念的三个不足》,载《涉外税务》1995年第5期。
④ 同上。
⑤ 〔美〕罗伊·罗哈吉:《国际税收基础》,林海宁、范文祥译,北京大学出版社2006年版,第1页。
⑥ 参见郑榕:《关于涉外税收和国际税收学科概念内涵和外延的再界定》,载《扬州大学税务学院学报》1999年第3期。

在概念移植的过程中,由于不同的法律体系和法制传统的影响,对同一概念在移植前后赋予不同的内涵是难以避免的,我们固然可以参考国外理论与实务界对国际税收的理解,但也未必要与之等同,国际税收这一概念毕竟也不为西方国家所特有。作为一种理论研究和学术探讨,除了要探求相关概念的本质以外,还要注重学科体系的科学性和完整性。本书认为广义的国际税收说比较全面地反映了其本质,具有其合理性,下文的论述均以广义的国际税收说为基础,即主张国际税收不仅包括不同国家之间的税收分配关系,同时还包括一国的涉外税收征纳关系。

(二)国际税法的概念

虽然目前国内学界普遍认为,国际税法是调整国际税收法律规范的总称,但在具体讨论时,往往对国际税收和国际税法二者的内涵和外延的界限缺乏必要的区分,这一点从目前国内主流教材的内容和体系安排可见一斑。不论是国际税收教材,还是国际税法教材,基本上都是以税收管辖权、国际双重征税、国际逃税与避税规制、国际税收协调等为主要内容,而且具体阐释也都大同小异。[①] 这种现象至少说明国际税收与国际税法之间的区别尚没有得到应有的重视和体现。

实际上,国际税法和国际税收是分属两个范畴的概念。国际税收是经济范畴,国际税法是法律范畴;国际税收是国际税法产生的经济前提,国际税法是规范和促进国际税收发展的法律保障。国际税法以国际税收为调整对象。严格说来,广义与狭义不是针对国际税法的概念而言,而是从其调整对象或法律渊源等其他角度来谈的。为了避免造成理解上的混乱,本书仍按照当前国内主流学说,将国际税法的概念分为狭义说、广义说和新国际税法说三种情形加以介绍。

1. 狭义说

狭义国际税法说认为,国际税法的调整对象仅限于国家间的税收分配关系,其渊源仅限于国家与国家之间的税收条约、协定,各国的涉外税法不能成为国际税法的渊源。

2. 广义说

该学说主张国际税法的调整对象不仅包括国家间的税收分配关系,而且还包括一国政府与跨国纳税人之间的涉外税收征纳关系。其法律规范除了包括调

[①] 参见程永昌主编:《国际税收学》(第2版),中国税务出版社2006年版;李志辉主编:《国际税收学》,科学出版社2006年版;刘剑文主编:《国际税法学》(第二版),北京大学出版社2004年版。

整国家间税收分配关系的国际税收条约以外,还包括各国国内的涉外税法。①

3. 新国际税法说

新国际税法说的内容包括:国际税法的调整对象是国际税收协调关系。所谓国际税收协调关系,是指两个或两个以上的国家或地区在协调它们之间的税收关系的过程中所产生的各种关系的总称。所谓税收关系,是指各相关主体在围绕税收的征管和协作等活动的过程中所产生的与税收有关的各种关系的总称。国际税法不调整国家与涉外纳税人之间的涉外税收征纳关系。国际税法的渊源包括条约、惯例和国际法院关于税收纠纷的判例,各国的涉外税法属于国内法,不是国际税法的渊源。新国际税法说还认为,涉外税法与国际税法的关系十分密切,决定了涉外税法是国际税法学的一个重要研究对象,涉外税法学也成为国际税法学中一个重要的组成部分,但涉外税法成为国际税法学的研究对象这一前提并不能当然地得出国际税法包括涉外税法的结论。②

尽管新国际税法说详尽地阐释了该学说与广义说和狭义说的区别,其视角也不乏独到之处,但从其内容看,新说与狭义说却极近相似,目前理论界在述及国际税法的概念时,仍然多提狭义说和广义说。在广义说与狭义说之间,绝大多数学者都主张广义说。本书在下文的论述中也主张广义的国际税法说,即国际税法作为国际经济法的一个独立法律分支,是调整国家涉外税收征纳关系和国家间税收分配关系的法律规范的总和。

二、国际税法的调整对象

简言之,国际税法的调整对象是国际经济活动中主权国家与跨国纳税人之间的税收征纳关系,以及由此产生的有关国家之间的税收分配关系。它包括两层含义:第一,它反映了一个国家对跨国纳税人的征税权及其征税制度;第二,它反映了国家之间税收权益的分配,两者互为条件,相互依赖。

由于两个或两个以上国家对税收具有管辖权,而同一纳税义务人在两个或两个以上国家负有双重纳税义务,因此,国际税收关系的内容必然具有双重性质,即一方面表现为主权国家与具有跨国所得的纳税人之间的税收征纳关系,另一方面则又表现为相关国家之间就纳税人的跨国所得的税收利益分配关系。

理论上说,税收分配关系和税收征纳关系是两个不同层面上的调整对象,如

---

① 参见刘剑文、李刚:《国际税法特征之探析》,载《武汉大学学报(哲学社会科学版)》1999年第4期。
② 参见翟继光:《国际税法学新论——兼论广义国际税法论的缺陷》,载《时代法学》2004年第4期。

果说前者侧重于国际税收基础理论,那么后者就是在基础理论指导下的特定国家的国际税收,但这两个不同层面之间的界限已越来越模糊,国际税法通常是对国家的涉外税收征纳关系和国家间的税收分配关系两个层次同时进行调整的。尽管从单个的国际税收法律规范看,其调整对象的单一性仍然存在,但实际上国家在对跨国纳税人的某项具体所得征税时,其中既包括了国家对跨国纳税人的跨国所得的征纳关系,也涉及国家之间的税收分配关系。[①]

三、国际税法的渊源

国际税法的渊源是指国际税法的表现形式。由于国际税收关系是以纳税人的跨国所得为基础所形成的一种特殊的经济分配关系,它既涉及国家与跨国纳税人的权益,又涉及相关国家的权益分配,因而调整国际税收关系的法律规范亦呈现出多样性的特点。总体上看,国际税法的渊源包括国际法规范和国内法规范,国际法规范又包括国际条约和国际惯例。

(一)国际税收条约

1. 概念及分类

国际税收条约(International Tax Treaty),亦称国际税收协定,是指两个或两个以上的主权国家,为了协调相互间在处理跨国纳税人征纳事务方面的税收关系,依照对等原则,通过政府间谈判所缔结的确定各自在国际税收方面的权利义务关系的一种书面协议。在税收国际化的历史条件下,国家税收权益关系的协调,主要是通过有关当事国之间缔结的国际税收协定来作出规范。国际税收协定已成为各国之间避免国际双重征税、调节国家之间的税收利益分配、促进国际经济合作的最有效手段之一。国际税收协定可以按照不同的标准加以分类。按照缔约方数量可以分为双边协定和多边协定;按照适用的税种可以分为所得税协定、关税协定等;按照协定的内容可以分为专项协定和综合协定。

2. 产生与发展

从根源看,国际税收协定的产生是以下三要素共同推动的结果:第一,随着国际经济合作的不断扩大,国际双重征税现象日趋突出,严重制约了国际经济合作和技术交流的正常进行,客观上需要以某种方式来规范和划分国家之间的税收管辖权。第二,国际上逃避税现象日趋猖獗,各国很难单独控制和防止跨国纳税人的逃避税活动,迫切需要加强国际税务合作,采取共同措施来防止国际逃避

---

① 参见刘剑文、李刚:《国际税法特征之探析》,载《武汉大学学报(哲学社会科学版)》1999年第4期。

税的发生。第三,为防止国际税收歧视,各国有必要通过协定安排来实现税收无差别待遇,为各国之间的经济合作扫除障碍。

正是在上述因素的推动下,早在19世纪中叶就开始出现了世界上最早的税收协定。通说认为,最早的税收协定是1843年法国和比利时缔结的双边税收协定。但最早旨在解决国际重复征税问题的税收协定是由英国与瑞士于1872年缔结的,该协定主要涉及遗产税,而1899年奥匈帝国与普鲁士王国缔结的双边税收协定则主要以解决对所得和财产重复征税为内容。二战之后,国家之间缔结税收协定的情况更多,已成为协调国家之间税收利益分配的主要手段。与现代税收条约不同的是,早期的税收协定是通过加强国家之间行政和司法协助以防止逃避税、增加财政收入,而现代税收条约则更多的是为了避免双重征税,这一差异反映了税收从单纯作为取得财政收入的手段发展成为促进实现国家经济目标的经济杠杆。除此之外,当代国际税收协定的发展,还呈现出以下几个方面的特征:

一是国际税收协定的内容不断充实。早期税收协定的条款一般较少,内容也过于狭窄,主要是为了解决某一单一问题,而近年来所缔结的税收协定,内容越来越广泛,在税种上,已由单一税种扩展到多项税种;在纳税客体上,已由少数所得扩展到几乎全部所得;在协定目标上,已由单纯的避免重复征税扩展到包括征税权的划分、消除双重征税、防止国际逃避税等内容。

二是国际税收协定日趋规范化。国际税收协定的规范化主要是通过国际组织制定的税收协定范本来实现的。1963年,经济合作与发展组织(Organization for Economic Co-operation and Development,简称"经合组织"或"OECD")的24个成员国草拟了一份避免双重征税协定,并于1977年4月11日正式颁布并命名为《经济合作与发展组织关于对所得和财产避免双重征税的协定范本》(简称《经合组织税收协定范本》或《OECD范本》,见附录2),该范本后来经过1992年、1994年、1995年、1997年、2000年、2003年、2005年、2008年、2010年和2014年十次修订,目前的2014年新范本不仅用来指导经合组织成员国之间的税收协定谈判,同时也为该组织成员国与非成员国在税收协定谈判中提供了示范基础。

除《OECD范本》以外,联合国经济及社会理事会1979年通过了《关于发达国家与发展中国家间双重征税的协定范本》(简称《联合国税收协定范本》或《UN范本》,见附录1),该范本从1997年开始修订,并于2001年公布修订后的新版本。历经十年,2011年再次作出修订。该范本在总体结构上与《OECD范本》相似,但扩大了收入来源国的税收管辖权范围,以平衡发达国家和发展中国家的税收利益。该范本在发展中国家的税收协定实践中得到广泛运用。

三是多边税收协定逐渐增多。20世纪70年代以前,国际税收协定的绝大多数都是双边协定,很少有多边协定,但进入1970年以后,伴随着区域经济集团化的发展,出现了区域税收一体化,一体化的税收加强了区域内、外多边税收协定的发展。① 尽管目前的多边协定仍是区域性的,还远不是全球性的协定或公约,但随着经济全球化的进一步发展,这些区域性的多边税收协定将来一定能在更大的跨区域范围内缔结,甚至在全球范围内缔结。② 值得一提的是,最早由经合组织和欧洲理事会于1988年制定的《多边税收征管互助公约》在2010年修订后,向所有国家开放,不再局限于经合组织和欧洲理事会的成员国。截至2013年8月底,已有包括中国在内的56个国家签署了该公约,使之成为一个真正意义上的全球性多边税收公约。

四是专项性国际税收协定迅速发展。作为国际税法渊源的国际条约除了以避免和消除双重征税为主要目的的综合性条约以外,还包括与国际税收相关的其他协定,尤其是21世纪以来发展最为迅速的国际税收情报交换协定。国际税收情报交换是指各国的税务主管当局之间为税收征管目的而彼此交换情报的行为。③ 在经济全球化和跨国经营日益普遍化的背景下,一国的税务部门要了解跨国纳税人的跨国经营状况及其他涉税信息,在很大程度上要依赖于他国协助提供的有关情报。2002年4月,经合组织出台了《税收情报交换协定范本》,对情报交流请求的实施、拒绝、保密、国内立法、执行程序等问题都作出了详细规定。该范本的出台极大地推动了国际范围内情报交换专项协定的签署步伐,截至2012年底,已有近千个以此范本为蓝本的情报交换协定得以签署。可以说,国际税收情报交换协定已经成为国际税法的一个重要国际法渊源。

3. 内容

如前所述,国际税收协定可以分为不同的类型,分别规定了不同的内容,这里仅结合《OECD范本》或以《OECD范本》为蓝本的综合协定看,此类协定通常包括以下几个方面的内容:④

(1) 协定的适用范围

① 主体范围。即协定适用于哪些人。早期的双边税收协定一般仅对缔约国双方的公民适用,即国籍是确定协定主体范围的标准,而并不考虑纳税人的住

---

① 参见苑新丽:《国际税收协定的发展及面临的新问题》,载《财经问题研究》2003年第10期。
② 参见刘永伟:《国际税收协定的几个重大发展及其展望》,载《中国法学》2005年第1期。
③ 参见廖益新主编:《国际税法学》,高等教育出版社2008年版,第301页。
④ 参见曹建明、陈治东主编:《国际经济法专论》(第六卷),法律出版社2000年版,第133页。

所或居所。随着跨国投资活动的增多，各国为捍卫自身的经济权益，都纷纷以住所或居所原则来行使税收管辖权。

② 客体范围。即协定适用于哪些税种。税收协定的客体主要是所得，但也不限于所得，对一些特定财产的占有行为课征的财产税也可列入协定的适用范围。协定的客体适用范围的确定主要取决于缔约国国内税制的特殊要求。

③ 地域范围。国际税收协定原则上对缔约国的全部国家领土有效，包括缔约国实施有关国内税收法律的所有领土、领海，以及缔约国根据国际法所拥有的勘探和开发海底和底土资源以及海底以上水域资源的主权权利的领海以外的区域。

④ 时间范围。一般国际税收协定以交换批准书为生效要件。缔约国双方经过谈判协商，达成协议文本草案，然后由双方主管部门草签，最后经缔约国各方的权力机关批准，双方互换批准书后方可生效。国际税收协定生效后，一般应长期有效，除非条约本身规定了有效期限。

(2) 税收管辖权的划分和协调

税收管辖权的划分是国际税收协定的核心条款。在征税涉及他国或多国的情形下，需通过税收管辖权划分规则来确定应由哪一国行使优先征税权，哪一些情形可由一国行使独占征税权等等。通过签订国际税收协定，缔约国双方确定对营业所得、投资所得、劳务所得及其财产所得等的管辖原则，以此来合理地划分缔约国各方的税收管辖权范围。

(3) 避免国际双重征税的方法

国际双重征税是由于有关国家对跨国所得同时行使不同的税收管辖权导致冲突所产生的，要解决国家间对跨国纳税人的双重征税问题，除了需要通过划分税收管辖权来防范双重征税以外，还需要规定消除双重征税的措施，即缔约国之间需要协商确定对行使居民管辖权的居住国应该如何采取有效的措施，最终消除双重征税。大多数协定都规定了免税法和抵免法两种方法。

(4) 税收无差别待遇原则

避免税收歧视，实行税收无差别待遇原则是国际税收的一项重要原则。事实上，有关禁止税收歧视的条款规定，其历史远比在当今国际税收协定中的条款规定来得悠久，早在1535年法国与奥斯曼帝国缔结的贸易协定中就有禁止对缔约国的另一方国民实行税收歧视的规定。《UN范本》与《OECD范本》都在第24条明确规定了税收的无差别待遇原则条款，以保证缔约国一方的人在缔约国另一方应负担的纳税义务，不与缔约国另一方的人在相同或类似的情况下所受到的纳税待遇不同或比其负担更重。税收无差别待遇原则在国际税收协定条款规定中具体表现为：国籍无差别条款、常设机构无差别条款、扣除无差别条款和所有权无差别条款等。

（5）加强国际合作，防止国际逃避税

鉴于跨国纳税人利用各国税制的差异及其立法漏洞进行逃避税的活动日益猖獗，防止国际逃避税已成为国际税收协定的重要内容。通过在国际税收协定中规定情报交换及其他形式的国际税务合作形式，有利于消除和防止国际逃避税现象。

4．国际税收协定的解释

国际税收协定作为法律规则，其解释的必要性除来源于一般法律需要解释的共同原因之外，还源于其本身存在的一些特点。各国在谈判过程的立场妥协和利益平衡、促进国际贸易和投资活动发展以及最大限度维护本国税收主权的张力等因素都造成条文的含糊不清和模棱两可，都决定了国际税收协定规则需要法律解释。

税收协定是国际条约，因此应根据条约法所规定的解释方法进行解释，即《维也纳条约法公约》（简称《条约法公约》）第 31 条至第 32 条规定的文义解释、体系解释、目的解释和历史解释方法，这应是税收协定一般解释规则。同时，大部分税收协定的第 3 条第 2 款都规定了应用协定用语的国内税法含义进行解释这一独特方法，这就构成了税收协定的专门解释规则。很多国家都制定了关于税收协定解释的国内法规定，如我国国家税务总局在 2010 年制定了《〈中华人民共和国政府和新加坡共和国政府关于对所得避免双重征税和防止偷漏税的协定〉及议定书条文解释》（国税发[2010]75 号），并且明确规定这个解释文件不但适用于《中华人民共和国政府和新加坡共和国政府关于对所得避免双重征税和防止偷漏税的协定》的解释，而且也适用于其他协定相同条款的解释及执行。虽然国内法对于税收协定的解释有重要作用，但是协定第 3 条第 2 款本身的解释还是应根据《条约法公约》进行，因此，第 3 条第 2 款的适用并没有排除《条约法公约》的适用。

在国际法上，国际条约的解释主体为缔约国全体或者经授权的某些专门机构。税收协定的解释虽然是对国际条约的解释，但其解释主要是由缔约国一方的税务机关和国内法院进行，而且税收协定的解释过程同时受到国际法和国内法的调整和制约，因此，必须同时结合国际法与国内法的规定才能全面地剖析税收协定的解释问题。例如，纯粹从国际法的角度来看，税收协定的解释在于查明和贯彻缔约国双方的共同意思。但在税收协定解释实践中，如果这一共同意思与本国立法机关立法意图不相符，缔约国国内法院最终不得不受制于本国宪法的规定,以本国立法机关的立法意图为准。① 但是,除非缔约国另一方明示接受,否则缔约国一方单方面的解释并非有权解释,对缔约国另一方不应有拘束力。

(二) 国际税收惯例

国际惯例是在长期国际交往中逐渐形成的不成文的法律规范,由具有法律约束力的"国际习惯"和尚不具有法律约束力的"通例"两部分组成。根据《国际法院规约》第 38 条第 1 款的规定,国际习惯是"作为通例之证明而经接受为法律者"。这就是说,一项规则要成为国际惯例必须具备两个条件:一是"物质因素",即长期实践中重复类似行为而形成普遍的习惯做法;二是"心理因素",即这种做法被国家和当事人认可而具有法律效力。

国际税收惯例是指在国际经济交往中处理国家间税收权益关系,反复出现并被各国广泛接受,因而具有法律约束力的税收通例,是国际税收关系的行为准则。② 一般认为,国际税收协定优先原则、在外国人税收待遇标准上的无差别原则、全面税收管辖权应限于居民纳税人原则、外交税收豁免原则等应视为国际税收惯例。③ 各国在协调处理税收权益的分配关系中,应当充分尊重和遵循这些国际税收惯例,只有这样才能体现国际税收关系中的平等互利原则,才能促进国际经济合作和技术交流的发展。④

(三) 国内法

国际税法的国内法渊源主要体现为各国的涉外税法,包括涉外所得税法和财产税法。它既包括各国立法和行政机关颁布的涉外税收法律法规,又包括英美法系国家司法机关的涉外税收判例。各国涉外税法虽有不少法律规范直接涉及国家间的税收分配关系,但国内法渊源在调整国际税收关系中的主要功能和作用,是调整该国与跨国纳税人之间的税收征纳关系,即确定国家对跨国征税对象的税收管辖权、征税范围和程度及课税的方式和程序。⑤ 判断一国税法是否属于国际税法的渊源,并不在于其法律名称是否冠以"国际"或"涉外"字样,而是看其内容是否调整国际税收关系。

---

① 具体案例可见本章阅读材料中的 Pierre Boulez v. Commissioner of Internal Revenue, 83 T. C. 584 (1984)。
② 参见刘志诚、王诚尧:《正确认识和运用税收国际惯例》,载《涉外税务》1995 年第 1 期。
③ 参见王选汇:《国际税收惯例纵横谈》,载《涉外税务》1995 年第 1 期。
④ 参见曹建明、陈治东主编:《国际经济法专论》(第六卷),法律出版社 2000 年版,第 5 页。
⑤ 参见廖益新:《国际税法学》,高等教育出版社 2008 年版,第 5 页。

四、国际税法的基本原则

原则可以分为基本原则和具体原则。国际税法的基本原则是指适用于国际税法的各个方面,构成国际税法的基础,并对国际税法的制定和实施等具有指导意义的信念。基本原则具有普遍适用性、基础性和稳定性,如果不满足这三个方面的特性,如某项原则只能适用于国际税法的某一个方面,或者不能构成国际税法的基础,则只能构成国际税法的具体原则。

区分国际税法的基本原则与具体原则具有非常重要的意义。基本原则由于具有稳定性,因而容易确定,而具体原则不具有稳定性,在国际税法的不同分支范围内,其具体原则有不同的内容。目前,关于国际税法的原则国内理论界分歧较大,权威学者之间也未能达成一致认识。产生这种分歧的主要原因就在于没有将基本原则与具体原则加以区分,而是笼统地讨论国际税法的原则。本书认为,国际税法的基本原则包括税收主权原则、国际合作原则和公平原则。

(一) 税收主权原则

税收主权是国家主权在国际税收领域的体现。国家主权是国家最重要的属性,是国家固有的在国内的最高权力和在国际上的独立权力。由于这种权力不可分割和不可让与,不从属于外来的意志与干预,因此,主权在国内是最高的,在国际上是独立的。质言之,国家独立自主地处理自己的内外事务、管理自己国家的权力就是国家主权。[①] 对内最高性和对外独立性是国家主权最重要的两个特征,对内最高性表现为国家对其领土内的一切人和物以及领土外的本国人享有属地优越权和属人优越权,主权国家可以通过立法等各种手段来实现自己的统治,而不受任何其他力量的干预和限制。独立性是指国家有权独立自主地处理其主权范围内的事务,国家处理这些事务不受外来的干涉。[②]

作为国家主权在国际税收领域的体现,税收主权有两个方面的含义:一是对本国涉外税收实施征管的权力,即指一国可以根据本国国情和自身发展需要独立自主地制定本国的涉外税法,包括确定税收管辖权的基础、税基与税率、税收优惠措施等。二是独立自主地参与国际税收利益分配的权力,包括参与国际税收条约的谈判与签订、参与国际税收争端的解决等。

(二) 国际合作原则

国际合作原则是指各国不论政治、经济、社会制度有何差异,在双边或多边

[①] 参见王铁崖主编:《国际法》,法律出版社 1981 年版,第 67 页。
[②] 参见杨泽伟:《主权论——国际法上的主权问题及其发展趋势研究》,北京大学出版社 2006 年版,第 7 页。

交往中都应该互相协助和合作。在国际税收中,按照税收主权原则,各国可以独立自主地制定本国的涉外税收法律,这就有可能导致不同国家税收法律之间的冲突,而这种冲突将具体表现为一系列的问题,如双重或多重征税,即不同国家对同一应税项目均实行征税。另外,各国税法冲突还会为国际逃避税提供操作空间,即跨国纳税人可以利用不同国家之间税收政策的差异,通过转移成本或利润等手段,将应税所得从高税率国家转移至低税率甚至是零税率国家。显然,这些都将严重影响正常的国际税收秩序,同时也不利于各国税收政策的实施。

解决上述冲突的有效途径便是加强国际合作。在国际税收中,国际合作的主要形式就是通过双边或多边协定确立合作框架,建立包括税收管辖权协调、信息交流、争端解决等在内的合作机制。目前,已有联合国、经合组织、东盟、安第斯共同体等国际组织制定了税收协定范本,各国在借鉴协定范本的基础上,结合各国具体情形,已签署各类税收协定六千多项。

这里需要指出的是,国际合作原则不仅体现在税收利益分配关系上,各国即便在制定本国的涉外税收征管法规时,也充分体现了国际合作原则,如税收抵免、饶让等制度都是国际合作原则的体现。正是从这个意义上说,国际合作原则贯穿各国涉外税收征纳和国际税收利益分配的全面关系中,构成国际税法的基本原则。

（三）公平原则

公平原则既是国内税法的基本原则,同时也是国际税法的基本原则。但公平原则在国内税法和国际税法中的含义是不一样的。国内税法中的公平原则主要是针对纳税人的纳税负担而言的,即指税收征纳关系中的公平。与此相比,国际税法中公平原则的含义要丰富得多,包括了国家间税收分配关系中的公平和涉外税收征纳关系中的公平。[①] 税收分配公平,是指各个主权国家在其税收管辖权独立的基础上平等地享有国际税收利益的分配。税收征纳公平又包括两个方面的含义,一是指跨国纳税人所承担的税收负担应与其经济状况和承受能力相适应,二是指经济情况相同的纳税人应承担相同的税收负担。

在国际税法中强调公平原则具有重要的理论和实践意义。当前由于不同国家的发达程度不一致,发达国家在资本输出的质和量方面都较发展中国家处于优势,如果发达国家利用自身的优势地位,强化居民税收管辖权,弱化来源地税收管辖权,则必将影响到广大发展中国家在国际税收利益分配中的应有份额,不

[①] 参见刘剑文、李刚:《国际税法特征之探悉》,载《武汉大学学报(哲学社会科学版)》1999 年第 4 期。

利于国际经济新秩序的构建。另外,有些国家在制定本国的涉外税收法律制度的过程中,对本国纳税人和外国纳税人区别对待,规定不同的税收负担,这样也人为地扭曲了市场环境,不利于企业之间展开公平竞争。① 只有坚持公平原则,才能既保证发达国家和发展中国家在国际税收分配关系中得到平等的对待,同时也为不同纳税人提供公平有序的竞争环境。

第二节 国际税法的产生与发展

一、国际税法的产生

税收作为一种历史现象,是国家的政治权力作用于经济的产物,反映着特定的社会分配关系。自从有了国家,国家为了实现其职能,就要向纳税人征税,取得财政收入。但这一数千年来的税收征纳关系,过去一般都严格限制在一国的疆域范围之内。因为一国的政治权力所管辖的范围一般仅限于本国的疆界,所以在税收产生之后的相当长的历史时期内,税收只能在一国领域内征收,不涉及其他国家的财政收入。

19世纪末20世纪初期,世界主要资本主义国家都纷纷步入垄断阶段,这一阶段的主要特征就是资本输出。一战以后,各主要资本主义国家大量的资本输出带来了大规模收入的国际化,国家与国家之间在税收问题上的矛盾不断产生且日益加剧。特别是二战后,资本和生产的国际化趋势愈加明显,纳税人收入的国际化规模不断扩大。这种收入和财产国际化现象的普遍存在和不断发展,为国际税收关系的产生和国际税收法制的形成提供了必要的经济基础。

由于纳税人收入的国际化,当主权国家采取不同的征税原则时,势必将出现对跨国纳税人的同一征税对象重复征税的情况。例如,一个在A国境内居住的A国公民甲,通过在B国从事经营活动从B国取得收入100万元,A国作为甲的居住国要对该笔收入征税,B国作为该笔收入的来源国也要对其征税,双重征税现象由此而产生。此外,由于各国存在税负水平和税收稽征水平的差异,这也很容易为跨国纳税人利用,从事国际逃税和避税活动。所有这一切,必然会引起相关国家如何对纳税人的跨国所得进行税收协调与分配的问题,即税收的国际化问题。在国际税收实践中,如果没有一个共同的准则作为指导,将直接影响到国与国之间的税收分配关系,影响到国际商品、劳务、技术和资金的流动,直接制

---

① 我国曾根据《企业所得税法》和《外商投资企业和外国企业所得税法》对内外资企业区别对待。从2008年1月1日起实行"两法合并",根据新的《企业所得税法》,内外资企业享受同等待遇。

约各国经济的发展。在这种情形下,主权国家一方面为维护自己的经济主权,另一方面也为了适应国际经济关系相互依存的格局,就必须和有关国家进行税收上的合作协调和调整,或者通过国内法上的单边调整,抑或通过国际上的双边或多边调整,并将两者有机地结合起来。于是,调整现代国际税收关系的国际税法便应运而生。[①]

二、当代国际税法的发展趋势

当代经济全球化背景下,国际税法的发展趋势呈现以下几个方面的特点:

(一) 国际税法规范不断充实和完善

国际税法是伴随着各国所得税制的创设而逐渐形成的,但国际税法的充分发展,特别是协调各国税收权益分配关系的国际税收法律规范的大量出现则是在二战以后。二战以来,国际双重征税与国际逃避税问题已给国与国之间的经济交往带来了重大障碍,各国政府都在努力寻求国际税收制度的健全途径和方法,并且取得了重大进展,具体表现为:

第一,国家之间缔结国际税收协定的步伐不断加快,协定的广度和深度不断发展。二战以后,各国政府为消除国际双重征税、国际逃避税以及税收歧视对国际经济合作产生的不利影响,深刻体会到必须缔结国际税收协定,并逐步使之向规范化方向演进。20世纪70年代末80年代初,《OECD范本》和《UN范本》的诞生标志着国际税收协定规范化的开始。

20世纪80年代以前,国际税收协定的缔结国主要是在发达国家之间。进入80年代之后,国际税收协定的缔结又出现了新的动向:首先,参与缔结国际税收协定的国家数量越来越多。当今国际税收协定已从发达国家向发展中国家扩展,并从双边协定向多边协定演进。截至2015年8月底,我国已与100个国家正式签署避免双重征税协定,其中97个协定已生效;另外,内地和香港、澳门两个特别行政区签署了避免双重征税安排,与台湾地区签署了《海峡两岸避免双重课税及加强税务合作协议》。[②] 尤为值得一提的是,一些过去对国际税收协定一向反应冷漠的国家或地区,如尼泊尔、卡塔尔、沙特阿拉伯、百慕大等也纷纷采取行动,积极与其他国家签署国际税收协定。其次,国际税收协定的内容也有所扩大。传统的国际税收协定的税种适用范围一般仅限于所得税和财产税,现在有

---

① 参见曹建明、陈治东主编:《国际经济法专论》(第六卷),法律出版社2000年版,第13—14页。
② 资料来源:http://www.chinatax.gov.cn/n810341/n810770/index.html,2015年12月1日访问。

些双边税收协定已将税种范围扩展到社会保障税、增值税和消费税等税种。总之,各国政府为协调解决跨国税收分配问题,通过谈判协商签署了大量的双边税收协定,国际税收协定网络已遍及发达国家和发展中国家,并且还在不断向纵深方向发展。

第二,各国的涉外税法日臻完善。目前,世界各国都致力于在国际经济合作与交往中运用税收管辖权来参与国际税收权益的划分和对其收益的分享,以维护各自的国家主权和经济利益。特别是那些对外国投资实行税收优惠原则的国家,出于某些税收政策上的考虑,往往制定了一些特别适用于涉外税收关系的专门单行法规。例如,我国七届人大第四次会议于1991年4月通过的《外商投资企业和外国企业所得税法》以及国务院于1991年6月发布的《外商投资企业和外国企业所得税法实施细则》就是专门调整涉外税收关系的单行法规。进入21世纪以来,随着国内和国际经济形势的变化,我国积极调整涉外税收政策,从2008年1月1日起实行新的《企业所得税法》,统一适用于外资和内资企业。当然,新法的通过并不是说就完全内外统一,甚至不存在涉外税法了,涉外税法不仅依然存在,而且是更加科学和完善了。

(二) 区域税收协调步伐加快

自20世纪80年代以来,随着国际经济合作与交往日益向集团化、区域化方向发展,特别是国际贸易的关税壁垒和非关税壁垒逐步得到消除,各国间商品、资本、技术和劳动力的跨国流动更为密切,出现了税收一体化的新格局。在推行税收一体化的进程中,欧共体国家一直走在世界前列。早在欧共体成立初期,就不断努力推动共同体成员国内部的政治与经济一体化进程。在税制方面,1968年,欧共体取消了工业品内部关税,并统一了对外关税税率。翌年又取消了农产品的内部关税。而后,欧共体在增值税方面也采取了一系列重大步骤,从1967年到1986年欧共体连续颁布了有关增值税的21个指令,以协调各成员国增值税,如缩小成员国之间的税率差别,规定统一的征税原则,规范清算制度等。目前,欧盟已开始就与所得税协调有关的股息转让定价、企业重组等问题展开协调。欧盟所采取的种种税收一体化措施,大大推进了欧洲统一市场的形成,同时也为世界其他地区的税收一体化提供了可资借鉴的经验。继欧盟之后,区域性经济组织相继成立,如中美洲共同市场、新西兰—澳大利亚自由贸易区、北美自由贸易区、东南亚国家联盟、安第斯共同市场、非洲统一组织等。目前,已形成西欧、北美和东亚三大经济区域,充分体现着不同国家间内外部的经济及税收利益矛盾与协调关系。① 长期以来，人们都期盼在全球建立一个统一的多边国际税收协调体系，而区域性的税收一体化创造了一个良好开端，为实现上述目标进行了有益的探索。当成立全球性税收管理组织尚不具备现实性时，在区域层面，由一些经济发展状况相近、经济体制和结构类似、经济交往密切的国家进行税收一体化的实践无疑更为重要。

（三）国际税收竞争依然存在，国际税收合作趋势凸现

税收竞争，是指各个国家或地区为了尽可能多地为本国或本地区吸引资本或经营活动，竞相降低税率或提供其他税收优惠措施，从而引发的一种竞争状态。税收竞争分为国内税收竞争和国际税收竞争，一国内部不同行政区划之间的税收竞争称为国内税收竞争，不同国家或地区之间的税收竞争称为国际税收竞争。在全球化背景下，国际税收竞争已成为当代国际税收中最重要的问题之一，日益受到国际社会的普遍关注。

欧盟早在20世纪60年代就已经开始了协调成员国税收政策的努力，到90年代，国际税收竞争已成为欧盟关注的焦点之一。为遏制税收竞争尤其是有害税收竞争的蔓延，1997年10月1日，欧盟发布了《税收一揽子计划》报告，其中《关于营业所得征税的指导法规》明确提出了判断成员国的某些税收措施是否有害的检测标准。欧盟还成立了一个审查小组，对成员国的税收措施予以审查。欧盟各成员国也都承诺不采用该指导法规指出的那些有害的税收竞争措施，并对现有法律法规和行政措施进行审查，修改那些不适当的税收措施。②

经合组织也一直致力于协调和规制其成员国和非成员国的税收竞争政策。1998年通过了题为《有害税收竞争：一个正在出现的全球性问题》的报告，要求对税收竞争加以规范和监督。随后又分别于2000年、2001年、2004年和2006年发布了关于规制有害税收竞争行为的工作进度报告，对成员国和非成员国在协调税收政策，防范有害税收竞争方面的工作进行阶段性的总结。③ 目前，经合组织对有害税收实践的规制主要体现在透明度和税收情报交换制度的建设上。

从2013年开始实施的税基侵蚀与利润转移（Base Erosion and Profit Shift-

---

① 参见汤贡亮主编：《2012年中国税收发展报告——中国国际税收发展战略研究》，中国税务出版社2013年版，第49页。
② 参见杨慧芳：《国际税法的新发展与趋向》，载《外交学院学报》2004年第3期。
③ 经合组织2000年、2001年、2004年和2006年的报告分别为：2000 Progress Report: Towards Global Tax Co-operation; Progress in Identifying and Eliminating Harmful Tax Practices; The OECD's Project on Harmful Tax Practices: The 2001 Progress Report; The OECD's Project on Harmful Tax Practices: The 2004 Progress Peport; The OECD's Project on Harmful Tax Practices: 2006 Update on Progress in Member Countries. 上述报告的详细内容可参见OECD网站：http://www.oecd.org。

ing,BEPS)项目中也涵盖了有害税收竞争问题。BEPS项目的第五项行动计划(打击有害税收实践)提出应该审议各国的优惠税制,确保任何税收优惠的获取都必须满足"实质性经营活动"要求,并且税收优惠政策必须具有透明度。经二十国集团(G20)领导人背书后,越来越多的发达国家、发展中国家和国际组织都参与到BEPS项目中,于是打击有害税收竞争也日益呈现出全球合作的趋势。

尽管包括欧盟和经合组织在内的国际社会一直致力于消除有害税收竞争,规范国际税收秩序,但全球范围内的税收竞争尚未得到根本性解决。可以预见,随着国际税收在国际经济秩序中扮演着越来越重要的地位,作为对国际税收秩序产生深远影响的国际税收竞争问题在一定时期内将更加复杂化,但合作仍是必由之路。税收竞争体现了各国积极通过税收优惠政策来吸引国际资本流入的动机,过度竞争是国家本位主义膨胀在国际税收领域的表现。在经济全球化的加速和深入发展的背景下,由竞争走向合作在经济和政治层面上都有其必然性。国际税收协调与合作的目的和作用主要是维护国家税收管辖权,维护税收公平竞争,维护纳税人权益。当前国际税收协调与合作紧密的特征正通过以下方式得以体现:(1)签订法律框架,包括税收协定、情报交换协议等;(2)建立磋商机制,包括定期、不定期互访,专题磋商等;(3)通过会议协调,包括共同选定专业税收议题、专题讨论等;(4)发挥组织作用,包括成立全球性或区域性组织,保障协调与合作。①

(四)国际税务合作模式从双边向多边发展

在国际税收合作领域,长期以来都是以双边协定为基础的合作模式,少有多边合作的安排,直到20世纪后半期才开始出现了一些区域性的多边协定。区域性多边协定虽然相较于双边协定而言是一个突破,但它仍然是建立在部分国家之间历史关联或政治经济制度相似性的基础之上的,与具有广泛包容性的全球性多边公约仍然相距甚远。全球性多边税收公约的缔结之所以如此困难,主要有两方面的原因:首先,各国的税制差异太大,不论是税种的选择、税收管辖权的确定,还是对纳税主体、征税对象等问题的规定都差别非常大,很难在国际范围内达成一致;其次,也是最根本的原因,各国担心融入多边体制会使本国的税收主权受到限制或侵蚀。

尽管上述制度和理念的障碍至今仍然存在,但是随着经济全球化的进一步发展,各国已普遍认识到传统的双边或区域性多边协定已不能满足调整新形势下国际税收秩序的需要,必须在更广泛的全球范围内通过多边协定来协调立场

---

① 参见郝昭成:《世界税收制度发展基本特征》,载《涉外税务》2011年第6期。

和加强合作。正是在这一背景下,经合组织于 2010 年对《多边税收征管互助公约》进行修订并向所有国家开放,使其成为一个全球性多边税务合作公约。

不可否认,《多边税收征管互助公约》还只是全球性多边税务合作的一个发端,公约本身也规定了多项保留条款,这注定了国际税务多边合作的路还很漫长,在当前不同国家之间尤其是发展中国家和发达国家之间税源竞争日趋激烈的背景下,对该公约寄予过高的期望是不现实的。但是,该公约的开放签署以及各国的积极姿态已足以表明国际税务多边合作已取得突破性进展,多边合作是各国在新的经济和政治环境中必然选择的道路和发展趋势。

(五)国际税务合作的深化要求各国在更大程度上让渡国家税收主权

在全球化趋势继续前行的基础上,国家间税收关系的协调始终是一个基本的发展趋势。近年来,在国际税收领域体现为反避税力度加大,在税收情报交换、征管互助等领域取得了突破性进展。同时,国际社会还加大了官方和非官方的国际税收交流与讨论,以加强各国税务机关的合作,共同应对金融危机背景下的国际税收挑战。[①] 截至 2013 年 4 月,经合组织"全球税收论坛"共有 120 个国家或地区参加。从 2006 年开始,论坛每年出版以税收透明度和情报交换为主的"税务合作"评价报告。自 2010 年 3 月开始至 2013 年 4 月,论坛已完成针对 100 个管辖区税收透明度与情报交换的同行评审(peer review)工作,透明度和税收情报交换的国际标准已被广泛认可。

在深化合作的同时也面临困境,尤其是如何协调维护国家税收主权、避免双重征税、打击国际避税三者之间的关系,要同时实现避免双重征税和打击国际避税两个目标,各国必须在税收主权上作出让步,深化国际合作。[②] 透明度和税收情报交换国际标准的建立是各国让渡税收行政主权的结果,但这种让步对于整个国际税收治理问题的解决仍然是不够的,还涉及税收立法主权和税收司法主权。2013 年的经合组织《税基侵蚀和利润转移报告》指出,导致税基侵蚀和利润转移的根本原因在于国际税收一般原则——分享税收管辖权与不断发展变化的商业环境不同步。国内和国际层面的国际税法规则还植根于低水平的跨国经济融合的商业环境,而非目前以知识产权作为价值驱动日益重要、信息及通讯技术不断发展为特征的全球纳税人环境。简而言之,各国税收制度融合的程度远远

---

① 参见汤贡亮主编:《2012 年中国税收发展报告——中国国际税收发展战略研究》,中国税务出版社 2013 年版,第 61—63 页。

② See Philipp Genschel and Thomas Rixen, The International Tax Regime: Historical Evolution and Political Change, June 1, 2012. 资料来源:http://ssrn.com/abstract=2139665,2013 年 7 月 11 日访问。

落后于各国经济的融合程度。鉴于国际税收领域内政策、制度等方面的协调内容日趋复杂,范围日益扩大,已有专家建议成立"世界税收组织",使其同世界贸易组织、国际货币基金组织一样发挥功能,就某些"世界性税基"征税,提供某些"世界性公共产品",并协调各国税制间的差异和运作矛盾。① 虽然真正意义上管理主权国家之间税收关系的国际税收组织短期内很难出现,但国际税务合作的进一步深化要求各国在更大程度上让渡国家税收主权,这已成为一个趋势。

(六)跨国电子商务的国际税务问题日益受到关注

电子商务是指采用数字化电子方式进行商务数据交换和开展商务活动。与传统经营模式相比,电子商务是一种网络化的新型经济活动。近年来,随着各国政府对电子商务市场的重视和信息技术本身的进步,电子商务得到飞速发展。根据联合国贸易和发展会议的统计,全球电子商务交易总额在1994年达到12亿美元,2000年增加到3000亿美元,2006年竟然达到12.8万亿美元,占全球商品销售的18%,2011年则达到40.6万亿美元,绝大部分的国际贸易额以网络贸易形式实现。② 日益风行的网络购物进一步推动了电子商务的发展,2012年中国电子商务市场整体交易规模为8.1万亿元,其中网络购物占16%,约为1.3万亿元。未来随着传统企业大规模进入电商行业、移动互联网的快速发展促使移动购物日益便捷,网络购物市场整体还将保持较快增长速度。③

目前,电子商务已经广泛深入到生产、流通、消费等各个领域,改变着传统经营管理模式和生产组织形态,影响到世界范围内的产业结构调整和资源配置。发达国家和新兴工业化国家把电子商务作为强化竞争优势的战略举措,制定电子商务发展政策和行动计划,力求把握发展主动权。④ 可以说,大力发展电子商务已成为各国参与全球经济合作的必然选择。

电子商务的广泛应用降低了企业经营、管理和商务活动的成本,促进了资金、技术、产品、服务和其他生产要素在全球范围的流动,推动了经济全球化的发展,给人类带来了巨大的经济和社会效益。另外,由于其经营模式的特殊性,电子商务的使用和推广也给包括法律制度在内的传统秩序和规则带来了全面的挑

---

① 参见汤贡亮主编:《2012年中国税收发展报告——中国国际税收发展战略研究》,中国税务出版社2013年版,第50页。
② 参见中国电子商务研究中心:《2011年全球电子商务交易额达40.6万亿美元》,http://b2b.toocle.com/detail—6075303.html,2013年6月11日访问。
③ 参见艾瑞咨询:《2012年中国电子商务交易额8.1万亿》,http://www.ebrun.com/20130131/67195.shtml,2013年6月11日访问。
④ 参见国家发展改革委员会和国务院信息化工作办公室2007年6月发布的《电子商务发展"十一五"规划》。

战和冲击。传统的知识产权法、合同法、侵权法、税法等法律的许多规定都不适用于电子商务的情形。就税法而言,正如有学者所归纳的,电子商务对税法的冲击可以概括为以下几个方面:传统的常设机构概念受到挑战;使得来源地税收管辖权和居民税收管辖权受到冲击,国际税收管辖权的冲突更加复杂;电子商务特有的经营模式使得有些商品、劳务和特许权的区别变得很模糊,导致税务处理混乱;由转让定价等引起的国际避税问题更加突出;电子商务环境下税收征管信息很难获取真实信息,给税务征管带来了困难;影响全球税收利益在国际上的分配秩序。① 由此可见,电子商务对国际税收法律制度的影响是全面的,如何确立电子商务环境下的国际税收规则和秩序将是国际社会亟待解决的重要问题之一。

经合组织为应对电子商务给国际税法规则带来的挑战,于 1999 年专门成立了技术咨询小组来指导关于营业利润征税条约规范的适用(The Technical Advisory Group on Monitoring the Application of Existing Treaty Norms for Taxing Business Profits,TAG),研究"现有的对营业利润征税的条约规则如何在电子商务环境下适用并提出替代性规则"。2000 年 12 月,经合组织财政事务委员会发布了《常设机构概念在电子商务背景下的运用:对经济合作与发展组织(OECD)税收协定范本第五条的注释的建议性说明》。② 2001 年 2 月,TAG 发布了《电子商务环境下常设机构的利润归属》讨论草案。③ 2002 年 11 月,TAG 向财政事务委员会提交了《电子商务引起的税收条约定性问题报告》。④ 2003 年 11 月,TAG 发布了《对营业利润征税的现有税收条约规则对电子商务而言是否适当》的讨论草案,并在各方评论的基础上进行完善,于 2004 年 6 月发布了最终报告。⑤ 该最终报告研究了作为 TAG 分析基础的电子商务环境下新的商业模式,概括了对营业利润征税的现有条约规则并予以评述,分析了一些替代性的方案并提出了建议。

---

① 参见"电子商务研究"课题组:《电子商务衍生的税收问题及其对策建议》,载《财政与税务》2000 年第 11 期。

② See The Committee on Fiscal Affairs: Clarification on the Application of the Permanent Establishment Definition in E-Commerce-[Proposed]: Changes to the Commentary on the Model Tax Convention on Article 5, 22 December 2000.

③ See Technical Advisory Group Discussion Paper: Attribution of Profit to a Permanent Establishment Involved in Electronic Commerce Transactions, February 2001.

④ See Technical Advisory Group Report to the OECD CFA WP No. 1: Tax Treaty Characterization Issues Arising from E-Commerce, November 2002.

⑤ See Technical Advisory Group Discussion Paper: Are the Current Treaty Rules for Taxing Business Profits Appropriate for E-Commerce? November 2003.

本章阅读材料

Pierre Boulez, Petitioner v. Commissioner of Internal Revenue, Respondent

Docket No. 12705-79

UNITED STATES TAX COURT

83 T.C. 584; 1984 U.S. Tax Ct. LEXIS 23; 83 T.C. No. 31
October 16, 1984.
October 16, 1984, Filed

DISPOSITION: *Decision will be entered under Rule 155.*
COUNSEL: *Allen Greenberg*, for the petitioner.
Barry Guberman, for the respondent.
JUDGES: Korner, *Judge*.
OPINION BY: Korner
OPINION

  Respondent determined a deficiency in petitioner's individual income tax for the calendar year 1975 in the amount of $20,685.61. After concessions, the sole issue which we are called upon to decide is whether certain payments received by petitioner in the year 1975 constitute "royalties," within the meaning of the applicable income tax treaty between the Federal Republic of Germany and the United States, and are therefore exempt from tax by the United States, or whether said payments constitute compensation for personal services within the meaning of that treaty, and are therefore taxable by the United States.

  The case was submitted to the Court under the provisions of Rule 122,[1] on the basis of a fully stipulated set of facts and exhibits, and our findings of

---

[1] All statutory references are to the Internal Revenue Code of 1954 as in effect in the year in issue, and all Rule references are to the Rules of Practice and Procedure of the Tax Court, unless otherwise noted.

fact herein are based upon said stipulation, the accompanying exhibits, and the facts established by the pleadings.

FINDINGS OF FACT

The petitioner, Pierre Boulez, resided in Paris, France, at the time the petition was filed in this case. Petitioner is a citizen of France, and during the calendar year 1975 was a resident of the Federal Republic of Germany (hereinafter FRG). For the taxable year 1975, petitioner was a nonresident alien of the United States for Federal income tax purposes, and he timely filed a Federal nonresident alien income tax return for that year with the Office of International Operations of respondent.

At all times relevant to this case, petitioner was a world-renowned music director and orchestra conductor. On February 19, 1969, petitioner entered into a contract with CBS Records, a division of CBS United Kingdom, Ltd., which is a subsidiary of CBS, Inc., a U.S. corporation. Said contract was modified as of September 13, 1971, and March 14, 1974, and, as so modified, was in effect during the year 1975. Under date of May 1, 1972, with the consent of CBS Records, the contract was assigned by petitioner to Beacon Concerts, Ltd., of London England, which acted as petitioner's agent and undertook to provide his services to CBS Records under the terms of the basic contract, as amended.

As relevant and material herein, the contract between petitioner and CBS Records, as in effect in the year 1975, provided in part as follows:

1. We [CBS Records] hereby agree to engage and you [the petitioner] agree to render your services exclusively for us as a producer and/or performer for the recording of musical and/or literary compositions for the purpose of making phonograph records. It is understood and agreed that such engagement by us shall include your services as a producer and/or performer with the New York Philharmonic for the recording of musical and/or literary compositions for the purposes of making phonograph records.

* * * *

3. (a) During the first two contract years of this agreement you will perform for the recording of satisfactory master recording [sic] sufficient in number to constitute two (2) 12 inch long-playing 331/3 rpm recordings, or

their equivalent, and we will record your performances; and during each contract year commencing September 13, 1971, you will perform for the recording of satisfactory master recordings sufficient in number to constitute three (3) twelve inch long-playing 331/3 rpm recordings, or their equivalent, and we will record your performances. Additional master recordings will be performed by you and recorded by us at our election.

* * * *

4. During the period of this Agreement you will not for any reason whatsoever give or sell your services under your own or any assumed name or anonymously to any other person firm or corporation but nothing herein contained shall preclude you for [sic] giving or selling your services for films personal appearances and broadcasting (whether or not accompanied by television) provided such services are not reproduced as records for sale to the public and you undertake to have this proviso included in any contract for such services. You will not during the period of five years after the expiration of the term of this Agreement give or sell your services for the purpose of making or assisting in the making of records of any of the compositions or works which you shall have performed under this Agreement. You acknowledge that your services are unique and extraordinary and that we shall be entitled to equitable relief to enforce the provision of this paragraph 4.

5. All master recordings recorded hereunder and all matrices and phonograph records manufactured therefrom, together with the performances embodied thereon, shall be entirely our [CBS Records] property, free from any claims whatsoever by you [petitioner] or any person deriving any rights or interests from you. Without limiting the generality of the foregoing, we (including other divisions of our company) and/or our subsidiaries, affiliates and licensees shall have the unlimited right, from time to time, to manufacture, by any method now or hereafter known, phonograph records and other reproductions, on any mediums or devices now or hereafter known, of the master recordings made hereunder, and to sell transfer or otherwise deal in the same throughout the world under any trademark, trade names and labels or to refrain from such manufacture, sale and dealing;

* * * *

6. We hereby agree to pay the accompaniment costs and studio charges in connection with the master recordings made hereunder.

* * * *

13. If, by reason of illness, injury, accident or refusal to work, you fail to perform for us in accordance with the provisions of this agreement, * * * we shall have the option without liability to suspend the application of paragraph 2 and/or paragraph 7 (including the payment of any royalties) of this agreement for the duration of any such contingency by giving you written notice thereof.

Under paragraph 7a of the contract, it was provided "For your services rendered hereunder and for the rights granted to us herein we will pay you the following royalties." There then followed an elaborate formula by which the petitioner was to be paid, based upon a percentage of the retail price derived by CBS Records from the sale of its phonograph records produced under the contract, with said percentage varying depending upon various factors, including, inter alia, whether the musical composition involved was in the public domain, whether the performance conducted by petitioner was made with the New York Philharmonic Orchestra, whether sales were made by direct sales or mail order through what was termed a "Club Operation," whether the record involved was a "re-issue," etc. In all cases, however, the payments or "royalties" which petitioner was to be entitled to receive were dependent upon future sales of recordings by CBS Records.

Pursuant to the February 19, 1969, contract with CBS Records, as amended, petitioner conducted various performances with the Cleveland Orchestra, the New York Philharmonic, and others in the recording of musical compositions for CBS Records. None of these recordings were from "live" performances (i. e. , performances before an audience). They were all private performances arranged solely for purposes of recording. CBS, Inc. , was responsible for and exercised control over the setting up of the recording session, employing and paying the members of the orchestra, providing and arranging the equipment and engineers and technicians needed to capture and electronically process the sounds rendered by the orchestra, and for compiling and editing the sounds to make master recordings, matrices, and phonograph records.

Petitioner exercised control over the manner in which the orchestra transposed into aural form the underlying musical composition which was the subject of each recording. He determined the placement of the musicians and the volume of aural sound to be rendered by the various musical instruments making up the orchestra. In conducting the orchestra, petitioner exercised his individual artistic talents of interpreting the musical work. Such interpretation, which is the function of the conductor, differs from conductor to conductor and is unique to each conductor's recording of a particular work.

Applications for the copyrights of all the master recordings, matrices, and phonograph records embodying the sound recordings of the musical compositions conducted by petitioner pursuant to the contract were filed by CBS, Inc., and all registrations thereof were issued by the U.S. Copyright Office registered in the name of CBS, Inc.

As the result of performances conducted by petitioner under the terms of the contract, CBS, Inc., paid to Beacon Concerts, Ltd., as petitioner's agent, the sum of $39,461.47 in the year 1975. Beacon Concerts, Ltd., in turn, paid such sum to petitioner in 1976. In his 1975 U.S. nonresident alien income tax return, petitioner disclosed the receipt of such amount, but excluded it as not being subject to U.S. income taxation. Petitioner reported the identical amount in his 1976 income tax return filed with the FRG as includable income subject to the German income tax, and petitioner paid German income tax thereon.

Upon audit of petitioner's 1975 U.S. income tax return, respondent determined, inter alia, that the entire amount of $39,461 was taxable to petitioner by the United States. Because of an apparent conflict between respondent and the FRG concerning the proper taxation of this income under the existing income tax treaty between the United States and the FRG, competent authority proceedings, pursuant to the provisions of the treaty, were instituted at the request of petitioner and were conducted by the FRG Ministry of Finance and respondent's Office of International Operations in an effort to resolve the issues arising under said income tax treaty.

The competent authorities of the two nations were unable to reach agreement on the correct treatment for income tax purposes of the income here involved. The position of the FRG was that these payments constituted "royalties," within the meaning of article VIII of the treaty, and therefore were taxable exclusively by the FRG. Respondent, on the other hand, took the position that said income was income from performance of personal services in the United States by petitioner, and therefore was taxable by the United States under the provisions of article X of said treaty, except that respondent here concedes that, of the total amount of $39,461.47, the amount of $9,000 was income from sources without the United States and was not subject to taxation by respondent, thus leaving the net amount of $30,461 in issue. ①

ULTIMATE FINDING OF FACT

The payments of CBS, Inc., to petitioner in 1975 were payments as compensation for personal services rendered by petitioner.

OPINION

Petitioner contends that the payments to him in 1975 by CBS, Inc., were not taxable by the United States, because they were "royalties" within the meaning of the applicable treaty between the United States and the FRG. Respondent, as noted above, contends that the payments in question were taxable to petitioner by the United States because they represented compensation for personal services performed in the United States by petitioner. The parties are in agreement that the outcome of this dispute is governed by the effective income tax treaty between the United States and the FRG.

Under date of July 22, 1954, there was executed a "Convention Between the United States of America and the Federal Republic of Germany for the Avoidance of Double Taxation with Respect to Taxes on Income," 5 U.S.T. (part 3) 2768, T.I.A.S. No. 3133. As amended by a Protocol, dated September 17, 1965, 16 U.S.T. (part 2) 1875, T.I.A.S. No. 5920, this convention (hereinafter the treaty) was in effect during the year 1975, and undertook to govern, in stated respects, the income taxation of natural and

---

① Petitioner concedes that, for U.S. income tax purposes, the payment of "royalties" by CBS, Inc., to Beacon Concerts, Ltd., in 1975 is to be treated as being paid directly to petitioner. Respondent's statutory notice determined the additional income in even dollars, thus accounting for the difference of $0.47.

juridical persons resident in either of the two nations, whose affairs might bring into play the taxing laws of both nations. Petitioner, a resident of the FRG, was a person within the coverage of the treaty. The relevant portions of the treaty provide, in part:

Article II

(2) In the application of the provisions of this Convention by one of the contracting States any term not otherwise defined shall, unless the context otherwise requires, have the meaning which the term has under its own applicable laws * * *

* * * *

Article VIII

(1) Royalties derived by a natural person resident in the Federal Republic or by a German company shall be exempt from tax by the United States.

* * * *

(3) The term "royalties", as used in this Article,

(a) means any royalties, rentals or other amounts paid as consideration for the use of, or the right to use, copyrights, artistic or scientific works (including motion picture films, or films or tapes for radio or television broadcasting), patents, designs, plans, secret processes or formulae, trademarks, or other like property or rights, or for industrial, commercial or scientific equipment, or for knowledge, experience or skill (know-how) and

(b) shall include gains derived from the alienation of any right or property giving rise to such royalties.

* * * *

Article X

* * * *

(2) Compensation for labor or personal services (including compensation derived from the practice of a liberal profession and the rendition of services as a director) performed in the United States by a natural person resident in the Federal Republic shall be exempt from tax by the United States if—[1]

---

[1] The treaty then enumerates several conditions which must be fulfilled before the exemption from tax by the United States is effective. The parties are in agreement that the exceptions do not apply in the present case, so that the payments in question, if held to be income from personal services, are taxable by the United States to petitioner.

Acknowledging that the provisions of the treaty take precedence over any conflicting provisions of the Internal Revenue Code of 1954 (sec. 7852(d); see also sec. 894), we must decide whether the payments received by petitioner in 1975 from CBS, Inc., constituted royalties or income from personal services within the meaning of that treaty. This issue, in turn, involves two facets:

(1) Did petitioner intend and purport to license or convey to CBS Records, and did the latter agree to pay for, a property interest in the recordings he was engaged to make, which would give rise to royalties?

(2) If so, did petitioner have a property interest in the recordings which he was capable of licensing or selling?

The first of the above questions is purely factual, depends upon the intention of the parties, and is to be determined by an examination of the record as a whole, including the terms of the contract entered into between petitioner and CBS Records, together with any other relevant and material evidence. *Beausoleil v. Commissioner*, 66 *T.C.* 244, 247 (1976); *Downs v. Commissioner*, 49 *T.C.* 533, 538 (1968); *McClain v. Commissioner*, 40 *T. C.* 841, 849 (1963); *Chilton v. Commissioner*, 40 *T.C.* 552, 562 (1963); *Karl R. Komarek v. Commissioner*, *T.C. Memo.* 1967-112.

The second question—whether petitioner had a property interest which he could license or sell—is a question of law. The treaty is not explicit, and we have found no cases or other authorities which would give us an interpretation of the treaty on this point. We are therefore remitted to U.S. law for the purpose of determining this question.

We will examine each of these questions in turn.

1. The Factual Question

By the contract entered into between petitioner and CBS Records in 1969, as amended, did the parties agree that petitioner was licensing or conveying to CBS Records a property interest in the recordings which he was retained to make, and in return for which he was to receive "royalties?" Petitioner claims that this is the case, and he bears the burden of proof to establish it. *Welch v. Helvering*, 290 *U.S.* 111 (1933); Rule 142(a).

The contract between the parties is by no means clear. On the one hand, the contract consistently refers to the compensation which petitioner is to be entitled to receive as "royalties," and such payments are tied directly to the proceeds which CBS Records was to receive from sales of recordings which petitioner was to make. Both these factors suggest that the parties had a royalty arrangement, rather than a compensation arrangement, in mind in entering into the contract. We bear in mind, however, that the labels which the parties affix to a transaction are not necessarily determinative of their true nature (*Kimble Glass Co. v. Commissioner*, 9 T.C. 183, 189 (1947)), and the fact that a party's remuneration under the contract is based on a percentage of future sales of the product created does not prove that a licensing or sale of property was intended, rather than compensation for services. *Karrer v. United States*, 138 Ct. Cl. 385, 152 F. Supp. 66 (1957).

On the other hand, the contract between petitioner and CBS Records is replete with language indicating that what was intended here was a contract for personal services. Thus, paragraph 1 (quoted in our findings of fact) clearly states that CBS Records was engaging petitioner "to render your services exclusively for us as a producer and/or performer * * * It is understood and agreed that such engagement by us shall include your services as a producer and/or performer." Paragraph 3 of the contract then requires petitioner to "perform" in the making of a certain number of recordings in each year. Most importantly, in the context of the present question, paragraph 4 of the contract (quoted in our findings) makes it clear that CBS considered petitioner's services to be the essence of the contract: petitioner agreed not to perform for others with respect to similar recordings during the term of the contract, and for a period of 5 years thereafter, and he was required to "acknowledge that your services are unique and extraordinary and that we shall be entitled to equitable relief to enforce the provision of this paragraph 4."

Under paragraph 5 of the contract (quoted *supra*), it was agreed that the recordings, once made, should be entirely the property of CBS Records, "free from any claims whatsoever by you or any person deriving any rights or interests from you." Significantly, nowhere in the contract is there any language of conveyance of any alleged property right in the recordings by petitioner to CBS Records, nor any language indicating a licensing of any such purported right, other than the designation of petitioner's remuneration as being "royalties." The word "copyright" itself is never mentioned. Finally, under paragraph 13 of the contract, CBS Records was entitled to suspend or terminate its payments to petitioner "if, by reason of illness, injury, accident or refusal to work, you fail to perform for us in accordance with the provisions of this agreement."

Considered as a whole, therefore, and acknowledging that the contract is not perfectly clear on this point, we conclude that the weight of the evidence is that the parties intended a contract for personal services, rather than one involving the sale or licensing of any property rights which petitioner might have in the recordings which were to be made in the future.

2. The Legal Question

Before a person can derive income from royalties, it is fundamental that he must have an ownership interest in the property whose licensing or sale gives rise to the income. Thus, in *Patterson v. Texas Co.*, *131 F. 2d 998*, *1001* (*5th Cir. 1942*), the Court of Appeals adopted the definition of a "royalty" as "a share of the product or profit reserved by the owner for permitting another to use the property." Likewise, in *Hopag S. A. Holding De Participation*, *etc. v. Commissioner*, *14 T.C. 38* (*1950*), this Court held that in order for a payment to constitute a "royalty," the payee must have an ownership interest in the property whose use generates the payment, citing the definition of royalties in *section 119(a)(4) of the Internal Revenue Code of 1939* (section 861(a)(4) in the 1954 Code is the same), which states:

Rentals or royalties from property located in the United States or from any interest in such property, including rentals or royalties for the use of or for the privilege of using in the United States patents, copyrights, secret processes and formulas, good will, trademarks, trade brands, franchises, and other like property, * * *

In its definition of royalties, the treaty embodies the same fundamental concept of ownership. Thus, in article VIII(3)(a), "royalties" are defined to mean "amounts paid as consideration for the use of, or *the right to use*, copyrights, artistic or [* * **21**] scientific works * * * *or other like property or rights*," and article VIII (3) (b) also states that the term "royalties" "shall include gains derived from the alienation of *any right or* property giving rise to such royalties." (Emphasis supplied.)

It is clear, then, that the existence of a property right in the payee is fundamental for the purpose of determining whether royalty income exists, and this is equally true under our domestic law as well as under the treaty.

Did the petitioner have any property rights in the recordings which he made for CBS Records, which he could either license or sell and which would give rise to royalty income here?① We think not.

As noted in our findings, the basic contract between petitioner and CBS Records was executed in 1969. At that time, petitioner had no copyrightable property interest in the recordings which he made for CBS Records under the Copyright Act of 1909 as amended, *17 U.S.C. sec. 1 et seq.*, and petitioner concedes that this was so. *Ingram v. Bowers*, 47 F. 2d 925 (S.D. N.Y. 1931), affd. 57 F. 2d 65 (2d Cir. 1932); *Capitol Records, Inc. v. Mercury Records Corp.*, 221 F. 2d 657 (2d Cir. 1955).

Petitioner contends, however, that the Copyright Act of 1909 was amended by the Sound Recording Amendment of 1971, Pub. L. 92-140, 85 Stat. 391 (1971), and by virtue of this amendment, petitioner then acquired copyrightable property interests in the recordings which he thereafter made for CBS Records.

We think that petitioner is correct, in that the Sound Recording Amendment of 1971, *supra*, did amend the Copyright Act of 1909 so as to create, for the first time, copyrightable property interests in a musical director or performer such as petitioner who was making sound recordings of musical works, a property right which had not existed theretofore. *17 U.S.C. secs. 1 (f), 5 (n), 26.*② In discussing the changes made by the Second Recording

---

① It is to be noted that the treaty classifies as royalty income both the income derived from the licensing of property as well as from the sale thereof. Although this definition is broader than the definition of royalty income for U.S. citizens (cf. secs. 1235, 1253), it corresponds to the treatment given to nonresident aliens by the Internal Revenue Code. Sec. 871(a)(1)(D); sec. 1.871-12(b)(1)(iii), *Income Tax Regs.* Petitioner herein does not make it clear whether he contends that he licensed a property interest which he had in the records which he made for CBS Records, or whether he sold his entire interest, but in view of the breadth of the treaty definition, it does not matter.

② The Copyright Act of 1909, *17 U.S.C. secs. 1 through 32*, was completely repealed and replaced by the present Copyright Act, Pub. L. 94-553, 90 Stat. 2541, effective Jan. 1, 1978. As to periods prior to that date, however, the former law remains in effect. Pub. L. 94-553, sec. 112.

Amendment of 1971, and the new property rights therein created in both record producers such as CBS Records and performers such as petitioner, the legislative history contains the following significant statement: "As in the case of motion pictures, the bill does not fix the authorship, or the resulting ownership, of sound recordings, but leaves these matters to the employment relationship and bargaining among the interests involved." H. Rept. 92-487 (1971), 1971 U. S. Code Cong. & Adm. News 1566, 1570.

In spite of this change in the law in 1971, however, petitioner's contractual relationship with CBS Records went on as before. Neither the amendment to that contract of 1971, nor the further amendment in 1974, made any reference to the change of the copyright laws, nor modified the basic contract in any respect which would be pertinent to the instant question. We conclude, therefore, that the parties saw no need to modify their contract because they understood that even after the Sound Recording Amendment of 1971, petitioner still had no licensable or transferable property rights in the recordings which he made for CBS Records, and we think this was correct.

The Copyright Act of 1909, even after its amendment by the Sound Recording Amendment of 1971, describes the person having a copyrightable interest in property as the "author or proprietor" (*17 U. S. C. sec. 9*), and further provides that "the word 'author' shall include an employer in the case of works made for hire." *17 U. S. C. sec. 26.* The above is a statutory enactment of the long-recognized rule that where a person is employed for the specific purpose of creating a work, including a copyrightable item, the fruits of his labor, carried out in accordance with the employment, are the property of his employer. The rule creates a rebuttable presumption to this effect, which can be overcome by express contractual provisions between the employee and the employer, reserving to the former the copyrightable interest.

Here, the petitioner, a musical conductor of world-wide reputation, was employed to make recordings for CBS Records, and in doing so, was to exercise his peculiar and unique skills in accordance with his experience, talent, and best judgment. In these circumstances, we do not think that petitioner was an "employee" in the common law sense, but rather was an independent contractor, with the same relationship to CBS Records as a lawyer, an engineer, or an architect would have to his client, or a doctor to his patient (see *Eicher v. Commissioner*, T. C. Memo. 1984-468). This, however, provides no grounds for distinction, since the "works for hire" rule applies to independent contractors just as it does to conventional employees. ①

In the instant case, the application of the "works for hire" rule means that petitioner had no copyrightable property interest in the recordings which he created for CBS Records, even after 1971. Petitioner was engaged for the specific purpose of making the recordings in question; his contract with CBS Records reserved no property rights in the recordings to him, and indeed made it specific that all such rights, whatever they were, were to reside in CBS Records. Under these circumstances, we do not think that petitioner has overcome the statutory presumption of the "works for hire" rule, nor that he has shown that he had any property interest in the recordings, either before 1971 or thereafter, which he could either license or sell to CBS Records so as to produce royalty income within the meaning of the treaty. This conclusion, in turn, reinforces our belief, which we have found as a fact, that the contract between petitioner and CBS Records was one for the performance of personal services.

It follows that respondent was correct in taxing this income to petitioner under the provisions of article X of the treaty.

Decision will be entered under Rule 155.

---

① In the case of an inventor who created patentable rights in the course of his employment as an independent contractor, in *Gilson v. Commissioner*, T. C. Memo. 1984-447, we recently stated that the "hired to invent" rule does not apply in the case of independent contractors. That case does not conflict with what we do here. In *Gilson*, the ultimate issue was factual, and we found on the facts that the taxpayer there had entered into a contract to be paid for the transfer of his rights in patentable designs, as opposed to a contract for personal services. We need not explore in the present case whether the "hired to invent" rule in the patent law is the same as the "work for hire" rule under copyright law, with respect to its application to independent contractors. As the above-cited cases make clear, the "works for hire" rule *does* apply to independent contractors in the copyright area, and can be negated only by affirmative evidence of a contrary intent of the contracting parties.

Global Business Models, Competitiveness, Corporate Governance and Taxation

—selected from 2013 OECD Report: Addressing Base Erosion and Profit Shifting

This chapter describes developments in the economy that have had an impact on the way businesses are organized and, as a consequence, on the management of their tax affairs. It also discusses the often relevant issue of country competitiveness and the impact these developments have on the rules for the taxation of cross-border activities.

Global business models and taxation

Globalisation is not new, but the pace of integration of national economies and markets has increased substantially in recent years. The free movements of capital and labour, the shift of manufacturing bases from high-cost to low-cost locations, the gradual removal of trade barriers, technological and telecommunication developments, and the ever-increasing importance of managing risks and of developing, protecting and exploiting intellectual property, have had an important impact on the way MNEs are structured and managed. This has resulted in a shift from country-specific operating models to global models based on matrix management organisations and integrated supply chains that centralise several functions at a regional or global level. Moreover, the growing importance of the service component of the economy, and of digital products that often can be delivered over the Internet, has made it possible for businesses to locate many productive activities in geographic locations that are distant from the physical location of their customers.

In today's MNEs the individual group companies undertake their activities within a framework of group policies and strategies that are set by the group as a whole. The separate legal entities forming the group operate as a single integrated enterprise following an overall business strategy. Management personnel may be geographically dispersed rather than being located in a single central location, with reporting lines and decision-making processes going beyond the legal structure of the MNE.

Global value chains (GVCs), characterised by the fragmentation of production across borders, have become a dominant feature of today's global economy, encompassing emerging as well as developed economies. Figure 3.1 is a simple illustration of these chains. Increasingly, the pattern of trade shows that a good produced in Economy 1 and exported to its market of final consumption involves inputs supplied by producers in other economies who themselves source their inputs from third economies.

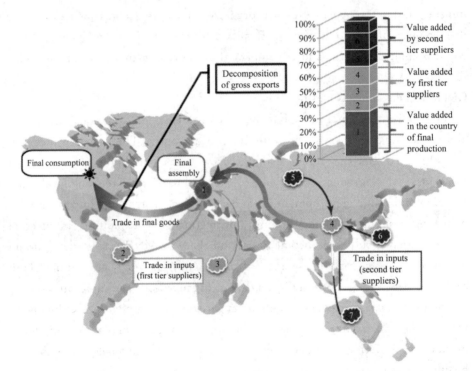

Figure 3.1. A simplified representation of a global value chain

Source: OECD (2012), "Global Value Chains: OECD Work on Measuring Trade in Value-Added and Beyond", internal working document, Statistics Directorate, OECD, Paris.

Another simple way to illustrate this is to consider how many production stages are involved to produce a given good or service. Figure 3.2 gives an average of these indices for all economies. Using an index that takes the value of 1 when there is a single stage of production in a single economy, the figure illustrates that supply chains in some sectors are long and that a significant share of this unbundling of production is international. The fragmentation of production is especially important in manufacturing industries but services are also increasingly produced within GVCs.

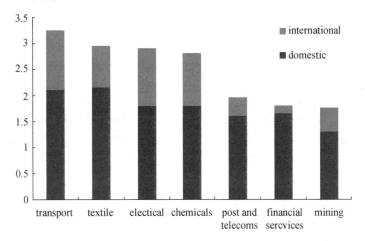

Figure 3.2. Index of the relative length of Global Value Chains, world average, selected industries, 2008

Source: OECD (2012), "Global Value Chains: OECD Work on Measuring Trade in Value-Added and Beyond", internal working document, Statistics Directorate, OECD, Paris.

The rise of GVCs has also changed the notion of what economies do and what they produce. It is increasingly less relevant to talk about the gross goods or services that are exported, while it is increasingly relevant to talk about tasks and stages of production. In a world where stages and tasks matter more than the final products

being produced, GVCs also challenge orthodox notions of where economies find themselves on the value-added curve. From an economic point of view, most of the value of a good or service is typically created in upstream activities where product design, R&D or production of core components occur, or in the tail-end of downstream activities where marketing or branding occurs. Knowledge-based assets, such as intellectual property, software and organisational skills, have become increasingly important for competitiveness and for economic growth and employment.

Globalisation has in effect caused products and operational models to evolve, creating the conditions for the development of global strategies aimed at maximising profits and minimising expenses and costs, including tax expenses. At the same time, the rules on the taxation of profits from cross-border activities have remained fairly unchanged, with the principles developed in the past still finding application in domestic and international tax rules (see also the second section of Chapter 4). In other words, the changes in business practices brought about by globalisation and digitalisation of the economy have raised questions among governments about whether the domestic and international rules on the taxation of cross-border profits have kept pace with those changes. Beyond cases of illegal abuses, which are the exception rather than the rule, MNEs engaged in BEPS comply with the legal requirements of the countries involved. Governments recognise this and also recognise that a change in this legal framework can only be achieved through international co-operation.

Competitiveness and taxation

Liberalisation of trade, the abolition of currency controls and technological advances have all contributed to a dramatic increase in the flows of capital and investments among countries. This has created unprecedented interconnectedness at all levels: individuals, businesses and governments. In striving to improve their competitive positions, businesses bring about the changes in investment, technological improvements and higher productivity that enable improvements in living standards. For a corporation, being competitive means to be able to sell the best products at the best price, so as to increase its profits and shareholder value. In this respect, it is just natural that investments will be made where profitability is the highest and that tax is one of the factors of profitability, and as such tax affects decisions on where and how to invest.

From a government perspective, globalisation means that domestic policies, including tax policy, cannot be designed in isolation, i. e. without taking into account the effects on other countries' policies and the effects of other countries' policies on its own ones. In today's world, the interaction of countries' domestic policies becomes fundamental. Tax policy is not only the expression of national sovereignty but it is at the core of this sovereignty, and each county is free to devise its tax system in the way it considers most appropriate. Tax policy and administration influence many of the drivers of increased productivity, ranging from investment in skills, capital equipment and technical know-how to the amount of resources required to administer and comply with the tax regime.

Governments work to ensure the highest level of growth for the highest level of well being. Growth depends on investments, which includes foreign investments. As investments take into account, together with several other factors, taxation, governments are often under pressure to offer a competitive tax environment. As already indicated in earlier OECD studies, experience shows that so-called "international competitiveness" concerns and pressures are felt in virtually all countries to somehow accommodate a relatively low corporate tax burden. Concerns over international competitiveness are often based on claims that accommodating treatment is available elsewhere.

Governments have long accepted that there are limits and that they should not engage in harmful tax practices. In 1998, the OECD issued a report on harmful tax practices in part based on the recognition that a "race to the bottom" would ultimately drive applicable tax rates on certain mobile sources of income to zero for all countries, whether or not this was the tax policy a country wished to pursue. It was felt that collectively agreeing on a set of common rules may in fact help countries to make their sovereign tax policy choices. The process for determining whether a regime is harmful contains three broad stages: (i) consideration of whether a regime is preferential and of preliminary factors, to determine whether the regime needs to be assessed; (ii) consideration of key factors and other factors to determine whether a preferential regime is potentially harmful; and (iii) consideration of the economic effects of a regime to determine whether a potentially harmful regime is actually harmful.

If a regime is considered preferential and within the scope of the work, four key factors and eight other factors are used to determine whether a preferential regime is potentially harmful. The four key factors are: (i) no or low effective tax rate; (ii) ring-fencing of the regime; (iii) lack of transparency; and (iv) lack of effective exchange of information. The eight other factors are: (i) an artificial definition of the tax base; (ii) failure to adhere to international transfer pricing principles; (iii) foreign source income exempt from residence country taxation; (iv) negotiable tax rate or tax base; (v) existence of secrecy provisions; (vi) access to a wide network of tax treaties; (vii) the regime is promoted as a tax minimisation vehicle; (viii) the regime encourages purely tax-driven operations or arrangements.

In order for a regime to be considered potentially harmful the first key factor, "no or low effective tax rate", must apply. This is a gateway criterion. However, an evaluation of whether a regime is potentially harmful should be based on an overall assessment of each of the factors and on its economic effects. Where a preferential regime has been found harmful, the relevant country will be given the opportunity to abolish the regime or remove the features that create the harmful effect. Where this is not done, other countries may then decide to implement defensive measures to counter the effects of the harmful regime, while at the same time continuing to encourage the country applying the regime to modify or remove it.

It is worth mentioning here that the recent past has witnessed major progress in relation to one of the four key factors, namely tax transparency. The Global Forum, which since 2000 has been the multilateral framework within which work in the area transparency and exchange of information has been carried out, was fundamentally restructured in 2009 to respond to a G20 call for action in this area. Since then more than 800 agreements that provide for the exchange of information in tax matters in accordance with the internationally agreed standard have been signed, 110 peer reviews have been launched and 88 peer review reports have been completed and published. The peer review outputs include determinations regarding the availability of any relevant information in tax matters (ownership, accounting or bank information), the appropriate power of the administration to access the information and the administration's capacity to deliver this information to any partner which requests it. Moreover, since the 2012 update of article 26 of the OECD Model Tax Convention, the standard on exchange of information clearly includes group requests. Finally, in the context of Foreign Account Tax Compliance Act (FATCA) agreements, a growing number of countries are moving towards automatic exchange of information. Needless to say, these developments provide opportunities to obtain better and more accurate information on BEPS instances that in the past were often not available.

Corporate governance and taxation

A key determinant of shareholder value under current corporate reporting standards is earnings per share (EPS). An important element of EPS is tax, which means that the net effect of having an ETR of 30% is that any earnings are reduced by 30%. In other words, the ETR significantly impacts EPS and therefore has a direct impact on shareholder value. Although excluded from earnings before interest, tax depreciation and amortisation (EBITDA), the ETR also has an impact on other financial indicators used by corporate analysts, such as the return on equity (ROE) or the weighted average cost of capital (WACC), and therefore on stock valuation.

The comparison between an MNE's ETR and that of its direct competitors often generates questions and therefore increased pressure on the MNE's tax department. At the same time, increased attention is being paid to risk, including tax risk, for financial reporting purposes. For example, under United States General Accounting Principles (GAAP), tighter accounting for uncertain tax positions under FIN 48 means that provisions for uncertain tax positions have to be made if it is more likely than not that the tax administration would not accept the position taken, assuming that it was in possession of all the facts.

An exposure draft on income tax was published by the International Accounting Standards Board (IASB) in March 2009 (ED/2009/2). It proposes that "an entity shall disclose information about the major sources of estimation uncertainties relating to tax..., including: a description of the uncertainty...". To the extent that financial accounting rules may increasingly require similar forms of disclosure, this means that adopting an aggressive tax position is unlikely to have a positive impact on the ETR and the profits available for distribution that can be reported in the published accounts of the corporation in the near term. As a result, the aggressive tax position does not enhance shareholder value immediately and does increase risk, including the reputational risk, if the tax planning becomes public, for example because the issue is the subject of litigation.

Several countries have recently taken a number of steps to address aggressive tax planning and rules requiring such schemes to be disclosed to the administration have been adopted by a number of them. As a result, aggressive tax strategies can be detrimental to shareholders' interests, particularly in the medium-to-long term, because they are high risk and the costs of failure can be significant, also from the point of view of reputation. Furthermore, for some years now there has been a clear trend in the relationship between tax administrations and large businesses away from a purely adversarial model towards a more collaborative approach. At the basis of these co-operative compliance programs there is an exchange of transparency for certainty, for both parties. Increased stringency of the accounting rules governing provisions for uncertain tax positions has only served to underline the commercial value of certainty.

As also recognised in the OECD Guidelines for Multinational Enterprises (OECD, 2011), which contain recommendations for responsible business conduct that the 44 adhering governments encourage their enterprises to observe wherever they operate, enterprises should treat tax governance and tax compliance as important elements of their oversight and broader risk management systems. In particular, corporate boards should adopt tax risk management strategies to ensure that the financial, regulatory and reputational risks associated with taxation are fully identified and evaluated. The guidelines underline that it is important that enterprises contribute to the public finances of host countries by making timely payment of their tax liabilities and recommend that enterprises comply with both the letter and spirit of the tax laws and regulations of the countries in which they operate.

第二章 国际税收管辖权

第一节 国际税收管辖权概述

管辖权是国家主权的体现。在税收领域,国家管辖权又称为税收管辖权,即国家有权决定由谁纳税、对什么征税、征多少税,以及如何征税。税收管辖权并不是国际税收特有的概念,自从有了税收,就存在税收管辖权的问题,在国际税收产生以前,税收管辖权局限在一国境内,问题相对简单。国际税收形成以后,就出现了不同国家都对同一征税对象征税的情形,于是形成了不同国家税收管辖权交叉重叠的情况。至此,税收管辖权问题开始引起国际社会的普遍关注,并成为国际税法的重要内容之一。

根据确定征税权力的原则不同,税收管辖权可分为居民税收管辖权、来源地税收管辖权和公民税收管辖权。

一、居民税收管辖权

居民税收管辖权,亦称"居住国税收管辖权",是指在国际税收中,国家根据纳税人在本国境内存在着税收居所这样的连结因素行使征税权力。它是属人管辖原则在国际税法上的体现,其确立是以纳税人与征税国之间存在着某种属人性质的联系为前提,这种根据纳税人的居民身份行使税收管辖权的原则,亦称为从人征税。

根据属人原则行使征税权的前提条件是纳税人与征税国之间存在着以人身隶属关系为特征的法律事实。这些属人连结因素,就自然人来说,主要有住所、居所、惯常居住地、国籍等等;就法人来说,主要有公司的注册登记所在地、公司的实际管理和控制中心所在地以及公司的总机构所在地等等。确定这类属人性质的连结因素在国际税法学上一般称作"税收居所"(tax residence)。凡是与征税国存在着这种税收居所联系的纳税人,便是该国税法上的居民纳税人,而这个征税国相应地被称作该纳税人的居住国。主权国家根据纳税人在本国境内存在着税收居所这一法律事实来行使征税的权力,这种根据税收居所联系对纳税人来自境内境外的全部财产和收入进行征税的原则,被称作"居住原则"或"居民税收管辖权原则"。

由于居民纳税人与居住国之间存在着居民身份的人身隶属关系,居住国可以主张对居民纳税人来源于和存在于居住国境内和境外的各种所得和财产价值征收所得税。因此,在征税国的居民税收管辖权下,纳税人承担的是无限纳税义务,即纳税人不仅要就来源于居住国境内的所得和财产承担纳税义务,而且还要就来源于居住国境外的所得和财产向其居住国承担纳税义务。[①]

各国确定本国的居民纳税人时所采用的标准并不完全一致,下一节将具体展开,这里仅以中国为例加以说明。中国区分企业和个人两种情形分别作出规定。就企业而言,中国规定了注册登记地和实际管理机构两种标准,即居民企业是指依法在中国境内成立,或者依照外国(地区)法律成立但实际管理机构在中国境内的企业,为中国的居民纳税人。[②] 这里的"实际管理机构",是指对企业的生产经营、人员、财务、财产等实施实质性全面管理和控制的机构。[③] 非居民企业是指依照外国(地区)法律成立且实际管理机构不在中国境内,但在中国境内设立机构、场所的,或者在中国境内未设立机构、场所,但有来源于中国境内所得的企业。[④] 这里所说的"机构、场所",是指在中国境内从事生产经营活动的机构、场所,包括:管理机构、营业机构或办事机构;工厂、农场或开采自然资源的场所;提供服务的场所;从事建筑、安装、装配、修理、勘探等工程作业的场所;其他从事生产经营活动的机构场所。非居民企业委托营业代理人在中国境内从事生产经营活动的,包括委托单位或者个人经常代其签订合同,或者储存、交付货物等,该营业代理人被视为非居民企业在中国境内设立的机构或场所。[⑤]

与国际通行做法一致,中国也规定居民企业承担无限纳税义务,而非居民企业承担有限纳税义务。居民企业应就来源于中国境内、境外的所得缴税。所得包括销售货物所得、提供劳务所得、转让财产所得、股息红利等权益性投资所得、利息所得、租金所得、特许权使用费所得、接受捐赠所得和其他所得。[⑥] 非居民企业在中国境内设立机构、场所的,应当就其所设机构、场所取得的来源于中国境内的所得,以及发生在中国境外但与其所设机构、场所有实际联系的所得缴纳企业所得税。非居民企业在中国境内未设立机构、场所的,或者虽设立机构、场所但取得的所得与其所设机构、场所没有实际联系的,应当就其来源于中国境内

---

① 参见刘剑文主编:《国际税法学》(第二版),北京大学出版社2004年版,第68页。
② 参见《企业所得税法》第2条。
③ 参见《企业所得税法实施条例》第4条。
④ 参见《企业所得税法》第2条。
⑤ 参见《企业所得税法实施条例》第5条。
⑥ 参见《企业所得税法》第3条、《企业所得税法实施条例》第6条。

的所得缴纳企业所得税。①

中国在界定个人居民纳税人时采用了住所标准和居住时间标准。在中国境内有住所或虽无住所但在境内居住满一年的个人为居民纳税人。在中国境内有住所的个人,是指因户籍、家庭、经济利益关系,而在中国境内习惯性居住的个人。在境内居住满一年,是指在一个纳税年度(即公历1月1日起至12月31日止)内,在中国境内居住满365日。在一个纳税年度内,一次不超过30日或者多次累计不超过90日的离境不扣减其在华居住的天数。居民纳税人对其无论是来源于中国境内还是境外的所得,都要在中国缴纳个人所得税。在中国境内无住所又不居住或居住不满一年但有从中国境内取得所得的个人为非居民纳税人。非居民纳税人仅就其来源于中国境内的所得,向中国缴纳个人所得税。②

二、来源地税收管辖权

来源地税收管辖权,亦称"从源征税",是指一国对跨国纳税人在该国领域范围内的所得课征税收的权力,它以征税对象与征税国领土之间存在着某种经济利益的联系为依据,是属地管辖原则在国际税法上的体现。

根据属地管辖原则行使税收管辖权的前提条件,是作为纳税人的各种所得与征税国之间存在着经济上的源泉关系。这些表示所得与征税国存在着某种渊源联系的地域连结标志,如不动产所在地,常设机构所在地,股息、利息、特许权使用费、租金等所得的发生地,以及债务人或支付人所在地等等,在国际税法上称作"所得来源地"(the source of income)或"所得来源国"。对那些在来源国没有税收居所,但却因取得上述所得而负有纳税义务的人,一般称为"来源国的非居民纳税人"。而在国际税法上,一国根据所得来源地这一连结因素对非居民纳税人征税的原则,称为"来源地原则"或"来源地税收管辖权原则"。

与居民税收管辖权下纳税人的无限纳税义务不同,如果一个国家行使的是来源地税收管辖权,纳税人承担的是有限的纳税义务,即只就来源于该国境内的所得向该国纳税。

由于来源地的认定直接关系到一国的税收利益,所以各国的来源地认定也不尽相同,本章第三节对此有详述,这里仅以中国为例加以阐释。企业所得来源地的确定遵循以下规则:(1)销售货物所得,按照交易活动发生地确定。(2)提供劳务所得,按照劳务发生地确定。(3)转让财产所得:① 不动产转让所得按

---

① 参见《企业所得税法》第3条。
② 参见《个人所得税法》第1条及《个人所得税法实施条例》第2、3条。

照不动产所在地确定;② 动产转让所得按照转让动产的企业或者机构、场所所在地确定;③ 权益性投资资产转让所得按照被投资企业所在地确定。(4) 股息、红利等权益性投资所得,按照分配所得的企业所在地确定。(5) 利息所得、租金所得、特许权使用费所得,按照负担、支付所得的企业或者机构、场所所在地确定,或者按照负担、支付所得的个人的住所地确定。(6) 其他所得,由国务院财政、税务主管部门确定。①

对于个人,下列所得属于来源于中国境内的所得:(1) 在中国境内任职、受雇而取得的工资、薪金所得;(2) 在中国境内从事生产、经营活动而取得的生产、经营所得;(3) 因任职、受雇、履约等而在中国境内提供劳务取得的劳务报酬所得;(4) 将财产出租给承租人在中国境内使用而取得的所得;(5) 转让中国境内的建筑物、土地使用权财产或者在中国境内转让其他财产取得的所得;(6) 提供各种特许权在中国境内使用而取得的所得;(7) 从中国境内的公司、企业以及其他经济组织或者个人取得的利息、股息、红利所得。②

三、公民税收管辖权

公民税收管辖权(citizenship based taxation),是指一国政府在行使征税权的过程中,以是否拥有该国国籍为标准,对拥有该国国籍者在全球范围内的所得以及财产价值行使征税权。与居民税收管辖权比较而言,公民税收管辖权也是属人管辖原则在国际税法上的体现。不同的是,公民税收管辖权仅以征税对象的国籍为标准,征税当局仅需考虑纳税人是否具有本国国籍,不论其所得与财产价值的来源与性质。本章第四节将具体介绍国籍的确认、公民税收管辖权的税法意义及其最新发展动态。

第二节 居民税收管辖权的行使

一、居民身份的确认

如前所述,如果纳税人在征税国境内存在税收居所,则其就是该国税法上的居民纳税人,因此居民纳税人身份的确定也就是税收居所的确定。

(一) 自然人居民身份的确认

根据各国的税法实践,在确认自然人居民身份的问题上,通常所采用的标准

---

① 参见《企业所得税法实施条例》第 7 条。
② 参见《个人所得税法实施条例》第 5 条。

主要有以下两种:

1. 住所标准

自然人的住所是指一个人以久住的意思而居住的某一处所。这一概念体现了住所的两个构成要件:一是自然人主观上有久住于某一地方的意思;二是自然人客观上有久住于一定地方的事实。有长住意图而无久住的事实,或者是有久住的事实而无长住的意图都难以构成一个人的住所。例如,一位美籍华人早已有归国定居的意图,但他一直居住在美国,并无在中国居住的事实,我们就很难认定该美籍华人的住所在中国境内。同样,如果一位美国商人长年在巴黎经商,但并无在巴黎定居的意图,与其家庭生活有关的一切都在美国,经商是他在巴黎的唯一动因,尽管该美国商人在巴黎居住,但他的住所是在美国而不是在法国。

由于住所具有永久性和稳定性的特点,采用住所标准以确定自然人的居民身份比较容易识别,但住所作为自然人永久居住的处所,却并不能反映出一个人真正的活动场所。在国际税收实践中,自然人离开自己住所而长期在外的现象屡见不鲜。鉴于住所标准存在的缺陷,有些国家或地区还采用其他辅助性规定来弥补住所标准的不足。例如,美国纽约州税法规定,凡在本州境内拥有一永久性的住宅,在纳税年度内又曾在该州境内居住六个月以上的,即视为本州的居民纳税人。

2. 居所标准

所谓居所,是指无久住的意思而暂时居住的处所。与住所不同,居所是住所以外的居住场所。各国法律都规定,一个人可以同时有几处居所,在无住所或住所无从查考的情况下,可视居所为住所。在各国税法实践中,居所也是用来判定自然人居民身份的主要标准之一。例如,英国、加拿大、澳大利亚等英美法系的国家就以该纳税人是否在本国境内拥有居所作为认定自然人居民身份的重要标志。

由于居所一般是自然人短暂逗留而临时居住并达到一定期限的处所,所以,居所并不具有永久居住的性质。因此,在国际税收实践中,居所标准一般与居留期限相结合,即自然人居民纳税人的身份,取决于其在一国境内的居留时间。例如,依照缅甸的税法规定,在缅甸国内实际停留 300 天以上的纳税义务人(不一定是连续停留 300 天),即视为缅甸税收上的居民纳税人。运用居所和居留时间相结合的标准,是国际上确定自然人居民身份的通常做法,只是各国税法规定的时间长短可能不同,停留时间连续或累计计算通常也并不一致。

(二) 法人居民身份的确认[①]

各国税法上判定法人居民身份，主要采用下列标准：

1. 注册地标准

注册地标准，是指法人的居民身份依法人在何国注册成立而定。采用这一标准的主要以美国、加拿大等国为代表。根据美国《国内税收法》(Internal Revenue Code, IRC) 第 7701 节 (a) 项的规定，在美国依法注册登记设立的公司，应就世界范围内的所得承担纳税义务。而不在美国注册成立的外国公司，仅就在美国境内从事贸易和经营活动有实际联系的所得或特定的投资所得承担纳税义务。例如，"国家纸张和铅字公司诉鲍尔斯" [National Paper & Type Co. v. Bowers (1924)] 一案中，原告国家纸张和铅字公司是一家依美国法注册登记成立的公司，其注册地位于新泽西州，并在纽约州经营进出口业务，将位于美国境内的货物运至国外销售，从中获取收益。美国税务当局不仅要求原告就其境内收入申报纳税，而且应将境外的销售利润包括在内。原告向法院起诉辩称，一些依外国法注册成立的公司，同样也在美国境内购买货物运至境外销售，其经营的业务范围同原告完全相同，但美国税务当局却对这些外国公司在美国境外的销售所得没有课征税收。据此，原告认为受到了税收的差别待遇。美国最高法院判决认定，美国政府应当保证依美国法注册成立的公司在世界范围内的利益不受到损害，因此美国政府有权要求美国公司就其世界范围的所得申报纳税。但美国政府无权对外国公司位于美国境外的收入行使课税权，因为外国公司根据外国法登记成立，在美国境外的活动并不受到美国法律的管辖。

采用法人注册地标准来确认法人的居民身份，其优点在于便于识别，因为法人的注册登记地只能有一个，但这种标准的缺点在于容易产生法律规避现象。目前，有许多跨国公司为了逃避所在国的沉重税负，纷纷在避税地设立"基地公司"以规避有关国家的税收管辖权。

2. 实际管理和控制中心所在地标准

实际管理和控制中心所在地标准，是指以法人在本国是否设有管理和控制中心来判定其居民身份。所谓管理和控制中心，主要指法人的董事会或监事会所在的地点。采用这一标准的主要以英国、德国、希腊、瑞士等国为代表。最被人广泛援引的经典判例是英国法院在 1906 年审理的"比尔斯联合矿业有限公司

[①] 这里所说的"法人"与民法或公司法上所说的"法人"并不是同一个概念，而是与"自然人"相对应的概念，包括公司和其他团体，不论它们是否符合民法或公司法上的"法人"概念。本注解也适用于本书下文中对"法人"的理解。

诉荷奥"(De Beers Consolidated Mines v. Howe)一案。① 在该案中,原告公司在南非注册登记,公司总部设在南非,其产品的开发与销售也在南非进行,但该公司的大部分股东却居住在英国本土,公司董事会也多在英国境内举行,公司经营与管理的重大决策均在英国境内作出。英国法院据此认定,该公司为英国居民公司,应承担居民纳税义务。与注册地标准一样,实际管理和控制中心所在地标准也存在弊端,实践中,有些企业为了税收利益而操纵选择管理中心所在地,以达到逃避税收的目的。

3. 总机构所在地标准

总机构所在地标准,是指凡总机构设在哪一国,便为该国居民公司。所谓总机构,就是指法人的总公司、总厂或总店,是负责管理和控制法人的全部日常经营业务活动并统一核算法人盈亏的中心机构。采用这一标准的主要有法国、日本等国。与实际管理和控制中心相比,总机构所在地标准强调的是法人组织结构主体的重要性,而实际管理和控制中心所在地标准确定的是法人权力中心的重要性。总机构所在地比较容易确定,但法人也容易通过使用改变总机构所在地的手段,达到变更居民身份的目的。②

二、居民税收管辖权冲突的解决原则

由于各国税法对纳税人居民身份的判定采用不同的标准,因此不可避免地会发生居民税收管辖权的冲突,导致在国际税收上产生双重居民的问题。税收上的双重居民加重了纳税人的税收负担,妨碍了国际经济的正常交往,同时也给国家税务当局行使税收管辖权带来一定的困难。于是,在缔结税收协定过程中,各国都在致力于解决对自然人和法人的双重居民身份问题。目前,对于居民税收管辖权的冲突主要靠各国在国际税收协定中规定冲突规则的方法加以解决。在这方面,《OECD范本》和《UN范本》确定的冲突原则具有代表意义。

(一)自然人居民身份冲突的解决方法

关于自然人居民身份的冲突,两大范本均规定,同时为缔约国双方居民的个人,其身份按以下规则确定:(1)应认为是其永久性住所所在国的居民;如果在两个国家同时有永久性住所,应认为是与其个人和经济关系更密切(重要利益中心)的国家的居民。(2)如果其重要利益中心所在国无法确定,或者在两个国家中任何一国都没有永久性住所,应认为是其有习惯性居处所在国的居民。

---

① 参见曹建明、陈治东主编:《国际经济法专论》(第六卷),法律出版社2000年版,第33页。
② 参见刘剑文主编:《国际税法学》(第二版),北京大学出版社2004年版,第84页。

(3) 如果其在两个国家都有或者都没有习惯性居处,应认为仅是其国籍所属缔约国的居民。(4) 如果其同时是两个国家的国民,或者不是两个国家中任何一国的国民,缔约国双方主管当局应通过协商解决。①

　　根据范本注释的解释,范本的规定将优先权给予了个人有永久性住所的缔约国一方。在范本的适用中(即当两国法律有冲突时),住所应是个人所拥有或占有"家"的地方,并且这个"家"具有永久性。也就是说,个人必须安排或保留这个"家"以用于永久性居住和使用,它不同于明显地为了作短期停留而在特定地点停留。至于"家"的概念,要考虑到任何形式的家(私人自有或租用的房屋或公寓、租用的带家具的房间),但住家的永久性是其本质要素,即个人已安排长期居住的住所,而不是为了某些原因(旅游、商务旅行、求学、到学校进修课程等)短期逗留而临时居住。②

　　如果某个人在缔约国双方都有永久性住所,上述原则将优先权给予了与个人的人身和经济联系更密切的国家,即重要利益中心地。如果利益中心地无法确定,则要考虑以下补充标准:首先是习惯性住处,然后是国籍。如果同时为两国国民或都不是两国国民,则应由两国共同协商解决。如果某人在缔约国双方都有一个永久性住所,有必要对事实加以分析以判定哪一国同这个人的人身和经济联系更为密切。这要考虑其家庭和社会关系、职业、政治、文化及其他活动、从事营业的地点、管理财产所在地等因素,这些情况应作为一个整体加以分析,并应特别注意个人的自身行为。如果他在一国已有住所,并在拥有该住所的同时在另一国又建一住所,但仍保留第一个住所且在此一直居住、工作,在那里拥有家庭和财产,这些事实加上其他一些因素可以表明,他在第一个国家保留其重要利益中心。③

　　上述原则还为以下两种情形的冲突提供了另一解决思路:第一种情况是个人在缔约国双方都有永久性住所,但不能确定其重要利益中心所在国,在一国而非另一国有习惯性住处的事实,足以使天平向该个人较常居留的国家倾斜。在判定习惯性住处时,不仅要注意这个人在所在国永久性住所的停留情况,还应考虑到在同一国家的任何其他地点停留的情况。第二种情况是此人的永久性住所不在缔约国的任何一方,如这个人不断地居住在各个旅馆之间。在这种情况下,要将此人在一个国家所有的停留时间加在一起进行判断,而不必问其停留的原

---

① 参见《UN 范本》和《OECD 范本》第 4 条第 2 款。
② 参见《OECD 范本》第 4 条注释第 12 段。
③ 参见《OECD 范本》第 4 条注释第 15 段。

因。在对这两种情况明确规定优先选择个人有习惯性住处的缔约国方面,上述原则没有明确规定应在多长的期间内比较个人在两国分别居住的时间长短,但应该理解为在足够长的期间内进行比较,以便能确定其在两个国家中的哪一个居所是属于习惯性的,同时确定停留的间隔时间。在前述两种情况中,如果这个人在缔约国双方都有或都没有习惯性住处,应优先选择其为国民的缔约国。如果这个人同时是缔约国双方国民或不是任何一方国民,则由主管当局通过相互协商解决这个问题。

(二) 法人居民身份冲突的解决方法

关于法人居民身份冲突的解决方式有两种:一是由双方协商确定该法人为哪一方的居民。二是在税收协定中确定一种标准,依此来判断法人是哪一方的居民。《UN 范本》和《OECD 范本》都规定,非个人纳税人同时为缔约国双方居住者的,应认为是其实际管理机构所在国的居住者。[①] 不过,两大范本均未对"实际管理"(effective management)一语作出明确的定义,留待各国在双边协定中协商确定。

范本注释表明,在实践中,一家公司被一个以上国家视为居民征税的事例虽然并不常见,但也时有发生。例如,缔约国一方根据公司的登记注册地,而缔约国另一方根据公司的实际管理机构所在地确定其居民身份,此时就会发生冲突,所以也应制定具体的规则加以解决。实际管理机构所在地,是指对企业实体的营业必不可少的关键性的管理与商业决策实质作出之地。这种实际管理机构所在地通常是企业高层(如董事会)作出决策的地方,以及决定企业整体行动的地点。在实践中还需进一步明确具体标准,所有相关的具体情况都必须予以考虑以便确定实际管理机构所在地。一个实体可能拥有多个管理机构所在地,但在任何特定时候只可能有一个实际管理机构所在地。

第三节 收入来源地税收管辖权的行使

一、所得来源地的认定

确认所得来源地,就是要认定所得的地域标志。根据这一地域标志,来源国有权对非居民纳税人取自本国境内的所得进行征税。目前,各国对所得来源地的认定,一般区分不同性质的所得采用不同的标准,主要分为营业所得、股息、利

---

① 参见《UN 范本》和《OECD 范本》第 4 条第 3 款。

息、财产收益和特许权使用费、个人劳务所得、不动产所得等收益的认定标准。

认定营业所得的来源地有下列几种：营业机构所在地、商品交付地、商品使用地、销售合同签订地、商品交付之前的储存地等等。例如，根据美国《国内税收法》的规定，销售购进存货的所得，其来源地是销售发生地，一般是所有权的转移地点。

各国一般以分配股息的居民所属国为来源地，有的国家则考虑分配股息的公司的利润实际来源地。例如，根据美国《国内税收法》的规定，国内公司支付的股息是美国来源所得，外国公司支付给外国股东的股息则不视为美国来源所得，但是如果该外国公司在美国从事贸易经营活动，则该支付的股息视为美国来源所得。

认定利息所得的来源地，各国主要采用以下标准：贷款的实际使用地、借款人所在地、利息支付地等，而对于债务发生地一般不予考虑。例如，根据美国《国内税收法》的规定，利息所得的来源地依支付人的居住地而定，据此，美国的国内公司、个人、联邦政府的代理人支付的利息为美国来源利息。

认定动产租金和特许权使用费的来源地标准一般有：财产的实际使用地、租赁人或被许可人所在地，以及租金或费用的支付地等。例如，根据美国《国内税收法》的规定，有形财产的租金所得，其来源地应是该租赁财产的所在地。

认定个人劳务所得的来源地标准一般有：劳务的提供地、劳动力的使用地、劳务报酬支付人的所在地等。例如，根据美国《国内税收法》的规定，在美国境内提供劳务所获取的报酬为美国来源所得，而在美国境外进行劳务活动的报酬所得是国外来源收入。

各国一般都以不动产所在地作为不动产所得的来源地。例如，根据美国《国内税收法》的规定，处置美国不动产或一家美国不动产控股公司股份的收入，视为美国来源所得，而出售位于美国境外的不动产所取得的所得视为外国来源收入。

目前，由于各国对各种所得的来源地的确认标准存在差异，就同一笔所得而言，可能因采用的标准不同而被认定为来源于两个国家，其结果必然导致国家来源地税收管辖权的冲突，需要借助税收协定的安排来加以协调。

二、收入来源地税收管辖权冲突的解决原则

不同来源地标准引起的来源地税收管辖权冲突以及来源地税收管辖权与居民税收管辖权冲突的解决方法将在第四章详述，在此仅作简要的概述。

(一) 跨国营业所得征税权冲突的协调

由于跨国营业所得是一种包罗各种生产经营业务在内的综合性所得,跨国营业所得来源地的认定标准极其复杂多样,很容易发生来源地税收管辖权的重叠,导致国际双重征税现象的产生。为了防止国际双重征税,在国际税法上,各国都根据"常设机构原则"(principle of permanent establishment)对非居民纳税人的跨国营业所得进行征税。所谓常设机构原则,是指来源国仅对非居民纳税人通过设在来源国境内的常设机构的活动所取得的营业所得实行征税。这一原则表明,来源国只能对非居民纳税人通过设在来源国境内的常设机构的活动所获取的所得行使征税权,而对于非居民纳税人不是通过常设机构的经营活动所产生的营业所得,则不视为来源于该国境内的营业所得,因而也无权征税。

(二) 跨国投资所得征税权冲突的协调

跨国投资所得通常是指纳税人从事消极投资活动所取得的股息、利息和特许权使用费等收入。来源地国对非居民的投资所得进行征税,首先必须确定上述投资所得的来源地是否在本国境内。由于各国在认定投资所得的来源地上所采取的标准不尽相同,如在股息来源地的确认上,有的国家以分配股息公司的实际管理或控制中心地为标准,有的国家则以分配股息公司的注册登记地为股息来源地,这必然使得各国在税收管辖权的行使上引发冲突,导致国际双重征税的产生。为了避免国际双重征税,各国有必要通过缔结国际税收协定,对各项投资所得的征税范围加以协调和确定。

从国际税收协定实践看,对于各项投资所得,国际上一般认为,不论是来源地国还是居住国,均有权对股息、利息和特许权使用费等投资所得行使征税权,但来源地国享有优先征税权。世界各国对非居民纳税人的投资所得,一般采用预提方式征税,即支付人在向非居民支付股息、利息、特许权使用费等款项时,有义务从中扣缴非居民纳税人应缴纳的所得税款。上述税收,在国际上通常称为"预提税",这是所得税的一种源泉控制征收的方式。预提税税率一般低于企业所得税税率,它往往根据收入全额计征,不扣除费用,具有估定预征的特点。那些适用"实际联系"原则的国家规定,如果非居民纳税人来源于其境内的投资所得与该非居民在其境内设立的常设机构有实际联系时,应归属于常设机构的所得中征税,而不适用预提方式征税。

(三) 跨国个人劳务所得征税权冲突的协调

个人劳务所得包括独立的个人劳务所得和非独立的个人劳务所得。前者主要指自由职业者所从事的专业性劳务活动或其他独立性质的活动而取得的收入,如从事独立的科学、文学、艺术、教育和教学活动,以及从事医师、律师、工程师、建筑师、牙医师和会计师等独立的活动而取得的所得;后者一般是指个人由于受雇而取得的薪金、工资和其他类似的报酬。

1. 跨国独立个人劳务所得征税权冲突协调的一般规则

对跨国独立个人劳务所得征税权的冲突协调问题,相关规定不尽一致。在2000年之前,《UN范本》和《OECD范本》对此都专设"第14条"加以规定,均采用了"固定基地原则"(principle of fixed base),只是二者在居住国和来源地国的税收利益分配问题上的规定有所不同。2000年,《OECD范本》删除了第14条,根据该范本注释的解释,删除第14条反映了在第7条使用的常设机构概念和第14条使用的固定基地概念之间,或者适用第7条或第14条计算利润和税收之间已经没有原先所预想的区别了,常设机构的概念可以适用于先前构成固定基地的情况。

与经合组织不一样,最新的《UN范本》仍然在第14条将对非居民纳税人的跨国独立个人劳务所得的征税单独作为一条加以规定,而且仍然实行"固定基地原则"。该范本第14条规定,对于非居民独立的个人劳务所得,应仅由居住国征税,但如有下述两种情形之一的,可由来源国征税:(1) 在来源国经常设有固定基地,并且其所得是归属于该固定基地的;(2) 在来源国停留期间在该会计年度中累计等于或超过183天,并且其所得是在该期间取得的。不过,两大范本均未对"固定基地"规定明确的定义,《OECD范本》只是在2000年以前的注释中规定固定基地应包括诸如医师的诊所、建筑师或律师事务所这样的从事独立劳务活动的固定场所或设施。

2. 跨国非独立个人劳务征税权冲突协调的一般规则

根据各国税收协定以及两大范本的相关规定,缔约国一方的居民由于受雇而取得的薪金、工资和其他类似的报酬,除了受雇于缔约国另一方的以外,应仅在该缔约国征税。由于受雇于缔约国另一方而取得的报酬,可以在缔约国另一方征税。但同时具备下述三项要件的,应由其居住国征税:(1) 收款人在该会计年度内的任何12个月中在缔约国另一方的停留期间累计不超过183天;(2) 该项报酬是由雇主自付或其代理人代付,而雇主并非缔约国另一方居民;(3) 该项报酬不由雇主设在另一国的常设机构或固定基地所负担。[①]

---

① 参见《UN范本》和《OECD范本》第15条。

3. 对特定人员的跨国劳务所得的征税规则

对于非居民独立个人劳务所得与非独立个人劳务所得的征税原则并不适用于一些特殊性质的所得,这些特殊性质的所得主要包括董事费以及艺术家和运动员所得等。

根据两大范本的第 16 条,缔约国一方居民作为缔约国另一方居民公司的董事会成员取得的董事费和其他类似款项,可以在该缔约国另一方征税。本条涉及缔约国一方居民作为缔约国另一方居民公司的董事会成员取得的报酬,由于有时难以判断董事的劳务活动在何地履行,因此,将公司的居民国作为该项劳务的履行地。根据范本注释,"其他类似性质的款项"包括个人以公司董事会成员的身份获得的其他实物利益(如股票期权、住宅或汽车的使用权、健康或人寿保险以及俱乐部会员资格等)。实践中,公司董事会成员往往还兼任公司的其他职务,如作为一般雇员、顾问、参事等等,第 16 条不适用于该人兼任董事以外的职务取得的报酬。

根据两大范本的第 17 条,缔约国一方居民作为表演家,如戏剧、电影、广播或电视艺术家、音乐家,或作为运动员,在缔约国另一方从事其个人活动取得的所得,可以在该缔约国另一方征税。表演家或运动员从事其个人活动取得的所得,并非归属于表演家或运动员本人,而是归属于其他人,该所得可以在该表演家或运动员从事其活动的缔约国征税。该条规定表明,对作为缔约国一方居民的表演家和运动员,可以在其从事个人活动所在地的缔约国另一方纳税,而不论这些活动是营业性质还是受雇性质。这样规定的结果,一方面有利于来源地国行使征税权,防止纳税人逃避税收,另一方面也能防止国际双重免税现象的产生。

(四) 跨国财产收益及财产价值征税权冲突的协调

1. 跨国财产收益征税权冲突的协调

所谓财产收益,一般是指在转移所有权的情形下,由于出售或转让财产而取得的所得。而跨国财产收益则是一国居民纳税人取得的来源于非居住国境内的财产转让所得。各国对于跨国财产收益的征税,一般以实际发生地或者是与常设机构或固定基地有关为准。根据两大范本的规定,缔约国一方居民从转让位于缔约国另一方的不动产所取得的所得,可由缔约国另一方征税,即由财产的所在国征税。缔约国一方的企业在缔约国另一方设有常设机构,或者缔约国一方居民在缔约国另一方设有从事独立个人劳务活动的固定基地,由于转让构成常设机构营业财产部分的动产或附属于固定基地的动产而取得的所得,包括由于转让整个常设机构(单独或随同整个企业转让)或固定基地取得的所得,可以在缔约国另一方征税。但是,转让在国际运输中运用的船舶、飞机和转让从事内河运输的船只,或转让与上述船舶、飞机或船只有关系的动产而取得的所得,应仅在该企业实际管理机构所在的缔约国征税,即由其居住国独占征税。缔约国一方居民转让股份取得收益,如果该股份50%①以上的价值直接或间接来自于位于缔约国另一方的不动产,则该收益可在该缔约国另一方征税。如果是转让前述财产以外的任何财产取得的收益,则应仅在转让者为其居民的缔约国征税。②

2. 跨国财产价值征税权冲突的协调

所谓跨国财产价值,一般是指一国居民纳税人所拥有的位于非居住国境内的那部分财产价值。两大范本都专门规定了对一般财产价值的征税协调规则,但两大范本所规定的协调规则主要调整的是跨国一般静态财产价值,仅涉及对财产的征税,不包括不动产税、遗产税、赠与税以及交易税。《OECD范本》注释表明,财产税通常构成对财产收益征税的补充,因此,原则上说,只有对财产的某个因素所产生的所得有权征税的国家,才能对该财产因素征税,但是不能单纯和简单地套用对这类所得征税的原则,因为一国并非对所有的所得项目都有独占征税权。

根据两大范本建议的课税协调规则,缔约国一方居民所有且坐落在缔约国另一方境内的不动产,以及缔约国一方企业设在缔约国另一方的常设机构营业财产部分的动产,或缔约国一方居民设在缔约国另一方从事独立个人劳务活动的固定基地的动产,都可以在缔约国另一方征税。但从事国际运输的船舶、飞机以及经营上述船舶、飞机的动产,应仅在企业的实际管理场所所在地一方征税。③ 对于上述财产以外的其他财产,两大范本的规定不尽一致。《OECD范本》规定应由财产所有人的居住国一方享有独占征税权,而《UN范本》则将这一问题留给有关国家在双边协定中协商确定。

第四节 公民税收管辖权的行使

虽然国内学界在界定公民税收管辖权时,多坚持以是否拥有一国国籍作为行使税收管辖权的标准,但从有关国家的实践看,国籍是重要因素,但不是唯一因素。另外,考虑到目前只有美国、荷兰等少数国家实行公民税收管辖权,而美

---

① 《OECD范本》规定该比例为50%,《UN范本》将这一问题留给有关国家在双边协定中协商确定。
② 参见《UN范本》和《OECD范本》第13条。
③ 参见《OECD范本》和《UN范本》第22条及相关注释。

国又是将此制度发挥到极致的国家,因此本节主要结合美国的立法和实践来对公民税收管辖权加以介绍。

一、国籍的确认

（一）自然人国籍的确认

在公民税收管辖权下,自然人国籍的确定具有重要意义。一个人拥有特定国家的国籍身份,从而可以享受该国所提供的人身、财产保护,并享有选举投票权、自由出入境权利等。正是这种特定的法律关系以及所涉及的国家主权和利益,为公民税收管辖权的实施奠定了理论基础。依据国际法基本理论,国籍认定问题属于各国主权范围内的管辖事项,每个国家都有权独立地制定本国国籍的取得、丧失、变更等相关规定。根据当今各国的立法和实践,自然人取得一国国籍的方式主要有:

(1) 出生地主义,即无论父母双方是否为该国公民,因出生而取得该国国籍。

(2) 血统主义,即父母双方或一方为该国公民,因血缘而取得该国国籍。

(3) 兼采出生地主义与血统主义,即父母双方或一方为该国公民,本人出生在该国,因而取得该国国籍。

(4) 申请入籍,即根据该国相关法律符合具体条件可以经申请批准,因而取得该国国籍。

在施行公民税收管辖权的国家,当税务行政部门依据本国国籍法确认一自然人具有该国国籍时,该自然人就负有无限的纳税义务,即使其在该国境内没有任何居所。

（二）法人国籍的确认

虽然有的学者因主张法人人格否定说而否认公司的国籍,认为只有公司的成员才享有国籍,但法人如自然人一样享有国籍在许多国家的立法与司法实践中已是不争的事实。关于法人国籍的认定,有下列学说:一是成员国籍主义。这种学说认为,法人的国籍应当依照组成法人的成员或董事会董事的国籍来确定,也就是以法人资本控制者的国籍来确定法人的国籍。二是设立地主义。这种学说认为,凡在内国设立的公司即为内国公司,凡在外国设立的公司即为外国公司。三是住所地主义。这种学说认为,公司的住所是公司的经营管理中心或主要活动中心,公司住所地决定公司的国籍。四是准据法主义。这种学说认为,公司依照哪国法律设立就是哪国法人。五是实际控制主义。这种学说认为,公司实际由哪国控制就是哪国公司。六是复合标准,即将上述不同标准相结合。①实践中,大多数国家都采用了设立地主义。例如,美国《国内税收法》规定,凡是根据美国各州法律注册成立的公司,均应就其国内国外的全部所得向美国承担税负。

二、公民税收管辖权的实施

自19世纪中叶以来,公民税收管辖权一直以其清晰的定义与显著的税收效果著称。在一定历史时期内,这种税收管辖权给相关国家的征税带来了积极的效果。然而,第二次工业革命以来,随着生产力的革新与发展,世界经济全球化进程不断提升,在此背景下,出现大量人口流动以及移居现象,这一现象使得公民税收管辖权的实际实施变得困难。

根据美国《国内税收法》第1节,每一个美国公民全球范围内的收入都将成为征税对象。② 为配合公民税收管辖权的具体实施,该法以及《国内税收条例》(Income Tax Regulations,ITR)首先就"美国公民"进行了完整的界定。对于自然人而言,根据《国内税收法》第7701节(b)项,税收法律意义上的"美国公民"是指符合"永久合法居住权"(lawfully admitted for permanent residence)的居民;满足"实际存在"(substantial present test)标准的居民;或者满足"第一年选择权"(first year election)的居民。③ 符合以上条件之一,该个人全球范围内的收入都将置于美国征税的范围以内。对于公司或者其他实体而言,根据《国内税收条例》第7701节2(b)项,税法意义上的美国国内公司是指根据美国联邦法律或是某一州法律而建立的公司。④ 但凡符合该项规定的公司就其全球收入向美国联邦政府缴税。

在具体实施公民税收管辖权的过程中,美国联邦最高法院1924年审理的Cook v. Tait一案对公民税收管辖权的理论基础与实施标准作了指导性的界定,并对后来的理论与实践产生了深远的影响。⑤ 该案涉及一位长期居住在墨西哥的美国公民,其所有收入与所得均来自墨西哥,然而,法庭经过审理后判决该美国公民应就其所得向美国政府纳税。判决指出,公民税收管辖权并不考虑纳税人的长期居住场所是否在美国,也不考虑收入来源地是不是美国,仅与相关

---

① 参见丁伟主编:《国际私法学》(第三版),北京大学出版社2013年版,第143页。
② See IRC §§ 1 and 11(a).
③ See IRC §§ 7701(b)(1).
④ See ITR §§ 301.7701-2(b)(1),(2),(3),(5),(6).
⑤ See Cook v. Tait, 265 U.S. 47.

纳税人的"公民身份"挂钩。① 根据《国内税收法》第7701节(b)(6)项,Cook具有永久合法居住在美国的权利,据此,他即为税法意义上的"美国公民",从而被归置于公民税收管辖权范围之内。根据此判决,公民税收管辖权的基础在于"美国政府对非长期居住在美国的美国公民征税是一个合理的行为,因为美国政府在全世界范围内对其合法公民都给予了一定人身和财产保护,因此,美国公民应就这份保护与收益向美国政府纳税"。

同时,为了调整公民税收管辖权所引起的双重征税的问题,美国国内收入局(Internal Revenue Service,IRS)与《国内税收条例》设置了"收入免除"(exclusion from gross income)与"国外税收抵免"(foreign tax credit)规则。"收入免除"是指就"合格纳税人"而言,在计算其应税收入时,可以适当免去其在海外的部分收入与相关住房补贴。② 与"收入免除"相比,"国外税收抵免"规则更为灵活,"国外税收抵免"具体来说是用限度内的国外已缴税款抵免国内应缴税款。

例如,一家根据美国联邦法律成立的公司在某一纳税年度全球范围内收入$100,000且全部来自美国境外,海外实际缴税$20,000。假设当年该公司收入所对应的美国税率为30%,那么在不考虑任何税收优惠的基础上,该公司应向联邦政府缴税$30,000($100,000×30%)。若根据"收入免除"规则,该公司的境外收入($100,000)可以免去$80,000(根据"收入免除"规则,每一个税收年度的"合格纳税人"的境外收入免额上限为$80,000)。据此,该公司向美国联邦政府缴税的税基缩减为$20,000,从而国内税收缩减为$6,000($20,000×30%)。因此,经过"收入免除"的调整,该公司这一税收年度的纳税总额为$26,000。若根据"国外税收抵免"规则,该公司境外所缴的$20,000转化为"抵扣额"折抵国内税收。据此,国内税收额度将缩减为$10,000($30,000－$20,000)。因此,该公司这一税收年度的纳税总额为$30,000。

不可否认,公民税收管辖权在一定时期内对美国的税收征管起到了积极的作用。然而,随着战后经济的不断发展与科技进步,如今公民税收管辖权的意义不断受到学界与实务界的质疑。美国政府税收政策顾问欧文·科恩(Irwin I. Cohn)教授就曾撰文指出美国现行公民税收管辖权已脱离了现今国际形势。由于经济全球化的发展,南北战争时期所涌现的仅富人阶级向外移居的现象早已不复存在,如今由于全球经济一体化的加强以及科技的不断发展,全球移居的特

---

① See Ray August, International Business Law, 3rd edition, Pearson Education North Asia Limited and Higher Education Press, 2002, pp. 707—708.
② See IRC§§911(a).

征不断明显。此外,根据美国移民和国籍法的规定,凡是在美国本土出生的自然人当然拥有美国国籍,部分拥有美国国籍的自然人可能从未真正在美国本土生活。在此背景下,坚持对全球范围内的美国公民征税已经失去了其当初确立时的社会基础,一味坚持公民税收管辖权还会给美国税收征管部门带来极大的行政支出负担,应及时废止。① 尽管质疑较多,但美国目前不大可能对其税收管辖权基础进行根本的变革。

三、公民税收管辖权的最新发展

2008 年金融危机以来,美国经济一直处于低迷期,其财政赤字问题也不断加剧。另外,美国每年大约有 11.5 万亿美元的应税收入隐匿于各"避税天堂"的离岸账户中,造成税款的大量流失。因此,如何完善税收体系、弥补税收漏洞成为美国政府一直着力解决的问题。与此同时,2007 年的"瑞银集团案"也促使美国执行更为严格的公民税收管辖权。②

2009 年 12 月 9 日,美国众议院通过《海外账户纳税法案》(Foreign Account Tax Compliance Act,FATCA)。《海外账户纳税法案》是美国《国内税收法》第四章"促进就业法案"(HIRE)第五标题的 A 副标题,法案原定于 2013 年 1 月 1 日正式生效,后因其引起全球范围内的争议,为了通过协调以更好地实施该法案,法案推迟到 2014 年 1 月 1 日起生效。

《海外账户纳税法案》是美国基于公民税收管辖权而向美国公民和具有美国永久居留权的人征缴税款的法案,其立法目的是防止纳税人将收入隐匿于离岸金融账户以避税。一方面,法案要求每一个拥有海外账户的美国公民,如果满足:(1) 上一个税收年度的最后一天账户上拥有超过 5 万美元;或(2) 上一个税收年度中的任何一天账户上曾拥有 15 万美元,必须及时申报他们的离岸账户信息,并及时缴税。如果符合条件的美国公民没有及时申报或者瞒报,那么他们将面临罚款。另一方面,法案要求全球范围内的金融机构与美国进行合作,具体而言,根据《海外账户纳税法案》,所有金融机构必须提供美国账户持有者的如下信息:身份、账户持有人地址、账户持有人的纳税人的身份证号或社保账号、账户存款数额、提交信息当天的资产价值。对不配合信息披露的外国金融机构和非金融外国组织,美国税务当局可以征收总收入 30% 的预扣税款。

---

① See Reuven S. Avi-Yonah, The Case Against Taxing Citizens, Public Law and Legal Theory Working Paper Series, March, 2010.

② United States v. UBS AG, see generally Jared Seff, Cracking Down on Tax Evaders-Swiss Banking: Secrets, Lies, and Deception, 38 S. U. L. Rev. 159 (2010).

《海外账户纳税法案》一经公布就引起了全球金融、法律、税务、财会以及政治领域的极大关注。在税收领域,《海外账户纳税法案》的实施使得公民税收管辖权废止问题又一次陷入热议。这一法案的公布表明美国政府仍坚持实施公民税收管辖权,但民众普遍担心该法案将增加那些长期移居海外的美国公民的税务负担,而且美国税务系统也将承受沉重的行政负担。此外,美国还有学者认为,《海外账户纳税法案》的公布与实施恰恰显示出公民税收管辖权的理论基础格外薄弱。[①] 对于一个长期居住在国外的美国公民或是仅因出生地而拥有美国国籍的自然人而言,其收入与所得均来自于居住国,拥有居住国金融账户应为合理之举,因为其近乎所有的生活要素都与居住国相关,理应向居住国纳税。对于这类公民,美国政府依据公民税收管辖权要求其向美国纳税,甚至凭借《海外账户纳税法案》强行要求该公民或者该公民账户所在的金融机构披露所得并缴税,着实凸显了公民税收管辖权在当今时代背景下的不合理性。

如前所述,虽然《海外账户纳税法案》的出台引起了关于公民税收管辖权合理性的又一轮争论,但从美国当局对法案的推进情况以及法案的具体内容可以看出,公民税收管辖权仍将是美国今后一段时期所要坚持的税收管辖权基础。

第五节 电子商务对传统税收管辖权制度的挑战

从20世纪后期开始,随着信息技术和网络技术的迅猛发展,电子商务逐渐风靡全球,成为一种全新的贸易方式。电子商务的出现,不仅给传统的贸易方式和企业经营模式带来冲击,而且也给包括税收制度在内的国际经济秩序提出了严峻的挑战。

电子商务与传统的商务模式相比,具有以下几个方面的特点:第一,全球性。互联网本身是开放的,没有国界,不存在地域范围限制,电子商务利用互联网的这一优势,开辟了巨大的网上交易空间。第二,流动性。任何人只要拥有一台电脑和相关的网络设备,就可以在全球任何地方从事国际贸易活动,不必依靠传统的固定基地。第三,隐蔽性。在电子商务环境下,越来越多的交易都被无纸化操作和匿名交易所代替,不用现金支付,也无须开具收支凭证。由于缺乏具有传统载体的交易证据,相关交易很难被跟踪或控制。第四,电子化或数字化。这也是电子商务区别于传统交易模式的最主要特征,电子商务以电子流代替实物流,传

---

① See Joanna Heiberg, FATCA: Toward a Multilateral Automatic Information Reporting Regime, Washington and Lee Law Review, Summer, 2012.

统的实物交易和服务被转换成数据后在互联网上传输和交易。①

电子商务的上述特点使得企业降低了经营成本,提高了交易效率,为企业创造了巨大的商业价值,但同时也给传统的税收制度带来了巨大的冲击。就税收管辖权而言,传统的居民税收管辖权和来源地税收管辖权受到严峻的挑战,探索适宜于电子商务环境的新的税收管辖权制度成为国际社会所面临的一项紧迫任务。

一、电子商务对居民税收管辖权的挑战

如前所述,确定纳税人居民身份是一国行使居民税收管辖权的前提。对自然人而言,确定其居民身份的"税收居所"有国籍、住所、居所等因素。电子商务具有高度流动性,特别是随着移动上网技术的普及,交易主体可以在任何一台联网的计算机上从事交易活动,其住所或居所的地理位置、居住时间的长短等已经不再与特定税收管辖区域产生必然联系,仍适用传统标准不仅无法有效确定自然人居民身份,而且会造成不同国家之间居民税收管辖权的冲突,导致国际税收关系复杂化。② 可见,电子商务的虚拟性和超越时空性使得传统的自然人税收居所标准已很难适用。

对于法人而言,实际管理或控制中心地、总机构所在地等是确定居民纳税人身份的重要标准。在电子商务环境下,由于信息技术得到广泛应用,公司的经营和管理可以不通过物理空间,而借助于电子信息互动交流技术来进行,如通过电子邮件、网络会议等形式来进行管理层之间的讨论和决策,远程办公和在线交易使得物理空间上的集中不再是公司经营管理上的必然要求。同一法人的不同分支机构即便分处全球各地,各分支机构的管理人员也可以通过互联网进行远程的实时沟通。在这种背景下,传统的总机构所在地、管理中心地等依赖地理上的特征对法人居民纳税人身份进行判断的标准逐渐失去原有的意义,使得法人的居民纳税人身份认定变得困难。

二、电子商务对来源地税收管辖权的挑战

(一)电子商务收入性质难以界定

各国所得税法通常将应税所得分为营业所得、劳务所得、投资所得、特许权使用费等种类,针对不同的应税所得适用不同的来源地确定标准及税收政策,因

---

① 参见张志超、李月平编著:《国际税收》,首都经济贸易大学出版社2005年版,第266页。
② 参见周昕、张翼:《电子商务对国际税收管辖权的挑战》,载《湖北社会科学》2002年第6期。

此,对于非居民纳税人所得的定性分类,是来源地国对所得实施征税必须解决的问题。但是,在电子商务环境下,非居民纳税人所得项目的划分界限变得模糊,因为书籍、报刊、音像制品等各种有形商品和计算机软件、专有技术等无形商品,以及各种咨询服务,都可以通过数据化处理而直接经过互联网传送,传统的按照交易标的性质和交易活动形式来划分区别交易所得性质的税法规则,对网上交易的数字化产品和服务难以适用。[①] 例如,网上在线销售软件的收入到底是营业所得还是特许权使用费?用户在线阅读电子数据而不下载,其行为是否构成租赁,支付的费用是不是租金?软件开发商为已售软件提供补丁程序所收取的费用到底是服务费用还是销售收入?不同的定性将决定税收管辖权的确定原则,从而影响到相关国家之间税收利益的划分,因而国际社会在电子商务收入的定性问题上争论颇多,目前仅就电脑软件的销售问题达成了有限的共识。根据经合组织 1992 年《电脑软件的税收处理》(The Tax Treatment of Computer Software)报告以及随后的一系列解释,通过电子商务方式销售软件并完全转让版权,所得收入是营业收入而不是特许权使用费;如果销售软件转让的只是软件的部分版权,则所获得的收入只能是特许权使用费,而不能算作营业收入。[②] 对于电脑软件以外的其他数字化产品交易的税收性质,目前国际社会仍然处于探讨之中。

(二)常设机构难以认定

所得来源地的确定是适用来源地税收管辖权的前提。如前所述,各国对不同种类的所得规定了不同的来源地,例如,营业所得通常以营业机构所在地或货物交付地等作为所得来源地;股息以分配股息的居民所属国为来源地;利息以贷款的实际使用地、借款人所在地或利息支付地等作为来源地;劳务所得则以劳务提供地、报酬支付人所在地等作为所得来源地。尽管电子商务所得的定性目前还存有争议,但一个不争的事实是,电子商务的特性使得各类所得来源地的确定规则都受到了全面的挑战,尤其是营业所得中的常设机构标准。

为了消除各国在营业所得来源地认定上的分歧,国际社会都坚持以常设机构所在地作为营业所得的来源地,联合国和经合组织的税收协定范本都对此作出了规定,并规定了常设机构的认定标准。电子商务出现以后,其特有的虚拟性使得常设机构的存在很难按照传统的标准来判断。企业从事电子商务活动可以

---

① 参见刘剑文主编:《国际税法学》(第二版),北京大学出版社 2004 年版,第 462 页。
② 参见〔美〕罗梅·罗哈吉:《国际税收基础》,林海宁、范文祥译,北京大学出版社 2006 年版,第 572 页。

不需要借助物理空间来完成,而直接进行网上交易,网上交易模式涉及的载体只有服务器和网址,而服务器或网址显然很难符合传统的常设机构标准,因为虚拟空间不能作为我们通常所说的"营业场所",而且这种虚拟空间具有高度流动性,缺乏固定性。目前,关于电子商务环境下的常设机构认定问题仍然是国际社会讨论的焦点,还没有一个普遍认可的结论。

经合组织为探讨电子商务中的常设机构问题,专门成立了工作组和技术咨询组,并发布了一系列的报告和解释说明。根据 2000 年 3 月发布的《常设机构概念在电子商务背景下的运用:对经济合作与发展组织(OECD)税收协定范本第五条的注释的建议性说明》以及随后的补充说明,经合组织对电子商务中的常设机构问题持以下立场:(1) 应对服务器与存储于其上的网址作出区分,互联网网址本身并不构成常设机构,而服务器则可能成为常设机构。(2) 服务器构成常设机构必须具有固定性,但这里的固定性不是看它是否有移动的可能,而应该看它在一段时间内是否移动过。(3) 如果电子商务交易仅限于预备性或辅助性活动,那么服务器计算机设备不构成该企业的常设机构。至于何谓预备性或辅助性活动,需要根据个案来决定,一般理解为包括收集信息、提供数据、广告宣传等。(4) 人的参与不是常设机构存在的必要条件,也就是说,即使没有人工参与运作,常设机构仍然可以成立。

在网址是否构成常设机构问题上,联合国国际贸易法委员会没有像经合组织那样采用一概否定的立场,而是在《电子商务示范法》中采用"功能等同"方法,即根据网址是否实际发挥了与固定、有形的机构、场所或营业代理人同样的功能作用来认定网址是否在来源地国构成常设机构。具体而言,常设机构的构成要同时满足以下三项标准:(1) 网址活动的时间延续性标准,即非居民的网址在互联网上活动存续的时间期限。它标志着网址的主人于一定期限内在互联网构成的虚拟市场上的主体存在,位于来源地境内的客户可以通过互联网点击相应的网址访问该网页进行交易。至于网址是否设置在位于来源地境内的某个服务器上,对访问该网址的来源地境内的客户而言并没有实质性区别,所以并不影响该网址构成常设机构的存在。各国可以在订立税收协定时规定网址构成常设机构的最短持续运营时间。(2) 网址活动的营业性标准,即非居民是否通过该网址实施了其全部或部分的营业活动。强调网址实际从事的活动内容的性质是否属于非居民纳税人本身的营业范围内容或是其中的一个部分,这种活动是否在该非居民纳税人的盈利过程中具有重要或不可或缺的作用。(3) 网址功能的系统性标准,即非居民控制的网址是否具有完成全部交易或主要的交易环节的功能,并且对来源地国境内的客户实际发挥了这样的功能作用。① 由此可见,不同的国际组织在此问题上尚存在争议,各国的观点也各不相同,如西班牙和葡萄牙就认为网址也可能成为常设机构,还有的国家认为服务器在任何情况下都不能作为常设机构。②

综上所述,电子商务对传统的税收管辖权原则提出了全面的挑战,国际社会为确立电子商务环境下的国际税收秩序进行了积极的探索和讨论,但由于相关方案的确定不仅关系到电子商务技术本身的发展,而且还最终影响到各国之间税收利益的划分,所以要确立能为国际社会所广泛认可和接受的电子商务税收秩序还尚需时日。

本章阅读材料

The Emergence of New Business Models

—selected from 2004 OECD report: Are the Current Treaty Rules for Taxing Business Profits Appropriate for E-Commerce?

6. The Internet has changed how business is conducted in local, national, and multinational environments. Through the development of various information and communication technologies, the Internet offers a reliable, consistent, secure, and flexible communications medium for conducting business. Whilst the use of the Internet as a marketing and sales tool receives the most publicity, the more significant economic consequences of the Internet arise from the ability of enterprises (including those in traditional sectors) to streamline various core business functions over the Internet. Business functions such as product innovation, production (including delivery of services), administration, accounting and finance, and customer service have all been made more efficient through the use of new communications

---

① 参见廖益新:《国际税法学》,高等教育出版社 2008 年版,第 376—380 页。
② See OECD: Taxation and Electronic Commerce: Implementing the Ottawa Taxation Framework Conditions, 2001.

technologies.

7. The following is an illustrative list of various categories of business models and functions enabled or impacted by the advent of Internet-related technologies.

—Outsourcing: new communications technologies allow enterprises to outsource the provision of services and to reach new suppliers of components and materials. A principal effect of outsourcing is to reduce costs for the enterprise, as the outsourcing service provider normally can provide the services, components and materials at lower cost than the enterprise, due to greater functional specialization, lower wage costs, or other factors. Another goal frequently is to improve quality, as functions are outsourced to enterprises which perform that function as a core competency.

—Commodity suppliers: The supply of raw materials is greatly facilitated by web-based systems that streamline the ordering, selling and payment systems for both small and large sellers/purchasers. These systems also extend the market for such products and ensure more competitive and transparent pricing.

—Manufacturing: New information technologies allow manufacturers to substantially reduce procurements costs. In turn, this allows their suppliers to access new customers or markets and reduce their transaction costs. These technologies also enable manufacturers to increase their direct sales to consumers, for instance by facilitating custom ordering of products. Similarly, they facilitate the outsourcing of non-core activities, such as manufacturing, of many product suppliers. Traditional manufacturers themselves can outsource manufacturing of components to lower cost locations.

—Retail distribution: Through their websites, enterprises may provide low cost products with a high degree of convenience and customization for their customers. Many business functions (e.g. procurement, inventory management, warehousing, shipping etc.) may be automated. This reduces costs for the consumer and allows him to have access to new customized services. This can be done by new businesses or by traditional retailers which want to supplement their traditional sales channels or improve services to their customers. Electronic marketplaces (e.g. online consumer auctions, electronic marketplaces operated by content aggregators or online shopping portals) allow consumers new ways to buy products or compare prices.

——Delivery: Shipping enterprises benefits from new technologies (e.g. online parcel order and tracking systems), which allow quicker and more accurate deliveries. This allows their business customers to outsource order fulfillment functions in order to concentrate on core activities.

——Marketing and customer support: Through the Internet, enterprises can present information about their products or services to a larger audience in a more efficient and cost effective manner. This allows small and remote businesses to enter new markets. Customer support also greatly benefits from new technologies, which allow worldwide access to call centers and customer-related operations, which can be provided by any jurisdiction that offers an educated and highly skilled employment base or presents cost-effective opportunities.

——Information: New technologies have made possible a vast array of new approaches to the delivery and treatment of information. Computer networks such as the Internet allow worldwide and almost instantaneous delivery of information in various forms to individuals and businesses. Some countries get access to information not previously available and the costs of accessing and searching information are substantially reduced for all. E-learning and interactive training allow a more generalized access to education and training, whether general or labour-oriented. The treatment of information is greatly facilitated, for instance through data processing, information storage systems and application service providers.

——Financial Services: Financial services, such as banking, brokerage and life insurance, are now routinely offered through the Internet. This can be done by traditional financial institutions or by new businesses, which can now enter markets without incurring the enormous expenses of setting up a brick-and-mortar branch network. Further, financial institutions can now offer new functions related to the security of e-commerce transactions.

——Other services: Various other types of services have greatly benefited from web-based network. This has been the case, for instance, in the areas of travel (e.g. flights booking, car rental and hotel reservations) and health-care (better information on health issues and products, greater access to health specialists, improved treatment of health expenses and patient information).

—Digital products: Various digital products (e. g. software, music, video, games, news, ebooks, etc.) can be marketed and, in some cases, distributed through web-based systems in direct purchase, rental, or pay-per-use transactions.

8. These examples show that new information technologies create opportunities and benefits for business and private consumers, even though businesses have so far made a greater use of these technologies. Indeed, all available data show that e-commerce at the consumer retail (B to C) represents, at the present time, only a fraction of e-commerce between businesses (B to B). The new information technologies create and facilitate business opportunities for traditional as well as high-tech enterprises, and for enterprises in all economies. For example, those opportunities include outsourcing non-core functions to related or unrelated entities enjoying cost advantages (which is a main advantage of new information technologies for business). Similarly, some businesses have gained the flexibility through the Internet to structure production, service, administration, financial or other operations in the most cost-effective and efficient manner. As a result, businesses have located personnel and other value producing activities in those places which yield the greatest return on investment. For other businesses, barriers to entry have been significantly reduced so as to allow them to conduct new profit seeking activities and/or to compete on an international scale. Finally, businesses have also been able to decentralize major business functions so as to address and provide for the needs of customers in remote jurisdictions. In most instances, such local presence has remained a necessity to maintain a competitive advantage and to provide the desired product or service to the recipient in the quickest and most cost-effective manner.

9. Whilst the development of such new business models based on new information technologies illustrates the significant changes in the way that business is carried on, the question is whether and to what extent the existing tax treaty rules can deal appropriately with these changes or will require modification.

DESCRIPTION OF THE CURRENT TREATY RULES FOR TAXING BUSINESS PROFITS

10. Whilst there are significant differences between bilateral tax treaties, the principles underlying the treaty provisions governing the taxation of business profits are relatively uniform and may be summarized as follows.

A. Liability to a country's tax: residents and non-residents

11. Under the rules of tax treaties, liability to a country's tax first depends on whether or not the taxpayer that derives the relevant income is a resident of that country. Any resident taxpayer may be taxed on its business profits wherever arising (subject to the requirement that the residence country eliminate residence-source double taxation) whilst, as a general rule, non-resident taxpayers may only be taxed on their business profits to the extent that these are attributable to a permanent establishment situated in the country (see below for the exceptions to that general rule).

12. Residence, for treaty purposes, depends on liability to tax under the domestic law of the taxpayer. A company is considered to be a resident of a State if it is liable to tax, in that State, by reason of factors (e. g. domicile, residence, incorporation or place of management) that trigger the widest domestic tax liability. Since the reference to domestic factors could result in the same company being a resident of the two countries that have entered into a treaty, treaties also include so-called "tie-breaker" rules that ensure that a taxpayer will have a single country's residence for purposes of applying the treaty. The tie-breaker rule of the OECD Model Tax Convention provides that a company that is considered to be a resident of two countries is a resident only of the country in which its place of effective management is situated.

B. Permanent establishment: the treaty nexus/threshold for taxing business profits of non residents

13. Treaty rules for taxing business profits use the concept of permanent establishment as a basic nexus/threshold rule for determining whether or not a country has taxing rights with respect to the business profits of a non-resident taxpayer. That threshold rule, however, is subject to a few exceptions for certain categories of business profits (see below). The permanent establishment concept also acts as a source rule to the extent that, as a general

rule, the only business profits of a non-resident that may be taxed by a country are those that are attributable to a permanent establishment.

14. The basic treaty definition of "permanent establishment" is "a fixed place of business through which the business of an enterprise is wholly or partly carried on". That definition incorporates both a geographical requirement (i. e. that a fixed physical location be identified as a permanent establishment) as well as a time requirement (i. e. the presence of the enterprise at that location must be more than merely temporary having regard to the type of business carried on).

15. In order to be able to conclude that part or the whole of the business of an enterprise is carried on through a particular place, that place must be at the disposal of that enterprise for purposes of these business activities. The treaty definition of permanent establishment provides, however, that if the place is only used to carry on certain activities of a preparatory or auxiliary character, that place will be deemed not to constitute a permanent establishment notwithstanding the basic definition.

16. The basic definition of permanent establishment is supplemented by a rule that deems a non-resident to have a permanent establishment in a country if another person acts in that country as an agent of the non-resident and habitually exercises an authority to conclude contracts in the name of the non-resident. That rule, however, does not apply to independent agents acting in the ordinary course of their business.

17. The interpretation of the current treaty definition of permanent establishment in the context of e-commerce has raised some questions. The OECD has now clarified how it considers that the definition should be applied with respect to e-commerce operations. The main conclusions that it has reached in that respect are as follows:

—a web site cannot, in itself, constitute a PE;

—web site hosting arrangements typically do not result in a PE for the enterprise that carries on business through the hosted web site;

—except in very unusual circumstances, an Internet service provider will not be deemed (under the agent/permanent establishment rule described above) to constitute a permanent establishment for the enterprises to which it provides services;

—whilst a place where computer equipment, such as a server, is located may in certain circumstances constitute a permanent establishment, this requires that the functions performed at that place be such as to go beyond what is preparatory or auxiliary.

18. As already mentioned, there are a number of exceptions to the permanent establishment nexus/threshold general rule as regards some categories of business profits.

19. On the one hand, some categories of profits may be taxed in a country even though there is no permanent establishment therein. This is the case of:

—profits derived from immovable property (e. g. hotels, mines etc...), which, in all or almost all treaties, may be taxed by the country of source where the immovable property is located;

—profits related to the performance of entertainers and athletes, which, in all or almost all treaties, may be taxed by the country of source where the performance takes place;

—profits that include certain types of payments which, depending on the treaty, may include dividends, interest, royalties or technical fees, on which the treaty allows the country of source to levy a limited tax based on the gross amount of the payment (as opposed to the profit element related to the payment);

—under some treaties, profits derived from collecting insurance premiums or insuring risks in the source country;

—under some treaties, profits derived from the provision of services if the presence of the provider in the country of source exceeds 183 days in a 12-month period.

20. On the other hand, all or almost all treaties also provide that profits from the operation of ships and aircraft in international traffic may not be taxed by the source country even though there is a permanent establishment situated in that country. Most treaties also provide that capital gains (except on immovable property and business property of a permanent establishment) may not be taxed by the country of source.

C. Computation of profits: the separate entity accounting and arm's length principles

21. The treaty principles for computing the business profits that may be taxed by a country are similar whether a country has taxing rights over business profits because these profits are those of a resident taxpayer or because these business profits are attributable to the permanent establishment of a non-resident taxpayer. In both cases, the rules for computing the business profits that may be taxed by the source country are based on the separate entity accounting and arm's length principles. Thus, each legal person or permanent establishment is generally treated as a separate taxpayer regardless of its relationship with other entities or parts of an entity. Each branch or subsidiary that is part of a multinational enterprise is therefore treated separately for purposes of the computation of profits under tax treaties, with the important proviso that, for purposes of determining the profits of each such branch or subsidiary, the conditions (i. e. primarily the price) of intra-group transactions may be readjusted to reflect those that would prevail between independent enterprises (the arm's length principle). The OECD, in its Transfer Pricing Guidelines (1995, in paragraphs 5 and 6 of the preface), identifies the "separate entity approach as the most reasonable means for achieving equitable results and minimizing the risk of unrelieved double taxation," notes that, "to apply the separate entity approach to intra-group transactions, individual group members must be taxed on the basis that they act at arm's length in dealing with each other," and concludes, "To ensure the correct application of the separate entity approach, OECD Member Countries have adopted the arm's-length principle..."

22. The "traditional" methods of determining arm's length prices (contained in Chapter II of the OECD Transfer Pricing Guidelines) are a) comparable uncontrolled prices (CUP), b) resale price (minus a margin), c) cost plus (a mark-up). In recent years, reflecting problems in applying the traditional methods, two additional "transactional profits methods" have been added to the OECD Transfer Pricing Guidelines: the "profit split method" and the "transactional net margin method."

23. Profit split method. The profit split methodology first identifies the combined profit to be split between the affiliated enterprises from controlled

transactions and then seeks to divide that profit based on the functions performed, assets used and the risks assumed by each. The profits to be split may be either the total combined profits from the controlled transactions or the residual profits that cannot be easily assigned to any of the enterprises on some appropriate basis, after providing a basic return to each entity for the activities performed.

24. Transactional net margin method. The transactional net margin method examines profit margins, relative to an appropriate base such as costs, sales, or assets. Thus it operates in a manner similar to the cost plus and resale price methods.

25. The OECD notes at paragraph 3.49 of the Transfer Pricing Guidelines that traditional transaction methods are to be preferred over transactional profit methods. It is however recognised at paragraph 3.50 that there are cases of last resort where traditional transaction methods cannot be applied reliably or exceptionally at all and so where transactional profit methods have to be applied. The paragraph concludes that as a general matter the use of transactional profit methods is discouraged. Since 1995, however, there has been a much wider use of profit methods by both taxpayers and tax administrations, especially to deal with the integration of functions within a multinational group (see the 1998 OECD Global Trading Report) and with unique and highly valuable intangibles. Further, the OECD is currently reviewing the treatment of profit methods as part of the process of monitoring the Transfer Pricing Guidelines.

D. The treaty rules for sharing the tax base between States where there is nexus

26. Since tax treaty rules allow for business profits to be taxed by both the source and residence countries in some cases, the same business profits may be subject to competing claims by these countries. Such competing claims are addressed by giving priority to source taxation. This priority is ensured by rules that either provide for the exemption from residence taxation of items of income with respect to which a tax treaty grants source taxation rights to the other State or that allow the source country's tax to be credited against the residence tax on such items.

27. As treaty rules also allow certain categories of profits to be taxed by a source country where there is no permanent establishment (see above), there can be, in certain cases, taxation in the State of source, in the State where the permanent establishment to which such profits are attributable is located and in the State of residence of the taxpayer to which that permanent establishment belongs. Tax treaties provide for the elimination of such triple taxation by giving priority (through the exemption/credit rules described above) to source taxation, then to taxation in the State where the permanent establishment is located, with residual taxation rights being given to the State of residence.

第三章 国际双重征税

第一节 国际双重征税概述

一、国际双重征税的概念与类型

双重征税是同一征税主体或不同的征税主体,对同一纳税义务人或不同的纳税义务人的同一征税对象或税源所进行的重复课征。就其性质看,双重征税可以划分为税制性双重征税、法律性双重征税和经济性双重征税三种基本类型。

税制性双重征税是由于复税制所造成的重复课税,如对同一税源既征收流转税,又征收所得税。法律性双重征税是在不同征税主体对同一纳税人的同一纳税客体进行课征的条件下产生的。经济性双重征税则是由于对相互关联的不同纳税人的同一征税对象课征所引起的,通常是指对两个不同的纳税人就同一项所得或财产的重复课税,即征税客体是同一的,而纳税人则不相同,所以,经济性双重征税亦称为重叠征税或双层征税。

在国际税收实践中,对跨国所得的双重征税,主要是指法律性国际双重征税和经济性国际双重征税,这是国际税法亟须解决的重要问题。[①] 因此,我们可以给国际双重征税下一个简单的定义,即指两个或两个以上的主权国家各自依据自己的税收管辖权,对同一或不同的跨国纳税人的同一征税对象或税源所进行的重复征税,主要包括法律性国际双重征税和经济性国际双重征税。[②] 国际双重征税的实质,是国家之间税收管辖权在同一征税对象或同一税源上重叠而发生的法律冲突。

---

① 理论界关于国际双重征税的概念存在广义和狭义之分,狭义论主张国际双重征税不包括经济性双重征税,而广义论则主张国际双重征税包括法律性双重征税和经济性双重征税,本书取广义论。

② 本书出于简明之考虑,对国际双重征税作如上定义。实际上,关于法律性双重征税和经济性双重征税的概念曾一度存在分歧。目前,普遍接受的法律性双重征税的概念是经合组织1963年在《关于对所得和财产避免双重征税协定范本草案的报告》中所给出的,根据该报告,法律性双重征税是指两个或两个以上的国家对同一纳税人就同一征税对象在同一时期内课征相同或类似的税收。该定义表明,法律性双重征税应包含五个构成要件,即存在两个或两个以上的征税主体;存在同一个纳税主体;针对相同的课税对象;处于同一征税期间;课征相同或类似的税种。经济性双重征税是指两个或两个以上的国家对不同的纳税人就同一课税对象在同一时期内课征相同或类似性质的税收。与法律性双重征税相比,经济性双重征税只是不满足"同一纳税主体"这一要件,其余四个要件与法律性双重征税相同。

二、国际双重征税的产生原因

(一) 法律性国际双重征税的产生原因

法律性国际双重征税的产生,主要是基于两个方面的原因:首先,纳税人收入的国际化以及各国所得税制的普及是国际双重征税产生的客观基础;其次,各国税收管辖权冲突是导致国际双重征税的直接原因。

就第一方面看,二战以后,随着跨国投资经营活动的迅猛发展,商品、资本和生产的国际化已成为国际经济发展的主要特征。这一特征也带来了纳税人收入的国际化,收入已不再局限于一国境内,具有跨国的属性,纳税人也不再限于在一国承担纳税义务,而应承担跨国的纳税义务。此外,自1799年英国创设所得税制以来,世界各国纷纷效仿,许多发达国家都建立了以所得税为核心税种的税收制度。于是,有关国家根据各自税收管辖权对跨国纳税人的跨国所得行使征税权,从而使双重征税成为可能。

根据国家主权原则,任何主权国家都可以自主确定本国的税收管辖权制度。各国从本国利益出发,竞相扩大管辖范围,必然导致各国税收管辖权之间的冲突,这种冲突主要有下列表现形式:

1. 居民税收管辖权之间的冲突。由于各国国内法在居民纳税人确认标准上的规定不同,某一跨国纳税人可能同时被两个或两个以上国家认定为具有各自国家的居民身份,这些国家均依据其国内税法对该居民纳税人行使全面的税收管辖权,即对该纳税人的境内外所得或财产进行征税,从而引发法律性国际双重征税。

2. 居民税收管辖权和收入来源地税收管辖权之间的冲突。居民税收管辖权和收入来源地税收管辖权之间的冲突表现为:一方面居住国对居民纳税人来自世界范围的全部所得行使征税权;而另一方面收入来源地国对非居民纳税人来源于其境内的所得进行征税,居住国和来源地国都根据国内税法进行征税势必导致法律性国际双重征税的产生。

3. 收入来源地国税收管辖权之间的冲突。这主要是由于各国对所得来源地的认定不一所致。例如,对营业所得的来源地的认定,有的国家以营业机构所在地为其来源地,有的国家以销售合同的签订地为其来源地。这样,同一所得就有可能被不同国家认定为来源于本国而进行征税,产生法律性国际双重征税。

(二) 经济性国际双重征税的产生原因

经济性双重征税通常是指对两个不同的纳税人就同一项所得或财产的重复征税。这种重复征税的现象不仅在两国或多国之间会发生,同样也发生在一国境内。经济性国际双重征税主要表现为下述两种情况：

1. 对公司利润和股息的征税。在广泛实行所得税制的国家，均对公司、企业所取得的营业利润征收公司所得税或企业所得税。此外，各国税法还规定，对股东所取得的股息红利应征收个人所得税，这实际上就是对公司利润再分配过程中的重复征税。这种重复课税并非是各国税收管辖权发生重叠所致，而是由于公司利润的再分配所形成的。

2. 对财产与股权财产的征税。在甲乙两国都有以财产为征税对象的税种，并对其居民纳税人的境内外财产行使征税权的条件下，如果甲国居民拥有设在乙国的公司的股权，该项股权应与其境内财产一并计入缴纳财产税。但该项股权所代表的财产又是设在乙国境内公司财产的组成部分，乙国也有权对该公司财产征收财产税。这样就形成了甲乙两国分别对不同的纳税主体就同一项财产所得进行征税，从而引发经济性国际双重征税现象。

不论是法律性还是经济性国际双重征税，都违背了税收公平原则，加重了跨国纳税人的税收负担，挫伤了跨国投资者的积极性，制约了国际经济正常交往的顺利进行，同时也不利于发展中国家更有效地吸引外资和引进先进技术。可以说，双重征税是当前国际税收实践中必须解决的主要问题。

第二节 法律性国际双重征税的解决方法

双重征税问题可以通过某个国家采取单边措施来解决，也可以通过两个或两个以上的国家在平等协商的基础上签订税收协定来协调解决。解决法律性国际双重征税的具体方法主要包括免税法、扣除法、抵免法。

一、免税法

免税法(method of tax exemption)，亦称"豁免法"，是指居住国政府对本国居民来源于国外的所得或财产免予征税。免税法实质上是居住国对收入来源地国行使属地税收管辖权的那部分所得放弃居民税收管辖权，承认来源地税收管辖权的独占权，从而避免两种税收管辖权的重叠交叉，防止双重征税的发生。根据实行免税法采用的税率的不同，免税法可分为两种形式：

（一）全额免税法

全额免税法(method of full exemption)，是指居住国政府在对其居民纳税人来源于国内的所得征税时，不考虑该居民纳税人已被本国免予征税的国外所得额，仅按国内所得额确定适用税率计征税收的方法。其计算公式为：

居住国应征所得税税额＝居民的国内所得×适用税率

（二）累进免税法

累进免税法（method of exemption with progression），是指居住国政府在对其居民纳税人来源于国内的所得征税时，将该居民纳税人已被本国免予征税的国外所得额考虑在内，适用其免税所得额未扣除前应适用的税率征税的方式。其计算公式为：

居住国应征所得税税额＝居民的国内和国外所得×适用税率×（国内所得／国内外总所得）

与全额免税法相比，累进免税法是以居民纳税人的国内外的所得总额求得适用税率，其结果是仅对居民纳税人的国外所得免除了国际双重征税，而不会使其国内所得因扣除国外所得后落入较低税率档次。

在免税法下，由于居住国对居民纳税人来源于国外的所得完全放弃了征税权，因此可以彻底地消除国际双重征税，但是免税法的运用并未能平衡兼顾居住国和来源地国的税收利益，因为免税法是使居住国单方面放弃行使居民税收管辖权，而使来源地国的地域征税权处于独享地位，这必将导致居住国的财政利益受到一定的影响，特别是在居住国税率高于来源地国税率的情况下，采用免税法使实际免除的税额大于应免除的国内纳税税额。此外，在来源地国的税率低于居住国税率的情况下，针对相同数额的所得，在居住国所需缴纳的税收要高于在来源地国缴纳的税收，这违背了税收中性原则，会在一定程度上促使纳税人通过转移资产和利润来实现避税的目的。由此可见，免税法并不是最佳的国际双重征税的解决方法，实践中采用免税法的国家并不多见。

二、扣除法

扣除法（method of tax deduction），是指居住国政府对居民纳税人因国外所得而向来源地国缴纳的所得税款，允许作为扣除项目从应税所得额中扣除，就其余额适用相应的税率计算应纳税额。其计算公式为：

居住国应征所得税额＝（居民的跨国总所得－国外已纳所得税额）×适用税率

居住国适用扣除法，并不能使跨国纳税人享受到从应纳居住国所得税中扣除已缴全部外国所得税款的权利，因而不能完全消除由于税收管辖权重叠交叉所造成的国际双重征税，其给予跨国纳税人扣除的一部分税额，只能对解决国际双重征税问题起一定的缓解作用，所以采用扣除法解决国际双重征税问题的国家也为数不多。

三、抵免法

所谓抵免法（method of tax credit），亦称"外国税收抵免"（foreign tax credit），是指居住国政府按本国居民纳税人在世界范围内的所得汇总计算其应纳税款，但允许其将因国外所得而已向来源地国缴纳的税款在本国税法规定的限度内从本国的应纳税额中抵免。

居住国运用抵免法对本国居民纳税人的跨国所得进行课税时，既承认了来源地国税收管辖权的优先地位，又行使了居民税收管辖权，因此抵免法是各国政府消除和解决国际双重征税的一种最主要的方法。

根据国际税收实践，外国税收抵免必须具备一定的条件和范围。第一，居住国政府允许抵免的，必须是来源地国政府征收的税，而不能是费或其他付款。第二，居住国允许抵免的必须是所得税，诸如销售税、增值税、关税等间接税则不在抵免范围之列。第三，居住国允许抵免的所得税，必须是针对纳税人的净所得，即从纳税人的毛收入中扣除成本、费用和损失的净额。如果不是对净所得所课征的税，居住国政府一般不予抵免。此外，适用抵免法的国家一般都以互惠为前提，实行对等原则，而且抵免的范围一般仅限于跨国所得的税收。

根据可以抵免的外国所得税的程度不同，可将抵免法分为全额抵免和限额抵免两类。

（一）全额抵免

所谓全额抵免（full credit），是指居住国政府对本国居民纳税人的国内外所得汇总征税时，允许跨国纳税人将其已向外国政府缴纳的所得税税额，在应向本国政府缴纳的税额中全部扣除，即抵免额等于纳税人在国外所缴纳的全部税收总额。

全额抵免的特点是简便易行，纳税人所属的居住国税务当局无须按本国税法计算和审核来源于国外所得以确定适用本国税率的税基，可省却计算中的繁琐问题。全额抵免的不利之处在于会导致超税负抵免情况的产生，尤其是在来源地国税率高于居住国税率的情形下，会以减少国内税收为代价来抵免国外税收，形成国家税收权益的外流。所以，实行全额抵免的国家极少。

（二）限额抵免

所谓限额抵免，亦称"普通抵免"（ordinary credit），是指居住国政府对本国居民纳税人国内外所得汇总征税时，允许该纳税人将其向外国政府缴纳的所得税税额在国外所得依照本国税法规定的税率计算税额的限度内，在应向居住国政府缴纳的税额中扣除。在采用抵免法消除国际双重征税的国家中，大多数均采用限额抵免法。

在限额抵免计算中,允许抵免的已缴来源地国税额的概念相当重要。抵免限额只是外国税收抵免的最高限度,并不是一定要按照抵免限额来抵免外国税收。因此,当抵免限额小于跨国纳税人已缴来源地国税款时,抵免限额即为允许抵免额;当抵免限额高于跨国纳税人已缴来源地国税款时,则纳税人已缴来源地国税款即为允许抵免额;当抵免限额与跨国纳税人已缴来源地国税款数额相等时,则纳税人已缴来源地国税款即为允许抵免额。因此,允许抵免的已缴来源地国的税额等于抵免限额与纳税人实际缴纳的来源地国税款两者之间数额较小者。

实践中,限额抵免又可以分为分国限额、综合限额与专项限额:

1. 分国限额

所谓分国限额(per country limitation),是指把应抵免的外国所得税税额分国别单独计算的抵免限额。其计算公式为:

某一外国税收抵免限额＝按来自国内外全部应税所得计算的向居住国缴纳的税款×(某一外国的应税所得/来自国内外的全部应税所得)

2. 综合限额

所谓综合限额(overall limitation),是指将居民纳税人向所有来源地国缴纳的所得税税款合并起来计算可以抵免的限度。其计算公式为:

综合抵免限额＝按来自国内外全部应税所得计算的向居住国缴纳的税款×(来自所有外国的应税所得/来自国内外的全部应税所得)

综合限额抵免方法和分国限额抵免方法在不同的情形和条件下,对跨国纳税人和居住国的利弊影响各不相同。当纳税人在各个非居住国的投资经营活动均有盈利,并且各个非居住国的税率水平相对纳税人的居住国税率水平有高有低的情况下,居住国实行综合限额抵免方法,对跨国纳税人较为有利。因为在这种情况下,纳税人可以将在高税率非居住国发生的超限额与在低税率的非居住国出现的不足限额相互抵补,从而使在各个非居住国的抵免限额得到充分利用。这样的结果是增加了跨国纳税人可以获得抵免的外国税额,减少了其最终应汇总缴纳居住国的税额,对跨国纳税人显然有利。但是,在跨国纳税人投资经营的各个非居住国的税率均高于或均低于居住国的税率的情况下,不存在各国限额间相互抵补的可能性,故实行综合限额和分国限额抵免方法的结果是一致的。当跨国纳税人在各个非居住国的投资经营结果有盈有亏的情况下,居住国采用分国限额抵免方法,对纳税人较为有利。此时不同非居住国的盈亏无须相抵,盈利分公司的抵免限额不会降低,所以能减轻该跨国纳税人的税收负担。

3. 专项限额

有些实行分类所得税制的国家还采用专项限额,即跨国纳税人的居住国,在对纳税人已向外国缴纳的税款进行抵免计算时,将某些低税率项目,与其他项目分开,单独计算的抵免限额。其计算公式为:

分项限额＝抵免前按境内境外全部应税所得应向居住国缴纳的税款×(来自国外某一专项的应税所得/来自居住国境内境外的全部应税所得)

居住国实行专项抵免限额方法,使居民纳税人来源于境外的低税率项目所得的不足限额与高税率项目所得的超限额不能相互冲抵,从而使纳税人可以从居住国应纳税额中得到抵扣的外国税额,较之不分项限额抵免方法下可以抵扣的外国税额要少。这对于维护居住国的税收权益较为合理有利,因为居住国本来对居民纳税人来源于非居住国的适用高税率的项目所得发生的超过抵免限额的那部分外国税额是不应承担抵扣义务的。但从跨国纳税人的角度考虑,居住国对纳税人来自国外的高税率项目所得发生的超限额不予抵免,而对低税率项目所得出现的不足限额却要补征税款,这样的外国税收抵免结果不尽公允合理。①

与全额抵免相比较,限额抵免具有一定的合理性。一是限额抵免的税基应依居住国国内税法规定计算来源地国的应纳税所得额,这样不但体现了居住国的国家主权,并且能够合理确定跨国纳税人的利润归属和划分国内外费用的分摊。二是限额抵免使跨国纳税人国外投资所得的税负不低于缴纳国内投资所得的税负水平,避免了对国内投资活动的冲击。但限额抵免也有其局限性,因为限额抵免计算繁琐,实际操作难度大,增加了居住国的税务成本。

四、不同方法的比较

抵免法、免税法、扣除法都是避免和消除法律性国际双重征税的重要手段,但三者在防止国际双重征税的效果上各有不同。

首先,在抵免法下,居住国仅承认来源地国税收管辖权的优先权,而不是独占权,对居民纳税人来自国外并已向来源地国纳税的那部分所得仍享有居民税收管辖权,这样就不至于因避免国际双重征税而过分牺牲居住国政府的财政利益。而免税法实质上是居住国对收入来源地国行使属地税收管辖权的那部分所得放弃居民税收管辖权,承认来源地国税收管辖权的独占权,是以牺牲居住国税

---

① 参见廖益新主编:《国际税法学》,高等教育出版社2008年版,第58页。

收利益为代价的。显然,抵免法比免税法更具合理性,尤其是当居住国和来源地国直接决定对纳税人的某些所得必须分享税收利益时,抵免法的适用优于免税法。

其次,在扣除法下,居住国对居民纳税人因国外所得而向来源地国缴纳的税款,允许作为一个扣除项目从其应税所得中扣除,它并不完全承认来源地国税收管辖权的优先权,因而不能完全解决跨国纳税人的双重税负问题。而在抵免法下,居住国在本国税法规定的限度内,对来源地国已征收本国居民的所得税予以抵免,从而基本上免除了跨国纳税人的双重税负。所以,在防止国际双重征税的效果上,抵免法优于扣除法。

第三节 经济性国际双重征税的解决方法

经济性国际双重征税的产生是因为各国实行公司所得税之后,把公司和股东分别视为两个不同的纳税实体予以课税,即对公司利润征收所得税后,又对股东从公司税后利润中分得的股息征收个人所得税,从而导致对同一利润两次征税。目前,应对经济性国际双重征税的方法主要有以下几种:

一、股息扣除制

所谓股息扣除制(dividend-deduction system),是指在计算公司所得税时,将股息视同费用开支一样,准许从公司税前所得中扣除,仅对扣除后的利润部分征收所得税。以美国税法为例,在股东为公司时,美国法律允许美国公司将它从应纳所得税的国内公司获得的股息从所得中扣除。瑞士联邦所得税法也规定,控股公司从子公司的投资收益中取得的股息的一定比例准予从应税所得中扣除。[①]

在实行股息扣除制时,不论是全部免税还是部分免税,各国都规定了一些限定条件:第一,拥有子公司一定数额的股份或最低金额。如瑞典要求25%以上的有表决权的股份。瑞士联邦规定,至少拥有子公司股份的20%,或账面价值至少达到200万瑞士法郎。第二,股份的持有应有一定的期限。一般要求在收到股息的纳税年度前,已持有股份至少12个月。如法国要求持股两年。

[①] 参见刘剑文主编:《国际税法学》(第二版),北京大学出版社2004年版,第178—179页。

二、分劈税率制

所谓分劈税率制(split-rate system),亦称"双税率制",是指对用于分配股息的利润和不用于分配股息的利润分别按不同的税率征收公司所得税,对分配利润适用的税率较低。分劈税率制的特点在于用减轻公司税负的方式来缓解经济性国际双重征税的矛盾。

例如,德国在1994年税制改革前,对留存利润的公司税税率为50%,而对已分配利润的税率为36%;1994年税制改革后,对前者的税率为45%,对后者则为30%。税率间的差异体现了对收取股息方所给予的减除。再如,日本对一般公司未作股息分配的普通所得课征30%或40%的基本税率,对作为股息分配的普通所得课征24%或32%的税率。

三、间接抵免制

相对于法律性双重征税的直接抵免方法,间接抵免是指适用于跨国公司母公司与子公司不同法律主体之间的一种抵免方法。区别直接和间接抵免的标准在于,用于抵免的税款是不是纳税人自己缴纳的。即母公司所属的居住国政府,允许母公司将其子公司已缴来源地国的所得税款中,应由母公司分得的股息承担的那部分税款,来冲抵母公司的应纳税款。间接抵免法之所以称为间接,是因为母公司所在的居住国政府允许母公司抵免的税额,并不是由母公司直接向子公司所在国政府缴纳的,而是通过子公司间接缴纳的。

适用间接抵免通常须具备三个条件:(1)能享受间接抵免的纳税人必须是法人公司,自然人不能享受间接抵免。(2)享受间接抵免的纳税人是其外国子公司的积极投资者,并且其拥有所属子公司的股权必须达到规定的最低限额。例如,美国《国内税收法》第902节明确规定,美国国内公司至少必须拥有国外子公司10%以上有表决权的股份,才能享受间接抵免,对于第二层和第三层的外国公司,则至少必须拥有5%的有表决权的股份。(3)享受间接抵免的跨国纳税人必须收到其所属子公司的股息。

间接抵免适用于母公司来自外国子公司的股息所承担的那部分所得税。母公司在向本国政府缴纳所得税时,不是将外国子公司的全部所得汇总计算,而只是将其从国外子公司取得的股息还原出毛收入合并计征所得税。母公司从本身应纳的所得税额中抵免的,仅是按照其取得的股息占国外子公司纳税后所占的比例。因此,间接抵免的计算相当复杂,分为以下几个步骤:

1. 计算应归入母公司的外国子公司所得额：

应归入母公司的外国子公司所得额①＝收到外国子公司的股息额/（1－外国子公司所得税税率）

2. 计算应由母公司承担的外国子公司所得税额：

应由母公司承担的外国子公司所得税额②＝外国子公司已纳所得税额×（母公司所获毛股息/外国子公司税后所得）

3. 计算抵免限额：

抵免限额③＝应归入母公司的外国子公司所得额×母公司所在国适用税率

4. 确定允许抵免的子公司已缴税额：

用②和③相比较，取值小者即为允许抵免的税额④。

5. 计算母公司所在国应征母公司所得税额：

应征税额＝（母公司所得额＋应归入母公司的外国子公司所得额①）×适用税率－允许抵免的外国子公司应纳税额④

可见，间接抵免旨在消除不同的纳税主体因同一税源重复课税所导致的双重征税，即国际重叠征税。目前，一些主要的发达国家在国内税法上都实行间接抵免法，以避免和消除经济性国际双重征税。此外，间接抵免还适用于母公司通过子公司来自外国孙公司以及孙公司下属的多层外国附属公司的重复征税问题，这种抵免亦称多层次间接抵免。由于多层次间接抵免的原理和方法与上述间接抵免大致相同，在此不再赘述。

与间接抵免相关的一个概念是"归集抵免制"（imputation credit system）。所谓归集抵免制，是指在对公司所得和股息的征税方面，所有的应纳税公司利润，不论是否用于分配，都要按法定税率缴纳公司所得税，公司用于分配的那部分利润已纳的公司所得税的一部分或全部，可以从股东收到的股息应纳的所得税额中予以抵扣；如果公司已纳的那部分所得税超过股东（包括公司股东）对那部分股息应纳的个人或公司所得税额，则要退给股东。① 归集抵免与间接抵免的原理相同，都是用股东收到的股息承担的分配股息的公司所在国所得税来抵扣股息所应当缴纳的股东所在国税收。两者的区别在于：(1) 间接抵免仅适用于公司股东，而归集抵免还可以适用于个人股东；(2) 间接抵免的适用以一定的持股比例为前提，而归集抵免无持股比例要求。

---

① 参见董根泰：《试论归集抵免制》，载《涉外税务杂志》1996年第5期。

第四节 税收饶让抵免

一、饶让抵免的概念及特点

国际税收饶让抵免(international tax sparing credit),是指一国政府(居住国政府)对本国纳税人在国外的投资所得由投资所在国(收入来源地国)减免的那一部分税收,视同已经缴纳,同样给予税收抵免的待遇。税收饶让抵免的主要目的是在运用抵免法消除国际双重征税的条件下,保证资本输入国为吸收外国投资所提供的各种税收优惠政策与措施得到真正落实。由于税收减免优惠主要是发展中国家在吸收外资的过程中较多采用的一种措施,所以,税收饶让抵免经常成为两个国家特别是发展中国家与发达国家在谈判缔结双边税收协定中的一个焦点问题。

税收饶让抵免是税收抵免的延伸和扩展,其作用已经超出了避免重复征税的范围。与一般的外国税收抵免不同,税收饶让抵免具有以下特点:第一,税收饶让抵免是缔约国之间意志妥协的产物,必须通过双边或多边安排方能实现。第二,税收饶让抵免制度一般反映在各国所缔结的双边或多边税收协定中。第三,税收饶让抵免的目的并不在于避免和消除法律性或经济性国际双重征税,而是为了使来源地国利用外资的税收优惠政策与措施真正收到实际效果。没有居住国政府提供税收饶让抵免措施作为屏障,来源地国对跨国投资者的税收减免优惠就会被居住国政府在计算抵免限额时所抵消,来源地国的税收优惠政策和措施就无从发挥其真正效用。第四,税收饶让抵免是在抵免法基础上发展起来的一种特殊的抵免制度,饶让抵免与一般的抵免法的根本区别在于:前者是居住国政府对其居民纳税人在来源地国所得到减免的那部分税收,视同已经缴纳;而后者则是对已经在来源地国实际缴纳的所得税款的免除。

二、税收饶让抵免的适用范围

纵观国际税收饶让抵免实践,处于居住国地位的发达国家都出于自身国内税收政策考虑,对国际税收饶让抵免的适用范围作出了限定。大致有以下三种情况:一是对股息、利息和特许权使用费等预提税的减免税予以税收饶让抵免;二是对营业所得的减免税给予税收饶让抵免;三是对税收协定缔结以后,来源地国政府依据国内税法规定的新出台的税收优惠措施所作出的减免税,经缔约国双方一致同意,给予饶让抵免。上述三方面的税收饶让抵免,在有关国家所缔结的双边税收协定中,或限定其中一个方面,或兼而有之。①

在税收饶让抵免的幅度上,各国做法也不尽相同,主要有下述两种方式:一是居住国将来源地国国内税法上规定的适用税率与国际税收协定中适用的限制税率之间的征税差额视为已征税额,按照国内税法规定予以饶让抵免。二是居住国一方不考虑本国居民纳税人在缔约国对方实际获得多少减免税优惠,均按照双边税收协定中确定的固定免税率给予税收饶让。在这种饶让抵免方式下,纳税人的有关所得是否得到了饶让抵免以及受益于饶让抵免的程度,取决于税收协定中对各类所得规定的固定抵免税率的高低。协定中的固定抵免税率就是确定税收饶让的界限和标准,而不管纳税人在缔约国对方实际缴纳了多少税额。② 这种方法可以避免居住国与来源地国因各自的税收制度不同而导致饶让抵免计算上的复杂性。

三、税收饶让抵免的合理性之辩

税收饶让抵免制度产生于 20 世纪 50 年代,当时西方工业化国家急于通过扩大对外直接投资来抢占海外市场,而发展中国家在发展过程中又普遍面临资金缺乏的困境,急需吸收外资来支撑本国经济的发展。在这一背景下,英美等发达国家首先提出对发展中国家提供的外资税收优惠实施饶让抵免。

进入 20 世纪 90 年代以来,随着世界经济格局的转变,一些发达国家开始质疑税收饶让抵免的合理性,认为它违背了资本输出中性原则,扭曲了全球资本的有效配置,影响了全球资本配置的效率,损害了居住国的税收利益,同时还认为税收饶让是一种不适当的援助发展中国家经济发展的措施,税收协定中的饶让抵免条款容易为纳税人滥用进行国际避税安排。随着一些发展中国家经济地位的提升,资本输出国与输入国之间的界限已经不再有明显的区别,实行饶让抵免的基本前提已发生改变。③

在部分发达国家的推动下,经合组织在 1998 年公布了其对税收协定中税收饶让制度实施效果的调查报告,该报告反映了发达国家对饶让抵免制度以下三方面的质疑:(1) 税收饶让引发滥用的可能性;(2) 税收饶让作为一项促进来源国经济发展的外国援助工具的有效性;(3) 对税收饶让可能激励各国采用税收优惠方式。经合组织建议成员国在税收协定的谈签过程中要权衡饶让抵免制度

---

① 参见刘剑文主编:《国际税法学》(第二版),北京大学出版社 2004 年版,第 201 页。
② 同上书,第 203 页。
③ 参见廖益新主编:《国际税法学》,北京大学出版社 2001 年版,第 334 页。

的利弊,通过对饶让抵免的范围和幅度进行限制,来重新设计合理的饶让抵免条款。①

尽管发达国家在最先提出税收饶让抵免制度后又改弦易辙,质疑或否定这一制度,背后都是基于对特定的国际国内政治和经济背景的考虑,但我们应该看到,税收饶让抵免的实质,是居住国对来源地国所实施的税收优惠措施的认可和配合,不论是对于资本输出国还是资本输入国而言,都体现了各自的利益。就资本输入国而言,它以本国财政收入的减少为代价换取了外资的进入,不仅解决了发展中所面临的资金短缺问题,而且从长远看也扩大了本国的税收来源;就资本输出国而言,它不仅为本国的剩余资金找到了市场,而且还可以增加本国的外汇收入。至于一些发达国家所主张的税收饶让损害居住国税收利益之说是缺乏依据的,因为税收饶让只是居住国对来源地国税收优惠政策的一种认可而已,其所饶让的本来就是来源地国政府应征收的税款,来源地国仅仅是出于本国的政策目标而放弃了该税收收入,整个过程并没有影响到居住国的税收利益。

当然,我们也应该看到,税收饶让抵免制度在有些情况下确实可能被纳税人用来作为避税的一种途径,我们在保留和运用这种制度的时候,也有必要对这一制度加以改进和规范。前述经合组织在1998年公布的关于税收协定中饶让制度实施效果的调查报告中提出以下改进方法:(1) 税收饶让不能给予股息、利息和特许权使用费等消极投资所得。(2) 在税收协定中明确规定饶让抵免仅适用于特定的行为,如对来源地国公共设施的投资行为等等,不对银行和保险服务提供税收饶让。另外,税收饶让不得给予来源地国的出口导向型企业,以防止该类企业在没有税负的情况下与其他国家承担全部税负的企业竞争。(3) 在税收协定中加入税收饶让反滥用条款(Tax Sparing Anti-Abuse Clause)。(4) 在税收协定中规定"日落条款"(Sunset Clause),即限定给予税收饶让的时间,如给予5—10年。② 需要注意的是,由于该报告主要体现的是发达国家的立场,上述有些方法与其说是作为一种反避税措施,不如说是要限制甚至取消整个饶让抵免条款,我们在具体应用中对此要予以关注。

---

① See Tax Sparing: A Reconsideration, Report by the Committee on Fiscal Affairs, OECD, 1998.
② Ibid.

本章阅读材料

PNC Financial Services Group, Inc., d/b/a Riggs National Bank, and Subsidiaries, Appellant v. Commissioner of Internal Revenue Service, Appellee.

HEADNOTE

Foreign tax credits—Brazilian withholding tax—net loans—proof of payment—indirect subsidies. Tax Court properly determined in remand decision that taxpayer/U.S. lender's FTC for Brazilian taxes paid on its behalf by Brazilian Central Bank pursuant to net loan arrangement had to be reduced by amount [pg. 2007-5780] of simultaneous "pecuniary benefit" Central Bank received back from Brazilian govt.; pecuniary benefit, which effectively rebated 40% of stated tax, qualified as indirect subsidy to "another person" in transaction with taxpayer within meaning of Reg § 1.901-2(e)(3), as in effect for years at issue. Taxpayer's argument that Central Bank couldn't be considered "another person," since it was essentially same as/part of Brazilian govt., failed in face of prior decisions deeming Central Bank to be standing in for private borrowers for purposes of subject transactions.

United States Court of Appeals FOR THE DISTRICT OF COLUMBIA CIRCUIT,

Appeal from the United States Tax Court (No. IRS-24368-89)

Before: Rogers, Brown and Griffith, Circuit Judges.

Judge: Brown, Circuit Judge.

Opinion for the Court filed by Circuit Judge Brown.

Dissenting opinion filed by Circuit Judge Griffith.

In prior litigation, PNC Financial successfully claimed a foreign tax credit for taxes paid on its behalf in Brazil. That credit, the Internal Revenue Service argues, must be reduced by the amount of an indirect subsidy PNC received from the Brazilian government. The Tax Court agreed, and we now affirm.

I

In an international tax case as complicated, economically and litigiously, as this one, we do well to start with the basics. When a U. S. bank makes a loan abroad, the interest income is susceptible to tax in both the United States and the foreign state. Congress avoids double-taxing international business by giving a credit for taxes paid to the foreign government, less any credit, refund, or subsidy given the taxpayer by the foreign government. I. R. C. § 901; Treas. Reg. § 1. 901-2 (e). Interest income of $100,000, for example, where the relevant tax rate in the U. S. was 50% and in the foreign country was 25% with a 10% refund, would work out to $15,000 to the foreign country and $35,000 to the IRS. Were the foreign rate 50% with no refund, $50,000 would flow to that country and nothing to the IRS. Thus the two countries are on a see-saw: When one country's tax revenue goes up, the other's goes down.

This case, or rather this iteration of this case (for it is the third time we have heard an appeal from the Tax Court concerning the same transaction), is a peculiar elaboration of these simple principles. During the 1970s and early 1980s, in an effort to increase its reserves of foreign currency, Brazil's government borrowed and (using tax breaks) encouraged its people to borrow substantial amounts from foreign lenders. In 1982, fiscal crisis led nearly to default on the loans, and Brazil embarked on a debt restructuring plan with an international consortium of banks. According to the plan, Brazil's government-controlled Central Bank stepped in as common debtor for the foreign banks, becoming a middleman on the old loans (paying the creditors what was owed to them from the original borrowers and in turn receiving payments from the original borrowers) and, since Brazil still needed foreign credit to function, borrowing billions of dollars in additional funds. Appellant PNC Financial Services Group, Inc. (formerly Riggs National Corporation and Subsidiaries) lent a portion of those additional funds. In 1984 and 1985, Brazil taxed PNC's interest income at a 25% rate, which came to $166,415 in 1984 and $181,272 in 1985. But a provision of Brazilian law, hanging on from happier economic days when the Brazilian government incentivized borrowing from foreign lenders, gave subsidies for these taxes worth 40% of the total— $66,566 in

1984, and $72,509 in 1985. This appeal is about the U. S. tax treatment of that $139,075 in subsidies. At first glance, it seems obvious enough that PNC should receive a credit of $166,415 less $66,566 toward its 1984 U. S. income tax, and $181,272 less $72,509 toward its 1985 U. S. income tax. But three factors complicate the picture. [pg. 2007-5781]

First, PNC's loans to the Central Bank were "net," not "gross." Riggs II gives a matchless explanation of the difference, which we will not belabor here. Suffice it to say that in a gross loan agreement, the lender pays local (Brazilian) taxes on his interest income (or the borrower withholds it), while in a net loan, the borrower "contractually agrees not only to pay interest to the lender, but also to pay any local (Brazilian) tax that the lender owes on that interest income." Riggs II, 163 F. 3d at 1364. This is not necessarily a boon to lenders, for all else being equal, lenders must compensate borrowers for paying lenders' taxes with lowered interest rates. "The real difference between gross loans and net loans," Riggs II explains, "lies not in who licks the stamp on the envelope to the Brazilian government, but in who bears the economic burden of the tax." Id. With a net loan, the borrower bears that burden, for the borrower faces the risk of change in local tax rates, while the lender's net income (the interest payments) is stable. With a gross loan, the lender suffers the loss or reaps the benefit of change; it is his net income that might vary with taxes. Either way, however, the foreign government imposes legal liability for the local tax on the lender, and so either way the IRS credits the foreign tax payments. Treas. Reg. § 1.901-2(f).

Second, the Central Bank is, as Riggs II put it, "no ordinary Brazilian borrower." 163 F. 3d at 1366. Created by law to implement Brazil's monetary and fiscal policies (including issuing currency), required to act on behalf of Brazil's government and prohibited from acting on behalf of anyone else, able to contract in the name of the National Treasury, responsible for managing foreign lending to Brazilian borrowers, and under the control of the Minister of Finance, the Central Bank is 100% a part of Brazil's federal government, as all parties agree. The Federal Constitution of Brazil makes the Central Bank immune from tax on its own income, and in fact until 1988 the Central Bank operated, along with the National Treasury and the Banco de Brasil (in which

Brazil's government held a controlling share), a centralized system for funding Brazil's government that jointly controlled Brazil's tax revenue (although it was the Banco de Brasil that actually held the government's tax revenue in its coffers). Thus, if it were legally possible for the Brazilian government to impose a tax on its Central Bank, it is not clear how it would be economically possible for the Central Bank to pay it: At most, the money would go from the Brazilian government's right pocket to its left. And so when the Central Bank takes out net loans from a U.S. lender, certain questions arise: Will Brazilian law, in keeping with the principle that tax payments incidental to net loans are payments on behalf of lenders, require the Central Bank to pay despite the Bank's constitutional immunity from taxes? If so, should the IRS credit those payments? If the Brazilian government refunds a portion of them to the Central Bank, should the IRS subtract some of the refund from the credit?

We must pause at this point to understand PNC's and the Central Bank's (or rather, Brazil's) interests on the eve of their lending arrangement. Only if the Central Bank was subjected to compulsory tax payments on PNC's behalf could PNC qualify for the § 901 credit. See Riggs II, 163 F. 3d at 1365-66. And such payments would represent no economic burden for Brazil even if the Central Bank actually moved cash from its (government-controlled) vaults to the Banco de Brasil's (government-controlled) vaults. See id. at 1369. So both PNC and Brazil had an interest in seeing the Central Bank subjected to the compulsory payments. For PNC, every cent thus paid to the Brazilian government was money PNC would not have to pay to the IRS, and for Brazil, the "tax" just meant, so far as we can tell, more credit at a lower interest rate. The only loser in the arrangement was the IRS, which, economically speaking, would simply have transferred wealth to Brazil for Brazil and PNC to split. See id. The IRS ends up on the wrong end of the see-saw.

Only the Central Bank's constitutional immunity from taxes stood in the way, and the third [pg. 2007-5782] complexity in this case concerns how that immunity was overcome. Given their interest in the foreign tax credit, PNC and other banks went to Brazil's highest ranking authority on tax matters, the Minister of Finance, to request definitive guidance on whether the Central Bank would be subjected to the compulsory tax payments on their behalf. The most natural way for the Minister to answer "Yes" would have been to hold the Central Bank's tax immunity inapplicable in net loan arrangements, since the tax-immune entity pays standing in the lender's shoes. But this way was closed: Brazilian law already had authority for the opposite proposition. Id. at 1366. Another way, however, was open, for the money PNC loaned the Central Bank was available and officially intended for re-lending to private borrowers in Brazil. If the Central Bank could not stand in for the private lenders, perhaps it could stand in for these private borrowers. The Minister issued a private letter ruling, not available to the public but binding on the parties under Brazilian law, which Riggs II describes:

The Minister deemed it appropriate to "look through" the Central Bank to those ultimate private borrowers—so-called "borrowers-to-be"—for purposes of deciding the proper tax treatment of the loans. And it was settled Brazilian law that a private borrower in a net loan was required to pay the tax obligation it had contractually assumed from the lender. The Minister concluded that the "borrowers-to-be" aspect of the loans compelled an analogy to the garden variety private borrower situation, and that the Central Bank must "as a substitute for such borrowers [to-be] pay the income tax incident on the interest..."

Id. (first alteration in original). This reasoning further complicates the IRS's § 901 question. If the Brazilian Revenue Service looks through the Central Bank's tax-immune status because the Central Bank stands in for borrowers-to-be, should the IRS follow suit in granting credits and subtracting subsidies? Should it matter that, in the event, none of the money ever was reloaned?

As a statutory matter, these questions shape up as interpretations of I. R. C. § 901 and associated portions of the 1984 and 1985 Tax Code and regulations. In Riggs I, the issue was whether to permit the foreign tax credit at all, and it turned on whether the Central Bank's tax payments were compulsory, as the Minister had ruled, or voluntary. The Tax Court, viewing the Minister's private letter ruling as nothing more than "perhaps an administrative advisory opinion," conducted its own analysis of Brazilian law, concluded that the payments were voluntary, and denied PNC the credit. 1996

U. S. Tax Ct. LEXIS 49, at 119. We reversed in Riggs II. As we saw it, the Tax Court had sat in judgment on and effectively declared invalid the Minister's order to the Central Bank to pay taxes—a foreign sovereign's official act within its own territory. The act of state doctrine shields such acts from American courts' review. 163 F. 3d at 1367-68. We remanded "so that the Tax Court may determine in the first instance... whether the taxes were in fact paid by the Central Bank, and whether Riggs' credits must be reduced by the amount of any subsidies that the Central Bank may have received." Id. at 1369.

Riggs III and IV resolved the first of those two questions. In Riggs III, citing accounting irregularities, the Tax Court held that PNC "failed to establish that the withholding taxes in issue were paid by the Central Bank on petitioner's behalf." 2001 Tax Ct. Memo LEXIS 20, at 66. Since PNC was (again) ineligible for the credit, the Tax Court did not reach the subsidies issue. But in Riggs IV, we reversed. PNC had submitted official Brazilian receipts stating that the tax had been paid. These receipts were entitled to the common law's "presumption of regularity" for "the official acts of public officers," and while this presumption was rebuttable, the accounting irregularities that moved the Tax Court weren't the sort of "clear or specific evidence" needed to rebut it. Riggs IV, 295 F. 3d at 21 (internal quotation marks omitted). There could no longer be any question that PNC was entitled to a foreign tax credit. Riggs IV remanded "to determine whether the tax credits should be reduced by any subsidies that may have been paid to the Central Bank." Id. at 23.

Riggs V takes up this last issue. In 1984 and 1985, recall, Brazil had a subsidies system (sometimes called a "pecuniary benefits" system in this litigation) that effectively returned 40% of any tax payment Brazilian borrowers in international net loans made on their foreign lenders' behalf. Mechanically, the two halves of the transaction—making the tax payments and receiving the subsidy—were "simultaneous," both occurring "before paying the interest to the foreign lender" and in such a way as to credit Brazil's national treasury "only with the amount by which the withholding tax exceeded the subsidy." Riggs V, 2004 Tax Ct. Memo LEXIS 110, at 34-36 (quoting Nissho Iwai Am. Corp. v. Comm'r, 89 T. C. 765, 770, 1987 U. S. Tax Ct.

LEXIS 142, at 11). In the Tax Court, no one doubted that this arrangement would have amounted to an indirect subsidy [pg. 2007-5783] and properly reduced PNC's foreign tax credit had the borrower been a private party; past litigation in what have come to be called "the Brazilian tax cases," Amoco Corp. v. Comm'r, 138 F. 3d 1139, 1145 [81 AFTR 2d 98-998] (7th Cir. 1998), laid that question to rest. See Norwest Corp. v. Comm'r, 69 F. 3d 1404, 1407-10 [76 AFTR 2d 95-7409] (8th Cir. 1995) (finding an indirect subsidy to the extent that the Brazilian government rebated a portion of the taxes Brazilian borrowers paid on U. S. lenders' behalf); Cont'l Ill. Corp. v. Comm'r, 998 F. 2d 513, 519-20 [72 AFTR 2d 93-5308] (7th Cir. 1993) (same); First Chi. Corp. v. Comm'r, 61 T. C. M. (CCH) 1774[91,044 PH Memo TC], 1991 Tax Ct. Memo LEXIS 63, at 18-19, 21 (same); Nissho Iwai, 1987 U. S. Tax Ct. LEXIS 142, at 24, 27 (same). What makes this case unique is the presence of and role played by the Central Bank standing in for private borrowers. The financial identity between the Central Bank and the Brazilian government, the same thing that had made it puzzling to think of the Central Bank making compulsory tax payments, also makes it puzzling to think of the Central Bank receiving governmental subsidies. But taking its cue from the Brazilian Minister of Finance's private letter ruling, the Tax Court held that the Central Bank received the subsidy "not... as an agent of the Brazilian Government, but rather on behalf of the borrowers-to-be," so that it was "proper to treat the Central Bank as separate from the Brazilian Government" for purposes of the subsidy regulation. Riggs V, 2004 Tax Ct. Memo LEXIS 110, at 56.

PNC has appealed and now the issue of the subsidy is before us.

II

PNC's position in this appeal is that the Brazilian government cannot give its Central Bank a subsidy because the two are, for tax purposes, one and the same. The subsidy regulation applicable at the time, Treas. Reg. § 1. 901-2 (e)(3) (1984), has, functionally, three parts. First, it defines a foreign subsidy as a payment "by any means (such as through a refund or credit)," by the foreign country to the taxpayer or someone engaged in a transaction with the taxpayer, where the payment "is determined, directly or indirectly, by reference to the amount of income tax." Second, it regulates direct subsidies: If a foreign country pays a subsidy directly to a taxpayer, that amount must be subtracted from the taxpayer's foreign tax credit. Third, distinguishing indirect subsidies, it states that "[a] foreign country is considered to provide a subsidy to a taxpayer if the country provides a subsidy to another person that... [e]ngages in a transaction with the taxpayer"; here too the subsidy must be subtracted from the credit. The Brazilian government's payments to its Central Bank, calculated by taking 40% of the income tax PNC owed Brazil, fit the definition of a subsidy but clearly are not direct subsidies, as all parties agree. The question is whether those payments qualify as indirect subsidies. PNC claims they do not because "[t]he Central Bank is part of the Brazilian government; indeed, as far as Brazil's finances are concerned, the Central Bank is the Brazilian government." Appellant's Reply Br. 1 (emphasis in original). Therefore "the Brazilian government paid the subsidy in question to itself," which, PNC argues, puts the payments outside the indirect subsidy regulation. The sole issue before us is whether, in the circumstances of this case, the Brazilian government's subsidy was paid "to another person" within the meaning of Treasury Regulation § 1.901-2(e)(3).

As a threshold matter, we must determine what it means for the recipient of a subsidy to be "another person": Does this mean a person other than the foreign country, or other than the taxpayer? Read in isolation, § 1.901-2(e)(3), with its careful distinction between direct and indirect subsidies, appears to ask whether the recipient is the taxpayer. However, because the indirect subsidy regulation seems on the whole to contemplate a transaction with three parties (foreign government, U.S. taxpayer, and U.S. taxpayer's local partner), the opposite approach—which PNC advocates—is also plausible, especially as it avoids the notion of a government paying a subsidy to itself. As the Commissioner has not opposed PNC's reading, we shall assume for purposes of this appeal that PNC's § 901 credit should be reduced if and only if the recipient of the subsidy (the Central Bank) is a person other than the Brazilian government.

PNC points to evidence that "the Central Bank is part of the foreign country," Appellant's Reply Br. 6, and hence cannot be "another person." If we faced this question in a [pg. 2007-5784] vacuum—without the borrowers-to-be arrangement, without the Minister of Finance's private letter ruling, and without the five hearings, appeals, and remands that preceded this appeal—we might well answer it as PNC proposes. There is, after all, no denying the Central Bank's part-to-whole relationship to the Brazilian government. But we do not operate in a vacuum; we are bound by determinations in earlier iterations of this case. PNC's factual argument, however convincing it might be, was properly before the court in Riggs II, not here. We cannot ignore the holding in that case and consider the facts de novo. See K. N. Llewellyn, The Bramble Bush 29, 35 (Oceana Publications 1981) (1930) (explaining how, depending on legal context or posture, the facts in a case can be far "from the reality of raw events" and "miles away from life").

PNC's proposed outcome would make a virtue of inconsistency, applying disparate treatment to two legs of a simultaneous transaction. Had the Central Bank handed $10 to the Brazilian government and the Brazilian government handed $5 back—or, even more accurately, had the Central Bank netted the transaction out itself and only handed over $5 in the first place—PNC would have us take legal account of the $10 and ignore the $5 given back.

"Inconsistency is the antithesis of the rule of law." LaShawn A. v. Barry, 87 F. 3d 1389, 1393 (D. C. Cir. 1996) (en banc). Of the various doctrines, principles, and practices we use to police inconsistency, some of which go to the root of what law is, law-of-the-case doctrine is most applicable here: "[T]he same issue presented a second time in the same case in the same court should lead to the same result." Id. (emphasis in original); see also Arizona v. California, 460 U. S. 605, 618 (1983) ("As most commonly defined, the doctrine posits that when a court decides upon a rule of law, that decision should continue to govern the same issues in subsequent stages in the same case."); Crocker v. Piedmont Aviation, Inc., 49 F. 3d 735, 739 (D. C. Cir. 1995) ("When there are multiple appeals taken in the course of a single piece of litigation, law-of-the-case doctrine holds that decisions rendered on the first appeal should not be revisited on later trips to the appellate court."). Law-of-the-case doctrine encompasses issues decided both explicitly and "by necessary implication." LaShawn A., 87 F. 3d at 1394 (quoting Crocker, 49

F. 3d at 739). The identity or non-identity of the Central Bank and the Brazilian government for purposes of the tax arrangement in this case was decided by necessary implication in Riggs II.

Riggs II was a subtle case. The issue was whether the Central Bank's payments to the Brazilian government on PNC's behalf should be regarded as voluntary or compulsory in light of the Foreign Minister's private letter ruling stating that the payments were compulsory. The court applied the act of state doctrine, which in its classic formulation holds that "the courts of one country will not sit in judgment on the acts of the government of another done within its own territory," Underhill v. Hernandez, 168 U. S. 250, 252 (1897), and in its modern formulation "precludes the courts of this country from inquiring into the validity of the public acts a recognized foreign sovereign power committed within its own territory," Banco Nacional de Cuba v. Sabbatino, 376 U. S. 398, 401 (1964). Since Banco Nacional, the doctrine has been understood to arise from the separation of powers, reflecting "the strong sense of the Judicial Branch that its engagement in the task of passing on the validity of foreign acts of state may hinder the conduct of foreign affairs." W. S. Kirkpatrick & Co. v. Envtl. Tectonics Corp., Int'l, 493 U. S. 400, 404 (1990) (internal quotation marks omitted).

Applying this doctrine to the Minister of Finance's private letter ruling was not straightforward. For one thing, the doctrine is typically applied to tangible acts, like the expropriation of property, rather than the ruling of a government official. See Riggs II, 163 F. 3d at 1368. For another, applying the doctrine to a foreign official's ruling might run contrary to Federal Rule of Civil Procedure 44. 1, directing courts to independently determine issues of foreign law, and its tax law equivalent, U. S. Tax Court Rule 146. In a crucial passage threading these obstacles, the Riggs II court reasoned that whether or not it can be said that the Brazilian Minister of Finance's interpretation of Brazilian law qualifies as an act of state, the Minister's order to the Central Bank to withhold and pay the income tax on the interest paid to the Bank goes beyond a mere interpretation of law. The Minister, after all, ordered that the Central Bank "must, in substitution of the future not yet identified debtors of the tax [i. e., the borrowers-to-be], pay the income tax..." Such an order has been treated as an act of state. The Tax Court's conclusion on Brazilian law—that no tax is imposed on a net loan transaction involving a governmental entity as borrower—implicitly declared "non-compulsory," i. e., invalid, the Minister's order to the Central Bank to pay the taxes. The act of state doctrine requires courts to abstain from even engaging in such an inquiry.

Id. (bracketed text in original) (internal citations omitted). Put in the affirmative, the holding here is that American courts must accept as given that the Brazilian government levied a compulsory tax payment on the Central Bank, where the Central Bank stood in for borrowers-to-be. Thus what Riggs II resolved by necessary implication was the status of or role played by the Central Bank with respect to the PNC transaction. That resolves the present appeal, for if the Central Bank stood in for borrowers-to-be when it paid PNC's taxes, it also stood in for them when it received 40% of those tax payments back in subsidies.

PNC tries to avoid this conclusion by arguing that the Riggs II court disavowed the borrowers-to-be rationale when it refused to hold that the "Minister of Finance's interpretation of Brazilian law qualifies as an act of state." The act of state at issue in Riggs II, as PNC interprets the case, was solely the Minister's order, the bare imperative to the Central Bank to pay taxes. Indeed, as PNC sees it, the act of state doctrine cannot encompass the rationale behind a foreign government's acts. The holding of Riggs II, on this argument, would be that American courts must accept as given that the Brazilian government levied a compulsory payment on the Central Bank-period.

But the borrowers-to-be rationale and the Minister's interpretation of Brazilian law are not one and the same, and the court's refusal to call one an act of state in no way implies rejection of the other. The Minister's private letter ruling has three parts: the bare imperative, the borrowers-to-be rationale, and a broader discussion of the Central Bank's legal situation in various types of financial transactions. The last of these is the likely antecedent for Riggs II's reference to an interpretation of Brazilian law—which makes good sense when one notices that the borrowers-to-be rationale is not an interpretation of law at all. Far from rejecting the borrowers-to-be logic, Riggs II in fact repeated that rationale—indeed, restated the Minister's order in such a way as to incorporate it—immediately after disclaiming the Minister's interpretation of Brazilian law as an act of state: "[W]hether or not it can be said that the Brazilian Minister of Finance's interpretation of Brazilian law qualifies as an act of state...[t]he Minister... ordered that the Central Bank must, in substitution of the...[borrowers-to-be], pay the income tax..." Id. (internal quotation marks omitted).

In concluding that the Central Bank is "another person" in the sense of the treasury regulation, we need not apply the act of state doctrine. Rather, in the interest of consistency, we need only adhere, as a law-of-the-case matter, to the necessary implications of Riggs II. There, the court held that, based on the act of state doctrine, American courts had to accept the Minister's determination that the Brazilian government had compelled the Central Bank to remit tax payments on PNC's behalf, standing in for the borrowers-to-be. In that role, the Central Bank was distinct from the Brazilian government. Thus, as the payment and the subsidy are both part of the same indivisible transaction, Riggs II necessarily implies the Central Bank is likewise distinct for purposes of the subsidy.

Two last points round out this argument. First, law-of-the-case doctrine is prudential; the Supreme Court has instructed that courts may "reopen what has been decided," though they should "as a rule... be loath to do so in the absence of extraordinary circumstances such as where the initial decision was clearly erroneous and would work a manifest injustice." Christianson v. Colt Indus. Operating Corp., 486 U.S. 800, 817 (1988) (quoting Messinger v. Anderson, 225 U.S. 436, 444 (1912))(internal quotation marks omitted), and Arizona, 460 U.S. at 618 n.8); see also LaShawn A., 87 F.3d at 1393. PNC has failed to persuade us that there is error or injustice, particularly when every previous court to address the issue has regarded PNC's tax arrangement in Brazil as a stratagem for avoiding U.S. taxes. See Riggs I, 1996 U.S. Tax Ct. LEXIS 49, at 41; Riggs II, 163 F.3d at 1369; Riggs III, 2001 Tax Ct. Memo LEXIS 20, at 64-66.

Second, the root principles at work here—the principle that courts must be consistent with one another and the principle that governmental entities may in some circumstances be treated as private when taking on a private role or function—have a venerable lineage. See Republic of Argentina v. Weltover, Inc. , 504 U. S. 607, 611, 614 (1992) (putting a distinction between a government's exercises of uniquely sovereign power and ordinary private power at the heart of foreign sovereign immunity); Alfred Dunhill of London, Inc. v. Republic of Cuba, 425 U. S. 682, 695 (1976) (plurality opinion) (recognizing a traditional distinction "between the public and governmental acts of sovereign states on the one hand and their private and commercial acts on the other"); Bank of the U. S. v. Planters' Bank of Ga. , 22 U. S. (9 Wheat) 904, 907 (1824) (Marshall, C. J.) ("[W]hen a government becomes a partner in any trading company, it devests itself, so far as concerns the transactions of that company, of its sovereign character, and takes that of a private citizen. "); Henry J. Friendly, Indiscretion [pg. 2007-5786] About Discretion, 31 Emory L. J. 747, 758 (1982) ("[T]he most basic principle of jurisprudence [is] that we must act alike in all cases of like nature. " (internal quotation marks omitted)).

III

In place of the analysis above, PNC asks us to follow the Seventh Circuit's approach from Amoco Corp. v. Commissioner, 138 F. 3d 1139 [81 AFTR 2d 98-998] (7th Cir. 1998). But as described below, Amoco shares none of the factual circumstances we find dispositive here, for which reason we decline to follow it in the instant case.

Virtually every page of PNC's briefs is studded with references to Amoco, which involved the tax consequences of a complicated oil exploration arrangement between Amoco, a U. S. oil company operating in Egypt, and the Egyptian General Petroleum Corporation, an entity owned and controlled by the Egyptian government for the purpose of managing Egypt's oil wealth. EGPC contracted to pay Amoco's Egyptian income tax on Amoco's behalf—as in a net loan arrangement—and then took a credit on its own Egyptian taxes exactly equal to what it paid for Amoco. (EGPC had no tax immunity and ordinarily paid income taxes as if a commercial entity.) The question for the Seventh Circuit was whether Amoco should be permitted a foreign tax credit on its U. S. taxes under §901, or whether the credit EGPC took in Egypt should, under the same subsidy regulation at issue in our case, count as an indirect subsidy, reducing Amoco's U. S. credit to zero. The Tax Court had found no indirect subsidy because "EGPC was part of the Egyptian government, and thus by definition it was incapable of receiving a subsidy from itself." Id. at 1146. The Seventh Circuit affirmed, but on somewhat more modest reasoning. Finding "[t]he question of how to treat state-owned enterprises... exceedingly complicated," the court favored a "functional approach" over "bright-line rules" and refused to decide "whether it is impossible in all circumstances for a government to grant a subsidy to one of its wholly or majority owned enterprises." Id. at 1146-47. In Amoco's case, the court found no indirect subsidy for two reasons: first was EGPC's economic identity with the Egyptian government ("EGPC's profits go straight to the treasury, and it would never feel any losses, because the treasury would absorb them."), and second was the fact that, as an economic matter, EGPC alone received the benefit of the credit while "Amoco unquestionably bore the economic burden of the taxes imposed on its operations by Egypt." Id. at 1148-49.

PNC argues that its situation is identical to the one in Amoco: It too contracted with a foreign governmental entity that agreed to pay its American partner's local taxes, received some of the tax money back, and shares an economic identity with the foreign government. Thus it too should benefit from the idea that, as PNC characterizes Amoco's holding, "when the benefit of the subsidy is provided to the foreign government, there is no subsidy within the meaning of the regulations since it is impossible for the foreign government to subsidize itself." Appellant's Br. 21.

But to start with, that isn't Amoco's holding—or rather, it is only half of Amoco's holding. The other half is the economic analysis concluding that the U. S. taxpayer bore all the burden of the foreign tax and received no benefit from the foreign credit—whereas in our case, the tax Brazil formally levied on its Central Bank represented only a benefit to PNC. Even more importantly, Amoco lacked every factual feature we have found decisive in this appeal: no tax immunity, no private letter ruling or equivalent, no borrowers-to-be or analogue for them, and no controlling precedent. Unless we ignore the facts and the history of this case, we are bound to regard the Central Bank as standing in for private parties. Indeed, PNC's comparisons between the

Central Bank in this case and EGPC in Amoco are premature: Logically prior to any such comparison—indeed the first analytic step in many cases that turn on someone's or something's governmental status—is fixing on the role that person or entity played in the particular circumstances of the case. The Seventh Circuit itself said as much ("[T]he kind of legal issue presented and the context of the suit has been more important than the label 'governmental' or 'non-governmental,'" Amoco Corp. , 138 F. 3d at 1147) and was careful to cabin its conclusions accordingly.

IV

Both PNC and the dissent would have us answer the question of the Central Bank's status as if indifferent to all context and background. This we cannot do. As we agree with the Tax Court that, under the facts of this case, it is "proper to treat the Central Bank as separate from the Brazilian government" and deem the bank "another person" within the meaning of the subsidy regulation, the judgment of the Tax Court is Affirmed.

Judge: Griffith, Circuit Judge, dissenting: I share the majority's frustration with this, the latest of what seems to have become a judicial [pg. 2007-5787] mini-series, "Riggs VI: Return of the Subsidy." We are unanimous in the hope that it is the last of the sequels. We disagree, however, about what our role in this case should be, and I think it a disagreement worthy of some discussion. While I share my colleagues' unease over PNC's "stratagem for avoiding U. S. taxes," Op. at 17, such discomfort alone cannot determine the outcome of a case. Both facts and law are fundamental to our conclusions, and although the facts of this case are complicated, the law is simple. This case turns entirely on the plain language of controlling U. S. tax regulations. That language is clear, unambiguous, and dispositive. Its effects—whatever they may be—are not within our power to forestall, and its neutral application does not, as the majority suggests, create any inconsistency. On the contrary, our abandonment of a textual approach creates inconsistencies galore, putting us conspicuously at odds with the text of both U. S. and relevant Brazilian law, our own precedent, and the reasoned decision of a sister circuit. The court's analysis also obscures two important principles it seeks to clarify: the act of state doctrine and the law-of-the-case doctrine. Accordingly, I dissent.

第四章　不同类型跨国所得的征税规则

第一节　对跨国营业利润的征税

一、对跨国营业利润征税的基本原则——常设机构原则

在国际税法上，跨国营业利润是指一国的居民纳税人在居住国境外取得的营业利润。对于该项所得，企业的居住国根据居民税收管辖权，要求该企业就其全球范围内取得的收入纳税，而那些非居民企业在其境内从事生产经营活动的国家，也会根据收入来源地税收管辖权，要求该非居民企业就在其境内从事生产经营活动取得的收入纳税，由此产生了对该企业的跨国营业所得的重复征税问题。

从目前的国际实践看，坚持常设机构原则是解决对跨国营业利润双重征税问题的基本原则。《OECD范本》和《UN范本》均规定：缔约国一方企业的利润仅在该缔约国征税，除非该企业通过设在缔约国另一方的常设机构进行营业活动。如果该企业通过设立在缔约国另一方的常设机构进行营业活动，对于可归属于该常设机构的利润，可以在缔约国另一方征税。[①] 该规定表明，居住国企业如果在收入来源国设立了常设机构，那么该企业通过该常设机构实施营业活动所取得的营业利润就应当在常设机构所在国纳税。该原则涉及定性和定量两个方面。定性的方面意味着，只要有常设机构的存在，常设机构所在国就可以对常设机构所隶属的企业的营业利润征税，也就是说，是否设有常设机构是确定收入来源国能否享有征税权的标准。定量的方面意味着，在常设机构所在国有权征税的前提下，居住国企业的营业利润中哪部分可以在常设机构所在国征税，即常设机构的利润归属问题，是确定收入来源国享有的征税权范围和程度大小的标准。

在理解和运用常设机构原则的过程中，关键要把握以下几个方面的内容：一是常设机构的认定，二是常设机构所在国征税权范围的确定方法，三是可归属于常设机构的利润的确定方法，四是常设机构原则的例外。

---

① 参见《OECD范本》和《UN范本》第7条。

二、常设机构的概念和范围

根据经合组织范本第 5 条有关常设机构概念的规定,常设机构包括场所型常设机构和代理型常设机构,前者以营业场所为核心要素,后者以代理人为核心要素。

(一)场所型常设机构

根据该范本第 5 条,场所型常设机构是指企业进行其全部或部分营业的固定营业场所。根据该定义,场所型常设机构需满足以下三个方面的构成要件:(1)必须有营业场所,如场地、房屋或者建筑物,在某些情况下营业场所也可以是机器、设备等设施;(2)该营业场所必须是固定的,即该场所必须是建立在一个确定的地点,并且具有一定的永久性;(3)企业通过该固定营业场所开展营业活动。结合税收协定范本及其注释,对前述三个构成要件理解如下:

1. "营业场所"的含义

虽然两大范本都没有对"营业场所"作出定义,但均通过列举的方式对其加以界定。根据两大范本第 5 条第 2 款,"常设机构"一语特别包括管理场所、分支机构、办事处、工厂、作业场所、矿场、油井、气井以及其他任何开采自然资源的场所。另外,《OECD 范本》第 5 条第 3 款规定,建筑工地或建筑、安装工程,如果持续存在 12 个月以上,构成常设机构。《UN 范本》第 5 条第 3 款规定,建筑工地或建筑、安装工程,以及与此相关的监督活动,如果持续存在 6 个月以上,构成常设机构;提供服务,如果在任何 12 个月中连续或累计 183 天以上,也构成常设机构。由此可见,上述建筑工地、建筑、安装或装配工程及与其有关的监督活动的场所,还有提供服务的场所,都属于营业场所的范围,在满足其他要件的情形下,将被认定为常设机构。

《OECD 范本》注释认为,上述列举表明应对"营业场所"作广义理解,它涵盖了所有用于从事企业营业的厂房、设施或装置,不论它们是否也用于其他目的。如果某企业没有厂房,或从事生产经营不需要厂房,而仅有一定可支配的空间,也可视为具有营业场所。厂房、设施或装置是为该企业自有或租用,或通过其他形式支配均无关紧要。因此,营业场所可以由市场上的某一摊位,或长期使用的海关仓库的一部分(用于存放应税物品)构成。此外,营业场所还可设在另一企业的营业设施中。例如,某外国企业持续地支配使用另一企业拥有的某座厂房或者其中的一部分的情形。只要企业拥有其支配的用于营业活动的一定的空间,这一事实就足以构成营业场所,并不要求其具有使用该场所的正式法律权利。可见,即使某企业非法占有某一特定地点并在那里进行营业,也可能构成常设机构。①

2. "固定"的含义

构成常设机构的营业场所必须是"固定"的。根据范本注释的解释,这里的"固定"包括两个层面的含义:一是空间上的固定性,即该营业场所必须是建立在一个确定的地点;二是时间上的非临时性。某一营业场所只有同时符合这两个标准,才能称之为"固定"的营业场所。

所谓营业场所在空间上的固定性,是指这个营业场所通常必须和某个特定的地理位置存在联系。若缔约国一方的企业不是在某确定的场所进行营业活动,那么不论其在缔约国另一方经营多久,都不能被认为具有固定性。② 两大范本在其注释中同时指出,空间上的固定性并不是要求构成常设机构的设备一定要实际定着于土地上,而是只要存在于某一确定的场所即可。③ 因此,空间上的固定,可以是指构成营业场所的设施、设备固定在土地上(或海床上),如房屋等建筑物、永久性石油生产设施等,也可以是指企业具有一个能稳定开展营业活动的场地和空间,如市场上的一个摊位等。若某企业从事的营业活动经常在相邻的地点之间移动,那么在判断是否存在一个单一的"营业场所"时,则要考虑这种营业的性质,如果一个营业活动在其内移动的特定地域,可被认为在商业上和地理上构成了关于该营业的不可分割的整体,那么一般可以认定存在一个单一的营业场所。相反,如果没有商业上的内在联系,仅在一个有限的地域范围内从事营业活动的事实,不足以导致该区域被认定为单一营业场所。例如,某油漆工人在某办公大楼里依据一系列不相关的合同,为一些不相关的客户连续工作,不能认为构成给该大楼刷油漆的单一项目,因而该建筑物不应被认为是该项工作的单一营业场所。然而,若油漆工人在一个单一合同下,为一个客户在整个大楼内工作,该项工作则会构成该油漆工人的单一项目,并且该建筑物整体由于此时在商业和地理方面构成不可分割的整体,因而可以被认为是该项工作的单一营业场所。④

所谓时间上的非临时性,或者说一定程度的永久性,是指该营业场所并不是一个临时性的营业场所。然而,由于构成企业营业场所的场地、设施和设备的不同,时间上持久性的判断,存在着主观标准和客观标准的差别。根据主观持久标准,所谓营业场所具有一定的持久性,并非是指构成营业场所的设备本身必须是

---

① 参见《OECD 范本》第 5 条注释第 4 段。
② 参见《OECD 范本》第 5 条注释第 5 段。
③ 同上。
④ 同上。

永久存在的,而是指企业对于营业场所应该具有长期使用的目的,即企业打算通过该营业场所长期进行营业活动。如果一个营业场所的建立是以长期使用为目的,即使由于企业活动本身的特殊性质或者由于特殊情况的发生(如纳税人死亡、投资失败等)而提前清算,该营业场所仍然构成常设机构。相应的,如果一个营业场所是以临时使用为目的,但是其存在的期限已经使得该营业场所不能被视为属于临时性场所时,该营业场所也可以构成一个固定营业场所,从而构成常设机构。[1] 根据客观期限标准,用于企业营业活动的营业场所只要在客观上存续一个确定的时间期限,那么该营业场所就构成税收协定意义上的固定营业场所。当前各国对外签订的税收协定对固定营业场所作一般性定义时,不仅制定了一个主观性的持久标准,同时又对某些特定的营业活动的营业场所规定了一个明确的时间期限,作为该营业场所符合固定营业场所的标准。这类营业场所主要包括上述的建筑工地,建筑、安装或装配工程以及与此有关的监督活动的营业场所,提供劳务和咨询劳务的营业场所,以及自然资源的勘探开发活动和与此有关的活动的营业场所。[2]

3. 企业通过该营业场所开展营业活动

为了使一个营业场所构成常设机构,使用该营业场所的企业必须通过该场所进行其全部或部分的营业活动。然而,并非所有用来开展营业活动的固定营业场所都可构成常设机构,《OECD范本》第5条第4款规定,以下营业场所不构成常设机构:(1) 专为储存、陈列或交付本企业货物或商品的目的而使用的设施;(2) 专为储存、陈列或交付的目的而保存本企业货物或商品的库存;(3) 专为通过另一企业加工的目的而保存本企业货物或商品的库存;(4) 专为本企业采购货物或商品或者收集情报的目的而设有的固定营业场所;(5) 专为本企业进行任何其他准备性或辅助性活动而设有的固定营业场所;(6) 专为本款第1至5项所规定的各项活动的结合而设有的固定营业场所,只要这种结合使得固定营业场所的全部活动属于准备或辅助性质。值得注意的是,《UN范本》虽然作出了与以上内容相似的规定,但将"专为交付本企业的货物或商品的目的而使用设施,以及专为交付的目的而保存本企业商品或货物的库存"从常设机构否定清单中删除。之所以作出这样的删除,是因为在制定该范本时,一些发展中国家的代表指出,为现货交付保存商品库存,促进了产品的销售,并且使设有设施的企业在所得来源国取得了利润,出于对发展中国家来源地税收管辖权的维护,这

---

[1] 参见《OECD范本》第5条注释第6.3段。
[2] 参见廖益新主编:《国际税法学》,高等教育出版社2008年版,第99—100页。

种用于交付货物的场所应当视为常设机构。而一些发达国家的专家则对此表示反对,认为交付货物这一环节在一般情况下所能分配的利润数额很少,因此坚持《OECD范本》的规定更加合理。由于发展中国家和发达国家的代表在此问题上意见对立,专家小组最终虽然同意在范本的条文中删除交付货物的活动,但同时建议,缔约国双方在签订税收协定的谈判中应考虑到这一分歧。①

从范本中列举的否定清单可以看出,如果企业通过固定营业场所进行的只是准备性或辅助性的活动,虽然这种活动对企业的生产具有贡献,但所提供的服务离利润的实现较远,以致难以将任何利润划归到这样的营业场所,因此,从事这些活动的固定营业场所不能被视为常设机构。这里的关键问题是要判断企业通过固定营业场所进行的活动是不是准备性或辅助性的。在实践中,由于企业活动的多样性,企业通过固定营业场所进行的营业活动是不是准备性或辅助性的,需要结合不同企业的具体情形来判断,决定性的标准是固定营业场所的活动本身是否构成企业整体活动的基本的和重要的部分。例如,如果一个企业所设的固定营业场所从事活动的目的与整个企业的目的相同,那么该场所的活动不能被认为是准备性或辅助性的活动。如果企业设立的某个固定营业场所的职责是管理一个企业,甚至是一个企业或财团的一部分,那么,不论其活动的范围是否被限制在某一地区,该管理活动都不能被认为是准备性或辅助性的活动。又如,企业专为向客户交付其销售的机器的零配件,并维修保养本企业销售机器所设的固定营业场所,应视为常设机构,因为这一活动超出了纯粹的交付货物的范围,这种售后活动是企业为客户服务的基本及重要的方面,因而不是单纯的辅助性活动,该营业场所构成企业的常设机构。②

关于开展营业活动的时间,《OECD范本》注释规定,企业从开始通过其固定营业场所进行营业活动起即构成常设机构,为使该场所成为永久性经营场所而在该场所进行的准备活动应包括在内,但若企业筹建固定营业场所的活动与营业场所日后从事的永久性活动有本质上的区别,那么企业建立该固定营业场所本身的时间不应包括在内。随着固定营业场所的转让,或者通过该场所进行的所有活动的停止,即当所有与常设机构过去的活动有关的行为和措施终止的时候,常设机构停止存在。然而,如果业务活动只是暂时中断,则不能视为营业的终止,常设机构继续存在。如果企业将其固定营业场所出租给另一企业,则该固定营业场所通常只为另一企业而非出租方的活动服务,一般认为,此时出租方的

---

① 参见《UN范本》注释对第5条第4款的解释。
② 参见《OECD范本》第5条注释第24、25段。

常设机构即告终止,除非其继续通过该固定营业场所进行自身的营业活动。①

(二) 代理型常设机构

与场所型常设机构不同,代理型常设机构反映的是企业通过代理人而不是固定营业场所从事营业活动,即使企业在一国没有固定营业场所,也可能因为代理人的存在而被认定为存在常设机构。按照代理人是否独立于被代理人,税收协定将代理人分为两类,一类是独立地位代理人,另一类是非独立地位代理人。② 在判断营业代理人是否构成常设机构时,针对独立地位代理人和非独立地位代理人的标准不尽一致,因此有必要掌握独立地位代理人与非独立地位代理人的划分标准。根据《OECD范本》注释的解释,独立地位代理人是指在法律上和经济上都独立于其所代理的企业的代理人。③ 非独立地位代理人是指除独立地位代理人以外的任何形式的代理人,不论该代理人是个人还是公司,是不是代理活动履行地国家的居民,是否在从事代理活动的国家设立营业场所,是否与被代理企业之间存在雇佣关系。④

1. 非独立地位代理人

缔约国一方企业通过非独立地位代理人在缔约国另一方进行活动时,根据《OECD范本》的规定,该非独立地位代理人构成常设机构必须同时符合以下条件:(1) 该非独立地位代理人在缔约国另一方代表该企业进行准备性或辅助性活动以外的活动;(2) 有权以企业的名义签订合同并经常行使这种权利。⑤ 根据《OECD范本》注释的解释,并非任何非独立代理人都可被认定为常设机构,只有那些由于其职权范围或活动性质使其所代理的企业在一定程度上参与了所在国家的经济活动的代理人,才应视为构成常设机构。根据该范本规定,代理人只有在有权缔结合同时,才能认定为该企业的常设机构,因为在这种情况下,代理人有足够的权利约束所代理的企业参与所在国家的商业活动。有学者将此种情形下的代理人称为缔约代理人。需要指出的是,缔约代理人只有经常行使缔约代理权时才能构成常设机构,如果只是偶尔或个别情况下代理签署合同,则不能认定为常设机构。

《UN范本》规定非独立地位代理人在以下三种情况下均可以构成常设机构:(1) 在缔约国另一方代表企业进行准备性或辅助性活动以外的活动,并且有

---

① 参见《OECD范本》第5条注释第11段。
② 参见《OECD范本》第5条注释第32段。
③ 参见《UN范本》第5条注释第37段。
④ 参见《UN范本》第5条注释第32段。
⑤ 参见《OECD范本》第5条第5款。

权以企业的名义签订合同并经常行使这种权利(即缔约代理人);(2)虽然没有缔约权,但是经常在缔约国另一方保存货物或商品的库存,并且代表企业经常从该库存中交付货物或商品(即交付货物代理人);(3)如果企业是保险企业时,除再保险外,在缔约国另一方收取保险费或接受保险业务(即保险代理人)。①

2. 独立地位代理人

对于独立地位代理人,两大范本均规定,只有在该代理人并非按照其营业常规从事代理活动时,方可认定为常设机构。② 也就是说,如果独立地位代理人代理企业进行活动时是按照其营业常规进行活动,那么该独立地位代理人不能被认定为被代理企业的常设机构。至于何谓独立地位代理人按照"营业常规"进行活动,《OECD范本》注释给出了解释:独立地位代理人按照"营业常规"进行活动,首先指的是独立地位代理人开展的营业活动本身在经济上不能直接归属于被代理企业。例如,如果一个佣金代理人不仅以其自身的名义销售某一企业的货物或商品,而且经常以该企业具有缔约权的常设代理人的身份进行活动,那么该代理人的这一活动超出其营业常规,应当视为该企业的常设机构。③ 其次,是否按照"营业常规"活动的判断,还取决于独立地位代理人是否按照"行业活动惯例"进行活动,即所谓"营业常规",主要是指独立地位代理人的行业活动惯例,该惯例是该行业当前已经存在的惯常活动。④ 虽然某种代理人行业的惯常活动是通常的比较对象,但在特定情形下,如在某个代理人的活动与通常行业无关的情况下,其他补充性的检测标准可以一并或选择性地适用。⑤ 如代理人所从事的代理活动是属于新兴行业的代理活动,由于此类行业往往存在着不同于其他行业的特点,加之参与此类行业的代理人较少,因此,应该给予营业常规解释方面的扩展性,即如果独立地位代理人所从事的活动在将来可能发展为该行业的惯常活动,那么该活动也可以解释为按其"营业常规"进行活动。⑥

最后需要指出的是,虽然《OECD范本》中对常设机构的认定规则作了如上详尽的规定,但在这些规则的解释和应用过程中还有许多问题有待进一步明确。为此,经合组织财政事务委员会下属工作组在2011年10月公布了一份名为《关于经合组织协定范本第5条"常设机构"的解释与应用》的讨论草案,内容涉及常

---

① 参见《UN范本》第5条第5、6款。
② 参见《OECD范本》第5条第6款、《UN范本》第5条第7款。
③ 参见《OECD范本》第5条注释第38.7段。
④ 参见朱炎生:《国际税收协定中常设机构原则研究》,法律出版社2006年版,第120页。
⑤ 参见《OECD范本》第5条注释第38.8段。
⑥ 参见廖益新主编:《国际税法学》,高等教育出版社2008年版,第105页。

设机构的存在时间要求、家庭办公与常设机构的认定、准备性与附属性活动的认定问题、数字产品和数据是否属于商品或货物、代理签约等诸多问题。2012年10月,经合组织根据公开的讨论意见对该草案进行了修订,并于2013年2月12日收到了各方就该更新后草案的修改建议。① 草案内容是对现行《OECD范本》第5条及其注释的修订与补充,将在下一次修订协定范本时采纳,因此对草案的具体规定需要予以关注。

三、常设机构所在国征税权范围的确定

缔约国一方的企业在缔约国另一方设有常设机构的情况下,在缔约国另一方取得的营业利润,包括通过常设机构产生的利润以及未通过常设机构而是以其他方法产生的利润。作为来源国的缔约国另一方可以对哪些部分的营业利润征税?对此,《OECD范本》采取"实际联系"标准,规定常设机构所在国可以征税的利润范围仅仅限于居住国企业通过常设机构产生的那部分利润,居住国企业通过常设机构以外的其他途径取得的利润,常设机构所在国不能对之征税。② 而《UN范本》则采取"限制性引力"原则,规定来源国不仅可对归属于常设机构的利润征税,而且当居住国企业在来源国销售与通过常设机构销售的货物或商品相同或类似的货物或商品时,或者开展与通过常设机构从事的经营活动相同或类似的其他经营活动时,来源国还可以对该销售活动或者其他经营活动产生的利润征税。③ 不难发现,按照《UN范本》的"限制性引力"原则,来源国有权征税的利润范围要比按照《OECD范本》规定的"实际联系"标准确定的征税范围广得多。

对于《UN范本》确定的引力原则,《OECD范本》虽然没有采纳,但在其范本注释中对此原则作了较为详尽的描述。它将引力原则区分为限制性引力原则和一般性引力原则,限制性引力原则仅适用于来源于与常设机构营业活动相类似的营业活动所产生的营业利润,它在一定程度上是基于反避税的需要。而根据一般性引力原则,收入来源国对来源于其境内的营业利润、股息、利息和特许权使用费等各项所得,只要所得的受益人在其境内设有常设机构,即使这些所得很明显不能归属于该常设机构,它们也完全可以对这些所得征税。一般性引力原

---

① See Public Comments Received on the Revised Discussion Draft on the Definition of "Permanent Establishment" (Article 5) of the OECD Model Tax Convention. 资料来源:OECD网站,http://www.oecd.org,2013年5月3日访问。
② 参见《OECD范本》第7条第1款。
③ 参见《UN范本》第7条第1款。

则在国际税收缔约实践中已经被否定了。经合组织认为,在对一个外国企业取得的来源于特定国家的利润征税问题上,该来源国的税务机关应注意区分外国企业从本国获取的利润的不同来源,应对每一项所得适用常设机构的检测标准,除非可能适用协定的其他条款。这种处理方法使税收征管与税法遵从更为简便和有效率,更适应商业经营的通常方式。现代经营组织形式是非常复杂的。有相当多的公司在同时从事各种不同的营业活动,每个公司可在许多国家进行广泛的商业活动。一个公司可以在另一国设立常设机构以进行产品的生产制造,同时该公司又可能通过独立代理人在该另一国境内销售不同的产品。该公司完全有充分的商业理由这么做,例如,这可能是基于公司传统的经营模式或者是基于商业便利。如果常设机构所在国为了将通过独立代理人从事每笔交易中的利润因素都并入到该常设机构的利润范围,将严重干扰正常的商业活动,与协定的宗旨亦是相违背的。[1]

四、可归属于常设机构的利润的确定方法

可归属于常设机构的利润是指对该常设机构从事的全部活动产生的盈亏进行核算的结果,包括常设机构与独立企业的交易和与关联企业的交易,以及常设机构与其所属企业的其他部分之间的内部交易。在确定常设机构利润归属的问题上,两大范本均坚持独立交易原则,即可归属于该常设机构的利润,是指假如该常设机构是一个在相同或类似情况下从事相同或类似活动的分设独立企业时可以预期获取的利润。经合组织在 2010 年修订其范本时,对此又补充规定:在运用独立交易原则时,采用虚拟独立分设企业假设,必须考虑到企业通过该常设机构和企业的其他部分所履行的职能、使用的资产和承担的风险。[2] 这一补充规定主要是吸收了 2008 年经合组织《常设机构利润归属报告》的内容,该报告对常设机构利润的归属作了极为详尽的规定。在 2010 年《OECD 范本》修订通过后,经合组织财政事务委员会还通过了 2008 年报告的修订版,以确保该报告的结论能与新版范本第 7 条措辞和编号协调一致。

经合组织《常设机构利润归属报告》旨在对如何在两个基本的和存在潜在冲突的目标之间取得合理的平衡给出实用性指导,即一方面要将常设机构和企业其他部分间的关系类比成两个独立的关联企业间的关系,另一方面又要使常设机构区别于一个法律意义上独立的企业。报告对确定常设机构利润过程中以下

---

[1] 参见《OECD 范本》第 7 条注释第 12 段。
[2] 参见《OECD 范本》第 7 条第 2 款。

关键问题作了规定:常设机构应就其执行的哪些职能获得补偿?应将哪些风险视为由常设机构承担?应将哪些资产视为由常设机构持有?应将多少无息资本视为由常设机构拥有?应将哪些内部交易视为发生于常设机构和企业其他部分之间?这些内部交易应如何定价?应将哪些与第三方的交易视为已由常设机构承担?

2010年的《OECD范本》将确定常设机构的利润分为两个步骤。第一个步骤为通过职能和事实分析得出以下结果:(1)将常设机构所隶属企业与独立企业间的交易产生的权利和义务相应适当地分配至该常设机构;(2)确认与资产经济所有权的归属相关的重要人员职能,并向常设机构分配资产的经济所有权;(3)确认与风险承担相关的重要人员职能,并向常设机构划归风险;(4)确认常设机构的其他职能;(5)确认和确定可合理确认的常设机构与所属企业其他部分间的内部交易的性质;以及(6)根据划归于常设机构的资产和风险向常设机构分配资本。在第二个步骤下,关联企业间的交易中归属于常设机构的交易部分,应当依照《OECD转让定价指南》(以下简称《指南》)中的指导进行定价,而常设机构与企业其他部门之间的内部交易,则类推适用《指南》。该过程通过下述工作,确认为按独立交易原则定价:(1)通过直接适用《指南》中规定的可比性因素(财产或服务的特征、经济环境和商业战略)或根据常设机构的特定事实情况类推适用《指南》中规定的可比性因素(职能分析、合同条件),确认常设机构的内部交易与非受控交易的可比性;以及(2)在考虑到常设机构和所属企业的其他部门各自所履行的职能、拥有的资产和承担的风险的同时,通过类推适用《指南》中规定的转让定价方法,对常设机构与所属企业其他部门之间的内部交易确定符合独立交易原则的回报。在《常设机构利润归属报告》中对各步骤涉及的各种操作方法有更为详细的讨论,特别是对广泛存在的通过常设机构进行营业活动的金融行业中的常设机构利润归属问题进行了分析。[①]

在确定常设机构利润归属时,《UN范本》以及2010年以前的《OECD范本》还规定了费用扣除原则。对于为常设机构实际发生的费用,不论它们发生在何处,均允许从属于常设机构的收入中扣除。这些费用包括行政和一般管理费用。此外,《UN范本》在此基础上,还进一步规定常设机构向企业总机构或任何其他办事处支付的如下款项,除属于偿还实际发生的代垫费用外,均不得扣除:(1)因使用专利或其他权利支付的特许权使用费、费用或其他类似款项;(2)因

---

① 经合组织《常设机构利润归属报告》第II部分主要讨论银行业的常设机构;第III部分主要涉及从事全球贸易企业的常设机构;第IV部分涉及经营保险业务企业的常设机构利润分配。

特定劳务的提供或管理而支付的酬金;(3)因借款而支付的利息(除银行企业外)。同样,在确定常设机构的利润时,除属于偿还实际发生的代垫费用外,也不考虑常设机构从总机构或任何其他办事处:(1)因使用专利或其他权利而取得的特许权使用费、费用或其他类似款项;(2)因提供劳务或管理而取得的手续费;(3)因为借款而收取的利息(银行企业除外)。① 范本中规定费用扣除原则,本意是要阐明在确定常设机构利润时,应考虑直接或间接为常设机构受益所发生的费用,即使这些费用是在常设机构所在国境外发生的。但该规定在实践中经常被误读,认为对使常设机构间接受益的费用扣除应限制在实际发生的费用范围内。鉴于此,2010年版的《OECD范本》删除了这一规定,不过,这一删除并不影响在确定可归属于常设机构的利润时应考虑到企业各种有关的费用,无论它们在何处发生。②

五、常设机构原则的例外——对国际运输利润的征税

(一)国际运输利润的征税权划分规则

尽管在各国相互签订的避免重复征税的税收协定中,常设机构原则是跨国营业所得征税协调的基本原则,但是此项原则并不适用于对国际运输利润课税的协调。对于国际运输利润的征税权协调,存在着企业实际管理机构所在国独占征税原则、居住国独占征税原则、综合适用居住国标准和实际管理机构所在地标准,以及运输活动所在国与实际管理机构所在税收分享原则的区别。

主张由一国独占征税的原则,主要是基于对此类国际运输经营活动特点的考虑。因为企业的船舶或飞机从事国际运输业务,其经营活动涉及众多国家,并经常在各国设有常设机构处理运输业务。船舶或飞机在单一的国际航程中往往在几个外国境内停留,按照常设机构课税的困难是如何将企业的运输利润适当地分配给在各国境内的常设机构。同时,将此类运输企业的利润分配给各地的常设机构,将导致征税的零散性,不符合集中和效益原则,容易滋生逃税、漏税的弊病。将这类涉及在众多国家境内发生的国际运输经营利润征税权,统一划归企业的实际管理机构所在地或企业的居住国行使,可以避免适用常设机构原则分配征税权可能产生的上述问题。

由企业的实际管理机构所在地而非居住国独占行使征税权,是为了保证这种独占征税权归属于实际参与此类国际运输业务活动的企业所在地国一方行

---

① 参见《UN范本》第7条第3款。
② 参见《OECD范本》第7条注释第38—40段。

使,防止第三国居民通过在缔约国一方境内注册成立一家挂牌的居民公司,将实际在缔约国境外进行的航运或空运业务和管理活动虚构在该公司名下,从而享受到税收协定的优惠待遇。

考虑到上述因素,《OECD范本》采用了实际管理机构所在地独占征税原则,其第8条规定:"一、以船舶或飞机从事国际运输取得的利润,应仅在企业实际管理机构所在缔约国征税。二、以船只从事内河运输取得的利润,应仅在企业实际管理机构所在缔约国征税。三、如果船运企业或内河运输企业的实际管理机构设在船舶或船只上,应以船舶或船只母港所在缔约国为所在国;或如果没有母港,应以船舶或船只经营者为其居民的缔约国为所在国。四、第一款的规定也适用于参加合伙经营、联合经营或参加国际经营机构取得的利润。"同时,范本在注释中对于居住国独占征税原则、综合适用居住国标准和实际管理机构所在地标准的协调方法作出了说明。

有些国家倾向于由居住国独占征税权。这些国家可以用以下规定替代《OECD范本》第1款:"缔约国一方企业以船舶或飞机从事国际运输取得的利润,应仅在该缔约国征税。"有些国家倾向于综合适用居住国标准和实际管理机构所在地标准,即如果企业实际管理场所所在国能够对企业的利润总额征税,那么该国具有优先征税权,而企业居住国按照《OECD范本》第23条的规定消除双重征税;如果企业实际管理场所所在国不能对企业利润总额征税,则企业居住国应具有优先征税权。[①]

《UN范本》则提供了两种可供缔约国双方在谈判时进行选择的方案。该范本第8条A与《OECD范本》的规定完全一致,采用企业实际管理机构所在国独占征税的原则。该范本第8条B则采缔约国双方分享征税原则,对船舶运输活动所在国的征税权益给予了一定程度的考虑。根据该范本第8条B第2款的规定,船舶从事国际运输取得的利润,应仅在企业实际管理机构所在的缔约国征税,但是经常在缔约国另一方从事业务的船运活动除外。如果这种船运活动比较经常地在缔约国另一方发生,上述利润可以在缔约国另一方征税。在缔约国另一方应税的利润,应以该企业从船运业务取得的全部纯利润为基础作适当的划分。这种划分计算的税额应减去一定的百分数(这个百分数可通过双方谈判确定)。

值得注意的是,国际运输利润征税权划分规则实际上是对国际运输业务活动发生地国来源地税收管辖权的排除(独占征税规则)或限制(分享征税规则),

---

① 参见《OECD范本》注释对第8条第1款的解释。

是对来源地优先征税原则——常设机构原则的排除,因此,"国际运输"概念的内涵和外延的宽窄以及国际运输利润范围的大小,将与国际运输业务活动发生地国行使来源地税收管辖权的范围大小有着内在的联系,两者之间呈现出负相关的关系。①

(二) 国际运输的含义

关于国际运输,两大范本均在第3条专门作出了定义,即国际运输是指"在缔约国一方设有实际管理机构的企业以船舶或飞机经营的运输,但不包括以船舶或飞机仅在缔约国另一方各地之间的经营"。根据《OECD范本》注释对第3条的解释,"国际运输"的定义比通常理解的含义要广。较广泛的定义意在保护实际管理机构所在国拥有对纯粹的国内运输和两个第三国之间的国际运输的征税权,并允许缔约国另一方仅对往来于其境内的运输征税。该意图可以由下述实例予以清楚的阐述。假设缔约国一方企业或在缔约国一方有实际管理机构的企业,通过在缔约国另一方的代理人出售航程全部限在缔约国一方境内,或者是航程全部限于在第三国境内的客票,本条规定不允许缔约国另一方对上述任何一种航程业务的营业利润征税。只有在运输业务仅限于缔约国另一方各地之间的运输的情况下,该缔约国另一方才能对上述缔约国一方企业征税。②

至于何为"以船舶或飞机仅在缔约国另一方各地之间的经营",《OECD范本》注释对此作出解释:如果船舶或者飞机的出发地和目的地都在缔约国另一方境内,则这样的航程即属于仅限于在缔约国另一方境内两地之间的营运。但是,"国际运输"的概念范围也涵盖构成船舶或飞机的更远航程一部分的在缔约国另一方境内两地之间的航程,如果该船舶或飞机的出发地或目的地在缔约国另一方境外。例如,作为同一航程的一部分,一飞机首先从缔约国一方某地飞向缔约国另一方境内某地,然后继续飞行至该缔约国另一方境内另一目的地,则该航程的第一和第二航程都属于"国际运输"的概念范围。③

有些国家认为"国际运输"这一定义更应倾向于指旅客或货物的运输,因此,任何仅在同一缔约国境内的旅客或货物的运输不应视为"国际运输"定义涵盖之范围,即使是由经常从事国际运输的船舶或飞机担任本次航程。持有该观点的缔约国经双方协商同意可以删除在定义中的例外规定里的"船舶或航空器"用语,并使用下述定义:"'国际运输'用语意指由实际管理机构在缔约国一方的任

---

① 参见廖益新主编:《国际税法学》,高等教育出版社2008年版,第117—118页。
② 参见《OECD范本》第3条注释第6段。
③ 参见《OECD范本》第3条注释第6.1段。

何企业运营的船舶或航空器所进行的运输,仅在缔约国另一方各地之间的运输除外。"①

(三) 国际运输业务利润范围的确定

根据《OECD范本》的注释,从事国际运输业务的利润包括:(1) 企业以其在国际运输经营的船舶或飞机(不论是其所有的、租赁的或以其他方式处于该企业的支配之下)从事客运或货运直接取得的利润;(2) 从事与国际运输活动直接相关的活动取得的利润;(3) 与以船舶或飞机从事国际运输经营具有附属性质的活动取得的利润。"直接相关的活动"是指主要为企业以其在国际运输中经营的船舶或飞机从事客运或货运而进行的活动。"附属性质的活动"是指具有如下特征的活动:虽然不为企业本身在国际运输中经营船舶或飞机所需,但对此类经营具有次要的贡献,并与此类经营关系密切,以至于不应被认为是该企业的一项不同的业务活动或所得来源。②

此类直接相关活动或附属性活动主要包括以下情形:(1) 出租装备、人员及供应配备齐全的船舶或飞机的活动;(2) 企业在从事国际运输活动中附带性地光租船舶或飞机的活动;(3) 根据代码共享、集装箱货位租用权协议,或者为了能享受更早发货或者提早出发的利益,某从事国际运输的企业利用另一企业经营的船舶或飞机搭载它的一些旅客或货物进行国际运输;(4) 某航空公司为了方便其国际航班乘客往返机场而提供市区与机场之间的巴士服务;(5) 企业在出发地国或目的地国为旅客或货物安排经营内陆运输的其他企业提供搭载、运输、交付服务而提供的服务活动;(6) 企业在其主要为以船舶或飞机从事国际运输而设置的售票场所为其他运输企业售票;(7) 企业在其经营的船舶或飞机或其营业场所(如售票处)提供的杂志上为其他企业进行广告;(8) 从事国际运输的企业从事出租集装箱、为其他企业提供集装箱短期存放活动;(9) 企业利用其为在国际运输中经营船舶或飞机而在某外国拥有资产或工作人员,在该国为其他运输企业提供货物或服务,如工程师、地面以及设备维修人员、货物搬运工、给养人员以及客户服务人员的服务;(10) 从事国际运输的企业,为了降低在其他国家为经营它们的船舶或飞机而维持设施的成本而参与的合营安排,如根据国际航空公司技术合营协议,某航空公司同意向在特定地点降落的其他航空公司提供备用的零件或者维修服务(这将使该航空公司在其他地方也能够受益于此

---

① 参见《OECD范本》第3条注释第6.2段。
② 参见《OECD范本》第8条注释第4.1—4.2段。

类服务)。①

此外,《OECD范本》注释还进一步主张,如海运或空运企业的投资所得(如来自股票、债券、股份或者贷款的所得)据以产生的投资是在该缔约国以船舶或飞机经营的国际运输业务的不可或缺的组成部分,以至于这种投资可以被认为与上述国际运输经营直接相关,那么也可以将该投资所得归属于国际运输利润范围内。例如,在缔约国从事国际运输业务所需的现金所产生的利息所得,或为从事国际运输业务依照法律规定要求担保的债券所产生的利息所得。但不适用于为下列机构处理现金流通或其他资金调度活动的过程中取得的利息所得:为企业的常设机构且这种利息所得不可归属于该常设机构,或者为关联企业(不论这些关联企业是否位于该缔约国境内),或者为总机构(资金调度和投资活动的中心);由企业当地经营产生的利润进行短期投资产生的利息所得,如果用于投资的资金并不是该企业为经营国际运输业务所要求的。② 由实际管理机构设在缔约国另一方的海运企业在缔约国一方经营造船厂的利润也不包括在内。③

第二节 对跨国个人劳务所得的征税

国际税法上将个人劳务所得区分为独立劳务所得和非独立劳务所得,分别规定了不同的征税原则。独立劳务所得是指个人以自己的名义独立地为他人提供某种专业服务或从事其他独立性活动而取得的劳务收入,如以个人名义开业的医师、律师、建筑设计师或会计师等为他人提供相应的专业技术性服务所获取的服务报酬,以及个人独立从事某种科学、文艺、娱乐或教育活动而取得的收入。非独立劳务所得是指个人由于任职或受雇于他人从事劳动服务工作而取得雇主支付的工资或薪金报酬。

两大范本曾在第14条和第15条分别对独立劳务所得和非独立劳务所得的征税规则作出规定。2000年1月,经合组织财政事务委员会通过了一份题为《经合组织税收协定范本第14条的相关问题》的报告。根据该报告,《OECD范本》第14条被删除,即不再对独立劳务所得的征税作出单独规定。经合组织认为,这个决定反映了这样的事实:第7条使用的"常设机构"的概念与第14条使用的"固定基地"的概念,及如何根据第7条或第14条计算利润和税额,已经没

---

① 参见《OECD范本》第8条注释第5—10.1段。
② 参见《OECD范本》第8条注释第14段。
③ 参见《OECD范本》第8条注释第12段。

有原先所预想的区别了。另外,纳税人的哪些活动属于第 14 条的适用范围而非第 7 条的规范范围,也并不总是清楚的。删除第 14 条意味着来自个人专业服务或具有独立特征的其他活动的所得将按第 7 条作为营业利润按照常设机构原则处理。① 如此一来,两大范本关于个人劳务所得的征税规则在形式上就出现了差异,即《UN 范本》仍在第 14 条和第 15 条分别对独立劳务所得和非独立劳务所得作出规定,而《OECD 范本》仅在第 15 条对非独立劳务所得作出规定,对独立劳务所得适用第 7 条关于营业利润的规定。②

一、对跨国独立劳务所得的征税规则

目前,对于跨国独立劳务所得的征税,修订后的《OECD 范本》采用的是常设机构原则,鉴于该原则已在第一节作了详尽阐述,本节不再赘述。

《UN 范本》中对于跨国独立劳务所得仍采用固定基地原则进行征税,即缔约国一方居民由于专业性劳务或其他独立性活动取得的所得,原则上应仅由其居住国一方征税,来源国一方不得征税。但如果缔约国一方居民在缔约国另一方境内设有经常从事独立劳务活动的固定基地,作为来源国的缔约国另一方可以对属于该固定基地的那部分所得征税。考虑到通常情况下作为跨国独立劳务所得来源国的广大发展中国家的利益,《UN 范本》在采用固定基地原则的同时,又适当扩大了来源地国对跨国独立劳务所得的征税范围,规定缔约国一方居民个人即使在缔约国另一方境内未设有固定基地的情况下,只要缔约国一方居民在有关会计年度开始或结束的任何 12 个月中在该缔约国另一方停留连续或累计超过 183 天,缔约国另一方就可以对该居民征税。也就是说,作为缔约国一方居民的个人如果在缔约国另一方境内从事独立劳务服务活动,只要在任何 12 个月内在缔约国另一方境内连续或累计停留时间达到或超过 183 天,则不论该个人在缔约国另一方境内是否设有固定基地这样的营业设施或场所,也不论其获得的独立劳务报酬是否由缔约国另一方的居民支付或由设在缔约国另一方境内的常设机构或固定基地负担,以及该个人获得的劳务报酬数额的多少,对该缔约国一方居民个人在缔约国另一方停留期间所取得的来源于缔约国另一方境内的独立劳务所得,作为所得来源地国的缔约国另一方均有权优先课税。

不难看出,《UN 范本》中关于跨国独立劳务所得的征税规则相对于采用常

---

① 参见《OECD 范本》第 14 条注释。
② 《OECD 范本》在删除第 14 条后,将第 15 条的标题改为"关于受雇所得的征税",取代此前的"关于非独立劳务所得的征税",但这一改变并不影响该条的适用范围。

设机构原则的《OECD范本》而言,更多地照顾到了来源地国一方的税收利益,体现了广大发展中国家的立场。

二、对跨国非独立劳务所得的征税规则

税收协定中所说的跨国非独立劳务所得,是指作为一国居民的纳税人因受雇于他人从事劳务活动所取得的来源于居住国境外的工资、薪金或其他类似性质的劳动报酬,但不包括董事费、退休金和政府服务费用。对于这类所得,纳税人的居住国和所得来源地国都有权征税,为了协调由此产生的征税权冲突,两大范本都规定了"183天规则":缔约国一方的居民由于受雇取得的薪金、工资或其他类似的报酬,除在缔约国另一方从事受雇的活动以外,应仅在该缔约国一方征税。在缔约国另一方从事受雇的活动取得的报酬,可以在该缔约国另一国征税。但在同时具备以下三项条件时,缔约国一方居民由于受雇于缔约国另一方取得的报酬,应仅在其居住国一方征税:(1) 收款人在有关会计年度开始或结束的任何12个月中在缔约国另一方停留连续或累计不超过183天;(2) 该项报酬由并非缔约国另一方居民的雇主支付或代表雇主支付的;(3) 该项报酬不由雇主设在缔约国另一方的常设机构或固定基地负担。① 在对这一规则的理解和应用过程中,关键是要把握以下几个方面的问题:

(一) 183天期限的计算

经合组织在1992年之前的范本以及早期的《UN范本》均规定,"收款人在有关财政年度中在缔约国另一方停留连续或累计不超过183天",该规定给财政年度不一致的缔约国各方造成了困难,而且在实际操作中给纳税人通过有意安排在缔约国一方境内停留的天数进行避税提供了机会,如纳税人在缔约国另一方在一年中的后半年停留5个半月,然后在次年的上半年停留5个半月,如此一来,虽然累计超过了183天,但仍使来源地国不能取得征税权。

为了防止纳税人利用这种方式来实施避税,两大范本对183天的计算方法作了修订,即按现在规定的"收款人在有关会计年度开始或结束的任何12个月期限内,在缔约国另一方境内停留累计不超过183天"。据此,183天期限的计算可以跨年度计算和移动计算。例如,作为缔约国一方居民的个人前往缔约国另一方从事非独立劳务工作期间,存在着往返于两国之间停留的情形或在第三国境内停留的情形。例如,某人从2001年6月起的12个月内,在缔约国另一方停留的天数累计不超过183天,但在从2001年7月起的12个月内停留的天数

---

① 参见《OECD范本》和《UN范本》第15条第1、2款。

累计超过183天,这种情况下作为劳务履行地的缔约国另一方,可以对该人在该国境内从事劳务活动取得的非独立劳务所得行使来源地税收管辖权征税。如果按跨年度计算和移动计算的结果,这个人没有在任何一个12个月期间内在缔约国另一方境内停留累计超过183天,则该个人的非独立劳务所得,如果并非是由缔约国另一方居民的雇主支付或代表雇主支付的,并且也不是由雇主设在缔约国另一方境内的常设机构或固定基地所负担的,缔约国另一方不得对其征税。可见,对183天实行跨年度或移动计算,扩大了劳务履行地国的征税范围,也能在一定程度上防止纳税人通过人为地安排在有关缔约国境内的停留天数进行避税。

至于183天期限的计算方法,各国在实践中曾使用过不同的方法,主要是"实际停留天数法"和"实际活动期间法"两种。前一种方法是按纳税人实际在缔约国一方境内停留的天数计算183天,纳税人中间离境或在境外休假的日期应予扣除;后一种方法则以纳税人前往缔约国一方从事劳务活动起始到结束的实际期限来计算183天,不考虑扣除中间的临时离境和在境外度假的天数。

目前,两大范本都采用了"实际停留天数法"。根据范本注释的规定,下列日子应计算在183天停留期限内:不足一天的时间、抵达日、离境日,以及在劳务履行地国境内度过的其他日子如星期六和星期日、国家法定节假日、在劳务活动开始前和劳务活动期间及劳务活动结束后在该国境内度过的休假日、短期离岗(包括由于培训、罢工、无法入厂、停工待料等原因而暂停工作的天数)、生病(但如果纳税人是因为生病而不能按原定时间离境返回以致超过183天期限,这种情形下生病的天数应予剔除)及家人死亡、生病等。然而,183天的计算不应包括纳税人在一次起点和终点均不在劳务履行地国境内的旅行途中在劳务履行地国境内度过的天数。根据上述原则,对其在劳务履行地国境外度过的全天数,不论是度假、公差,还是任何其他原因,均不应计算在183天以内。但是,纳税人只要在缔约国一方停留即使是一天中极短的时间,在计算其在该国逗留183天时也作为一天计算。[1]

(二) 雇佣关系的认定

如果缔约国一方的居民个人受雇在缔约国另一方从事劳务活动的时间未超过183天,其所收取的工资、薪金等跨国非独立劳务所得要依照税收协定规定的"183天规则"在劳务活动履行地国享受免税待遇,还必须同时符合另一条件,即有关的工资、薪金等非独立劳务报酬是由并非缔约国另一方居民的雇主支付或

---

[1] 参见《OECD范本》第15条注释第5段。

是代表该雇主的其他人所支付的,并且该项报酬不由雇主设在该缔约国另一方的常设机构所负担。这里最关键的就是对雇佣关系的认定,即判断报酬支付人与收款人之间是否存在雇佣关系。在认定雇佣关系的过程中,除了按照雇佣关系的特征进行定性外,还需将个人在雇佣关系(劳动合同)下对某个企业提供服务的情形与个人根据两个不同企业之间签订的服务提供合同(服务合同)而对某个企业提供服务的情形区别开来,后者比较典型的例子就是国际劳务租用。在国际劳务租用情形下,缔约国一方企业通过在缔约国另一方境内的劳务中介机构招收外国雇员来为企业服务,这些外国雇员形式上只与缔约国另一方的劳务中介机构签订雇佣合同,他们的工资、薪金也是由该劳务中介机构支付,如果他们在有关年度内被派遣到缔约国一方境内为企业工作一次或多次停留的时间未超过183天,从表面上看,这些外国雇员符合税收协定中"183天规则"所要求具备的三个条件,从而其在缔约国一方工作期间取得的工资、薪金等非独立劳务所得可以要求缔约国一方给予协定规定的免税待遇。由于这种国际劳务租用方式经常容易被纳税人滥用来规避在劳务履行地国的纳税义务,1992年修订后的《OECD范本》注释对此作了专门的说明,指出"雇主"应是指对雇员的工作拥有权利并承担该项工作所产生的责任和风险的人。在国际劳务租用情形下,雇主的这些职能作用,往往在很大程度上是使用这些外国雇员的企业而非由外国劳务中介机构承担和行使的。按照实质重于形式的原则,应该具体审查这些职能究竟主要是由劳务中介机构还是使用外国雇员的企业来行使的,以确定真正的雇主。是否存在雇佣关系,主要由劳务履行地国按照其国内法标准来进行认定,劳务履行地国在按照其国内法进行认定时,必须坚持客观的标准,例如,如果相关的事实情况清楚地表明,有关的服务是根据两个不同的企业间签订的提供服务的合同而提供的,则一国不能根据其国内法将这种服务视为雇佣服务。在明显不存在雇佣关系的情形下,如果允许缔约国将服务认定为受雇劳务,或明显是企业通过它自己的人员对某个居民经营的企业提供服务的情形下,如果允许缔约国否定某个非居民经营的企业的雇主资格,将使得协定所规定的缓解征税权冲突的规则毫无意义。

在判断个人提供的劳务是以雇佣身份提供还是根据两个企业间的服务合同提供时,通常要考虑提供服务的性质,即个人提供的服务是否构成接受该服务的企业的营业活动不可或缺的组成部分,如果构成了其重要组成部分,并由该企业承担责任和风险,那么应被认为存在雇佣关系。此外,下列补充因素也应予以考虑:谁有权指挥该个人关于工作应以何种方式进行;谁控制和对履行工作的地点负责;个人工作的报酬是否由形式上的雇主向接受服务的企业直接收取;谁向该个人提供工作的工具和必需的材料;谁决定开展工作的人员数量和资质;谁有权选择履行工作的人员和终止为开展此项工作与此人之间所签的合同;谁决定该个人的休假和工作计划等。对这些综合因素的考虑,有助于透过各种形式上的安排从实质上准确判断雇佣关系的存在与否。[①]

(三) 非独立劳务报酬是否系由设在劳务履行地国的常设机构或固定基地负担的认定

根据两个范本规定的"183天规则",跨国非独立劳务所得在劳务履行地国享受免税待遇必须同时符合的第三项条件,是这种非独立劳务报酬并不是由雇主设在劳务履行地国的某个常设机构或固定基地负担的,即这种跨国非独立劳务报酬在劳务履行地国的常设机构或固定基地计算其应税所得额时,并未作为其一项营业费用列支扣除。此项限制条件规定的目的在于防止损害劳务履行地国的课税权益,因为缔约国一方居民来源于缔约国另一方境内的非独立劳务所得,如果构成在缔约国另一方境内的某个常设机构或固定基地在税前列支扣除的成本费用,尽管跨国履行劳务活动的缔约国一方居民个人在缔约国另一方境内停留的时间未超过183天,但由于其所获得的工资、薪金所得影响到缔约国另一方对常设机构或固定基地的税收利益,在这种情形下限制缔约国另一方对非居民的跨国劳务报酬不得征税,显然是不公平合理的。

虽然两个范本建议的有关非独立劳务所得课税协调的"183天规则"为各国间的双边税收协定所普遍采用,但在执行"183天规则"的实践中,对于如何理解认定非居民的劳务所得是否系由劳务履行地国境内的某个常设机构或固定基地负担这个问题,并不完全一致。《OECD范本》注释中指出,"由……负担"一语必须根据本项的目的进行解释,也就是要保证第15条第2款提供的例外(同时满足三项条件时无须在来源国征税)不适用于根据第7条(营业利润)的原则和报酬的性质,在计算设在实际履行劳务的缔约国境内的常设机构的利润时可构成一项成本费用支出而扣除的那部分报酬。[②] 典型的事例是由某个常设机构或固定基地直接对非居民雇员支付工资、薪金性质的劳务报酬,并且此种劳务报酬的费用开支在常设机构或固定基地的账面上体现为一项营业成本费用支出。但如果非居民雇员的工资报酬并非由劳务履行地国的常设机构或固定基地直接支付,是否足以认定常设机构没有负担这种劳务报酬,这个问题还要结合具体情况进行分析。

[①] 参见《OECD范本》第15条注释第8.13—8.14段。
[②] 参见《OECD范本》第15条注释第5段。

有些情况下,虽然在劳务履行地国境内的常设机构或固定基地工作的非居民雇员的工资报酬并非是由该常设机构或固定基地直接支付给非居民雇员本人,而是由在居住国的企业总机构或雇主支付的,从而在该常设机构或固定基地的账簿上并没有体现出这项工资、薪金费用支出,但常设机构或固定基地可能通过某种间接的方式而实际承担了上述情形下非居民雇员的工资、薪金费用。例如,常设机构或固定基地接受了总机构分摊的一般管理费用,而且常设机构或固定基地所在国也允许这部分分摊的管理费用可以在常设机构或固定基地方面列支扣除;或者常设机构以向总机构支付特殊劳务费的方式,实际负担了由总机构雇用并派遣到常设机构工作的非居民雇员的工资、薪金。在这类情形下,尽管非居民雇员的工资、薪金并不是由劳务履行地国境内的常设机构或固定基地直接支付的,但由于常设机构或固定基地实际上是负担了他们的工资、薪金费用支出,并因此而影响到劳务履行地国对境内的常设机构或固定基地的所得课税,应该认定劳务履行地国根据"183天规则",对上述情形的非居民雇员取得工资、薪金报酬有优先课税权。①

在认定缔约国对方居民个人来源于中国境内的工资、薪金所得是否由中国境内的机构、场所负担这一问题上,中国税务机关实践中采用了一种比较简单明确的判断标准。根据国家税务总局的有关规定,在有关税收协定规定的期间,在中国境内连续或累计居住不超过183天的缔约国对方居民个人,应仅就其实际在中国境内工作期间由中国境内企业或个人雇主支付或者由中国境内机构负担的工资、薪金所得申报纳税。凡是由该中国境内企业、机构属于采取核定利润方法计征企业所得税或没有营业收入而不征收企业所得税的,在该中国境内企业、机构任职、受雇的个人实际在中国境内工作期间取得的工资、薪金,不论是否在该中国境内企业、机构会计账簿中有记载,均应视为该中国境内企业支付或由该中国境内机构负担的工资、薪金。② 采用这种简单明确的认定标准,虽然有利于维护劳务履行地国的税收权益,有助于防止非居民雇员与雇主之间通过人为地安排工资、薪金支付地点和方式进行国际逃避税,但其中对在中国境内没有营业收入而不征收企业所得税的外国机构、场所任职、受雇的短期来华工作的非居民雇员取得的境外雇主支付的工资、薪金报酬,也视为系由境内的机构、场所负担而要求在中国纳税,与前述此类税收协定中有关非独立劳务所得课税的"183天

---

① 参见廖益新主编:《国际税法学》,高等教育出版社2008年版,第145页。
② 参见国家税务总局《关于在中国境内无住所的个人取得工资薪金所得纳税义务问题的通知》(国税发【1994】148号)第2条。

规则"的宗旨似有不符。

三、对特定人员的跨国劳务所得的征税规则

由于国际人员交往的情况复杂多样,各国政府出于某些政策因素的考虑,对于某些从事特定的跨国业务活动的人员所取得的劳务报酬,往往通过税收协定作出一些不同于劳务所得一般课税规则的特别规定。在涉及对这些特定人员的跨国劳务所得征税时,税收协定中的这些特别协调规则,具有优先于前述有关独立劳务和非独立劳务所得课税协调的一般原则的适用地位。

(一)跨国董事费所得的征税

董事费(directors' fees)是公司法人支付给它的决策领导机构——董事会的成员的劳务酬金。担任公司董事的人员区别于公司的一般雇员,又不同于那些独立从事专业性劳务活动的自由职业者,他们主要通过董事会议参与公司重要经营决策活动和监督公司的经营管理业绩,除非同时兼任公司某种具体的行政管理职务,董事一般并不常在公司里工作。尤其是跨国担任公司董事的人,他们往往在公司所在国以外的居住国内从事本身的职业活动。这些人虽并不常在公司里工作,但他们每年从公司取得的董事费或其他类似性质的劳务报酬数额不少,按照劳务履行地原则很难确定他们所取得的董事费是在哪个国家提供的劳务活动产生的。因此,在对缔约国一方居民跨国担任缔约国另一方的居民公司的董事所取得的董事费和其他类似性质报酬的征税问题上,两大范本都主张背离对跨国劳务所得的一般征税原则,按支付者所在地原则确认支付董事费的公司所在国一方有权对此类跨国劳务所得征税,而不管纳税人在公司所在国境内停留期限的长短和实际履行董事职务的活动地点何在。当然,作为纳税人的居住国一方仍然有权对纳税人来源于境外的董事费所得课税,但应承担税收协定中规定的采取避免双重征税措施的义务。两个范本所建议的上述征税协调规则,已为大多数国家签订的税收协定所采纳。

按照《OECD范本》第16条的注释,上述由支付公司所在国一方课税的协调规则的适用范围,仅限于缔约国一方居民(包括自然人和法人)作为缔约国另一方居民公司的董事成员而取得的董事费和其他类似款项,包括个人以董事会成员身份获得的实物利益(如股票期权、住宅或汽车的使用权、健康或人寿保险以及俱乐部成员资格等),但不包括董事成员兼任公司其他职务(如公司职员、顾问、参事等)而取得的报酬。[①] 后者仍应按协定中有关独立劳务或非独立劳务所

---

① 参见《OECD范本》第16条注释第1.1、2段。

得的一般课税原则处理。所谓董事费或其他类似款项,范围包括董事人员在辞去董事职务时从公司收取的辞职金,即使这种辞职金可能是采用某种终身年金的形式支付,并不构成《OECD范本》第18条规定的退休金所得。

在各国税收协定实践中,上述适用于跨国董事费所得的支付公司所在国课税原则可否扩大到对跨国担任公司高级管理职务人员取得的工资、薪金所得的征税,目前尚存在较大分歧。按照《UN范本》第16条第2款,缔约国一方居民由于担任缔约国另一方居民公司的高级行政管理职务工作取得工资、薪金或其他类似报酬,亦可按公司所在国课税原则由缔约国另一方行使优先课税权,而不问纳税人在缔约国另一方境内停留时间的长短和是否实际在该公司工作。但《OECD范本》对这类人员的工资、薪金所得未作出特别规定。就各国间的税收协定看,有些国家间的双边协定采用了《UN范本》第16条第2款的规定。① 但多数国家认为,这类跨国担任公司高层管理职务人员所取得的工资、薪金报酬,明显属于非独立劳务性质所得,仍应适用协定中有关非独立劳务所得课税协调的一般原则处理。

(二)对跨国从事表演活动的艺术家、运动员的所得的征税

跨国从事戏剧、影视、音乐等各种艺术表演活动的艺术家和跨国参加体育竞赛活动的运动员,一般在表演竞技活动地所在国停留的时间较短,很少出现超过183天的情况,也不会设有固定基地。但是,这类人员通过短期的表演活动取得的收益报酬往往相当可观。对这类人员上述跨国所得如果按前述有关独立劳务或非独立劳务所得的一般征税原则处理,实际上将排除作为所得来源地的表演活动地所在国对这类跨国所得行使征税权。为了合理地协调缔约国双方的税收权益,两大范本的第17条在这个问题上作了相同的如下规定:"一、虽有第14条(《OECD范本》第7条)和第15条的规定,缔约国一方居民,作为表演家,如戏剧、电影、广播或电视艺术家或音乐家,或者作为运动员,在缔约国另一方从事其个人活动取得的所得,可以在另一国征税。二、表演家或运动员从事其个人活动取得的所得,并非为了表演家或运动员本人而是为了其他人的,虽有第7条、第14条和第15条的规定,其所得可以在表演家或运动员从事活动的缔约国征税。"

按照上述规定,缔约国一方居民作为表演家或运动员,在缔约国另一方从事某种带有娱乐性质的文艺或体育表演活动而产生的所得,无论是归属于其本人

---

① 中国与挪威、瑞典、加拿大等少数国家之间签订的税收协定采纳了《UN范本》的做法,但与其他大多数国家之间的税收协定在这个问题上是按《OECD范本》第16条规定的模式未作出特别规定。

的还是归属于其他人的,都可不受范本第7条有关营业利润、第14条有关独立劳务所得和第15条有关非独立劳务所得的课税规定限制,由表演活动所在地的缔约国另一方行使优先课税权。作为表演家或运动员的居住国的缔约国一方虽然仍可根据本国税法对其所得行使居民税收管辖权进行征税,但应按税收协定规定采取相应的消除双重征税的措施。包括中国在内的许多国家在对外签订的双边税收协定中都采用了上述协调规则。

上述协调规则中所称的"表演家",并不仅限于两大范本第17条第1款中所列举的那几种人员,凡从事具有公众表演娱乐性质的各种文化艺术活动的人员都属于上述"表演家"概念范围。但为表演活动提供行政管理、技术服务或辅助工作的人员,如影视剧片的摄像或制片人员、行政后勤服务人员、技术人员等,并不在这一协调规则适用范围之内。这些人员所取得的工作报酬,按照有关独立劳务或非独立劳务所得的一般征税协调规则处理。而所谓运动员,也不局限于参加像篮球、排球、田径比赛等传统的体育竞技活动的人员,还包括高尔夫球手、象棋或桥牌选手、赛马骑手和网球选手等运动人员,无论他们是职业或业余运动人员,也不管他们所参加的表演或竞赛活动是否具有政治、社会、宗教或慈善背景色彩,只要这种表演活动具有公众娱乐性质,他们通过这些活动所取得的报酬所得即属于两大范本第17条规定的适用范围。跨国从事表演活动的艺术家或运动员除了取得与他们的表演竞赛活动相应的劳务报酬外,可能还经常收取一些以特许权使用费、赞助费(sponsorship fee)或广告费等形式支付的款项。这些性质的收入,如果与表演家或运动员的演出活动并没有直接联系,一般应适用范本中其他相关的条款处理,不在第17条的调整范围。但如果这些收入款项与他们在缔约国一方境内从事的表演活动有直接联系,亦应将其纳入演出活动所获得的劳务报酬范围。[①]

作为缔约国一方居民的表演家或运动员有时并非独立以个人名义而是以受雇于某个公司团体或其他人的非独立身份前往缔约国另一方从事表演活动,表演活动所产生的收入并非直接归属于表演家个人,而属于该公司团体或其他人所得。在这类情形下,根据两大范本第17条第2款的规定,表演活动所在地的缔约国另一方同样对该公司团体或其他人的上述所得征税,并不受范本中有关营业利润课税的常设机构原则或有关独立个人劳务所得课税的固定基地和"183天规则"的限制。范本作出这种规定的目的,在于防止纳税人假借公司团体或其他人的名义规避在演出活动地国履行纳税义务,保证演出活动地所在国一方对

---

① 参见《OECD范本》第17条第1款注释第3、4、9段。

此类跨国所得应有的税收权益,同时也有助于避免造成双重免税的不公平结果。因为在演出活动的收入并非归属于表演家或运动员个人而是某个公司团体或其他人所有的情况下,如果没有上述第 17 条第 2 款的规定,演出活动地国一方只能对表演家或运动员从受雇的公司团体或其他人支付的少量报酬征税,而对取得演出收入的公司团体或其他人,依照范本第 7 条、第 14 条或第 15 条的规定,则只有当他们在演出活动地设有常设机构、固定基地或停留超过 183 天的情况下才能取得行使来源地课税权进行征税。这样的结果容易使跨国表演家或运动员假借受雇于某个公司团体或其他个人的名义规避演出活动地国对演出活动收入的课税。同时,在演出收入归属于某个公司团体或其他个人的情况下,如果他们在演出活动地国不存在常设机构或固定基地,而他们的居住国税法对居民来源于境外的营业所得或劳务报酬实行免税或规定不征税,则将造成双重免税的后果。①

为了促进缔约国双方政府间的文化体育交流合作计划的实施,许多国家间签订的税收协定往往规定,上述由演出活动地国课税的规则不适用于按照政府间文化交流计划安排的或由缔约国一方政府或其他地方政府公共基金资助进行的跨国表演活动。在这种情况下,缔约国一方居民作为表演家或运动员,按照缔约国双方政府的文化体育交流计划安排,或受缔约国一方政府或其他地方政府公共基金的资助前往缔约国另一方进行表演活动,由此而产生的所得不论是归属于本人或是归属于其他人,在缔约国另一方都应给予免税待遇。②

(三)对退休金和政府职员所得的征税

退休金是个人根据有关国家和社会保险或公共福利制度因过去的雇佣或工作关系在退休以后继续取得的一种劳务报酬所得。在跨国退休金所得,即一国的居民因过去在另一国的雇佣或工作关系而从另一国取得的退休金的征税协调问题上,各国政府的观点主张并不一致。一些国家基于跨国退休金的受益人退休后并不在原先受雇国境内居住的事实情况,主张应仅由受益人居住国征税,而支付退休金的来源地国不应征税。因为由受益人的居住国独占征税更能综合考虑受益人的负担能力,体现量能课税原则。如果由过去的雇佣关系所在国征税,由于纳税人并不在境内居住,当地税务机关并不了解并掌握纳税人的负税能力,难以保证征税公平合理。同时,如果受益人过去曾在多个国家受雇而有多处来源的退休金所得,要在以前受雇的各个国家履行纳税义务,也有诸多不便。但主

---

① 参见《OECD 范本》第 17 条第 2 款注释第 11.1、11.2 段。
② 参见《OECD 范本》第 17 条注释第 13、14 段。

张退休金应在来源国课税的国家则认为,跨国退休金所得实质上是受益人因过去在雇佣关系所在国提供劳务所取得的延期支付的劳动报酬,应与一般非独立劳务所得一样,原则上可以在所得来源地即劳务履行地国征税。另外,退休金的支付在支付人方面通常要作为一种税前列支的费用扣除,在计算支付人的应税所得额时予以扣除从而影响支付人所在国的所得税收入,因此对受益人的退休金所得,作为来源地国一方应当拥有征税权。

由于在跨国退休金所得的征税权划分问题上存在着不同的主张,各国在两大范本中对这个问题的处理也不一致。《OECD范本》第18条主张,除政府职员的退休金外,因过去受雇于一般企业、事业单位或社会团体的退休人员,包括雇于政府经营的企业或事业单位的人员所取得的退休金或其他类似报酬,应仅由受益人居住国一方独占征税。而《UN范本》第18条在这个问题上则是提出了供缔约国双方选择的两种征税协调方案。其中一种方案即第18条A款在上述《OECD范本》第18条规定的基础上增补了作为例外的第2款规定,即如果缔约国一方居民来源于缔约国另一方的退休金,是从缔约国另一方政府或地方当局按照公共福利计划建立的社会保险基金中支付的款项,则这部分退休金应仅在支付者所在国即缔约国另一方征税,作为受益人的居住国的缔约国一方应予免税。第二种方案即第18条B款规定,跨国退休金所得可以在受益人的居住国征税,如果系由缔约国另一方居民或设在该国的常设机构支付的情况下,也可以在缔约国另一方征税,即受益人的居住国和支付者所在国双方均有权征税,但从缔约国另一方政府或地方当局建立的社会保险基金中支付的退休金所得,应仅由缔约国另一方独占征税。显然《UN范本》建议的上述两种征税协调方案,与《OECD范本》的第18条相比,均较多地照顾了来源地国一方对跨国退休金的征税权益。

各国税收协定对政府职员的退休金和工资、薪金报酬的课税规定比较一致。两大范本第19条都规定,缔约国一方政府或地方当局支付给向其提供服务的个人的工资、薪金报酬,应该仅在该国即支付者所在国征税,缔约国另一方不得征税,尽管取得上述工资、薪金报酬的个人按缔约国另一方税法规定构成在该国境内居住的居民。但如果这种服务是在缔约国另一方提供的,并且提供服务的个人不仅是缔约国另一方的居民,而且是其国民,或者并非仅由于提供该项服务而成为缔约国另一方的居民,该个人取得的由缔约国一方政府支付的工资、薪金,应仅由缔约国另一方征税。上述所谓"并非仅由于提供该项服务而成为缔约国另一方的居民",是指该个人原本就是缔约国另一方的居民,不是仅由于受雇于该缔约国一方政府或地方当局在缔约国另一方境内从事工作或提供服务的缘故,在缔约国另一方居留而成为该缔约国另一方的居民。对政府雇员的退休金所得,两个范本也主张适用与上述工资、薪金所得同样的规则处理,即缔约国一方政府或其地方当局支付的或从其建立的基金中对向其提供服务的个人支付的退休金,应仅在该缔约国一方征税。但如果提供服务的个人是缔约国另一方的居民,并且是其国民,该项退休金应仅在缔约国另一方征税。各国税收协定中对政府雇员的跨国工资、薪金报酬和退休金所得原则上适用由支付者独占征税规则,主要是考虑与有关外交和领事关系的国际公约规定和外交豁免的国际习惯保持一致。中国在对外签订税收协定中也采用了两个范本的上述协调规则。

(四)对学生和企业实习生的跨国所得的征税

为了促进国际教育科技和文化的交流合作,照顾跨国求学和接受培训的学生和企业实习生的生活,各国相互间往往在税收协定中对这些人员给予区别对待,对他们为接受教育或培训目的在缔约国一方居留期间所获得的款项、报酬等,在一定条件或范围内给予免税待遇,只是在各个具体协定中确定的免税范围和条件可能有所不同。

两大范本第20条均规定:"学生或企业实习生是,或在直接前往缔约国一方之前曾是缔约国另一方居民,仅由于接受教育或培训的目的停留在该缔约国一方,其为维持生活、教育或培训收到的来源于该国以外的款项,该国不应征税。"根据这一规定,作为缔约国另一方居民的学生或企业实习生,为接受教育或培训目的前往并居留在缔约国一方期间,其所取得的来源于该缔约国一方境外的为维持生活、教育或培训目的而支付的款项,该缔约国一方不得对之课税,而只能由缔约国另一方根据其税法规定决定对上述人员的所得是否课税。这一规则的适用,应注意以下一些条件限制和范围问题:

首先,适用的人员范围仅为学生或企业实习生,包括前往缔约国一方从事接受某种教育或培训活动的各种人员,即这些人员必须是以学生或企业实习生的身份在缔约国一方境内居留,至于他们在前往缔约国一方之前是否已具有学生或企业实习生的身份并不影响这一规则的适用。所谓"以学生或企业实习生的身份在缔约国一方居留",要求这些人员在缔约国一方境内居留的唯一或主要目的,是接受教育或培训。如果他们主要是出于其他目的在缔约国一方境内居留,接受教育或培训只是次要目的,则不能依据上述规定在缔约国一方要求得到免税待遇。因为税收协定限制缔约国一方的征税权的目的,是照顾跨国求学或接受技术培训的学生和企业实习生的生活。不过,上述所谓以接受教育或培训为唯一或主要目的,并不排除这类跨国求学或接受技术培训的学生和企业实习生在业余时间从事某些劳务工作,以获取报酬补充其在缔约国一方境内的生活费用的不足。

其次,是对上述人员的居民身份限制,即这些学生或企业实习生在前往缔约国一方接受教育或培训之时或之前,必须是缔约国另一方的居民,才能适用两大范本第 20 条规定的免税待遇。这种居民身份的条件限制是为了保证税收协定提供的免税优惠待遇仅能由缔约国居民享受,防止让第三国居民"沾光"。因为有些国家的税法规定,居民个人移居境外一年以上,即丧失本国居民身份。而这种移居到另一个国家的个人经过在该国境内半年或一年以上的居住时间,又会成为另一国的居民。这种已经丧失了原居住国居民身份的个人,就不能要求享受原居住国与其他国家签订税收协定中规定的这种免税待遇。

最后,缔约国一方根据协定给予的免税范围,仅限于这类学生或企业实习生从缔约国一方境外收到的为了维持生活、接受教育或培训而支付的款项。这一限制条件有两层含义。其一,可以给予免税的这些款项应是为了这些人员在缔约国一方境内的生活、教育或培训的目的而支付的。例如,来自缔约国另一方提供的学费、助学金、奖学金等性质的款项。如果不是属于为上述目的而支付的款项,则不能给予免税待遇。例如,这些人员从缔约国一方境外的某家银行取得的存款利息,尽管这种利息可能是用来贴补在缔约国一方的生活、教育或培训费用的不足所需,但因为利息支付的原因依据是存款的孳息,而非出于收款人接受教育或培训的原因,所以不能免税。① 其二,这些款项必须是这些人员从缔约国一方境外收到的款项,即应是来源于缔约国一方境外(包括来自缔约国另一方或来自第三国)的款项,才能依协定规定在缔约国一方享受免税待遇。如果这些学生或企业实习生收取的是来自缔约国一方境内的款项,尽管这种款项是为他们在境内接受教育或培训目的而支付的,也不能根据税收协定的这一规定要求免税。

《UN 范本》在这个问题上虽然也采用了《OECD 范本》第 20 条的规定,但考虑到这类跨国接受教育或培训的学生或企业实习生从缔约国一方境外收取的奖学金、助学金等类似性质的款项往往不足以应付他们生活、教育或培训的费用开支,通常需要在缔约国另一方境内从事某些劳务或服务活动以获取一定的劳务报酬来补贴生活、教育或培训开支的实际情况,在第 20 条中增设了第 2 款,规定:"第一款所述学生或企业学徒取得不包括在第一款的赠款、奖学金和雇佣报酬,在接受教育或培训期间,应与该缔约国一方居民享受同样的免税、扣除或减税。"这一款规定的主要目的在于防止对来自缔约国另一方的学生或企业实习生

---

① See Klaus Vogel, Klaus Vogel on Double Taxation Convention, Kluwer Law International, Third Edition, 1997, p. 1059.

在缔约国一方接受教育或培训期间,受到与当地学生或企业实习生不同的税收待遇。

第三节　对跨国投资所得的征税

国际税法上的投资所得是指纳税人将其资产或技术提供给他人使用而取得的各种所得,主要包括股息、利息和特许权使用费三种。通常而言,股息所得是指纳税人因对被投资企业出资入股或购买股票而拥有股权、股份或其他非债权关系分享利润的权利而取得的所得或收益。利息所得是指纳税人因提供贷款或拥有其他形式的债权而获得的收入。特许权使用费则是指权利人因提供专利、商标、专有技术、著作权等无形资产的使用权而获取的报酬。投资所得区别于前述营业所得和劳务所得的主要特点在于,投资所得的受益人只是通过向公司企业投资入股,购买股票或债券,提供贷款和转让财产、设备或技术的使用权等方式取得收益,投资人本身并不直接参与被投资企业的经营管理,尤其是那些证券投资人,更是如此。因此,投资所得属于权利所得性质,具有消极、被动、支付人一般相对固定而受益人往往比较零散的特点。

一、跨国投资所得课税协调的基本原则——税收分享原则

为了协调纳税人的居住国和所得来源地国针对跨国投资所得的征税权冲突,两大范本对跨国股息、利息所得都采用了税收分享原则,即可以在受益人的居住国征税,也可以在所得来源地国一方征税。但对于跨国特许权使用费,《OECD范本》规定应仅由居住国一方独占征税,而《UN范本》采用与股息、利息相同的税收分享原则。为了保证居住国一方能分享到一定的税收利益,国际税收协定在确认所得来源地国对各项投资所得有权课税的同时,限定其源泉扣缴的预提税税率不得超过一定的比例,具体比例由双方在协定的签订过程中协商确定。

之所以对投资所得采取税收分享原则,而不采用独占征税原则,这是由投资所得的特点所决定的。就投资所得的来源国而言,由于有关的资金、财产和技术是在其境内得到实际运用,所得的实现与来源国的经济活动有着密切的联系。来源国一方有充分的理由对非居民来源于其境内的各种投资所得行使属地征税权。对于作为纳税人的居住国一方来说,虽然产生投资所得的资金、财产或技术并不是在本国境内实际运用,但有关资金的筹集、财产的购置和技术的研究开发,往往是在居住国境内进行的。这些投资的成本费用一般已在纳税人的居住

国得到了摊销扣除,因此也应保证纳税人的居住国对其居民来自境外的投资所得能分享到适当的税收利益,这样的结果才公平合理。在税收协定确认来源国一方可以依据其税法规定对缔约国另一方居民有关的投资所得行使优先课税权的情况下,如果协定没有同时限定来源国一方征收预提税的税率,在来源国预提税税率较高的条件下,居住国方面在对纳税人已缴的来源国预提税给予税收抵免后,将无法实际分享到适当的税收利益。

两大范本第 10 条和第 11 条以及《UN 范本》第 12 条规定的这种对有关投资所得通过限定来源国一方可以课征预提税的最高税率,以实现税收分享的协调原则,已为绝大多数国家的双边税收协定实践所采用。只是各国在具体签订的各个双边协定中对有关投资所得确定的限制税率高低略有不同。至于《OECD 范本》第 12 条第 1 款主张的跨国特许使用费应仅由受益人的居住国一方独占征税的分配规则,仅是在少数彼此间技术交流的数量规模大体平衡相当的发达国家之间的双边协定中采用。因为,彼此间的资金或技术交流水平相等的两个国家之间,对某些投资所得规定相互免除在来源地征税,仅由受益人的居住国一方征税,最终的国际税收利益分配结果,也是大体对等的。但在经济技术发展水平相差较大的国家之间,由于彼此间的资金和技术交流数量规模悬殊,将有关跨国投资所得的征税权划归受益人的居住国独占行使,对处在资金和技术输入国地位的缔约国一方会形成极不合理的税收权益分配结果。[①]

二、税收分享原则适用的前提——受益所有人必须为缔约国一方的居民

双重征税协定就所得来源国一方对各项跨国投资所得项目源泉扣缴预提税税率的限定,为从事跨国间接投资的缔约国另一方居民纳税人提供了较为稳定的协定税收优惠待遇。然而,此类协定中对有关投资所得项目的限制税率规定,是缔约国双方在对等互惠原则的基础上经过谈判确定的,其适用的纳税人范围,应仅限于具有缔约国一方居民身份的跨国投资所得的受益人。如果为第三国居民纳税人享受此种协定限制税率的优惠,则有违缔约国双方设定这些协定条款的初衷,损害有关投资所得来源国一方的正当税收利益。为了防止协定的优惠待遇被第三国居民不当利用,自 20 世纪 80 年代以来,各国间签订的双边税收协定在有关投资所得限制税率的条款中,普遍参照两个范本的建议,采用了"受益所有人"这一概念,即如果有关跨国投资所得的受益所有人不是缔约国另一方的居民纳税人,而是某个第三国的居民,尽管有关跨国投资所得的收款人具有缔约

---

① 参见廖益新主编:《国际税法学》,高等教育出版社 2008 年版,第 166 页。

国另一方的居民身份,只要他不是缔约国另一方税法意义上有关投资所得的受益所有人,则来源国一方对其来源于境内的跨国投资所得,可以适用国内所得税法规定的预提税率进行源泉课税,不受协定中规定的限制税率的约束。

《OECD范本》注释中指出,来源国没有义务仅因投资所得是被缔约国另一方居民所直接获取的而放弃其对该股息所得的征税权。"受益所有人"一语不是在一种狭隘的技术层面上运用的,而应结合其上下文以及协定的目的和宗旨来理解,包括避免双重征税和防止逃税与避税,并明确了代理人、指定人以及"导管"公司不属于受益所有人的范围,但未能进一步给出明确具体的标准。在一项所得是由作为代理人或指定人的缔约国一方居民所接收的情形下,如果来源国仅因为该所得的直接接收人具有缔约国另一方居民的身份而给予减税或者免税,这将违背本协定的目的和宗旨。这种情形下该所得的直接接收人虽具有居民身份,但他的地位并不致引起任何可能的双重征税,因为该接收人在居住国的税法上不被视为该所得的所有人。同样地,如果缔约国一方的某个居民不是通过代理人或指定人关系,而只是为另一个实际取得股息利益的人作为接收相关所得的"导管"行事,此时,要求来源国给予其减税或免税的做法,也与本协定的目的和宗旨不符。因此,经合组织财政事务委员会题为《双重征税协定与"导管"公司的运用》的报告的结论是:"导管"公司一般不能被认定为受益所有人,尽管它形式上是特定资产的所有人,但它对资产的权力非常有限,使得其实际上仅仅是一个为利害关系人的利益行事的受托人或者执行人。[①]

关于"受益所有人"的概念和认定标准,目前还存在分歧,有学者将这种分歧归纳为以下几种情形:(1) 税收协定中的受益所有人用语是否具有其独立的协定法意义,还是应适用缔约国的国内法概念来解释认定;(2) 税收协定意义上的受益所有人的判定应该依据的是一种法律性质的认定标准,还是可以是一种事实性或经济实质性的检测标准;(3) 受益所有人的认定应仅考察的是收款人对所得的控制支配权,还是应扩大考虑其对产生所得的基础财产或权利的控制支配权;(4) 在受益所有人问题上是否应考虑缔约国国内特别反避税规则或实质优于形式等一般反避税原则的适用。结合经合组织先后于 2011 年 4 月 29 日和 2012 年 12 月 25 日公布的两份题为《经合组织税收协定范本中"受益所有人"含义的说明》的讨论稿,有学者总结出在受益所有人认定分歧问题上的未来发展趋向:(1) 税收协定中的受益所有人用语应具有其相对独立的协定法概念含义;

---

① 参见《OECD范本》第10条注释第12—12.1段、第11条注释第9—10段、第12条注释第4—4.1段。

(2) 虽然确认受益所有人原则上应该依据一种法律性质的标准进行判定,但也不排除可以适用某种事实性的检测标准来认定某种法律义务的存在;(3) 明确了受益所有人的认定应关注考察收款人对有关所得款项的控制支配权,并不扩及其对产生所得的基础财产或权利的控制支配权;(4) 虽然确认在受益所有人概念解释上并不适用缔约国国内法上的特别或一般反避税规则,但同时明确获得受益所有人资格的认定并不等于即可自动获得协定规定的减免预提税优惠待遇。

三、税收分享原则适用的例外——与常设机构有实际联系的投资所得

以限制来源地国预提税税率为核心的税收分享原则的重要例外是,作为缔约国一方居民的受益所有人,如果在所得来源国另一方境内设有常设机构进行营业或设有固定基地从事独立个人劳务,并且据以支付股息、利息和特许权使用费的股权、债权和权利财产与该常设机构或固定基地有实际联系,这种情况下取得的股息、利息和特许权使用费所得,不适用协定中有关投资所得的预提税限制规定,而应适用协定中有关营业所得课税条款,将其并入常设机构的营业利润课税或适用协定中有关独立劳务所得的征税协调规则,将其并入固定基地的个人所得征税。

该例外规定实际上是对两大范本第 7 条第 2 款独立企业原则的补充和发展。根据确定常设机构利润范围的独立企业原则,应将常设机构视作相对独立于总机构或其他分支机构的一个独立实体,常设机构运用其所属资产从事经营活动取得的营业利润和营业外收益,包括与总机构或其他分支机构之间的业务往来按独立交易原则应当收取的利润,都应归属于常设机构的利润范围。而所谓与常设机构或固定基地有实际联系的投资所得,是指产生这些投资所得的股权、债权、知识产权和设备财产等属于常设机构或固定基地直接拥有的资产,或常设机构或固定基地与产生有关投资所得的资产有实际经营管理关系。

根据《OECD 范本》的解释,股权、债权和权利财产的持有与常设机构存在"实际联系"这一要件不仅限于要求在会计核算上常设机构账簿中有记载。据以支付投资所得的股权、债权和权利财产持有必须与常设机构有实际联系,如果股权、债权和权利财产的"经济"所有权按照《常设机构利润归属报告》中为适用第 7 条第 2 款而提出的原则分配给该常设机构,则这种与支付股息有关的股份持有将因此而构成常设机构的部分营业资产。股权、债权和权利财产的这种"经济"所有权相当于一个独立企业在所得税意义上拥有的所有权,包括随之产生的

收益和负担。① 由于缔约国一方居民的上述投资所得与其在来源国境内设置的常设机构或固定基地存在这样的实际联系,按照独立计算常设机构或固定基地所得的原则,作为来源地国一方应将这类投资所得认定为归属于常设机构或固定基地的利润范围,与常设机构或固定基地的营业所得合并课税,而不能像对一般非居民来源于境内的投资所得那样,以源泉扣缴预提所得税为在来源国的最终税收。

四、对各项投资所得的征税规则

(一)对股息的征税规则

1. 税收分享原则的应用

对于缔约国一方居民公司支付给缔约国另一方居民的股息,《OECD范本》第10条首先确立了税收分享原则:"一、缔约国一方居民公司支付给缔约国另一方居民的股息,可以在该缔约国另一方征税。二、然而,这些股息也可以在支付股息的公司是其居民的缔约国,按照该缔约国法律征税。但是如果股息受益所有人是缔约国另一方的居民,则所征的税款:(1)如果受益所有人是直接持有支付股息公司至少25%资本的公司(不是合伙企业),不应超过股息总额的5%;(2)在其他情况下,不应超过股息总额的15%。"② 由于母子公司的特殊关系,对子公司支付给母公司的股息适用较低利率从轻征税是合理的,这不仅避免了重复征税,也促进了国际投资,但能否实现这一意图,还主要取决于母公司为其居民的国家对股息的税务处理。③ 但需要注意的是上述条款中"资本"的认定。

"资本"一语是指与股息即分配给股东的利润征税相关的资本。此处这一用语意味着在上述第1项规定意义上,即在对股东(在特定情形下指母公司)进行分配的意义上使用的。因此,作为一般原则,该用语应按它在公司法中的含义范围来理解,即在大多数情况下为以资本的形式反映在公司资产负债表上的所有股票的票面价值。对于所发行的各种不同股票(普通股、优先股、多重表决权股、无表决权股、无记名股、记名股等)的区别及其他因素,特别是企业提留的各种储备金,均不予考虑。当向公司提供的贷款或其他形式的出资,严格按公司法不构成资本,但按国内法或惯例(资本弱化或将贷款视同股本),由此而获得的所得被

---

① 参见《OECD范本》第10条注释第32—32.1段、第11条注释第25—25.1段、第12条注释第21—21.1段。
② 《UN范本》第10条第2款未明确规定支付股息的公司所在国一方对股息的预提税比例,而是规定这一协定限制税率由缔约国双方通过谈判具体确定。
③ 参见《OECD范本》第10条第2款注释第10段。

作为第 10 条规定下的"股息"处理时,这种贷款或出资也将被作为第 1 项意义上的"资本"看待。对那些不拥有公司法意义上的资本的实体而言,第 1 项规定意义上的"资本",是指在计算分配利润方面应予考虑的对这些实体的所有投入总额。在双边谈判中,缔约国可不采用第 1 项的"资本"标准,而换用"表决权"标准。①

但该项规定没有要求收取股息的公司必须在股息分配前的相对长的一段时间内至少拥有 25% 以上的资本。这说明关键是在产生第 10 条第 2 款所适用的纳税义务时的股票持有状况,大多数情况下即指股东合法获得股息时的持股状况。这主要是希望制定的条款能够尽可能广泛地被适用。如果要求母公司在利润分配前一段时间就拥有最低限额的股份,则可能涉及大量的调查工作。某些经合组织成员国国内法规定股息接收公司必须持有股份的最低期限,才能获得股息上的免税或者减税待遇。有鉴于此,缔约国双方在其协定中可加入类似的条件。但在滥用本款规定的情形下不应给予第 1 项所规定的减税待遇。例如,主要是为了获得上述条款所给予的优惠,持股在 25% 以下的公司在股息支付前的短时间内增加它在分配股息公司中的持股份额,或者主要是为了获得减税而安排符合要求的股份占有数。为防止这类人为操纵情形,缔约国可在第 1 项中增加以下规定:"但以上述持股份额的取得主要目的不是为了利用本项规定的优惠为限"。②

另外,对股息征税规则的把握除前述受益所有人的认定、与常设机构有实际联系的股息所得例外以外,还需要掌握以下两点:一是"股息"的定义和范围;二是禁止对股息境外征税以及对未分配利润征税。

2. 股息的定义和范围

股息是指从股份、"享受"股份("Jouissance" Shares)或"享受"权利("Jouissance" Rights)、矿业股份、发起人股份或非债权关系而是分享利润的其他权利取得的所得,以及按照分配利润的公司是其居民的国家的法律,视同股份所得同样征税的其他公司权利取得的所得。③ 由于各国国内法差别很大,所以不可能对"股息"作出充分和详尽的定义。因此,《OECD 范本》仅列举了在经合组织大多数成员国法律中均能找到且在任何情形下都会给予同样对待处理的例子,继而再概括出一个一般定义规定。④ 由于大多数国家合伙企业不具有法人地位,

---

① 参见《OECD 范本》第 10 条第 2 款注释第 15 段。
② 参见《OECD 范本》第 10 条第 2 款注释第 16—17 段。
③ 参见《OECD 范本》和《UN 范本》第 10 条第 3 款。
④ 参见《OECD 范本》第 10 条第 3 款注释第 23 段。

合伙企业的利润分配不属于股息的定义范围,而是作为合伙人的营业所得征税,除非合伙企业在其实际管理场所所在地国家的税收地位实质上与股份有限公司的地位相似。①

对于股息的认定,主要应当考虑以下三点:首先,与利润的分配有关;其次,参与利润分配的债权不包括在内,可转换债权的利息也不是股息;最后,应注意在贷款人实际分担公司风险的情况下,即当支付的回报主要是基于企业经营的成功与否时,有关贷款利息的处理问题。《OECD 范本》并不阻止借款人所在国根据资本弱化的国内法将利息作为股息处理。贷款人是否分担企业风险的问题必须根据个案中的所有情况来判定。例如,该贷款大大超过企业资本中的其他投资形式(或被用以弥补重要的资本损失),并与公司可变现资产严重不匹配;债权人将分享公司的任何利润;利息的支付水平取决于公司的利润;所签订的贷款合同没有对具体的偿还日期作出明确规定。②

股息支付不仅包括每年股东大会所决定的利润分配,也包括其他货币或具有货币价值的收益分配,如红股、红利、清算收入以及变相利润分配。只要支付公司居住国将该收益作为股息征税,就可适用《OECD 范本》第 10 条。至于公司所付的是当年利润还是历年结存利润,即以往会计年度的利润,这一问题无关紧要。公司减少股东权益的分配形式,如构成返还出资的任何形式的付款,通常都不被当作股息。作为一般原则,仅股东自身享有公司股份所授予的收益分配权。然而,这种收益如果分配给公司法上不认为是股东的人,也可视为股息,如果此类人与该公司的法律关系类似于在公司中持有股份(隐蔽持股),且收益接收人与股东关系极其密切,如接收人是股东的亲戚或是一家与拥有该股份的公司同属于一个集团的公司。③

3. 股息来源地的认定

考虑到能够直接分配股息的一般是具有独立法人地位的公司,这种公司的总机构或实际管理机构必然是设在缔约国一方而成为该国的居民公司。两大范本及各国签订的双边税收协定采用以居民公司支付为准的原则,即凡是缔约国一方居民公司支付的股息,应认定该股息发生在该缔约国,该缔约国对居民公司支付给缔约国另一方居民股东的股息,可以按税收协定规定的限制税率课征预提税。将在缔约国一方境内的常设机构取得的利润汇给位于缔约国另一方境内

---

① 参见《OECD 范本》第 10 条第 3 款注释第 27 段。
② 参见《OECD 范本》第 10 条第 3 款注释第 24—25 段。
③ 参见《OECD 范本》第 10 条第 3 款注释第 28—29 段。

的总机构，由总机构支付股息，应认定该股息的发生地在总机构所在的缔约国另一方，而不考虑股息的实际利润来源地为常设机构所在的缔约国一方境内。这也是下文即将阐述的禁止对股息境外征税的原因。避免双重征税协定统一以分配股息的公司的居住地作为股息的发生地，并相应确定由该公司所在地的缔约国一方行使源泉扣缴预提税的权利，这样就避免了因缔约国各自国内税法关于股息来源地认定标准的差异而可能导致协定条款适用的争议。

4. 禁止对股息境外征税以及对未分配利润征税

两大范本第10条第5款均规定："缔约国一方居民公司从缔约国另一方取得利润或所得，该缔约国另一方不得对该公司支付的股息征收任何税收（但支付给该缔约国另一方居民的股息或者据以支付股息的股份与设在缔约国另一方的常设机构有实际联系的除外），也不得对该公司的未分配的利润征收任何税收，即使支付的股息或未分配的利润全部或部分是发生于该缔约国另一方的利润或所得。"该款否定了两种类型的征税。首先，禁止对股息境外征税，即缔约国不能仅因为用于分配的利润来源于本国境内（如通过那里的常设机构来实现）而对非居民公司所分配的股息征税。因为如前所述，税收协定意义上的股息来源地为分配股息的公司居住地，即使该股息的利润来源于公司设在其他国家的常设机构。当然，当公司利润来源国对支付给本国居民股东或境内常设机构的股息征税时，则不存在境外征税问题。其次，对非居民公司的未分配利润不应征收特别税种。①

有人可能会认为，纳税人居住国依照其受控外国公司立法或其他具有类似效果的规则，寻求对未分配利润进行征税的做法是与上述第5款的规定相违背的行为。然而，应注意的是，第5款仅是对来源地国征税的限制。因此，对居住国按此类立法或规则所进行的征税没有任何影响。此外，该款仅涉及对公司的税收问题而不包括对股东的税收问题。然而，此类受控外国公司立法或规则的适用可能会使第23条（免税法和抵免法）的适用复杂化。②

在股息实际由基地公司分配的情况下，双边税收协定有关股息的规定必须按正常方式适用，因为存在协定意义上的股息所得。因此，基地公司所在国可以对股息征收预提税。股东居住国将按通常的方法消除双重征税（即给予税收抵免或免税）。这意味着即使对所分配利润（股息）在以往年度根据受控外国公司立法或其他具有类似效果的规则已被征税，股东居住国仍应对该股息所征收的

---

① 参见《OECD范本》第10条第5款注释第34、36段。
② 参见《OECD范本》第10条第5款注释第37—38段。

预提税给予抵免。然而,这种情形下的抵免义务仍存在疑问。通常这种股息是免税的(因为根据相关立法或规则已对这笔所得征了税),而且有人可能认为此时提供税收抵免缺乏基础。另外,如果只要通过受控外国公司规则这类防范性立法对股息提前征税就可以避免税收抵免责任,协定的目的就会落空。上述基本原则建议抵免应被给予,尽管具体执行还取决于相关立法或规则的技术性、外国税收抵免国内税收的制度,以及个案的具体情况(如对"推定股息"征税后所经过的时间)。然而,对那些依赖于人为安排的纳税人来说,则要承担不能得到税务当局充分保证的风险。①

(二) 对利息的征税规则

1. 税收分享原则的应用

对于缔约国一方居民公司支付给缔约国另一方居民的利息,《OECD 范本》第 11 条第 1、2 款确立了税收分享原则:"一、发生于缔约国一方并支付给缔约国另一方居民的利息,可以在该缔约国另一方征税。二、然而,这些利息也可以在该利息发生的缔约国,按照该国法律征税。但是,如果利息的受益所有人是缔约国另一方的居民,则所征税款不应超过利息总额的 10%。缔约国双方主管当局应通过相互协商,确定实施该限制税率的方式。"《UN 范本》第 11 条第 2 款未明确规定支付利息的公司所在国一方对利息的预提税比例,而是规定这一协定限制税率由缔约国双方通过谈判具体确定。10% 的税率限制被认为是合理的,因为考虑到来源国已有权对在本国境内通过借入资金的投资所产生的利润或所得征税。②

在某些情况下,《OECD 范本》第 11 条第 2 款所采用的允许对利息支出进行源泉课税的方法,可能构成国际贸易的一个障碍,或者因其他原因而被认为是不适当的。例如,当利息受益人据以产生利息的业务提供的资金是向他人所借时,以利息形式实现的利润将远远小于名义上收到的利息;如果所付出的利息等于或超过所获得的利息,则没有任何利润,甚至产生亏损。这种情形下的问题居民国是无法解决的,因为受益人在该国是以其从交易中所获取的净利润纳税的,所以该国征收很少的税或根本征不到税。产生这个问题的原因在于,来源国是按利息的毛收入额计算征税,并不考虑为了获取该利息而产生的费用。为了避免这样的问题,实践中债权人倾向于将来源国对利息的课税负担转移给债务人,从而增加债务人所负担的利率,债务人也随之增加了与应纳来源国税额相对应的

---

① 参见《OECD 范本》第 10 条第 5 款注释第 39 段。
② 参见《OECD 范本》第 11 条第 2 款注释第 7 段序言。

财务负担。①

双边税收协定的缔约国还可能在协定中给予下列利息以免税待遇：支付给一国、其所属行政区和中央银行的利息；由一国或其所属行政区支付的利息；根据出口融资计划支付的利息；支付给金融机构的利息；赊销利息；支付给某些免税实体的利息（如退休基金）。

2. 利息的定义和范围

根据《OECD 范本》第 11 条第 3 款，"利息"是指从各种债权取得的所得，不论其有无抵押担保或者是否有权分享债务人的利润；特别是指从政府证券取得的所得、从债券或者信用债券取得的所得，包括附属于这些证券、债券和信用债券的溢价和奖金。由于延期支付的罚款，不应视为本条所规定的利息。② "各种债权"一语显然包括现金存款、货币形态的有价证券以及政府证券、债券和信用债券。参与利润分配债券的利息一般不应视为股息，可转换债券在没有转换成股份前，通常其利息也不被认为是股息。然而，如果该项债券贷款实际分担了债务人公司的风险，则其利息应被视为股息。也就是说，区分股息和利息的关键在于是否分担了债务人的风险。在推定资本弱化的情形下，有时难以区分股息和利息。为避免任何第 10 条和第 11 条所涉所得类别重叠的可能性，应注意第 11 条的"利息"一语不包括按第 10 条"股息"处理的所得项目。③ 该利息的定义通常也不适用于某些非传统的缺乏基础性债务交易的（如利率掉期）金融工具的支付。然而，如果根据"实质优于形式"规则、"权利滥用"原则，或者任何类似原则，认为存在贷款，则该定义仍将适用。④

此外，不同于股息的定义，第 11 条第 3 款有关利息的定义在原则上是穷尽性的。在条文规定中不附属提及这方面的国内法规定被认为是更为可取的。其理由有以下几方面考虑：(1) 本定义实际上涵盖了各国国内法上视为利息的所有类型的所得；(2) 从法律角度讲，该定义更具保障性，并能保证协定不受国内法今后变化的影响；(3) 协定应尽可能避免援引国内法。然而，缔约国双方在双边协定中可以扩大利息的定义范围，使之包括定义没有涉及的但按任一方国内法视同利息征税的各类所得。在此情况下，则可选择援引国内法。⑤

需要指出的是，由于支付利息的人与受益所有人之间或者他们与其他人之

---

① 参见《OECD 范本》第 11 条第 2 款注释第 7.1 段。
② 《UN 范本》第 11 条第 3 款也作了上述规定。
③ 参见《OECD 范本》第 11 条注释第 18、19 段。
④ 参见《OECD 范本》第 11 条注释第 21.1 段。
⑤ 参见《OECD 范本》第 11 条注释第 21 段。

间的特殊关系,就有关债权所支付的利息数额超出支付人与受益所有人没有上述关系所能同意的数额时,利息仅包括后面提及的数额,超过该数额的部分不得视为协定中所说的"利息",应按各缔约国的国内法律征税,但应考虑协定中其他条款的规定。① 这种特殊关系包括不同于因法律关系而支付利息的任何共同利益关系,如关联企业关系、血缘和婚姻关系。②

3. 利息来源地的认定

根据《OECD范本》第11条第5款,如果支付利息的人为缔约国一方居民,应认为该利息发生于该缔约国。然而,如果支付利息的人不论是不是缔约国一方居民,在缔约国一方设有常设机构或固定基地,支付该利息的债务与该常设机构或固定基地有联系,并由其负担利息,上述利息应认为发生于该常设机构所在缔约国。③

本款明确了利息来源国是利息支付人为其居民的国家这一原则。然而,该款也规定了一个例外情形,即该项贷款与该利息支付人在缔约国另一方拥有的常设机构有明显的经济联系。如果是应常设机构的需要而签订贷款合同,且支付的利息由该常设机构承担,本款认为利息的来源地应是常设机构所在的缔约国,不管该机构的所有者为何国居民,即使其居住在第三国。但只有在贷款和与常设机构的经济联系足够清晰的情形下,才具有正当性。

在这一点上,可以区分如下可能出现的情况:(1)常设机构的管理部门按该常设机构的具体要求签订贷款合同,将借入款项作为该机构的债务,并由其直接将利息支付给债权人;(2)企业总机构为设在另一国的常设机构单独使用的贷款签订合同并代付利息,但所付利息最终由该常设机构承担;(3)该贷款合同是由企业总机构签订的,所贷资金用于设在不同国家境内的数个常设机构使用。上述第1、2种情形符合常设机构例外的条件,常设机构所在国可视为利息发生国。然而,第3种情形超出了第11条第5款规定的范围,因为该款文字规定排除了同一笔贷款可有多个来源地的情形。同时,这种做法将会导致管理上相当大的复杂性,并使债权人无法事先计算出该利息所要承担的税收。当然,缔约国双方可根据意愿将该款的适用范围限制在第1种情形或者扩大到第3种情形。④

但是,上述第11条第5款对下述被其排除的情形没有提出解决方案,即利

---

① 参见《OECD范本》和《UN范本》第11条第6款。
② 参见《OECD范本》第11条第6款注释第33—34段。
③ 参见两大范本第11条第5款。
④ 参见《OECD范本》第11条第5款注释第26—27段。

息支付人和受益人均为缔约国居民,但贷款是为支付人设在第三国的常设机构的需要而借入,并由该常设机构负担利息的情况。因此,按照本款的现有规定,只有其第一句将适用于这种情形,即利息发生国被视为利息支付人为其居民的国家,而不是使用贷款并承担利息的常设机构所在的第三国。因此,这笔利息将在利息支付人为其居民的缔约国和受益人为其居民的缔约国双方征税。但是,虽然可按本条的安排避免以两个国家的形式征税的双重征税情形,但不能避免若第三国对其境内常设机构所负担的贷款利息征税而导致的支付人和受益人的国家与第三国之间的重复征税。[1]

(三)特许权使用费的征税规则

对于特许权使用费的征税协调原则,两大范本的规定不尽一致,《UN范本》第12条规定:"发生于缔约国一方并支付给缔约国另一方居民的特许权使用费,可以在另一国征税。然而,这些特许权使用费也可以在其发生的缔约国,按照该国法律征税。但是,如果收款人是特许权使用费受益所有人,所征税款不应超过特许权使用费总额的__%(百分数通过双边谈判确定)"。《OECD范本》第12条则规定:"发生于缔约国一方并由缔约国另一方居民受益所有的特许权使用费,应仅在该缔约国另一方征税"。显然,《UN范本》体现的是所得来源地国和受益所有人居住地国税收利益分享的原则,而《OECD范本》则规定由受益所有人居住地国独占征税。

总的来说,特许权使用费是指由于使用或有权使用以下权利而支付的款项,无论这些权利是否已经或者必须在公共注册部门登记:构成各种形式的文学与艺术的权利和财产;有关工业、商业和科学经验的文本和情报资料中确定的知识产权要素。该定义既包括了在有许可的情况下所支付的款项,也包括了某人由于欺诈性复制或侵犯这项权利而被责令支付的赔偿款。[2] 在理解该概念时要特别注意的是,作为特许权使用费支付的报酬须是为了"使用或有权使用"某种规定的权利,而不是为了取得该项权利的完全所有权,如果是为了取得完全所有权而支付的报酬,原则上应认定为营业利润或资本利得,而不是特许权使用费。尽管上述关于特许权使用费的定义中突出了与其他类型所得的区别,但在实践中由于交易的复杂多样性,通常需要结合具体情形来加以辨别。

纳税人因传授某种专有技术而收取的特许权使用费与提供某种专业技术服务而获得的劳务报酬往往很难区分,尤其是在既包含提供专有技术又包括提供

---

[1] 参见《OECD范本》第11条第5款注释第28段。

[2] 参见《OECD范本》第12条注释第8段。

技术服务的混合合同中,这两者的界限更是微妙,对此,《OECD 范本》注释给出了一些参考标准:提供专有技术的合同涉及的是在特许权使用费的定义中所述的已经存在的那类情报资料,或者涉及的是在开发或创造出那类情报资料后提供那类情报资料,并且合同中有关这类情报资料保密性的具体规定;在提供服务的合同中,服务提供方允诺提供服务,该服务也许需要服务提供方使用特殊知识、技能和专门技术,但并不将其转让给另一方;在涉及提供专有技术的大多数情况下,根据合同,提供方除了提供现有情报或复制现有材料之外,通常不参与受让方的生产经营活动,而在服务合同中,多数情况下,服务提供方为了履行其合同义务,需要独立地完成为另一方服务的工作。在包括提供技术和提供服务的混合合同中,原则上应根据合同内容或以合理的比例进行划分,对合同所规定的报酬总额进行分解,然后对各部分适用由此确定的适当的税收待遇。但是,如果混合合同中的一部分构成了合同中最主要的目的,而另一部分仅是辅助性的和大部分是不重要的,则一般可对报酬的总额按主要部分所适用的税收待遇处理。

关于计算机软件的报酬是否属于特许权使用费一直是实践中碰到的一个难题。经合组织在其范本注释中表明:对于计算机软件转让交易中所收取报酬的属性,取决于在有关程序使用及开发的具体安排下受让方获得的权利的性质。如果支付报酬是为了通过某种方式获得使用该软件的权利(没有此种许可将构成对版权的侵权),则为获取版权中部分权利(转让方没有转让全部版权权利)而支付的款项构成特许权使用费。如果获得的与版权相关的权利限于那些使用者能够对程序进行操作所必需的权利,无论这种权利是通过法律授予的,还是通过与版权所有人签订特许权协议授予的,将程序复制到计算机硬盘或随机存取到存储器上,或者为了存档的目的而做的拷贝,都是利用该程序的一个必要步骤。当与这些复制行为有关的权利只是为了使用户能对程序进行有效操作的情形下,为这些类型交易而支付的款项应作为营业利润而不是特许权使用费来处理。如果报酬是为转让版权权利的全部所有权目的而支付时,该款项不构成特许权使用费,而应视具体情形分别定性为营业利润或财产收益。

电子商务的发展促使数字产品交易越来越多,上述关于软件报酬的原则也适用于其他种类数字产品的交易,如影像、声音或文本等。在决定产生于这些交易的款项是否构成特许权使用费时,主要是要辨别有关款项实质上的支付目的。

与利息征税规则一样,如果由于特许权使用费的支付人与受益所有人之间或他们与其他人之间的特殊关系,就有关使用、权利或情报信息支付的特许权使用费数额超出支付人与受益所有人没有上述关系所能同意的数额时,对于超出部分则不适用特许权使用费的征税规则,应按各缔约国的法律征税,但应考虑协定中其他条款的规定。

第四节 对跨国财产收益和其他所得的征税

一、对跨国财产收益课税的一般规则

一般而言,两大范本中的财产收益,主要是指作为缔约国一方居民的纳税人转让位于缔约国另一方境内的具有资本性质的财产的所有权而取得的收益。

目前,各国对跨国财产收益的税收待遇规定的差异较大,有些国家对财产收益不征税;有些国家对企业财产收益和个人财产收益区别对待,对企业发生的财产收益要征税,但对个人从其贸易或营业以外取得的财产收益则不征税。此外,各国对财产收益征收的税种也不同,有的国家将财产收益作为一般所得与其他种类的所得合并征收,而有的国家则对财产收益单独征收特别税。对于纳税人所从事的涉及转让财产所有权的交易所得到底是财产收益还是营业收入的问题,范本认为没有必要作统一规定,应由缔约国的国内法来确定,因为正常情况下应将对某类财产的财产收益征税的权力赋予按照协定有权对该类财产和由该类财产而取得的所得征税的国家,对转让营业财产所得征税的权力必须给予同一个国家而不论该项收益是财产收益还是营业利润。也就是说,不论是财产收益还是营业利润,都由同一个国家来征税,到底按哪一类所得来征税,由该国国内法确定即可。

多数对财产收益征税的国家,都是在资产转让发生时才征税,但也有一些国家仅对所谓实现的财产收益征税。在某些情况下,虽然发生了财产转让,但在税收上认为没有实现财产收益(如转让收益被用于取得新的资产)。财产收益是否实现,应根据国内法来确定。财产收益原则上不包括与转让资产无关的增值,这是因为只要所有权人仍持有上述资产,资产增值收益就还只是存在于纸面上,但有些国家的税法规定即使没有转让行为发生,对资产增值和营业资产的重估也要征税。

考虑到各国立法的差异较大,范本并不试图对此作统一规定,而是将财产收益是否应征税,以及如果征税又应如何征收的问题,留待各缔约国国内法去解决。如果缔约国国内法中未赋予对财产收益征税的权力,那么无论如何都不能将协定中的规定解释为赋予了该国对财产收益征税的权力。

两大范本均规定,除对不动产、常设机构财产、船舶、飞机及其附属动产、股

份的转让有特殊规定外,转让其他任何财产取得的收益,应仅在转让者为其居民的缔约国征税。也就是说,除特殊财产的转让外,其他财产的转让适用转让方居住国独占征税原则。下面将就跨国财产收益的特殊规则作介绍。

二、对跨国财产收益课税的特殊规则

(一) 对跨国不动产转让所得的征税规则

两大范本均规定,缔约国一方居民转让位于缔约国另一方的不动产取得的收益,可以在该缔约国另一方征税。据此规定,作为缔约国一方居民的企业或个人转让其坐落于缔约国另一方境内的不动产所产生的所得,作为不动产所在地的缔约国另一方有优先征税的权力,即可以依照其国内税法规定的税率和方式进行征税。作为纳税人的居住国的缔约国一方对上述跨国转让不动产收益同样也可以行使居民税收管辖权征税,但应按范本规定采取必要的消除重复征税措施。

关于不动产的概念,根据两大范本第 6 条的规定,原则上按照财产所在地的缔约国国内法律来解释。应该指出的是,这里适用财产所在地国一方国内法上的不动产概念含义来解释范本中不动产用语的含义,性质上不同于两大范本第 3 条第 2 款规定的协定解释规则,适用缔约国国内有关税法概念来解释协定本身未明确定义的概念用语。前者情形不是协定本身未就不动产这一用语作出明确定义,而是协定以财产所在地国的国内法上的不动产概念的含义,作为协定中不动产概念的含义。因此,在这种情况下尽管适用财产所在地国一方的国内法上不动产概念认定的结果,与适用缔约国另一方国内不动产法律概念识别的结果不一致,但纳税人或缔约国另一方也不得提出异议。而后者情形下适用缔约国一方国内有关税法概念来解释协定中未明确定义的用语含义,如果与适用缔约国另一方国内有关税法概念解释协定中同一用语的结果不同,纳税人或缔约国另一方税务机关是可以提出异议或要求通过相互协商程序解决由于解释冲突而引起的有关争议。[①]

考虑到各国国内法对不动产的定义和范围规定的差异较大,为了尽可能减少因为这类差异带来的税收利益分配上的不均衡,两大范本均规定,不动产在任何情况下都应包括附属于不动产的财产,农业和林业所使用的牲畜和设备,有关地产的一般法律规定所适用的权利,不动产的用益权,以及由于开采或有权开采矿藏、水源与其他自然资源而取得固定或不固定的收入的权利,但船舶和飞机不应视为不动产。

---

① 参见廖益新主编:《国际税法学》,高等教育出版社 2008 年版,第 197 页。

(二) 对转让常设机构或固定基地财产所得的征税

根据两大范本的规定,转让缔约国一方企业在缔约国另一方的常设机构营业财产部分的动产取得的收益,以及缔约国一方居民个人转让他在缔约国另一方从事个人独立劳务的固定基地的动产所获取的收益,包括转让整个常设机构(单独或随同整个企业)或固定基地所取得的收益,可以在该缔约国另一方征税。

这里关键是要把握以下两点:一个是关于常设机构和固定基地的概念,二是动产的范围。关于前一个问题,前文已有详述,这里不再赘述。关于常设机构或固定基地的动产的范围,根据《OECD范本》注释的规定,"动产"一语是指范本所规定的不动产以外的所有财产,既包括机器设备、库存商品、原材料等有形财产,也包括无形财产,如商誉、许可证等。如果转让的是可归属于常设机构或固定基地的不动产,则要适用前面关于不动产转让所得的征税规则。

(三) 对转让船舶、飞机及附属动产收益的征税

对于转让从事国际运输的船舶、飞机、从事内河运输的船只或附属于经营上述船舶、飞机或船只的动产取得的收益,两大范本均规定应仅在该企业实际管理机构所在的缔约国征税。范本注释中特别指出,这里的规定仅适用于转让财产的企业本身经营中的船舶、飞机或船只,而不论是为其自有的运输业务或是依据租约出租配齐设备、人员和补给的船只、船舶或飞机。如果企业虽然拥有船只、船舶或飞机但不从事运输经营的情形(如除偶尔从事范本第8条注释第5段所指的光船租赁外,企业只是将财产租给其他人),则不能由企业的实际管理机构所在的缔约国独占征税,而应该按照转让常设机构动产所得或转让其他财产所得,由常设机构所在地的缔约国或转让者为其居民的缔约国征税。

(四) 对转让公司股份和其他财产所得的征税

关于转让公司股份所取得收益的税收协调原则,两大范本规定的差异较大。《OECD范本》第13条第4款规定,缔约国一方居民转让股份取得收益,该股份50%以上的价值直接或间接来自于位于缔约国另一方的不动产,该收益可在该缔约国另一方征税。经合组织之所以这么规定,主要是为了使转让这类股份所获得的收益与转让股份构成基础的不动产取得的收益,同样可在该缔约国一方征税。

《OECD范本》对转让公司股份收益的上述税收协调原则是在2003年确立的。在2003年之前,《OECD范本》只是对转让不动产,转让从事国际运输的船舶、飞机、从事内河运输的船只或附属于经营上述船舶、飞机或船只的动产,以及转让缔约国一方企业在缔约国另一方的常设机构营业财产部分的动产这三种情形作了特别规定,对于转让前述三种财产以外的所有财产,包括所有转让公司股权或股票的收益,均由转让人的居住国一方独占征税,被转让股份的公司的居住

国一方不得征税。这一规定在具体实践中可能出现一个问题,即如果公司股份的构成基础主要或全部是不动产,这时转让公司股份实际上只是一种外在形式,而实质是转让不动产,但如果按照股份转让,则应由转让人的居住国征税,若按照不动产转让,则应由不动产所在国征税。两者在实质上是同一回事,但税收管辖权却截然不同。正是考虑到这一问题,经合组织在 2003 年对范本作出修订,以弥补这一漏洞。

对于转让股份的收益,《OECD 范本》只规定了股份价值主要来自于不动产的情形,对于其他情形则没作特别规定。与《OECD 范本》不同,《UN 范本》主张对转让股份收益区分以下两种情况处理:(1) 转让某个公司的财产股份取得的收益,如果该公司的财产主要直接或间接由位于缔约国一方的不动产所组成,应适用关于不动产转让所得的征税协调规则处理,即可以在该不动产所在地的缔约国一方征税。(2) 转让公司企业的其他股份或股票取得的收益,如果被转让的股份或股票在转让前的 12 个月内任何时间达到公司股权的一定比例(具体的比例数可由缔约国双方在协定中谈判确定),可以在被转让公司企业为其居民的缔约国一方征税。① 至于未达到协定规定比例的股份转让收益,则应与其他财产转让所得一样,由转让者的居住国一方独占征税。

可见,《UN 范本》所规定的第一种情形与经合组织的规定相近似,但第二种情形是《OECD 范本》没有涉及的。不过,即便对于两大范本都采纳的原则,也并非所有国家都认同,针对《OECD 范本》第 13 条第 4 款,诸多经合组织成员国都提出了保留意见。例如,法国、芬兰、瑞典、日本、西班牙和墨西哥等国分别要求保留对转让位于本国境内的不动产的公司财产股份收益或转让本国居民公司中的重大股份所得征税的权力。②

三、对其他所得的课税规则

其他所得,在各国国内所得税法上是一个富有弹性的概念,一般是指纳税人取得的虽不在税法明确规定的有关应税所得项目范围,但属于所得税课税对象的各种所得或收益。例如,我国《个人所得税法》第 2 条第 11 项规定的"经国务院财政部门确定征税的其他所得";《企业所得税法》第 6 条第 9 项规定的"其他收入",即企业取得的除第 6 条第 1 项至第 8 项规定的收入外的其他收入。但是,在各国相互签订的税收协定中,其他所得则是指此类协定有关所得税条款未

---

① 参见《UN 范本》第 13 条第 4 款、第 5 款。
② 参见《OECD 范本》注释第 13 条第 33、35、36、39、42、45、49 和 51 段。

涉及的其他所得或收益。

对协定意义上的其他跨国所得的课税协调,《UN 范本》在第 21 条作出规定:"一、缔约国一方居民的各项所得,无论其发生于何地,凡本协定上述各条未作规定的,应仅在该缔约国一方征税。二、第六条第二款规定的不动产所得以外的其他所得,如果所得的收款人是缔约国一方居民,通过设在缔约国另一方的常设机构进行营业,或者通过设在缔约国另一方的固定基地从事独立劳务,据以支付所得的权利或财产与该常设机构有实际联系,则不适用第一款的规定。在这种情况下,应适用第七条或第十四条的规定。"①

本条对范本其他条款未涉及的所得规定了一般规则,故被称为"一揽子兜底条款"。这些所得不仅包括未明确其待遇的某类所得,也包括来源未加明确的所得。本条适用范围并不限于发生于缔约国一方的所得,还包括来自第三国的所得。本条第 2 款规定了第 1 款规定的例外情况,即该所得(除来源于不动产外)与缔约国一方居民设在缔约国另一方的常设机构或固定基地的活动有联系,也包括来源于第三国的所得。在这种情况下,征税权赋予该常设机构或固定基地所在的缔约国。至于如何判定常设机构或固定基地与之有实际联系,前文已作阐述,本节不再赘述。

本章阅读材料

Statement of Principles Used to Attribute Profits to a Permanent Establishment

—selected from 2010 OECD Report on the Attribution of Profits to Permanent Establishments

B-1. The "functionally separate entity approach"

8. The authorised OECD approach is that the profits to be attributed to a PE are the profits that the PE would have earned at arm's length, in particular in its dealings with other parts of the enterprise, if it were a separate and independent enterprise engaged in the same or similar activities under the same

---

① 《OECD 范本》第 21 条的规定与之相同,仅没有固定基地的规定,因为其对于独立劳务的规定已纳入第 7 条营业利润适用常设机构原则予以调整。

or similar conditions, taking into account the functions performed, assets used and risks assumed by the enterprise through the permanent establishment and through the other parts of the enterprise. The phrase "profits of an enterprise" in Article 7(1) should not be interpreted as affecting the determination of the quantum of the profits that are to be attributed to the PE, other than providing specific confirmation that "the right to tax does not extend to profits that the enterprise may derive from that State otherwise than through the permanent establishment" (i. e. there should be no "force of attraction principle"). Profits may therefore be attributed to a permanent establishment even though the enterprise as a whole has never made profits. Conversely, Article 7 may result in no profits being attributed to a permanent establishment even though the enterprise as a whole has made profits.

B-2. Basic premise of the authorised OECD approach

9. The authorised OECD approach does not dictate the specifics or mechanics of domestic law, but only sets a limit on the amount of attributable profit that may be taxed in the host country of the PE. Accordingly, the profits to be attributed to a PE are the profits that the PE would have earned at arm's length, in particular in its dealings with other parts of the enterprise, if it were a separate and independent enterprise engaged in the same or similar activities under the same or similar conditions, taking into account the functions performed, assets used and risks assumed by the enterprise through the permanent establishment and through the other parts of the enterprise, determined by applying the Guidelines by analogy. This is in line with one of the fundamental rationales behind the PE concept, which is to allow, within certain limits, the taxation of non-resident enterprises in respect of their activities (having regards to assets used and risks assumed) in the source jurisdiction. In addition, the authorised OECD approach is not designed to prevent the application of any domestic legislation aimed at preventing abuse of tax losses or tax credits by shifting the location of assets or risks. Finally, where their domestic law does not recognise loss transactions in certain circumstances between associated enterprises, countries may consider that the authorised OECD approach would not require the recognition of a loss on an analogous dealing in determining the profits of a PE.

10. The interpretation of Article 7(2) under the authorised OECD approach is that a two-step analysis is required. First, a functional and factual analysis, conducted in accordance with the guidance found in the Guidelines, must be performed in order to hypothesise appropriately the PE and the remainder of the enterprise (or a segment or segments thereof) as if they were associated enterprises, each undertaking functions, owning and/or using assets, assuming risks, and entering into dealings with each other and transactions with other related and unrelated enterprises. Under the first step, the functional and factual analysis must identify the economically significant activities and responsibilities undertaken by the PE. This analysis should, to the extent relevant, consider the PE's activities and responsibilities in the context of the activities and responsibilities undertaken by the enterprise as a whole, particularly those parts of the enterprise that engage in dealings with the PE. Under the second step, the remuneration of any dealings between the hypothesised enterprises is determined by applying by analogy the Article 9 transfer pricing tools (as articulated in the Guidelines for separate enterprises) by reference to the functions performed, assets used and risk assumed by the hypothesised enterprises. The result of these two steps will be to allow the calculation of the profits (or losses) of the PE from all its activities, including transactions with other unrelated enterprises, transactions with related enterprises (with direct application of the Guidelines) and dealings with other parts of the enterprise (under step 2 of the authorised OECD approach).

11. The hypothesis by which a PE is treated as a functionally separate and independent enterprise is a mere fiction necessary for purposes of determining the business profits of this part of the enterprise under Article 7. The authorised OECD approach should not be viewed as implying that the PE must be treated as a separate enterprise entering into dealings with the rest of the enterprise of which it is a part for purposes of any other provisions of the Convention.

12. These general principles are further discussed under Section D.

B-3. Step one: hypothesising the PE as a separate and independent enterprise

See Section D-2 for a more detailed discussion of step one of the authorised OECD approach.

(i) Functional and factual analysis

13. The functional and factual analysis under step two of the authorised OECD approach performs the same role in the comparability analysis in a PE context under Article 7 as it does in situations involving associated enterprises under Article 9. Notwithstanding this similarity, the functional and factual analysis has further applications under step one of the authorised OECD approach for purposes of hypothesising the PE as a "separate and independent enterprise engaged in the same or similar activities under the same or similar conditions, taking into account the functions performed, assets used and risks assumed by the enterprise through the permanent establishment and through the other parts of the enterprise". These further applications are necessary because a PE is not in fact legally separate from the rest of the enterprise of which it is a part in the way that an associated enterprise is legally separate from other enterprises within the same MNE group. This factual, legal difference gives rise to issues in a PE context that are not present in an associated enterprises context.

14. As between unrelated enterprises, the determination of which enterprise owns assets and which bears risk is determined by legally binding contracts or other ascertainable legal arrangements. Similar considerations apply to associated enterprises providing those contracts or legal arrangements reflect the underlying reality and meet the criteria in Chapter I of the Guidelines. Similarly, in a separate enterprise context no issues generally arise over determining which enterprise possesses the capital. The factual, legal position in a PE context, on the other hand, is that there is no single part of an enterprise which legally "owns" the assets, assumes the risks, possesses the capital or contracts with separate enterprises. The legal position is thus unhelpful in a PE context, since Article 7(2) requires the PE to be treated as if it were a separate and independent enterprise, performing its own functions, assuming its own risk and owning or using assets on its own. It is therefore necessary under the arm's length principle of Article 7 to develop a mechanism for attributing risks, economic ownership of assets and capital to the hypothetically separate and independent PE, for associating with the hypothetically separate and independent PE the rights and obligations arising

out of transactions between separate enterprises and the enterprise of which the PE is a part and for recognising and determining the nature of the "dealings" (i. e. the intra-enterprise equivalents of separate enterprise transactions) between the hypothetically separate PE and other parts of the enterprise of which the PE is a part.

15. As it is not possible to use a legal analysis as the required mechanism, another solution must be sought. After careful consideration, the OECD decided that a functional analysis should be used, as this concept underpins the application of the arm's length principle under Article 9 and there is already considerable guidance on how to conduct this analysis in the Guidelines. However, in order to address the issues created by the fact that legally the assets, risks, capital, and rights and obligations arising out of transactions with separate enterprises belong to the enterprise as a whole rather than to any one part of the enterprise and that there is no legal transaction between different parts of a single entity, it proved necessary to supplement the functional analysis of Article 9. Accordingly, the authorised OECD approach attributes to the PE those risks for which the significant functions relevant to the assumption and/or management (subsequent to the transfer) of risks are performed by people in the PE and also attributes to the PE economic ownership of assets for which the significant functions relevant to the economic ownership of assets are performed by people in the PE. The authorised OECD approach also sets forth approaches to attribute capital, including "free" capital (i. e. funding that does not give rise to a tax deductible return in the nature of interest), to the PE to support the functions it has performed, the risks assumed and assets attributed to it, as well as criteria for the recognition and characterisation of dealings between the PE and other parts of the enterprise to which it belongs.

16. The significant people functions relevant to the assumption of risk and the significant people functions relevant to the economic ownership of assets will vary from business sector to business sector (e. g. such functions are unlikely to be the same for an oil extraction company and a bank) and from enterprise to enterprise within sectors (e. g. not all oil extraction companies or all banks are the same). It should be stressed that a particular enterprise may

have one or more significant people functions relevant to the assumption of risk and to the economic ownership of assets, each of which has to be taken into account in the above analysis. The extent of the overlap between the significant people functions relevant to the assumption of risk and the significant people functions relevant to the economic ownership of assets will also vary from business sector to business sector and from enterprise to enterprise within sectors. For example, in the case of financial assets of financial enterprises, the same significant people functions will generally be relevant both to the assumption of risk and to the economic ownership of those assets. This special category of asset is discussed in Part II (bank loans), Part III (financial products of enterprises engaged in global trading), and Part IV (the assets representing the investment of reserves and surpluses derived from insurance business). Because of the special relationship between risks and financial assets in those specific sectors, the authorised OECD approach uses the "key entrepreneurial risk-taking function" ("KERT function") terminology in describing the functions relevant to the attribution of both risks and assets, but that terminology is not used for other sectors. Outside the financial enterprise sector, risks may be less intimately linked with assets, so that there may be less overlap between the significant people functions relevant to the assumption of risk and those relevant to the economic ownership of the assets.

17. Whilst it is important under the first step of the authorised OECD approach to identify the significant people functions relevant to the assumption of risk and those relevant to the economic ownership of assets, it is also important under the first step to analyse other functions performed by the PE. This is because the profits (or losses) of the PE will be based upon all its activities, including transactions with other unrelated enterprises, transactions with related enterprises (with direct application of the Guidelines) and dealings with other parts of the enterprise (under step 2 of the authorised OECD approach). Under the second step of the authorised OECD approach the Guidelines are applied by analogy to the PE's dealings with other parts of the enterprise to ensure that the performance of all of its functions in relation to these dealings is rewarded on an arm's length basis. The dealings of the hypothesised separate and independent enterprise will be compared to

transactions of independent enterprises performing the same or similar functions, using the same or similar assets, assuming the same or similar risks and possessing the same or similar economically relevant characteristics. The transfer pricing methods set out in the Guidelines are applied to determine an arm's length price for the dealings. It should be noted that there is no presumption that functions other than significant people functions relevant to the assumption of risk and significant people functions relevant to the economic ownership of assets are by nature of low value. This will be determined by the functional and comparability analyses based on the particular facts and circumstances.

(ii) Attribution of assets

18. Under the authorised OECD approach it is necessary to hypothesise the PE as if it were a separate and independent enterprise. This exercise entails, inter alia, the determination of which assets are "economically owned" and/or used by the PE and in what capacity. The factual position is that no one part of an enterprise owns assets; they belong to the enterprise as a whole. It is therefore necessary under the first step of the authorised OECD approach to find a means of attributing economic ownership. One possible approach would be to allow taxpayers to simply nominate which part of the enterprise economically owns the assets. This approach, though simple and administrable, would potentially provide an incentive for taxpayers to attribute economic ownership of assets in ways that would lead to inappropriate allocations of profit and thus has been rejected as not in accordance with sound tax policy. Instead there is a broad consensus that assets generally are to be attributed to the part of the enterprise which performs the significant people functions relevant to the determination of economic ownership of assets. The functional and factual analysis will examine all the facts and circumstances to determine the extent to which the assets of the enterprise are used in the functions performed by the PE and the conditions under which the assets are used, including the factors to be taken into account to determine which part of the enterprise is regarded as the economic owner of the assets actually owned by the enterprise. The attribution of economic ownership of assets will have consequences for both the attribution of capital and interest-bearing debt and

the attribution of profit to the PE.

19. The consequences of attributing economic ownership of assets under the first step for determining profits under the second step may depend upon the type of asset and the type of business in which the asset is used. For example, economically owning a tangible asset used in a manufacturing process does not necessarily, of itself, attribute to the economic owner of the asset the income from selling goods produced by using the asset. Attributing economic ownership of financial assets, on the other hand, attributes the income and expenses associated with holding those assets or lending them out or selling them to third parties.

20. In the case of financial assets of financial enterprises, the creation and management of such assets (and their attendant risks) is itself the significant people function relevant to determining the initial economic ownership of the assets, so the initial attribution of economic ownership of those assets to the part of the enterprise performing that function has primary importance not only for determining characterisation of the "separate and independent enterprise" under step one, but also to the attribution of profits under step two, since the attribution of income-generating assets also effectively determines which part of the enterprise receives the income and expenses associated with those assets. This special category of asset is discussed in Part II (bank loans), Part III (financial products of enterprises engaged in global trading) and Part IV (the assets representing the investment of reserves and surpluses derived from insurance business).

(iii) Attribution of risks

21. The functional and factual analysis will initially attribute to the PE any risks inherent in, or created by, the PE's own significant people functions relevant to the assumption of risks and take into account any subsequent dealings or transactions related to the subsequent transfer of risks or to the transfer of the management of those risks to different parts of the enterprise or to other enterprises. The term "risk assumption" refers to the initial assumption of risk but it is not necessary that the same part of the enterprise subsequently be treated as having retained the risk assumed. Being attributed risks in the Article 7 context means the equivalent of bearing risks for income

tax purposes by a separate enterprise, with the attendant benefits and burdens, in particular the potential exposure to gains or losses from the realisation or non-realisation of said risks. This raises the question of whether, and if so, in what circumstances, dealings resulting in the transfers of risks should be recognised within a single entity so that risks initially assumed by one part of the enterprise will be treated as subsequently borne by another part of the enterprise. The circumstances in which it is possible to recognise such a transfer are discussed in Section D-2(vi).

22. Depending on the nature of the enterprise's business, some risks will be related to the potential loss in value of assets attributed to the PE while some other risks will be created by activities and not necessarily linked to the simple existence of the assets (e.g. liability risks). The significant people functions relevant to the assumption of risks are those which require active decision-making with regard to the acceptance and/or management (subsequent to the transfer) of those risks. The extent of the decision-making will depend on the nature of the risk involved.

23. By way of illustration, take the example of an enterprise which consists of a head office in one jurisdiction and one PE in another jurisdiction. Assume products are manufactured at the head office location and delivered to the PE premises for sale to customers in the PE jurisdiction. Assume the manufacturing functions are performed by employees of the head office and the sales are concluded by employees of the PE. A functional and factual analysis is performed and concludes that in this particular instance this particular PE is acting as a distributor of the head office products. In this example it might be necessary to attribute, among others, excess inventory risk and credit risk.

24. Under the authorised OECD approach, the attribution of these risks within the single enterprise will follow from the identification of the significant people functions relevant to the initial acceptance and subsequent management of those risks:

- The excess inventory risk is likely to be regarded as initially assumed by that part of the enterprise which makes the active decisions related to inventory levels. Depending on the circumstances of the case, this may be either the head office or the PE.

- The credit risk is likely to be regarded as initially assumed by that part of the enterprise which decides to conclude a sale to a particular customer after having reviewed the creditworthiness of this customer. A question may arise however where a review of the creditworthiness of each customer is performed by one part of the enterprise before a sale is concluded by another part of the enterprise. In such a case, the functional and factual analysis would have to examine whether the people in charge of reviewing the customers' creditworthiness are in effect the ones making a decision that leads to the assumption of credit risk, or if they act as a support function for the PE which ultimately makes the decision of whether or not to sell to a particular customer.

25. Note that the fact that general parameters for inventory levels or credit risks might potentially be set by another part of the enterprise would not change the assumption of the risk, as the significant people functions relevant to the assumption of risks are those which involve active decision-making.

26. The attribution and measurement of risk is an important part of the functional and factual analysis since the presence of risk affects both the attribution of capital under step one of the authorised OECD approach and the attribution of profits to the PE under the second step. Under step one of the authorised OECD approach, since capital follows risks, the part of the enterprise that performs the significant people functions relevant to the assumption of risks (or that performs the significant people functions relevant to taking over and managing a risk initially assumed by another part of the enterprise) would be attributed the capital necessary to support these risks. Under the second step of the authorised OECD approach, the selection and application of a transfer pricing method will take into account risks assumed by the PE and by other parts of the enterprise it has dealings with.

27. The attribution of risk is particularly important in the financial sector where it has a substantial impact on the attribution of both capital and income and expenses to the PE, but it can also be important in other businesses. The financial sector, because of the nature of its business, has very sophisticated risk measurement tools. Outside the financial sector it will still be necessary—although often more difficult—to measure risk.

(iv) Attribution of free capital

28. The functional and factual analysis will attribute "free" capital (i. e. funding that does not give rise to a tax deductible return in the nature of interest) to the PE for tax purposes, to ensure an arm's length attribution of profits to the PE. The starting point for the attribution of capital is that under the arm's length principle a PE should have sufficient capital to support the functions it undertakes, the assets it economically owns and the risks it assumes. In the financial sector regulations stipulate minimum levels of regulatory capital to provide a cushion in the event that some of the risks inherent in the business crystallise into financial loss. Capital provides a similar cushion against crystallisation of risk in non-financial sectors.

29. A key distinction between a separate legal enterprise and a PE is that one legal enterprise can enter into a legally binding agreement to guarantee all the risks assumed as a result of the functions performed by another legal enterprise. For such a guarantee to have substance, the "free" capital needed to support the risks assumed would reside in a different legal enterprise from that in which the transactions giving rise to the risks are booked. In contrast one of the key factual conditions of an enterprise trading through a PE is that the "free" capital and risks are not segregated from each other within a single legal enterprise. To attempt to do so for tax purposes (i. e. to treat one part of an enterprise as able to guarantee a risk assumed by another part of the enterprise) would contradict the factual situation and would not be consistent with the authorised OECD approach. Capital needed to support risks must be regarded as following the risks. In other words, capital needed to support risks is to be attributed to a PE by reference to the risks attributed to it and not the other way round.

30. The attribution of "free" capital should be carried out in accordance with the arm's length principle to ensure that a fair and appropriate amount of profits is allocated to the PE. The purpose of the attribution is to inform the attribution of profits to the PE under Article 7(2). The Report describes a number of different possible approaches for applying that principle in practice, recognising that the attribution of "free" capital to a PE is not an exact science, and that any particular facts and circumstances are likely to give rise

to a range of arm's length results for the "free" capital attributable to a PE, not a single figure. There is a common premise to the authorised approaches to attributing "free" capital, that an internal condition of the PE is that the creditworthiness of the PE is generally the same as the enterprise of which it is a part.

31. The authorised OECD approach recognises a range of acceptable approaches for attributing "free" capital that are capable of giving an arm's length result, each with its own strengths and weaknesses, which become more or less material depending on the facts and circumstances of particular cases. Different methods adopt different starting points for determining the amount of "free" capital attributable to a PE, which either put more emphasis on the actual structure of the enterprise of which the PE is a part or alternatively, on the capital structures of comparable independent enterprises. The key to attributing "free" capital is to recognise:

• The existence of strengths and weaknesses in any approach and when these are likely to be present (discussed in more detail in Section D-2(v)(b)(2)).

• That there is no single arm's length amount of "free capital", but a range of potential capital attributions within which it is possible to find an amount of "free" capital that can meet the basic principle set out above.

(a) Funding costs

32. The PE requires a certain amount of funding, made up of "free" capital and interest-bearing debt. The objective is to attribute an arm's length amount of interest to the PE, using one of the authorised approaches to attributing "free" capital in order to support the functions, assets and risks attributed to the PE. These issues are discussed in more detail in Section D-2(v)(b)(3).

(v) Recognition of dealings

33. There are a number of aspects to the recognition (or not) of dealings between a PE and the rest of the enterprise of which it is a part. First, a PE is not the same as a subsidiary, and is not in fact legally or economically separate from the rest of the enterprise of which it is a part. It follows that:

• Save in exceptional circumstances, all parts of the enterprise have the same creditworthiness. This means that dealings between a PE and the rest of the enterprise of which it is a part should be priced on the basis that both share the same creditworthiness; and

• There is no scope for the rest of the enterprise to guarantee the PE's creditworthiness, or for the PE to guarantee the creditworthiness of the rest of the enterprise.

34. Second, dealings between a PE and the rest of the enterprise of which it is a part have no legal consequences for the enterprise as a whole. This implies a need for greater scrutiny of dealings between a PE and the rest of the enterprise of which it is a part than of transactions between two associated enterprises. This also implies a greater scrutiny of documentation (in the inevitable absence, for example, of legally binding contracts) that might otherwise exist and considering the uniqueness of this issue, countries would wish to require taxpayers to demonstrate clearly that it would be appropriate to recognise the dealing.

35. This greater scrutiny means a threshold needs to be passed before a dealing is accepted as equivalent to a transaction that would have taken place between independent enterprises acting at arm's length. Only once that threshold is passed can a dealing be reflected in the attribution of profits under Article 7(2). The functional and factual analysis must determine whether a real and identifiable event has occurred and should be taken into account as a dealing of economic significance between the PE and another part of the enterprise.

36. Thus, for example, an accounting record and contemporaneous documentation showing a dealing that transfers economically significant risks, responsibilities and benefits would be a useful starting point for the purposes of attributing profits. Taxpayers are encouraged to prepare such documentation, as it may reduce substantially the potential for controversies regarding application of the authorised OECD approach. Tax administrations would give effect to such documentation, notwithstanding its lack of legal effect, to the extent that:

• the documentation is consistent with the economic substance of the activities taking place within the enterprise as revealed by the functional and factual analysis;

• the arrangements documented in relation to the dealing, viewed in their entirety, do not differ from those which would have been adopted by comparable independent enterprises behaving in a commercially rational manner or, if they do so differ, the structure as presented in the taxpayer's documentation does not practically impede the tax administration from determining an appropriate transfer price; and

• the dealing presented in the taxpayer's documentation does not violate the principles of the authorised OECD approach by, for example, purporting to transfer risks in a way that segregates them from functions.

See paragraphs 1.48-1.54 and 1.64-1.69 of the Guidelines by analogy.

37. It is important to note, however, that the authorised OECD approach is generally not intended to impose more burdensome documentation requirements in connection with intra-enterprise dealings than apply to transactions between associated enterprises. Moreover, as in the case of transfer pricing documentation under the Guidelines, the requirements should not be applied in such a way as to impose on taxpayers costs and burdens disproportionate to the circumstances.

38. Third, where dealings are capable of being recognised, they may lead to a transfer of assets and/or risks between the PE and other parts of the enterprise to which it belongs. As a consequence the characterisation and recognition of dealings will affect the attribution of risks, assets and therefore capital to the PE.

B-4. Step two: determining the profits of the hypothesised separate and independent enterprise based upon a comparability analysis

See Section D-3 for a more detailed discussion of step two of the authorised OECD approach.

39. Where dealings are capable of being recognised, they should be priced on an arm's length basis, assuming the PE and the rest of the enterprise of which it is a part to be independent of one another. This should be done using by analogy the guidance on transfer pricing methods contained in the Guidelines.

40. The authorised OECD approach is to undertake a comparison of

dealings between the PE and the enterprise of which it is a part, with transactions between independent enterprises. This comparison is to be made by following, by analogy, the comparability analysis described in the Guidelines. By analogy with the Guidelines, comparability in the PE context means either that none of the differences (if any) between the dealing and the transaction between independent enterprises materially affects the measure used to attribute profit to the PE, or that reasonably accurate adjustments can be made to eliminate the material effects of such differences. Principles similar to the aggregation rules of Chapter III of the Guidelines should also apply to permit the PE's dealings to be aggregated, where appropriate, in determining the PE's attributable profit.

41. Under the authorised OECD approach, for purposes of determining the arm's length remuneration of dealings, the most appropriate method to the circumstances of the case should be selected and applied by analogy to the guidance in the Guidelines.

42. In an arm's length transaction an independent enterprise normally would seek to charge for making a provision in such a way as to generate profit, rather than providing it merely at cost, although there can be circumstances in which a provision made at an arm's length price will not result in a profit (e.g. see paragraph 7.33 of the Guidelines in connection with the provision of services).

43. Section D-3(iv) contains a discussion of some commonly occurring dealings which require special mention-dealings involving changes in the use of tangible assets, intangible assets, cost contribution arrangements and internal service dealings.

B-5. Summary of the two-step analysis

44. The attribution of profits to a PE of an enterprise on an arm's length basis will follow from the calculation of the profits (or losses) from all its activities, including transactions with other unrelated enterprises, transactions with related enterprises (with direct application of the Guidelines) and dealings with other parts of the enterprise (under step 2 of the authorised OECD approach). This analysis involves the following two steps:

Step One

A functional and factual analysis, leading to:

—The attribution to the PE as appropriate of the rights and obligations arising out of transactions between the enterprise of which the PE is a part and separate enterprises;

—The identification of significant people functions relevant to the attribution of economic ownership of assets, and the attribution of economic ownership of assets to the PE;

—The identification of significant people functions relevant to the assumption of risks, and the attribution of risks to the PE;

—The identification of other functions of the PE;

—The recognition and determination of the nature of those dealings between the PE and other parts of the same enterprise that can appropriately be recognised, having passed the threshold test; and

—The attribution of capital based on the assets and risks attributed to the PE.

Step Two

The pricing on an arm's length basis of recognised dealings through:

—The determination of comparability between the dealings and uncontrolled transactions, established by applying the Guidelines' comparability factors directly (characteristics of property or services, economic circumstances and business strategies) or by analogy (functional analysis, contractual terms) in light of the particular factual circumstances of the PE; and

—Selecting and applying by analogy to the guidance in the Guidelines the most appropriate method to the circumstances of the case to arrive at an arm's length compensation for the dealings between the PE and the rest of the enterprise, taking into account the functions performed by and the assets and risks attributed to the PE.

The pricing on an arm's length basis of any transactions with associated enterprises attributed to the PE should follow the guidance in the Guidelines and is not discussed in this Report. The order of the listing of items within each of the steps above is not meant to be prescriptive, as the various items may be interrelated (e.g. risk is initially attributed to a PE as it performs the significant people functions relevant to the assumption of that risk but the recognition and characterisation of a subsequent dealing between the PE and another part of the enterprise that manages the risk may lead to a transfer of the risk and supporting capital to the other part of the enterprise).

45. It can be seen that the functional and factual analysis is primarily needed to hypothesise the PE as a functionally separate entity, to identify the significant people functions relevant to determining which part of the enterprise assumes and/or subsequently manages particular risks and economically owns particular assets, and to attribute to the PE as a hypothetically separate entity an appropriate amount of capital. This step of the analysis is likewise necessary to identify which part of the enterprise should be hypothesised to have undertaken the enterprise's rights and obligations arising from transactions with other enterprises and what dealings should be hypothesised to exist between the PE and other parts of the enterprise. Secondly, it is important to identify the respective functions performed by both the PE and other parts of the enterprise with which it is hypothesised to have dealings in order to price those dealings under the second step of the authorised OECD approach.

B-6. Dependent agent PEs

46. This Report does not examine the issue of whether a PE exists under Article 5(5) of the OECD Model Tax Convention (a so-called "dependent agent PE") but discusses the consequences of finding that a dependent agent PE exists in terms of the profits that should be attributed to the dependent agent PE.

47. Where a dependent agent PE is found to exist under Article 5(5), the question arises as to how to attribute profits to the PE. The answer is to follow the same principles as used for other types of PEs, for to do otherwise would be inconsistent with Article 7 and the arm's length principle. Under the first step of the authorised OECD approach a functional and factual analysis determines the functions undertaken by the dependent agent enterprise both on its own account and on behalf of the non-resident enterprise. On the one hand the dependent agent enterprise will be rewarded for the service it provides to the non-resident enterprise (taking into account its assets and its risks (if

any)). On the other hand, the dependent agent PE will be attributed the assets and risks of the non-resident enterprise relating to the functions performed by the dependent agent enterprise on behalf of the non-resident, together with sufficient capital to support those assets and risks. The authorised OECD approach then attributes profits to the dependent agent PE on the basis of those assets, risks and capital.

第五章 国际避税与反避税

随着经济全球化的不断深化,跨国公司和个人为了追求利益最大化,纷纷利用各国税收体制的差异来实现减轻税负的目的,国际避税现象普遍存在。国际避税行为不仅侵害了国家的税收权益,也影响了正常的国际税收秩序。国际避税与反避税已成为国际税收关系中受到广泛关注的焦点。国际避税的常见方式包括滥用协定、资本弱化、转让定价、受控外国公司等。鉴于转让定价制度的内容较多,本书另辟一章介绍。

第一节 国际避税与反避税概述

一、国际避税的概念

对于避税概念的界定,需要在一个更为广泛的概念——策略性税收行为(strategic tax behaviors)下予以理解。策略性税收行为是指其目的在于减少税收义务的行为,该行为可以分为三类:逃税(tax evasion)、避税(tax avoidance)和合法的节税(licit tax savings)。[①] 对于这三种行为的定义,学术界争论已久,实践中也存在很多不明确之处。尽管如此,我们还是可以对这些术语的根本属性作出界定。

逃税是指有意的违法行为,如直接违反税法以逃避支付税款的义务。避税是指所有旨在减少纳税义务的不合理行为,这些行为并不违反法律的字面意思,但却明显违反法律的精神。合法的节税是指既不违反法律规定也不违反其精神,旨在减轻税收负担的可接受的税收行为,也被称为合理的税收筹划。国际避税则是指跨国纳税人利用各国税收法规的漏洞和差异,或利用国际税收协定中的缺陷,通过形式上不违法但违背税法精神的方式,来谋求减轻或规避税收负担的行为。

逃税的非法性和节税的合法性是明晰的,而避税行为是否合法则要对个案分别进行考量。每个国家都有自己的反避税政策和规则,都面临界定合法节税

[①] See Reuven Avi-Yonah, Global Perspectives on Income Taxation Law, Oxford University Press, 2011, pp. 101-102.

行为和非法避税行为的问题。由于标准缺乏明晰性和统一性,同一交易在一国可能被认为是符合税法的,而在另一国则可能与其税法相悖。因此,对避税概念的把握除了掌握其理论上的基本属性之外,更重要的是要在具体案例中去甄别。

二、国际避税产生的原因及主要方式

国际避税的产生是内外因共同作用的结果。首先,在内因方面,国际避税的出现是企业追求利润最大化的产物。通过规避税负以实现税后利润最大化,是跨国纳税人实现经营战略目标的重要手段。与非法的逃税方式相比,避税行为更具隐蔽性,因此为跨国纳税人所青睐。其次,国际避税又是外在因素影响的产物。这里的外在因素主要表现为各国税收制度的差异,如关于税收管辖权标准、征税对象和税率、税收优惠措施等方面的差异,跨国纳税人正是利用这些差异来实施避税。国际避税在形式上可以分为如下几种类型:

第一,利用纳税主体的跨国流动进行避税。这一方式主要是通过调整纳税主体在居民税收管辖权和公民税收管辖权方面的连结点,以期获得相应的避税好处,其具体表现形式依自然人和法人两类不同的纳税主体而有所差异。从自然人角度来说,由于一国一般以国籍、住所或居住时间为实施税收管辖权的依据,跨国纳税人可以借助改变国籍、迁移住所或者人为地缩短居住时间等方式来规避一国税收管辖权的适用,从而达到避税目的。从法人角度来说,主要是跨国公司,由于不同国家对于法人的管辖权适用不同的认定标准,跨国纳税人可以人为地选择法人登记注册地,或者改变法人的实际管理中心或控制中心所在地,将法人的注册地、实际管理中心或者控制中心调整到低税国甚至无税国,从而有效规避在高税国境内的纳税义务,以达到减轻税负的目的。

第二,利用征税对象的跨国移动进行避税。这是当前国际避税的重要方式,各国税收征管部门广泛关注的主要是以下两种形式:一种是利用国际避税地进行避税。跨国纳税人通过在国际避税地设立"基地公司",将在避税地境外获取的财产、收入和所得汇集到"基地公司"的账户下,从而利用避税地的低税率或者免税优惠达到避税的目的。另一种是跨国关联企业通过转让定价进行国际避税,这主要体现于跨国企业利用关联企业所在国家征税税率上的差异,人为地进行转让定价安排,将利润从高税负国移转到低税负国,从而大大减轻自身税负,获取高额的税后利润。转让定价是当前跨国纳税人采用最多的避税形式。

第三,通过改变征税对象的性质进行避税。这种形式在当前税务实践中主要体现为改变企业的资本结构,即利用债务资本和股权资本在税收待遇方面的差别,人为地调整债务资本和股权资本在公司资本结构中的比例。由于债务资本所需支付的利息在税收待遇方面优于股权资本所需支付的股息,利息可以作为费用在税前扣除,不像股息那样可能会遭受经济性双重征税,更多的企业选择通过提高债务资本的比例,实行所谓的"资本弱化",来实现减轻税负、增加企业税后利润的目的。

三、国际反避税的主要途径

国际避税严重侵害有关国家的税收利益,危及正常的税收秩序,规制国际避税已成为当前各国税收征管工作中的重要内容。从立法和实践看,各国的反避税措施可以分为国内法途径和国际法途径,国内法途径主要是制定和实施一般反避税规则和特别反避税规则,而国际法途径则主要是国际税务行政合作。

(一) 国内法途径

1. 一般反避税规则

一般反避税规则是指税务机关按照实质重于形式、禁止滥用法律等原则,对企业实施的以避税为目的的不合理行为进行审核评估和调查调整的规则。

(1) 实质重于形式原则(substance over form doctrine)。根据该原则,税务主管当局可以忽略交易的法律形式而审查交易的经济实质。如一项收入本来是经营性收入,但纳税人却通过交易步骤的设计使其成为资本利得,从而享受关于资本利得的税收优惠,税务当局则可以根据实质重于形式原则将该收入重新定性为经营性收入予以征税。

分步交易原则(step transaction doctrine)是对实质重于形式原则的发展,该原则认为,只要有合法的经济实质,对纳税人交易的形式一般应当予以尊重,即使采用另一种方式会产生更多的税收。然而,如果一项交易包括多个步骤,且这些步骤都专注于最终的结果,那么税务当局可以以将该多个步骤的交易视为一个整体,即可以忽视经济上没有意义的步骤,评估整个交易结果的税收待遇。实质重于形式原则的另一个发展是经济实质或商业目的原则(economic substance or business purpose doctrine),即要使一项交易在税法上有效,必须要有节税以外的商业目的(或善意目的或经济实质)。我国在制定2008年《企业所得税法》时首次引入了一般反避税规则概念。《企业所得税法》第47条将一般反避税规则所适用的安排定义为"企业实施其他不具有合理商业目的的安排而减少其应纳税收入或者所得额",同时在《企业所得税法实施条例》第120条中进一步解释"不具有合理商业目的,是指以减少、免除或者推迟缴纳税款为主要目的";《企业所得税法实施条例》第123条规定,对企业实施其他不具有合理商业目的安排的,税务机关有权在该业务发生的纳税年度起10年内进行纳税调整。

有些国家并没有规定完整意义上的一般反避税规则,而是直接应用实质重于形式原则来对避税行为进行调整。如美国,其立法中并没有确立一般反避税规则,法院采用实质重于形式原则来否定那些避税交易中的税收安排,并根据商业目的、经济实质、分步交易测试等原则和方法来进行调整。通常而言,一项交易只有在符合下列条件时才被认为具有经济实质:该项交易改变了纳税人的经济地位;该纳税人对于该项交易有实质性目的(除了税收目的)。如果一项交易没有经济实质,那么该项交易不但会被否定(或根据其实质重新定性),而且纳税人还将被处以相当于该项交易应纳税额一定比例的罚金。除了美国之外,英国、以色列等国也采用类似的做法。[①]

(2) 滥用法律原则(abuse of law doctrine)。该原则强调征纳双方利益的平衡,国家肯定纳税人有权追求税收负担最小化,采取合法形式来安排交易活动,但如果纳税人开展的交易活动除了追求避税目的以外不具有诚实信用的商业目的,这一交易行为将被认定为与立法意图和法律精神相违背,从而被界定为"滥用法律",应予以否定并按照正常交易行为进行征税。不难看出,该原则与实质重于形式原则有异曲同工之妙,德国、法国、巴西是采用该原则的典型国家。

实践中,很多国家采用上述两种原则结合的混合模式,如意大利、瑞典、日本、加拿大、澳大利亚、印度、俄罗斯等。

2. 特别反避税规则

针对特定的避税行为制定专门的规制办法是国际反避税实践领域的一大发展,与一般反避税规则不同的是,特别反避税规则针对的是特别类型化的避税行为。例如,针对跨国纳税人利用国际避税地进行避税制定专门的避税地规制办法;针对跨国企业利用转让定价行为进行避税制定出专门的转让定价规则;针对资本弱化的避税行为制定专门的资本弱化规则;针对跨国纳税人利用受控外国公司进行避税而制定专门的受控外国公司税制等等。这些特别反避税规则将在本章其他部分详细阐述。

(二) 国际法途径

基于国际避税的跨国性特征,任何单个国家都无法准确地掌握跨国纳税人位于境外的资产和收入状况,因此,要有效地打击国际避税行为,必须借助各国的合作。当前,国际反避税实践在这方面已经取得实质性进展,具体体现为以下两个方面:一是完善了国际税收协定的有关条款,防止第三国居民通过套用税收

---

① See Reuven Avi-Yonah, Global Perspectives on Income Taxation Law, Oxford University Press, 2011, pp. 104-105.

协定进行避税。例如,越来越多的国家在其对外签订的税收协定中制定了反滥用税收协定的专门条款,强化了受益所有人的认定等等。二是拓宽了国际税务合作的广度和深度,近年来越来越多的国家在税务情报交换、税收征收协助以及谈签预约定价安排等方面展开合作,使得国际税务合作不断向纵深发展。

第二节 滥用税收协定

一、滥用税收协定的概念和危害

在国际税收实践中,由于各主权国家的税收政策之间存在着差异,导致纳税人在进行跨国投资和贸易时往往会遇到双重征税的问题。双重征税会加重纳税人的税负,抑制国际投资和国际贸易的发展。为避免这种双重征税现象,各国均采取了不同的措施,其中最常见也最有效的方法便是签订税收协定。税收协定的签订促进了全球贸易和投资的发展,在充分尊重国家税收主权的同时又兼顾了对纳税人利益的保障。

迄今为止,税收协定以双边形式居多,但并非所有国家之间都签订了双边税收协定。按照互惠原则,通常只有协定缔约国的居民才能享受协定规定的税收优惠或抵免政策,非协定缔约国则不能享受这些优惠政策。于是,一些非缔约国的居民往往会采取各种手段,通过在协定缔约国境内设立非实际经营的公司,从而取得本不该属于其的税收优惠,这种行为便是滥用国际税收协定。简而言之,滥用税收协定是指非税收协定缔约国的居民通过在税收协定缔约国设立中介公司的做法获取其本不应享有的税收协定中的税收优惠。这些税收优惠通常包括税收抵免、延缓缴纳税金、差别优惠税率等等。

滥用国际税收协定具有多方面的危害性,具体体现为以下几个方面:

首先,滥用税收协定使得有关国家蒙受巨大的税收损失。税收是各国主要的财政收入,没有稳定的税收来源,国家财政支出就很难维系。然而,滥用税收协定的行为显然会使得有关国家税收收入下降,导致财政赤字甚至财政危机,影响到国家机器的正常运转。

其次,滥用税收协定违背了缔约双方的缔约初衷。税收协定是缔约国双方在对等互惠原则的基础上经过谈判确定的,其适用的纳税人范围,应仅限于具有缔约国一方居民身份的纳税人。如果第三国居民能够通过某种途径享受协定下的优惠,则有违缔约国双方签订协定条款的初衷,损害有关国家的税收利益。

最后,滥用税收协定不利于其他国家之间签订更多的税收协定。由于滥用税收协定的现象的存在,导致非协定缔约国居民也可以利用协定提供的便利,这种"搭便车"的现象会使得各国在签订税收协定之时产生更多的担忧,丧失签订协定的积极性。

二、滥用税收协定的主要方式

纳税人滥用税收协定的方式主要可分为以下两种:

（一）设立直接导管公司

所谓设立直接导管公司,是指营业地在第三国的滥用税收协定人通过在某一缔约国内设立非实际营业的导管公司,利用该公司所处国家与目标公司所处国家之间税收协定所提供的优惠税收待遇,达到避税的目的。如图5-1所示,营业地在A国的A公司与营业地在B国的B公司进行国际贸易,由于A、B两国之间并无税收协定,A公司选择在与A、B两国均有税收协定的C国内建立导管公司C公司,通过C公司来与B公司进行贸易。如此一来,A公司便享受到了本不能享受到的税收优惠,这里的C公司便是直接导管公司。

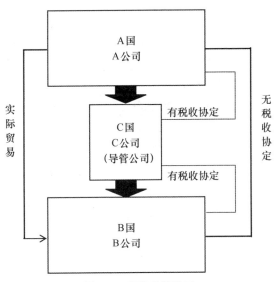

图5-1 直接导管公司

在选择导管公司所在地时,通常要综合考虑以下两个因素:一是税率较低,或者完全放弃对外来收入的征税权的国家或地区;二是该国家或地区与有关国家或地区之间具有关于税收抵免的税收协定。设立直接导管公司的避税方法表面上看是正常的商业行为,但它毕竟以避税为目的,不仅会扭曲跨国投资和贸易的流向,影响正常的经济秩序,同时对其他纳税人也有失公允。

(二) 设立间接导管公司

相比设立直接导管公司,设立间接导管公司则更为隐秘和间接。设立间接导管公司是指利用两个以上的非实际营业的导管公司进行避税的行为。这种滥用税收协定的做法往往涉及多个国家,纳税人为了逃避在与本国并无税收协定的国家的税收,往往在两个甚至更多的国家设立空壳公司,通过利用这些国家相互之间的税收协定中关于税收抵免等税收优惠条款,达到避税目的。如图5-2所示,营业地在A国的A公司与营业地在B国的B公司进行国际贸易。由于A、B两国之间并无税收协定,而设立直接导管公司的情形并不能使A公司达到避税的目的,于是A公司选择在C国、D国、E国等若干国家境内设立多个导管公司,导管公司之间并没有实质性的商业交易。其中,A与C、C与D、D与E等相邻国家间均有税收协定。A公司通过这一系列的导管公司,利用这些国家间的税收协定提供的便利和优惠,完成与B公司之间的交易,享受了其本不应享有的协定优惠,这就是间接导管公司避税方法。

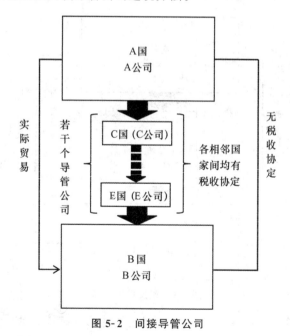

图 5-2　间接导管公司

三、滥用税收协定的规制措施

如前所述,滥用税收协定具有多重危害性,为了防止和消除这些危害,各国均依据本国法中的一般反避税规则或特别反避税规则来加以规制,瑞士还专门制定了《防止税收协定滥用法》。① 我国《特别纳税调整办法(试行)》在第92条专门作出规定,对于企业滥用税收协定进行避税安排的,税务机关可启动一般反避税调查。

除了各国国内法规定以外,两大范本及其注释中也详细规定了在条约层面防止滥用税收协定的措施。具体而言,协定层面的规制措施可分为以下几种:

(一)一般反滥用税收协定条款

一般反滥用条款是普遍适用的、不针对特定对象的协定滥用规制措施,具体包括:

1. 透视法(the look-through approach)

顾名思义,透视法是探求公司本身的实质,通过对公司实质的分析来判断是否适用税收协定。根据透视法,适用税收协定的公司不仅需要营业地(居住地)在缔约国,其主要股东的居所地也需要在缔约国。如此透视"公司面纱",就可有效避免第三国国民在缔约国设立公司继而利用税收协定的现象发生。透视法作为一般反滥用税收协定条款中的重要条款,为世界各国在签订税收协定时广泛采用。

《OECD范本》对透视法的规定见之于第1条的注释第13段,规定如果缔约国一方的某公司被非该缔约国的居民直接地或通过一个或多个公司(不管为何国居民)间接地拥有或控制,这种缔约国一方的居民公司的任何所得、收益或利润,不应享受本协定的税收减免待遇。

2. 征税法(the subject-to-tax approach)

征税法是指在一个国家享受税收协定优惠的前提是在另一国家已经就相同交易缴纳过一定税额的方法。由于税收协定的主要宗旨在于避免双重征税,征税法的考虑便在于只有在出现双重征税的情况下才能适用税收协定给予纳税人的税收抵免等优惠措施。《OECD范本》第1条注释第15段规定:"当发生于缔约国一方的所得由缔约国另一方居民公司取得,并且不在该缔约国另一方居住的一个或多个人:(1)直接或间接或通过一个或多个公司,不论其为何国居民,

---

① 瑞士《防止税收协定滥用法》规定,必须满足以下条件才能享受瑞士与其他国家签订的税收协定中的优惠待遇:在瑞士设立的公司的债务不得超过其股本金的6倍;该公司向居住在瑞士以外的纳税人以利息、使用费、广告费等形式支付的款项不能超过享受某一实施的税收协定优惠所得的50%;在如果有非居民在瑞士具有控制权益的情况下,非居民根据税收协定所享受的税收优惠的所得中,至少有25%应当作为股息分配而缴纳瑞士的预提税。综合上述条件可以看出,如果有第三国的纳税人控制了某一瑞士公司的大部分股权,那么将很难根据瑞士对外签署的税收协定享受到税收优惠。

以参股或其他形式拥有该公司的实质性股权;或者(2)直接或间接,单独或共同对该公司行使管理或控制,则本协定规定的任何给予免税或减税的措施仅适用于根据最后提及的国家之税法的一般性规定负有纳税义务的所得。"目前,瑞士、英国、德国等国家在实践中采用了这一方法。

3. 渠道法(the channel approach)

渠道法是指如果某一公司将特定比例的利润用作支付给第三国个人或公司,则这个公司的股息、利息等就不得享受税收协定所规定的税收优惠。渠道法主要针对的是设立间接导管公司的避税措施。间接导管公司避税措施虽然隐秘,但有一个共同点,均是利用设在某一国家的导管公司向位于第三国的个人或公司支付大额利润,从中获得税收利益。《OECD范本》第1条注释第17段规定:"发生于缔约国一方的所得由缔约国另一方的居民公司取得,并且由非该缔约国另一方居民的一个或多个人:(1)直接或间接或通过一个或多个公司,不论其为何国居民,以参股或其他形式拥有该公司的实质性股权;或者(2)直接或间接,单独或共同参与该公司的管理或控制。如果上述这种所得的50%以上用于偿付上述人的债权(包括利息、特许权使用费等),本协定给予的任何免税或减税规定应不适用。"实践中采用这一方法的国家很多,如瑞士与美国的双边税收协定中就有类似的规定,丹麦、德国、比利时等国家在其对外签订的税收协定中也采用了这种方法。

4. 善意条款(bona fide provision)

除上述三种方法外,《OECD范本》第1条注释中还规定了善意条款规则。善意条款是针对上述三种防范手段的一种保障措施,旨在防止上述措施的不当适用会干涉和影响到正常的投资或贸易活动。善意条款从某种角度上即为一种一般例外条款。根据《OECD范本》第1条注释第19段,善意条款是指虽然出现疑似滥用税收协定的现象,但如果交易在本质上仍是正常贸易,只要符合善意条款中规定的例外情形,则仍能享受协定下的税收优惠。这里的例外情形包括一般善意规定、营业活动规定、税额规定、证券交易规定、可替代减免条款等。这些条款可以综合适用,也可分别运用,各国在协定中需结合实际情况来决定。

(二) 特别反滥用税收协定条款

所谓特别反滥用税收协定条款,是指针对特定纳税人或者特定收益类型的反滥用措施。两大范本中关于代理人的界定,以及对"表演者公司"和"受益所有人"的规定都属于特别反滥用税收协定条款的范畴。① 其中,"受益所有人"概念的引入和界定是特殊反滥用税收协定条款中最重要的内容,也是《UN 范本》在最近一次修订中得以扩充和新增的主要内容之一。②

本书在第四章第三节讲到投资所得的征税规则时已提到"受益所有人"这一概念。就反滥用税收协定而言,它是指如果有关跨国投资所得的受益所有人不是缔约国另一方的居民纳税人,而是某个第三国的居民,尽管有关跨国投资所得的收款人具有缔约国另一方居民身份,只要他不是缔约国另一方税法意义上有关投资所得的受益所有人,则来源国一方对其来源于境内的跨国投资所得,可以适用国内所得税法规定的预提税率进行源泉课税,不受协定中规定的限制税率的约束。通过限定投资所得的受益所有人范围来防止协定滥用这一做法在两大范本中得到广泛的适用。

2010 年修订的《OECD 范本》第 10、11、12 条分别对股息、利息和特许权使用费中的受益所有人作了如下规定:"缔约国一方居民公司支付给缔约国另一方居民的股息,可以在该缔约国另一方征税。然而,这些股息也可以在支付股息的公司为其居民的缔约国,按照该国法律征税。但是,如果股息受益所有人是缔约国另一方的居民,则所征税款:(一) 如果受益所有人是直接持有支付股息公司至少 25% 资本的公司(不是合伙企业),不应超过股息总额的 5%;(二) 在其他情形下,不应超过股息总额 15%。缔约国双方主管当局应通过相互协商,确定实施该限制税率的方式";"发生于缔约国一方并支付给缔约国另一方居民的利息,可以在该缔约国另一方征税。然而,这些利息也可以在该利息发生的缔约国,按照该国法律征税。但是,如果利息的受益所有人是缔约国另一方的居民,则所征税款不应超过利息总额的 10%。缔约国双方主管当局应通过相互协商,确定实施该限制税率的方式";"发生于缔约国一方并由缔约国另一方居民受益所有的特许权使用费,应仅在该缔约国另一方征税。如果特许权使用费受益所有人是缔约国一方的居民,在特许权使用费发生的缔约国另一方,通过设在该缔约国另一方的常设机构进行营业,且据以支付该特许权使用费的权利或财产与该常设机构有实际联系,则应适用第七条关于营业利润的征税规则。"在 2011 年修订的《UN 范本》中,也对受益所有人问题作了类似的规定。由此可见,受益所有人不仅是限制收入来源地国对股息、利息、特许权使用费征税的条件,也是反

---

① 参见《OECD 范本》和《UN 范本》第 5 条和第 17 条第 2 款。
② See Secretariat Note: As Finalised by the UN Tax Committee by Written Procedure for Inclusion in the Next Version of the United Nations Model Double Taxation Convention Between Developed and Developing Countries-June 2009, Improper Use of Tax Treaties, paragraphs. 10,11.

滥用税收协定的重要手段。鉴于相关知识已在本书前面章节中详述,在此不再赘述。

第三节 资本弱化

企业融资渠道总体上分为权益性融资和债务性融资。权益性融资是指向其他投资者出售公司的所有权,即用所有者的权益来交换资金,最典型的方式就是发行股票。权益性融资并不增加公司的债务。债务性融资则是指企业以负债为主要代价来融通资金的融资方式,主要包括向银行等金融机构贷款、发行企业债券等。债务性融资后企业的债务增加。不同融资渠道的选择往往取决于企业的风险偏好、融资成本等因素。随着各国所得税制的普及和完善,税收因素在融资方式的选择中占据着越来越重要的地位。与权益融资相比,债务性融资能够起到降低税负的效果,于是,一些企业过度增加负债比例,降低权益资本的份额,这也就是本节所要介绍的资本弱化(thin capitalization)。资本弱化是企业逃避税的一种手段,因而也是各国立法和税务机关力求规制的对象。

一、资本弱化的概念及其对税收的影响

资本弱化又称为"资本隐藏"或"股份隐藏",是指企业为了实现避税或其他目的,在融资方式的选择上,降低权益资本的比重,提高负债的比重,从而增加利息获得更多的税前扣除,减少所得税的一种避税形式。企业及其投资者之所以实施资本弱化,是因为通过资本弱化可以实现一系列的好处,具体包括以下几点:

首先,减少公司的应税利润,降低税负。根据各国所得税法的规定,企业的借款利息通常可以作为财务费用在税前扣除,从而减少企业的应纳税所得额。而权益资本以股息形式获得的报酬属于税后净利润的分配,不能在税前所得中扣除。相比之下,债务资本产生的"税盾效应"降低了企业的税收成本。负债融资的这一优势可以通过表5-1的比较来进一步阐述。

假设不经过资本弱化法规的调整,某跨国企业追加投资100万,当年实现息税前利润100万,贷款利率为10%,适用的所得税率为30%,预提税率为10%,企业税后利润全部分配给投资者,不存在其他调整项目。在上述假设条件下,投资者以增加权益资本和提供贷款两种追加投资方式产生的实际税率相差甚大。

从表5-1可知,如果没有资本弱化法规的调整,投资者以增加权益资本和提

供贷款方式最后取得的收益是不一样的,后一种方式下由于降低了实际税负,从而提高了投资者收益。

表 5-1　权益融资和负债融资的税收效应比较

	增加权益资本(万元)	提供贷款(万元)
息前税前利润	100	100
利息	0	10
应税所得	100	90
所得税(30%)	30	27
税后净利润	70	63
预提税(10%)	0	1(10×10%)
投资者收益(股息利息之和)	70	73(10+63)
实际税率	30%	27%

其次,资本弱化可以避免经济性双重征税。① 如果通过权益融资,母公司作为投资者从子公司取得的股息收入来自于子公司的税后利润,通常要征两次税:一次是利润分配前作为企业应税所得缴纳企业所得税;另一次是利润分配后由子公司所在国征一次预提所得税。在没有实行免税或抵免制的国家,这种经济性双重征税必然降低母公司的投资收益。如果通过母公司提供贷款来融资,母公司取得的利息是来自于子公司的税前所得,虽然该利息收入在子公司所在国要缴纳预提税,母公司在其居住国还要就这一收入缴纳所得税,但对这种法律性双重征税,母公司通常可以获得其所在国的抵免或免税。可见,资本弱化可以防止经济性双重征税给企业带来税负的增加。

最后,股本在处分时会有资本利得税的产生,而借款在偿还时则无此种税负。②

除了上述税收利益之外,资本弱化还可以实现企业在经营战略上的其他便利,如取得稳定的投资收益、降低投资风险、维持股权结构稳定等。不难看出,这些因素的存在决定了资本弱化既有合理的一面,又有不合理的一面,各国资本弱化法规所要规制的是以避税为目的的不合理的资本弱化行为,而不是企业出于经营需要在合理范围内作出的资本结构安排。

---

① 参见张志超、李月平编著:《国际税收》,首都经贸大学出版社 2005 年版,第 178 页。
② 参见安然、罗艳:《对"资本弱化"进行规制的思考》,载《法学论坛》2006 年第 2 期。

二、资本弱化的规制措施

资本弱化作为一种避税手段,不仅破坏了税收中性原则,导致企业之间的不公平竞争,而且还损害了收入来源地国的利益,将本来应该归属于来源地国的税收利益转移到居住地国。为了防止企业利用资本弱化进行避税,许多国家都制定了相应的反避税立法,各国在这方面的做法并不一致,主要有独立交易法和固定比例法两种方法,下面对这两种方法加以简单介绍。

(一)独立交易法

独立交易法是指在确定贷款或募股资金的特征时,要看关联方的贷款条件是否与非关联方的贷款条件相同,如果不同,则关联方的贷款可能被视为隐蔽的募股,要按照有关法规对利息征税。根据独立交易法,对于关联企业之间的资金借贷,凡不按照独立企业原则故意提高利率、多列利息、转移利润的,税务当局有权进行合理调整,对超过规定标准支付的利息在计征所得税时不得作为财务费用税前扣除。

独立交易法是以转让定价的一般原则为基础的,这种方法也常被用来调整关联企业之间的转让定价行为。该方法在资本弱化规则的实际应用中,一般要解决三个问题:一是对关联企业间的控制与被控制关系的认定。两大范本都在第9条"联属企业"中进行了相关规定,各国大都以占有企业股份比例的多少或其他关联因素来进行认定。二是何为独立企业贷款利率或正常的贷款利率,其参照标准是什么。经合组织在有关"资本弱化"的报告中指出,通常有两种方式来判定:(1)针对具体个案,根据整个商业行为和借贷目的进行判定;(2)是否超过固定的债权比例。三是如何进行调整。通常是对超过界限支付的利息不予作为费用扣除,或将超额利息视为利润分配或股息。[①]

不难看出,独立交易法主要是针对关联企业之间的转让定价行为的,它能否有效适用于资本弱化避税情形,有学者提出了质疑,认为独立交易法的核心要素是审查关联企业之间的交易定价是否背离了公开市场上的独立交易价格标准,即是否存在着人为的故意提高或压低交易价格和费用的情形。具体就融资交易而言,只有在关联企业之间融资交易的利率过分高于或低于金融市场上同类贷款的正常利率时,税务当局才能适用独立交易原则进行调整。而资本弱化是将正常情形下应以股权资本形式投入的资金改为采用贷款形式投入,从而以支付贷款利息的方式提前抽取了借款公司的税前利润。关联企业之间资本弱化性质

---

① 参见安然、罗艳:《对"资本弱化"进行规制的思考》,载《法学论坛》2006年第2期。

的贷款完全可以按照公开市场上的正常商业贷款利率来进行,此时,独立交易法就难以取得管制效果。① 应该说,这种质疑是不无道理的,但我们也不能因此而完全否定独立交易法在规制资本弱化中的作用。尽管缺乏针对性,但独立交易法以及实质重于形式原则等传统的反避税原则在所有的反避税立法中都具有重要的指导意义。

采用独立交易法来规制资本弱化的国家不多,英国是实行独立交易法的典型国家,根据英国税法的规定,英国公司向关联方贷款时,如果没有按照独立交易条件支付利息,则支付的过量利息不得税前扣除,而且还要将不允许扣除的这部分利息视为股息予以征税。这里的过量利息是指借款公司实际支付的利息与按照独立交易法应该支付的利息之差。不过,英国的资本弱化法规只限制关联企业之间利息支付的税前扣除,而对向非关联企业支付的利息则一般没有税前扣除的限制。②

(二) 固定比例法

固定比例法又称为"安全港模式",即通过立法对公司债务资本和权益资本的比例加以限制,如果债务资本与权益资本的比例在立法规定的限制范围以内,则债务利息可以在税前扣除,如果债务资本与权益资本的比例超过了立法规定的比例,则超出部分的债务利息不得税前扣除,有的国家还规定将超出部分的债务利息视为股息予以征税。③ 适用固定比例法的过程中,以下三个方面的要素至关重要:

1. 贷款人范围的确定。资本弱化规则并不是要笼统地限制企业负债,而是要防止企业以避税为目的过度举债,也并不是把来自于所有贷款人的负债都作为限制的对象,而是对贷款人规定了一定的条件。综合各国立法看,绝大多数国家都要求贷款人与借款企业存在关联关系,有些国家还特别规定贷款人须是非居民股东,否则,在计算债务资本与权益资本的比例以决定是否适用资本弱化规则时,此类贷款人所提供的贷款不得作为适格的债务资本。

2. 债务范围的确定。债务范围的确定反映了立法机关适用资本弱化法规的宽严程度,债务范围规定得越宽,说明法规越严格,反之则说明越宽松。由于

---

① 参见廖益新、陈红彦:《论中国规制资本弱化税法的完善》,载《厦门大学学报(哲学社会科学版)》2007年第1期。

② 参见孙少岩、李响:《限制资本弱化的法律问题研究》,载《经济纵横》2006年第2期。

③ 目前国内著述中对固定比例法的概念表述不一,有的认为该方法是限制资产负债率,即债务与资产总额的比例,有的则认为是限制债务与权益资本的比例。上述两种提法本质上并无区别,固定比例法主要考虑的是债务在企业资本结构中的比重,至于以总资本中的哪一个变量作为参照物来衡量这一比重并不重要。

各国的立法态度不同,因此对固定比例法中的债务范围的规定也不一致。例如,在美国,债务范围包括一般性投资贷款、期限超过 90 天的短期贷款、无关联第三方提供的对股东有追索权的贷款、混合融资工具。在澳大利亚,债务范围包括一般性投资贷款、期限超过 30 天的短期贷款、混合融资工具。

担保是与债务紧密相关的一个问题,有些国家的资本弱化法规将特定的担保也视为债务,如意大利、荷兰就规定,即使贷款本身不是由适格的关联人作出的,只要该债务是由适格的关联人担保,那么也构成适格的债务。德国的规定更为严格,不仅企业对第三人的债务可以因该债务系由适格的关联人担保而使其构成适格债务,而且只要是实际提供贷款的人对实质性参股股东或者该股东的关联方(即适格的贷款人)享有追索权,都可以使得该贷款债务成为资本弱化规则意义上的适格债务。[①] 当然,并非所有的国家都如此规定,如根据加拿大的法律,居民公司从非关联的第三方取得的由居民股东担保的债务,不属于资本弱化规则下的债务范围。

3. 权益资本的确定。固定比例法以债务资本对权益资本的比例作为判定是否存在"资本弱化"的标准,因此权益资本的确定与债务范围的确定同样重要。根据会计学原理,权益资本包括实收资本、资本公积、盈余公积和未分配利润。由于权益资本一直处于变化之中,因此计算时点的确定十分关键,有的国家选择前一年的年末数,有的国家取全年平均数,也有一些国家取当年年末数,还有一些国家对不同的资本项目选择不同的计算时点,如在澳大利亚,未分配利润及资产重置价值一般在年初确定,但实收资本和股票发行溢价则在年末确定。[②]

最后需要提及的是,我国在经过长期的理论探讨和实践摸索之后,也在 2008 年的《企业所得税法》中规定了资本弱化规则,根据该法第 46 条,企业从其关联方接受的债权性投资与权益性投资的比例超过规定标准而发生的利息支出,不得在计算应纳税所得额时扣除。《企业所得税法实施条例》进一步规定,这里所说的债权性投资是指企业直接或者间接从关联方获得的,需要偿还本金和支付利息或者需要以其他具有支付利息性质的方式予以补偿的融资,包括:关联方通过无关联第三方提供的债权性投资;无关联第三方提供的、由关联方担保且负有连带责任的债权性投资;其他间接从关联方获得的具有负债实质的债权性

---

① See A. Korner, The New German Thin Capitalization Rules: Tax Planning Incompatibility with European Law, Intertax, 2004 (8/9): 401-415. 转引自廖益新、陈红彦:《论中国规制资本弱化税法的完善》,载《厦门大学学报(哲学社会科学版)》2007 年第 1 期。

② 参见〔美〕罗梅·罗哈吉:《国际税收基础》,林海宁、范文祥译,北京大学出版社 2006 年版,第 434 页。

投资。权益性投资是指企业接受的不需要偿还本金和支付利息,投资人对企业净资产拥有所有权的投资。① 但这些规则过于原则化,缺乏具体操作标准。基于这些不足,2009 年实施的《特别纳税调整实施办法(试行)》在《企业所得税法》及其实施条例基础上以"资本弱化管理"专章的形式作了系统规定。依据该实施办法的规定,我国对于资本弱化的规制办法同时采用"固定比例法"和"正常交易法"。首先对于固定比例的设立,我国以企业的性质是否为金融企业为划分标准,规定金融企业接受关联方债权性投资与其权益性投资的比例为 5∶1;其他企业为 2∶1。② 在实施固定比例法的基础上,我国资本弱化税制规定,若企业可以提供同期资料证明关联债权投资金额、利率、期限、融资条件以及债资比例等符合独立交易原则,那么其超过标准比例的关联方利息支出,不得在计算应纳税所得额时扣除。③

基于以上分析,尽管资本弱化税制在我国的确立时间相对较晚,但不可否认,它的确立体现了我国反避税意识和反避税能力的提高,对于规范我国税收征纳秩序具有重要的现实意义。从目前看,进一步规范和完善我国的资本弱化立法与实践仍将是一个长期的任务。

第四节 受控外国公司

居民纳税人通常应对其境内外所得纳税,但这里的境外所得是指已经收到的收入,对于还未收到的所得则不产生纳税义务。如此一来,居民纳税人就有可能通过在免税或低税地区设立一个实体来接收境外所得收入,从而达到在国内延期纳税甚至避税的目的。这种人为操纵的延期纳税不仅造成了不合理的税收流失,同时也使得投资国外的居民比那些投资国内的居民享有了更多的税收利益,破坏了税收中性原则。于是,许多国家开始通过受控外国公司立法来对这一现象加以规制。

受控外国公司(Controlled Foreign Company,CFC)规则的核心就是如果设在某些免税或低税地的外国公司为本国居民纳税人所控制,那么该公司取得的利润不论是否分配,都要对本国居民就其应享份额加以征税。CFC 规则极其复杂,涉及 CFC 的界定、可归属收入的确定等诸多方面。

---

① 参见《企业所得税法实施条例》第 119 条第 3 款。
② 参见《特别纳税调整实施办法(试行)》第 85 条、国家税务总局《关于企业关联方利息支出税前扣除标准有关税收政策问题的通知》第 1 条。
③ 参见《特别纳税调整实施办法(试行)》第 90 条。

一、受控外国公司的界定

适用CFC规则的前提是要界定何谓CFC。综合各国的立法看，总体上遵循两个方面的标准：严格控制标准和事实控制标准。严格控制标准要求本国居民对外国公司的资产所有权或重大事项投票权享有绝对的控制地位；事实控制标准则是指尽管本国居民对某一外国公司的资产所有权或重大事项投票权不享有绝对控制地位，但能对该外国公司产生实质性影响，或实施实质上的控制。前一个标准采用量化的指标来衡量，而后一个标准则无法量化，通常只能由税务机关在综合考量相关因素的基础上作出认定，比较灵活。实践中都是将二者结合使用，以严格控制标准为主，事实控制标准为辅，将后者作为一种兜底条款，最大限度地防止本国居民通过设立CFC的方式来拖延纳税或逃避税。

尽管各国都普遍采用控制标准，但各国立法所要求的控制程度并不一致，有的国家要求本国居民对外国公司拥有50%以上的资产或表决权，有的则规定在本国居民对外国公司拥有不足50%的资产或表决权时，如果其中一个居民股东对该公司具有实质性影响亦可。以澳大利亚立法为例，满足下列要求之一的即为CFC：(1) 5个或5个以下的居民股东直接或间接地拥有50%或以上的权益；(2) 单个居民股东直接或间接地拥有至少40%以上的权益，而且该外国公司不为其他非本国居民股东所控制；(3) 5个或5个以下的居民股东单独或共同控制外国公司。

上述标准看似简单，具体操作中却极其复杂。首先，由于不同的股东可能对不同的事项拥有不同的表决权，因此控制利益（control interest）很难量化。其次，表决权在不同时期可能发生变动，时间点的选择很重要。再次，有一些相关方虽然不拥有股权，但也有重大利益存在，如公司的债权人虽然不对公司拥有股权，但实际上也能对公司产生重大影响，此类主体的影响力或控制力不容忽视。最后，规则所规定的"间接控制"如何确定也是个问题，这里的"间接控制"主要是指通过关联企业控制，如果对"间接控制"方式规定得过于宽泛的话，则有可能将几个独立行事的实体也认定为关联企业，但如果规定得过于狭窄的话，又有可能使得相关规则易于规避。

在探讨CFC的判定标准时，还需要注意一点：从绝大多数国家的CFC规则看，有些公司虽然符合CFC的标准，但在满足一定条件时仍可以不适用CFC规则。适用这种例外情形的条件通常包括以下几个方面：(1) CFC每年将其一定比例的收入进行分配；(2) CFC主要是通过真实活动获得的积极收入，而且在该国也有商业存在；(3) 设立CFC的动机不是为逃避或延期缴纳在股东居住国应该缴纳的税;(4) CFC 股票在公认的股票交易市场上市;(5) CFC 总收入或已归属收入低于一个最低数额,或这种收入所占比例没有超过 CFC 总收入的一定比例。[①]

二、可归属收入的确定

可归属收入(attributable income)是指根据 CFC 规则,CFC 所得中可归入居民股东应税收入并予以征税的那部分收入。计算可归属收入的方法有地域法和交易法两种。

所谓地域法,是指将设在特定国家或地区的 CFC 的所得作为可归属收入。这里确定特定国家或地区的标准主要是看该国家或地区的税制是否与本国税制具有可比性。如果认为 CFC 所在地具有与本国相同或相近的税制与税率,通常不将该公司的所得视为可归属收入。相反,如果认为 CFC 所在地不具备完备的税制,或者规定的税率较低,甚至为大多数收入规定了免税优惠,则将该公司的所得视为可归属收入。之所以如此区别对待,主要是考虑到 CFC 立法的初衷是为了防止居民股东通过在境外成立实体来接收或持有所得以实现迟延纳税甚至是逃避税的目的,如果 CFC 所在地税制完备,而且税率与本国相当,那么本国居民股东就无法以这种方式来实现其目的,因而也就没有必要通过 CFC 规则来规制迟延纳税或逃避税行为。如果 CFC 所在地税制不健全,或者税率极低,则很容易为本国居民所利用,因此有必要通过 CFC 规则,将该公司的未分配收入归属到本国居民股东的应税收入中予以征税。

所谓交易法,则是将 CFC 特定类型的收入作为可归属收入,这些特定类型的收入主要是指不洁收入(tainted income),包括消极收入和少数积极收入。这种区分主要是考虑到积极收入中体现了更真实的商业意图,而不仅仅是以享受税收利益为目的,相比之下,消极收入更易被操纵用来实现税收利益,有必要通过 CFC 规则来规制。

实践中,上述两种方法常常结合使用,先根据税制是否完备以及税率是否合理将 CFC 所在地进行分类,然后在不同类别的国家中区别适用交易法来确定可归属收入。目前采用这种方法的国家较多,包括澳大利亚、德国、新西兰等。

三、受控外国公司规则与税收协定的关系

CFC 规则自产生以来,其与有关税收协定的关系就一直是争论的焦点,此

[①] 参见〔美〕罗梅·罗哈吉:《国际税收基础》,林海宁、范文祥译,北京大学出版社 2006 年版,第 411 页。

类争论至今不仅没有平息,而且比以往更加激烈。根据 CFC 规则,只要 CFC 当期产生了利润,不管这一利润是否分配给股东,股东所在国都可以对本国股东的应得利润进行征税。同时,由于利润是由 CFC 产生的,因此 CFC 所在地对公司利润享有优先征税权。如此一来是否就出现了双重征税?如果股东所在国与 CFC 所在地之间签有避免双重征税协定,那么 CFC 规则与此类协定之间是协调还是冲突?目前对这些问题都尚无定论。

2002 年 3 月,芬兰最高行政法院作出裁定,认为芬兰根据本国 CFC 规则对本国居民全资拥有的比利时公司的所得实施征税的行为没有违反两国之间的双边税收协定。无独有偶,同年 6 月,法国法院在 Schneider 一案中裁定,按照法国与瑞士之间的双边税收协定,法国不得根据本国的 CFC 规则对本国居民的瑞士子公司所得进行征税。芬兰与比利时之间的协定和法国与瑞士之间的协定都是以《OECD 范本》为蓝本而签署的,然而两个国家对相同的案情却作出了不同的判定,再次突出了各国在 CFC 规则与有关税收协定之间关系这一问题上的分歧。

其实,要分析二者之间的关系,首先要看 CFC 规则是否使股东所在国获得了额外的域外征税权,而这种域外征税权是否与税收协定的相关条款相冲突。以两大范本为例,两个范本的第 10 条第 5 款均规定,缔约国一方居民公司从缔约国另一方取得利润或所得,另一国不得对该公司支付的股息征收任何税收。但支付给另一国居民的股息或支付股息的股份与设在另一国的常设机构或固定基地有实际联系的除外。对于该公司的未分配利润,即使已支付的股息或未分配利润全部或部分是发生于另一国的利润或所得,另一国也不得征税。有人认为 CFC 规则使得一国可以对非居民公司的未分配利润征税,因而违反了范本的前述条款。实际上,正如经合组织在 1987 年《避免双重税收协定与基地公司的运用》(Double Taxation Conventions and the Use of Base Companies)报告中指出的,《OECD 范本》第 10 条第 5 款所限制的是对公司的征税,而没有涉及对公司股东的征税;另外,范本也没有限制一国为了反避税而对本国居民的征税。因此,CFC 规则并没有使股东所在国获得与范本条款相冲突的域外征税权。

CFC 规则与税收协定关系争论中的另一个问题就是,CFC 规则是否与条约所规定的避免双重征税的目标相冲突。应该看到,税收协定所力求避免的主要是法律性双重征税,而不是经济性双重征税,如果 CFC 规则导致双重征税,也只是经济性双重征税,即由不同的纳税人对同一项所得纳税,大多数税收协定对此类情形都是无能为力的。

从上面的介绍看,CFC 规则不仅十分复杂,而且争论较多。但不可否认的是,它作为一种新型的规制逃避税的手段,正日益受到越来越多国家的重视。在借鉴其他国家经验的基础上,我国也对 CFC 问题作出了规定。2008 年 1 月 1 日实施的《企业所得税法》第 45 条规定,由居民企业,或者由居民企业和中国居民控制的设立在实际税负明显低于本法第 4 条第 1 款规定税率水平的国家(地区)的企业,并非由于合理的经营需要而对利润不作分配或者减少分配的,上述利润中应归属于该居民企业的部分,应当计入该居民企业的当期收入。《企业所得税法实施条例》进一步对"中国居民"的概念、"控制"的判断标准等作出了规定。① 2009 年实施的《特别纳税调整办法(试行)》在《企业所得税法》及其实施条例的基础上,以第八章"受控外国企业管理"的专章形式对 CFC 问题作了系统规定。依据该办法,CFC 中为了避税而故意不作分配或者减少分配的利润,将被同股息分配额,计入中国居民企业股东的当期所得予以征税。② 基于以上分析,不难看出,我国在 CFC 税制方面已经有所进步,但同时我们必须清晰地认识到,与其他国家繁杂的 CFC 规则相比,我国的规定仍然非常笼统,对于如何确定可归属收入、何谓"少分配利润"等问题都没能明确,有些问题甚至根本没有涉及。这些问题都还有待于在进一步借鉴别国经验的基础上,结合国际经济实践以及我国的国情来加以完善。

第五节 税基侵蚀和利润转移

目前,尽管各国都针对国际避税行为制定了反避税规则,但这些反避税规则本身的不够完善和相互之间的差异却又为避税提供了机会。经合组织将这种利用反避税规则及各国税收管辖权差异进行避税的方式称为"税基侵蚀和利润转移"(Base Erosion and Profit Shifting,BEPS)。BEPS 是目前国际社会普遍面临的一个挑战,它对各国的税收收入、税收主权以及税收公平性来说都是非常严重的威胁,经合组织、二十国集团等国际社会已着手探索应对这一威胁的行动方案。

严格说来,BEPS 并不是一种独立形态的避税方式,可以说它是传统避税与现代避税方式的统称,但基于目前这一问题的严重性,国际社会将其作为一项系统的工作来对待,所以本书也在此将其单辟一节加以介绍。

---

① 参见《企业所得税法实施条例》第 116、117 和 119 条。
② 参见《特别纳税调整办法(试行)》第 80 条。

一、税基侵蚀和利润转移的产生原因和主要方式

经合组织关于BEPS的报告认为,导致BEPS产生的根本原因在于传统的国际税收规则落后于不断发展变化的商业环境,国内与国际层面的国际税法规则还根植于低水平的跨国经济融合的商业环境,不能适应当前以知识产权价值驱动作用日益显著、信息及通讯技术不断发展为特征的全球纳税人环境。简而言之,各国税收制度融合的程度远不及各国经济的融合程度。于是,各国税收制度的差异导致了国际税收制度中的漏洞和错配,跨国公司利用这些漏洞和错配使得应税利润"消失"或者转移到没有或几乎没有实际经营活动的低税地,这些行为就是BEPS。由此可见,除一些蓄意逃避税行为以外,BEPS的主要问题还是出在现行税法本身。BEPS已经在全球范围内造成了诸多国家财政收入的流失。同时,相比较发达国家而言,发展中国家在财政收入方面对企业所得税的依赖更为严重,因此受到影响也更为明显。

目前,BEPS在实施方式上可以归纳为以下两种情形:

(一)基于对各国税收管辖制度差异的利用

根据国家主权原则,每个国家都有权自主设计本国的税收政策,建立自己的税收法律体系。但各国在这一过程中应确保本国的征税不会对跨国贸易和投资带来扭曲的效果,也不会以不利于国内从业者的方式损害一国境内的竞争和投资。在一个全球化的世界,世界经济融合程度日益加深,各国独立设置的国内税收体系通常相互不一致,这就为错配(mismatch)带来了空间。这种错配可能导致双重征税,也可能导致双重不征税。在双重不征税的情况下,实际上就是这种错配使得收入在税收目的上消失,由此使整体的税负减少,尽管难以辨别出具体哪个国家的税收收入减少了,但所涉及的所有国家总体税收收入减少了。此外,这种错配也损害了正常的竞争秩序,某些跨国企业可以凭借其全球营销网络和税务专业知识从政策错配中获得更多的竞争优势。当前跨国公司利用政策错配的策略有:

1. 低税外国分支机构

一个在高税率国家境内设立的公司,如果总机构所在国根据国内法或税收协定,对外国分支机构的收入给予豁免,则可以通过向位于低税率国境内的分支机构提供贷款(许可或服务)实现很低的实际税率。分支机构所在国通常通过以下几种方式提供税收优惠:(1)分支机构所在国对其收入实行低税率或零税率;(2)分支机构所在国视在该国进行的活动不足以构成可对该外国公司征税的存在;(3)分支机构所在国给予分支机构对外支付的利息以抵扣待遇。

2. 混合实体(hybrid entities)

混合实体是指一个实体在一国被认为是可被征税的实体,而在另一国被认为是"透明"的免税实体。例如,A 国的母公司 A 向在 B 国的子公司 B 提供贷款,根据 B 国的税法规定,B 公司并非"透明"免税实体,而根据 A 国的税法,B 公司为"透明"实体,则 B 公司是"混合实体"。由此,当 B 公司向 A 公司支付利息时,该利息可在 B 国作税前抵扣,而 A 公司收到的该利息却不用在 A 国交税。因为,从 A 国的角度看,B 公司为"透明"实体,所以 A 公司根本就没有取得应税收入,也就无须纳税。但值得注意的是,如果情况正好相反(B 公司在 A 国不"透明",而在 B 国"透明"),那么就会产生双重征税。

3. 混合金融工具或其他金融交易

有些金融工具既有债权的典型特征,又有股权的典型特征。例如,A 国的 A 公司购买了 B 国的 B 公司发行的金融产品,该金融产品在 A 国被视为股权,而在 B 国被视为债务工具,故 B 公司向 A 公司支付的投资回报在 B 国可以用作利息税前扣除;而在 A 国,A 公司收到的投资回报被视为股息,享有税收豁免。如此一来,就享受了双重的税收优惠利益。其他金融交易包括担保或衍生品等等,也可以产生相似的效果。

(二)基于对反避税规则的利用

实践中存在很多规避反避税规则的税务筹划策略,如通过独立第三方提供融资来规避资本弱化规则,这一策略在资本弱化规则仅适用于关联方融资时尤为有效,在其他情形下,资本弱化规则也可以通过运用衍生品工具来规避。同样,各国 CFC 规则也可能被规避,包括通过改变跨国企业的公司结构,使得非居民公司设置于没有 CFC 规则的(低税或无税)国家。运用混合实体也可以使收入在税收目的上在母公司所在国"消失",从而规避该国 CFC 规则的适用。

在各国的转让定价立法中,也存在产生 BEPS 的空间,因为转让定价的基本原则为独立交易原则,该原则的假设之一就是:交易一方承担的功能、资产、风险越多,其预期的回报就越多,反之亦然。因此,独立交易原则为企业将功能、资产、风险转移至那些具有更优惠税收待遇的国家或地区提供了可能性。虽然功能转移比较困难,但转移有形资产和无形资产的风险和所有权则相对容易,实践中很多公司强调将重要的风险及很难评估的无形资产转移到低税率国家或地区,这种安排可能会导致 BEPS。此外,与风险转移有关的安排还产生了一系列转让定价问题,例如,风险如何在跨国公司集团成员间分配,转让定价规则应在何种程度上认可合同本身对于风险的分配,以及如果风险在集团成员间转移,是否需要补偿性支付等等。诚如有些专家指出的,当前的转让定价规则过于强调法律结构,而不注重统一的集团背后的经济现实,这可能为 BEPS 创造机会。

不管通过上述何种实施方式,任何旨在实现税基侵蚀和利润转移目标的税务安排通常都要包含一些相互协调的策略,这些策略包括以下要素:(1)通过交易结构的安排减少净利润,使得在营业地所在国或收入来源国境内的税收最小化;(2)来源地预提税较低或根本没有;(3)从利润转移中的利润接受方看,对于通过集团内安排获得的非常规利润,适用税率较低或零税率;(4)从母公司角度看,通过上述三个步骤实现的利润,在母公司所在国无须纳税。可见,任何对于 BEPS 的分析都要注意多重因素的存在及其相互作用和影响。①

二、应对税基侵蚀和利润转移的全球行动方案

2013 年 7 月,经合组织发布了《应对税基侵蚀与利润转移的行动方案》(OECD's Action Plan on Base Erosion and Profit Shifting)(以下简称《行动方案》),目标是重修税法以适应形势的发展并且确保利润在经济活动发生地和价值创造地征税。该方案要求根本性地改变现有机制,采取更有效的措施应对 BEPS,从协同跨境交易相关国法规、强化现有国际标准中对实质活动的要求并提高税收透明度、为正常经营活动增加税收方面的确定性这三个方面提出了以下 15 项计划:(1)应对数字经济带来的税务挑战;(2)使混合错配安排的税收效果中性化;(3)加强 CFC 立法;(4)通过规范利息扣除以及其他财务支出限制税基侵蚀;(5)更有效地抵制有害税收竞争;(6)反对滥用税收协定;(7)防止人为地隐匿常设机构;(8)确保无形资产转让定价与价值创造相一致;(9)确保风险与资本转让定价与价值创造相一致;(10)确保其他高风险交易中的转让定价与价值创造相一致;(11)建立一套收集与分析 BEPS 相关数据的方法;(12)要求纳税人披露税务筹划安排;(13)复核转让定价文档;(14)确保争端解决机制更加有效;(15)发展多边机制。《行动方案》为各国政府制订方案以应对 BEPS 提供了一个全球路线图,也必将为全球商业环境及国际税收秩序带来深远的影响。正如经合组织秘书长安赫尔·古里亚(Angel Gurria)在方案发布时所说的,《行动方案》标志着国际税务合作将进入历史性的转折时期,它将引领各国采取相互协调的、综合的、透明的标准以应对 BEPS。那些源于 20 世纪 20 年代的国际税法规则主要是为了避免双重征税,然而这些规则如今已被广泛用于双重免税的税收筹划。《行动方案》意在对此进行补救,确保跨国公司缴纳其应当缴纳的税款。

---

① See OECD (2013), Addressing Base Erosion and Profit Shifting, OECD Publishing.

2013年9月,《行动方案》在圣彼得堡举行的G20峰会上获得了各国领导人的背书,所有G20及OECD国家以平等身份共同参与重塑国际税收规则体系基本架构的相关工作,发展中国家也通过征询机制加入了新规则的讨论和制定。诸多区域性和全球性国际组织,如非洲管理论坛(ATAF)、税务部门负责人会晤与研究中心(CREDAF)、欧洲税收管理组织(IOTA)、美洲税收管理组织(CIAT)以及联合国(UN)、国际货币基金组织(IMF)、世界银行(WBG)等都参与了新规则的磋商。BEPS项目逐步演变成为一个在全球范围内由OECD国家、非OECD国家和众多国际组织共同参与的税收合作项目。

三、BEPS项目的2015最终成果报告

2015年10月5日,OECD发布了BEPS项目的最终成果报告,涵盖BEPS项目所有15项行动计划。虽然这些报告不具有法律约束力,但这些成果报告可以作为工作指引,促使各国在立法和征管上的趋同,来堵塞国际税收规则漏洞,防止跨国企业通过人为筹划向低税或无税地区转移利润。

BEPS项目的2015最终成果报告由以下13个报告组成,除了《无形资产转让定价指引》报告涵盖了三个行动计划(即第8—10项行动计划)的内容,基本上每个报告对应一个行动计划:

1. 报告《应对数字经济面临的税收挑战》对应第1项行动计划

数字经济是信息与通讯技术广泛传播与不断变革的结果。由于信息与通信技术对包括零售、金融服务甚至教育和传媒等各行业产生广泛影响,以至于数字经济不断演化成为"新经济"的同义语。

该报告分析了数字经济及其商业模式和主要特征,认为数字经济本身不会产生独特的BEPS问题,但某些特征会加剧BEPS问题产生的风险,如对于常设机构的定义、转让定价和受控外国企业税制等问题。因为数字经济中的虚拟联结度、数据发挥关键作用等特征对直接税与间接税都带来了巨大挑战,现行的国际税收框架已不能确保利润在经济活动发生地及价值创造地征税,因此,报告探讨了应对数字经济挑战的多种备选方案,包括基于"显著的经济存在"这一概念来判定新的联结度。依此方案,如果一个企业从国内消费者中获得大量收入,并且具备通过数字化方式连接该国目标客户,或与该国用户之间的联系互动大量发生,那么根据显著的经济存在原则,该企业可能会被认为在该国有应税活动的场所。另外,报告还从间接税的角度分析了对跨境B2C交易征收增值税所面临的挑战,建议此类交易应在消费者所在地征收。

2. 报告《消除混合错配安排的影响》对应第 2 项行动计划

混合错配安排是一种跨境税收筹划,它利用两国对相同金融工具、财产转让或实体规定的不同税务处理,以达到双重不征税或长期递延纳税的目的。常见的例子如混合金融工具,即某金融工具在一国(地区)被视为债权,而在另一国(地区)被视为股权,因而该金融工具下发生的付款在支付国可以抵扣,在收款国却被作为免税的股息处理。

该报告针对国内法反错配规则和税收协定范本条款给出了一般性建议和具体建议,包括各国采用"联动规则"(linking rules),即由支付方所在国不允许税前扣除作为首要规则,收款方所在国计入收入作为次要规则,确保该支付至少在一国纳税。另外,还建议修订税收协定范本和范本注释,确保混合错配安排不应造成滥用税收协定的优惠待遇,对相关收入应至少在一个国家被征税。

3. 报告《制定有效受控外国公司规则》对应第 3 项行动计划

受控外国公司(CFC)规则是为了应对纳税人将利润转移至其拥有控制权益的外国低税负子公司,导致避税结果的风险而制定的规则。CFC 规则可赋予税收管辖区对跨国集团所设立的外国低税负子公司取得的所得直接征税的权力,以打击上述避税行为。通过 CFC 规则,纳税人所在税收管辖区无须等待外国子公司实际分配其所得,即可对该所得拥有征税的权力,因为所得的分配往往可以无限期递延。

该报告提出了关于有效的 CFC 规则所需构成要件的建议,例如,根据受控外国子公司的实际所得税税率来判断子公司所在国是否为低税率国家,应使用投资者母国的规定来计算受控外国子公司应被视为分配的依据,母公司所在国应在制定外国税收抵免时充分考虑外国受控子公司视同分配的利润所负担外国税收的抵免,等等。该报告明确,这些建议并非强制各国施行的最低标准,而是集合各国经验以作参考的最佳实践。有意愿的国家可以将该建议引入作为其 CFC 规则,也可以参考该建议完善自身的 CFC 规则。

4. 报告《对利用利息扣除和其他款项支付实现的税基侵蚀予以限制》对应第 4 项行动计划

跨国公司利用利息和其他一些费用税前扣除的规定,通过将更多第三方债务转移到高税率国家、通过内部贷款产生超出实际第三方利息费用的利息扣除、利用第三方或集团内部融资为免税收入的产生进行融资等方式进行税基侵蚀。该报告推荐了相应的限制利息和费用扣除的措施,包括固定扣除率规则和集团扣除率规则以及用来支持一般利息限额规则并解决某些特殊风险的针对性规则供各国选择。固定扣除率规则允许实体扣除不超过基准净利息/息税折旧摊销前利润(EBITDA)比率的净利息费用,该基准固定扣除率可在 10%—30%的区间内设置。集团扣除率规则允许企业扣除不超过其所在集团的净利息/EBITD 比率的净利息费用,前提是该比率高于基准固定扣除率。

5. 报告《考虑透明度与实质性因素更有效地打击有害税收实践》对应第 5 项行动计划

该报告认为有害税收实践的根本问题在于滥用税收优惠而导致产生人为利润转移的风险,因此提出了从两个方面打击有害税收实践:一是任何税收优惠的获取都必须满足"实质性经营活动"要求,即要重新实现"利润的征税应与实质性活动产生利润的地方相一致"的原则。报告推荐采用"关联法",仅在纳税人从事了相关优惠制度所要求的核心业务活动并获取了与优惠制度相关的收入时,才能给予优惠。二是税收优惠政策必须具有透明度。对于与优惠制度有关的六大类税收裁定将进行强制性自发情报交换,这六类裁定包括关于优惠制度的裁定、跨境单边预约定价协议或其他单边转让定价裁定、调减利润的裁定、有关常设机构的裁定、导管公司的裁定和有害税收实践论坛(Forum on Harmful Tax Practices,FHTP)认定的因缺乏相关方面的信息交换会导致 BEPS 问题的其他裁定。

6. 报告《防止税收协定优惠的不当授予》对应第 6 项行动计划

"择协避税"一般是指并非缔约国税收居民的人,试图通过安排获取只给予该缔约国税收居民的协定优惠。这种策略通常在有合适税收协定的国家中设立公司来实施,因为这些公司仅在文件中存现,在现实中却没有或几乎没有任何实质存在,因此经常构成"邮箱公司""壳公司"或"导管公司"。因此,该报告提出,防止税收协定优惠不当授予的最低标准是通过修订双边税收协定来解决。报告建议,首先,协定的标题和序言中应明确,缔约国双方意在防止为通过逃避税(包括择协避税安排)所造成的不征或少征行为创造条件。其次,缔约国为执行这一共同意愿,要在协定中(1)结合采用"利益限制"规则(LOB,特别反滥用规则)和"主要目的测试"规则(PPT,一般反滥用规则);(2)纳入"主要目的测试"规则;或(3)纳入"利益限制"规则并辅之以应对导管安排的机制,如对导管融资安排适用主要目的测试,对于仅充当导管作用,将所得支付给第三国投资者的实体,不允许其享受协定优惠。

7. 报告《防止人为规避常设机构》对应第 7 项行动计划

该报告建议修改常设机构的定义,来应对不恰当地规避常设机构安排,包括以佣金代理人安排代替分销商,或实质在某国开展合同谈判,但不正式在该国订立合同,而是在国外确定或批准合同,或者经常代表外国企业行使订立合同权利的人,虽然全部或几乎全部代表紧密关联企业,却声称为"独立代理人"。另外,报告还建议将《OECD范本》第5条4款的特定豁免活动限定为准备性、辅助性活动,目的是要应对关联企业通过拆分活动内容来规避构成常设机构。

8. 报告《确保转让定价结果与价值创造相匹配》对应第8—10项行动计划

该报告涵盖了BEPS项目的第8项行动计划——确保无形资产转让定价与价值创造相一致、第9项行动计划——确保风险与资本转让定价与价值创造相一致和第10项行动计划——确保其他高风险交易中的转让定价与价值创造相一致。之所以把这三个行动计划的研究成果放在一个报告中,是因为它们都体现了要经济回报与价值创造保持一致的原则。

报告指出,独立交易原则是一项实用且公平的准则,纳税人和税务机关可以根据独立交易原则评估关联企业间的转让价格,并避免双重征税。然而,由于独立交易原则偏重于依据合同条款分配功能、资产和风险,这就导致现有的独立交易原则应用指南很容易被不当使用。但是,替代性原则,如公式分配原则,各国还很难在短期内达成共识,并且也不能防止不当使用和确保利润与价值的真正匹配。因此,目前来看,继续在现行的独立交易原则体系下解决具体BEPS问题仍是最有成效的。

同时,该报告也指出,还有必要从以下几个重要方面来修订目前的转让定价规则,加强对应用独立交易原则的指引,确保达到利润与相应经济活动所创造的价值相一致的结果:

- 涉及无形资产的交易,因为有价值的无形资产所产生的利润如果被不当分配,将导致BEPS问题;
- 合同约定的风险分配及相应的利润分配,与实际开展的经济活动所创造的价值不匹配的问题;
- 资本充裕的跨国集团成员作为资金提供者所获得的资金回报,与其从事的经济活动不匹配的问题;
- 当一项交易不具商业合理性时,该交易重新定性的问题;
- 集团劳务和大宗商品交易。

因此,经合组织将在2016年至2017年修订《OECD转让定价指南》,将该报告中的建议纳入该指南。

9. 报告《衡量和监控BEPS》对应第11项行动计划

该报告初步估计,2014年全球因BEPS导致的税收流失约1000亿至2400亿美元之间,相当于全球企业所得税总额的4%—10%。同时,由于BEPS的存在,实施激进税收筹划的跨国企业获得不正当的竞争优势,强化对公司债权的依赖,使得外商直接投资流向错误的目的地,影响了对部分急需的公共基础设施的财政支持。报告建议使用"BEPS 指标面板",运用六个指标来监测不同的 BEPS 方式,并且使用国别报告数据来估算 BEPS 的规模和监控 BEPS 项目应对措施的实效。

10. 报告《强制披露规则》对应第 12 项行动计划

强制披露规则要求筹划方和/或纳税人在早期向税务机关披露其使用的符合一定特征的筹划安排。该规则可使税务机关尽早获得激进或滥用性税收筹划安排以及安排使用者的信息,以便税务机关及时应对。针对强制披露规则如何制定,该报告给出了一系列的建议,包括报告义务责任人、税收筹划安排的特征、强制披露时间节点和罚则,目的是使各国可以根据其需要设计强制披露规则,以在早期获取激进或滥用性税收筹划安排和安排使用者的信息。但是,报告同时也表明,这些建议并非强制各国施行的最低标准,各国可自由选择是否引入强制披露规则。

11. 报告《转让定价文档和国别报告》对应第 13 项行动计划

关于转让定价文档,报告要求跨国企业向所有相关国家的税务机关提供"主体文档",内容包括概括性地介绍其全球运营信息和转让定价政策,并要求其向各国提交更具体的"本地文档",内容包括相关的重要关联交易、交易金额以及企业对于这些交易所做的转让定价分析。主体文档与本地文档由跨国企业直接提交给税务机关。

国别报告是税务机关实施高级别转让定价风险评估,或者评价其他税基侵蚀和利润转移风险的一项工具。报告要求跨国企业按年度向其实际经营所在的税收管辖区申报国别报告,包括其根据集团内部经营活动分布指标计算的全球收入分配和税款缴纳情况,以及在各税收管辖区从事经营活动的集团成员实体名单及其所从事的经营活动。国别报告将由最终控股企业提交给其居民国税务机关,并依据政府间情报交换机制,如《多边主管当局协议》、双边税收协定或情报交换协议,通过自动情报交换在国与国之间共享。在特定情况下,次要机制可作为替代方式,如本地提交,即国别报告由子公司提交给其所在国税务机关。

通过获取上述三个文档,即国别报告、主体文档和本地文档,税务机关可以获得纳税人转移定价信息,用于转让定价风险评估、税务调查资源的有效分配,以及调查目标的确定等。

12. 报告《使争议解决机制更有效》对应第 14 项行动计划

针对税收协定范本第 25 条规定的相互协商程序(Mutural Agreement Procedure,MAP)作为解决与协定解释或应用相关争议的机制,本报告提出了加强 MAP 效力与效率的最低标准和最佳实践的建议,并且提出建立一套监督机制来评估最低标准的执行,从而确保对最低标准承诺的有效实施。评估包括三项内容:各国由税收协定和国内法规构成的法律框架,相互协商工作指南以及实际履行最低标准的情况。

13. 报告《开发用于修订多边税收协定的多边工具》对应第 15 项行动计划

开发多边工具的目标是通过对双边税收协定的修订,使解决税基侵蚀和利润转移问题的措施得以迅速和顺利的执行。若能使用多边协议来修订现有的双边税收协定,BEPS 项目中与税收协定有关的各项措施,如混合错配安排、协定滥用、常设机构和相互协商程序等,都可以得到快速实施。因此,报告本身并未提出多边协议的具体内容,而是成立了一个专门小组,继续研究和开发用于修订税收协定的多边工具,并且决定将于 2016 年 12 月 31 日前完成多边工具的起草,并供各国签署。

除了继续开发多边工具,经合组织也宣布 G20 和经合组织成员国将在平等的基础上在 2016 年继续开展后续工作,包括金融交易领域转让定价方面的工作,完成利润分割法指引和难以估值的无形资产的定价方法,改变常设机构的定义来更准确地确定常设机构的利润归属,探索对非集合投资基金协定征税的解决方案,并完成保险业和银行业利息扣除的集团利息分配比例和其他特殊模式。

四、BEPS 项目的成就及影响

BEPS 各项措施在全面实施之前,其影响即已显现。一些大型跨国企业宣布对其税收架构作出重要调整,表明纳税人的行为已经有了变化。各项措施一旦全面实施,将提升跨境税收规则的一致性,强化对经济实质的要求,同时也确保税收透明度和确定性的提高。

1. 提升一致性

BEPS 项目更新了 OECD 范本规则,并确定了最佳实践,确保在国内政策设计中纳入对跨境交易的考量。相关措施还包括:建议了构建有效受控外国企业税制的几个关键要素;建议了利息扣除方面的通用性规定;建议了设立受控外国企业制度时的几个关键因素。此外,相关工作还将确保企业与政府处于平等地位,消除或修订存在有害因素的优惠税制规定,以及交换有关具体裁定方面的信息。

2. 强化实质性要求

转让定价规则已经得到更新,确保结果与实质经济活动相符;鉴于知识产权定价的困难,有关以估值无形资产,如商标和专利等的定价方法也已经制定出来。在产品交易和低附加值服务方面,则设计了简化机制,这两个领域与发展中国家尤其相关。在协定滥用方面,同意实施一项最低标准,以确保协定优惠仅给予那些合适的对象。最后,常设机构定义(设定非居民征税的门槛标准)也经过修订,以更好反映商业实质,防止发生筹划和避税行为。

3. 保障税收透明度和确定性的提高

BEPS 的规模和经济影响相关指标目前已经设计出来,这些指标为监控和评估 BEPS 各项措施实施的有效性和影响提供了工具;建立强制性披露制度的相关决议也已成形;对转让定价同期资料的要求已经过大幅修订,各方已就一个包含多个经济活动指标的国别报告模板达成共识。此外,各国还一致同意就大范围的裁定交换信息。有效争端解决机制也得到强化,其中包括部分国家有意使用仲裁方式解决争议。同时,各方就四个领域设立最低标准、构建公平环境达成共识,即协定滥用、国别报告、争端解决和有害税收实践。在这些领域,各国承诺将一致实施相关措施,防止由于个别国家的不作为而给其他国家带来负面溢出效应。

本章阅读材料

Counteracting Measures Against the Use of Tax Havens: An Overview

—selected from OECD report: International Tax Avoidance and Evasion, Four Related Studies

III. COUNTERACTING MEASURES AGAINST THE USE OF TAX HAVENS: AN OVERVIEW

46. Domestic legislative measures aimed at curbing the abuse of tax havens exist in many forms. Some of them are general in character and may apply to all types of tax avoidance or evasion. But these general measures tend not to be effective enough, and more "targeted" measures have been felt necessary, either for strengthening the tax authorities' hands (e. g. reversal of burden of proof, "extended" residence) or for submitting persons dealing with havens to stronger reporting requirements or new tax liability. The most sophisticated form of such specific legislation, which now exists in Canada, France, Germany, Japan, the United Kingdom and the United States, provides

liability to tax on certain types of unremitted income of companies set up in tax havens and controlled by residents (this type of legislation is hereafter referred to as "subpart F-type provisions"). Other forms of legislation, whether or not tailored to this particular problem are also reviewed in this chapter.

A. General provisions against international tax avoidance

1. Transfer pricing legislation

47. Most Member countries have transfer pricing legislation giving their tax administrations the authority to scrutinize international transactions between related persons and to reallocate income or disallow costs that are not determined on an arm's length basis. Though these provisions are not focused particularly on transactions with tax havens, they are an important instrument in preventing the artificial shifting of income to base companies established in tax havens.

48. Transfer pricing provisions are in some countries very detailed such as Section 482 of the United States Internal Revenue Code and its related regulations. A number of countries rely on more general provisions enabling them to correct transfer prices to figures which would have been agreed between unrelated persons dealing at arm's length. Since the publication of the 1979 OECD report on "Transfer pricing and Multinational Enterprises", however, there has been a tendency (e. g. in Canada, Demark, Germany, Italy and Japan) to supplement such general provisions by more detailed administrative guidelines to be applied in specific cases of transfer pricing. Explicit reference to transactions with low-tax countries is in particular made in the German guidelines. Related measures in certain countries include thin capitalization provisions under which diversions of funds to low-tax countries can be counteracted.

49. Specific steps taken by some administrations for improving efficiency in dealing with transfer pricing cases—such as the centralized auditing of large companies by specialized auditors, or industrywide investigations—are also relevant and are dealt with in paragraphs 92 to 97 below.

2. General provisions on tax avoidance

50. Some countries have general anti-avoidance provisions that are in principle applicable to the whole of their tax legislation. An example is the

Swedish general clause whereby the effect of a transaction would be disallowed if the taxpayer obtained a tax advantage contrary to the basic principle of the tax law which would have been applicable had he used the most natural way of carrying out the transaction. Another example of a general provision is the so-called "annihilation provision" found in New Zealand. According to this type of provision, any agreement shall be absolutely void insofar as "directly or indirectly, it has or purports to have the purpose or effect of in any way, directly or indirectly" avoiding tax. Australia until recently also used an "annihilation provision" but as from 28th May 1981 new general anti-avoidance provisions were introduced to overcome deficiencies found to exist in the previous legislation. Broadly speaking the new provisions apply to arrangements that are blatant, artificial or contrived and enable denial of a tax benefit obtained by a taxpayer as a result of entering into a scheme designed predominantly to achieve that benefit.

51. Though these general provisions may have their advantages, the courts of many countries are unwilling to look beyond the letter of the law, in which case recourse has to be made to specific legislation. This possible weakness of general provisions probably still exists, but there are indications in some countries that the attitudes of the courts may have changed somewhat in recent years (see paragraphs 83—85). Nevertheless, general provisions are unlikely to be the main legislative weapon used by tax authorities to counter the abuse of tax havens.

3. "Substance over form"

52. The concept of "Substance over form" which, in broad terms, can be defined as the prevalence of economic or social reality over the literal wording of legal provisions, has been used to counter the attempted circumvention of tax laws. This approach can be adopted by the courts as a principle of interpretation or explicitly set out in a statute. In many European countries, including France, Germany, the Netherland and Switzerland, it is embodied in the judicial concept of "abuse of law". In common law countries and the approach is a well-recognized principle of statutory interpretation which may be applied in certain circumstance to tax laws. Statutory forms of the principle of substance over-form are found in a number of countries: Australia, Belgium,

Germany, Luxembourg, the Netherland, Swizerland and the United States.

53. Taking the French legislation (Article L. 64 of the Livre des Procédures Fiscales) as an example, any transactions made in the form of a contract or any kind of legal instrument, the provisions which conceal profits or income arising or transferred, cannot be invoked against the tax administration. To reinstate the true nature of the disputed transaction and determine the basis for taxation accordingly, the tax administration may seek the opinion of a special consultative committee on the abuse of legal provisions. If tax is assessed in accordance with the opinion delivered by the committee, the burden of proof lies with the taxpayer in the event of a subsequent appeal.

54. This type of legislation can be effective only if the tax authorities are able to establish the economic reality of transactions or a series of transactions. Such a process requires information on international transactions which may be available only from sources such as foreign exchange control or international exchanges of information.

4. Maintaining the withholding tax on income paid to non-residents

55. High rates of withholding tax on incomes such as interest, royalties, dividends, rents, management fees and other similar payments, paid to non-residents may also be used as a general weapon in the arsenal of counteracting measures. The withholding tax is usually reduced or removed only under the terms of tax conventions and in some cases in return for a guarantee of administrative assistance.

56. The maintenance of withholding tax also prevents companies in a tax haven country from being used as "conduit companies", particularly for the collection of interest and royalty payments between a resident of a treaty partner and a resident of a third country. Tax would be withheld, in the absence of tax convention, at the rate chargeable under ordinary law on the relevant amounts paid through the conduit company to the resident in the third country. Obviously, the effectiveness of this measure depends either on the refusal to conclude tax conventions with tax havens or on having safeguarding clauses introduced into the conventions with tax haven countries so as to enable withholding tax reductions or exemptions to be refused in certain circumstances.

B. Legislation directed against the use of tax havens

1. Shifting the burden of proof

57. Usually the "burden of proof" (or the "burden of persuasion") lies with the tax authorities but in some countries it will normally rest with the taxpayer, who has to provide detailed evidence when claiming the benefit of tax provisions or challenging the assessment made by the tax authorities, for instance, in Australia, the Netherlands, New Zealand and the United States. However, even when the burden of proof is imposed on the tax authorities, in some instances it will be reversed to the taxpayer's side in the case of certain types of transactions with low-tax countries. Such provisions aim mainly at discouraging disguised transfers of profits abroad and the accumulation of income in tax havens. Measures taken for this purpose were introduced in Belgium in 1938(reinforced in 1973) and in France in 1974. A Special Council, created to consider the issues of organized and economic crime, proposed in 1980 that a similar requirement should be introduced in Sweden. However, the proposal was rejected by the government largely because of the difficulty of defining what should be regarded as a low-tax country, especially in view of frequent changes in foreign tax legislation and tax rates.

58. The measures taken in Belgium and France provide that interest, royalties and license-fee payments, or consideration for services paid by a person resident or established in Belgium (or France) to a person resident or established in a country or territory situated outside Belgium (or France) giving "preference taxation treatment" shall not be deductible for tax purposes "unless the payer furnishes proof that expenses correspond to genuine transactions and are not abnormal or excessive". In France, this provision also applies to payments made from accounts held by financial institutions set up in a country with a "privileged tax treatment", irrespective of the residence of the recipient of the payment (Article 238 of the C. G. I.). Where it has not been possible to establish that the operation had actually taken place, the expenses which cannot be justified are fully added back to taxable income. If the amount of such expenditure merely appears excessive, then it is the excess which is added back.

59. In contrast to subpart F-type legislation, these provisions do not place

any additional burden on the taxpayer when he is making his return of income tax. They allow the production of documentary evidence at this stage, but do not require it. In general, if individual cases are examined, the tax authorities will require such evidence. On the other hand, the subpart F-type legislation is usually more exacting in that it makes the taxpayer automatically render a detailed return of his transactions with related persons abroad.

60. These provisions have been found to be particularly effective in countering evasion techniques which use tax havens, since the person making the payments must both establish the genuineness of the purported transaction, and show that the amount of the payments is not abnormal or excessive. Evidently they deal only with one part of the problem, as in many cases the point of using tax havens is to avoid taxation on income generated by transferred property rather than to obtain a deduction for facilities provided or services rendered by the foreign entity. The burden they impose on the taxpayer is, however, likely to complicate his task considerably if the transactions in which he engages aim at tax avoidance. Tax authorities in Belgium and France have found that these provisions have succeeded in deterring tax avoidance through the medium of tax havens.

61. Belgian and French transfer-pricing legislations provide examples of the shifting of burden of proof in cases where enterprises established in those countries have related enterprises located in tax havens. Under Article 24 of the Belgian Code des Impôts sur le Revenu (and Article 57 of the French Code Général des Impôts), the tax administration has authority to include in the profits of Belgian (or French) enterprises which control, or are controlled by, enterprises located outside Belgium (or France), profits indirectly transferred to the latter, whether through overcharging or undercharging on purchase of sale prices or by any other means. To bring this legislation into play the tax administration must furnish proof that a dependence relationship with the foreign enterprise exists and then, that there has been a transfer of profits for the latter's benefit. However, in the case of transactions with firms established in a country or territory with preferential taxation treatment, the tax administration in not required to prove the existence of a dependence relationship.

2. Subpart F-type provisions

a) Background

62. This is the most significant type of tax legislation directly aimed at counteracting the tax advantages derived from the deferral possibilities offered by the use of tax haven subsidiaries. Broadly, this is achieved by taxing the subsidiary's income in the hands of its domestic shareholders. This type of legislation was initially enacted in the United States in the 1930s (personal holding company provisions in 1934 and foreign personal holding company provisions in 1937). Then Subpart F legislation was enacted in 1962 and expanded in 1975, 1982 and 1984. Subpart F legislation provides for the taxation of the United States shareholders of controlled foreign corporations on their pro rata share of certain categories of undistributed profits from tax haven activities and certain other activities of the foreign corporation. The German "Foreign Tax Law" (Aussensteuergesetz) of 1972 introduced detailed rules on the attribution to resident shareholders of base companies' passive income derived by a controlled intermediate company. Comparable provisions were enacted in Canada as part of the tax reform of 1972[Foreign Accrual Property Income (FAPI)—these provisions came fully into force in 1976]. Japan introduced counteracting measures in 1978 as part of the Special Taxation Measures Law with an exhaustive list of 27 tax havens in three categories. France enacted legislation in 1980 (now Article 209B of C. G. I.) and the United Kingdom in the 1984 Finance Act. An outline of all these provisions is presented in Annex II and their implementation is assessed in paragraphs 99 to 114 below.

b) Scope of the legislation

63. The approach taken in the provisions of the six countries described above is basically the same. However, reflecting the variety of their fiscal and economic concerns, there are differences in detail. Subpart F-type legislation generally refers to three factors (see Annex II).

i) Participation held by residents

The tax haven company must be owned to a large extent by residents of the State where the legislation is in force. Minimum ownership formulae vary and one of the main problems is apparently how to counter strategies used by taxpayers to avoid there criteria (e. g. by indirect participation and other specific devices).

ii) Nature of the income

Under the German and Canadian provisions, particular types of activities are regarded as "tainted" and only the income derived from such activities is attributed to the resident shareholders (so-called "shopping approach"). On the other hand, the Japanese, French and the United Kingdom provisions subject to tax all of the retained income of certain subsidiaries set up in tax havens as long as they do not satisfy certain criteria of exemption (so-called "exemption approach"). Even in the latter approach, the nature of the activities of the tax haven subsidiary is crucial in determining whether or not the criteria for exemption are satisfied, so the two approaches reach substantially the same result.

Income covered under the "shopping approach" is normally "passive income", that term usually being defined in the legislation. It would normally comprise dividends, interest, royalties, capital gains and profits arising from administrative and management functions as well as payments of convenience (bribes, etc.). However, some non-passive income from, for example, the following activities is also included under some domestic laws, for example

—Administration of assets: income from this type of activity is generally included in the legislation, insofar as the income is not effectively connected with "active" business (such as production, etc.);

—Financial pivots: income is generally included (see paragraph 30 above). There evidently exist, however, differences and "grey areas", especially where such pivots take the form of banks, insurance companies, etc.;

—Operational base companies: income seems to be included where they have a clearly auxiliary character, carrying out only administrative or management functions or receiving payments of convenience. Specific problems may arise in the field of trading or service companies where the respective scope of the legislation and of arm's length pricing rules may be unspecified.

iii) Low taxation

While low taxation is a characteristic of tax havens, it proves difficult to define it for the purposes of applying subpart F-type provisions. Countries, therefore, approach this problem in a variety of ways, which are summarized in Annex II below.

c) Specific provisions of relevance

64. The United States provisions concerning "foreign personal holding companies" were introduced with corporations domiciled in low-tax countries very much in mind. They provide that the shareholders of a foreign personal holding company are taxed on their proportionate share of the corporation's undistributed foreign personal holding company income (such as dividends, interest, royalties and capital gains from securities). A foreign corporation is a foreign personal holding company if at least 60 per cent of the corporation's gross income for that year is foreign personal holding company income, and if more than 50 per cent in value of the corporation's outstanding stock is owned (directly or indirectly) by not more than five individuals who are citizens or residents of the United States. After 1984, the Subpart F provision takes precedence over the Foreign Personal Holding Company provisions.

3. Other tax provisions

a) Emigration

65. Under German law, a new concept of "extended non-resident tax liability" has been introduced in the individual income tax, the general wealth tax and the inheritance tax. This concept (Sections 2 to 5 of the Foreign Tax Law) applies to German citizens or former German citizens who transfer their residence from Germay to a low-tax country and who, for five out of the last ten years, were German citizens or subject to German tax as residents. If such an individual retains a significant economic interest in Germany after transferring residence to a low-tax country (a country imposing less than two-thirds of the tax imposed in Germany), then he is subject to German income tax for ten years after the year of emigration on all income that would not be considered as foreign source income for the purpose of the foreign tax credit provision in the hands of a person subject to unlimited liability to German income tax. The income tax liability is thus narrower than for residents but wider than for non-residents. The most important effect of this provision is that the progressive income tax scale is applied to income for which tax of 25

per cent will otherwise be withheld. Although not directed at emigration to low-tax countries, special provisions also apply in Canada, Denmark, Sweden, and the United States, to taxpayers leaving the country on a permanent basis. Such taxpayers remain subject to taxation in their country of origin for a prescribed period after they leave. The United Kingdom also has special provisions which apply to companies ceasing to be resident in the United Kingdom.

b) "Rent-a-star" company

66. France has a specific provision aimed at dissuading artistes (entertainers or sportsmen) from incorporating themselves ("Rent-a-star" company) in low-tax countries and rendering services in France. Under Article 155A of CGI, persons can be taxed, regardless of whether they are resident in France for tax purposes or not, on the basis of the services they render for which remuneration is collected by an individual or corporate third party established in a country giving preferential tax treatment. The effect is to remove any interposed screen, whether by an individual or an entity, established in a tax haven.

c) Transfer of assets abroad

67. Ireland and the United Kingdom have some relevant provisions which although not expressly concerned with tax havens, in general terms are designed to stop the avoidance of tax through individuals transferring assets abroad and arranging for what is in substance their income to be paid to a person resident or domiciled outside Ireland or the United Kingdom. Typically the arrangement would result in income or a capital benefit being paid to a company or discretionary trust in a tax haven, either indirectly for the benefit of the individual who transferred the assets (or accruing for his benefit), or for the benefit of someone else ordinarily resident in these countries. The legislation taxes the relevant income concerned. If the benefit is for someone other than the transferor, the charge is limited to the benefits that person actually receives; if it is for the transferor, all the income as it arises outside the country is subject to tax. But before the rules can apply, the tax authorities have to establish a tax avoidance motive.

68. Belgium also has provision in its law to prevent artificial transfer of

assets although they are not exclusively directed at tax havens. Sales or contribution of shares, bonds debt-claims, patents, etc. to a foreign holding company, an individual or an enterprise subject to an abnormally favorable tax treatment as concerns the income derived from the transferred assets or rights, are deemed to be shams. According to these provisions, the taxpayer cannot invoke the argument that he is no longer owner of the transferred shares, bonds, debt-claims and patents. The taxpayer, would be subject to tax on income from the transferred assets as if the transfer had not taken place unless he proves that:

——The transfer has been made for a genuine financial or economic reason;

——The taxpayer has received normal consideration as a counterpart for the transfer and the income flowing from that consideration is effectively taxed in Belgium at a level which is normal as compared with the tax burden which would have existed if the transfer had not taken place.

69. The United States has two provisions which allow the tax administration to consider the motives of persons transferring assets abroad. In a number of cases the Internal Revenue Code excludes from tax gains on transfers of property between corporations or corporations and their controllers in specific circumstances, for instance, property distributed to a corporation upon liquidation of another corporation (section 332). Broadly speaking, section 367 of the Code makes the exclusions ineffective by deeming a recipient foreign corporation not to be a corporation for these purposes unless it is established that the transfer was not made in pursuance of a plan having as one of its principal purposes the avoidance of income tax. The second provision, section 1491, imposes a special tax at a rate of 35 per cent on the adjusted value of property (less any gain taxed as income) transferred by a United States citizen or resident, domestic corporation or partnership or a trust or estate (which is not a foreign trust or estate) to a foreign corporation as paid-in surplus or as a contribution to capital, a foreign trust or estate or a foreign partnership unless it is established that the transfer is not principally for tax avoidance purposes. Amongst other exemptions, this latter provision does not apply to a transfer subject to section 367.

d) Offshore investment funds

70. Financial institutions frequently set up mutual funds, unit trusts and similar investment vehicles in tax havens. The investment concern itself pays no, or nominal, tax in the haven. If income were totally distributed to the investors, they would pay tax on it year by year in the countries in which they are resident. However, the income is often not distributed, instead being accumulated and increasing the value of investors' holdings so that, when the investor eventually disposes of his holding, he has a capital gain which will reflect the accumulated income. In many countries less tax will be paid on a capital gain than on income. In the absence of counteracting legislation, investment vehicles in tax havens can therefore be used to convert income into capital gain, with a substantial tax saving for the investor.

71. The popularity of such investment vehicles has caused a number of countries to take legislative action. These include the Netherland, the United States and Germany and they have been followed more recently by Canada[see paragraph 108 and note 26] and the United Kingdom. These counteracting measures reveal two basic approaches to the problem: first, in Canada, the Netherlands and Germany investors are taxed annually under rules for calculating the amount of income relating to the year in question; second, the United Kingdom and the United States tax the investor's gain Canada as income at the time when the holding in the investment concern is disposed of.

4. Foreign exchange control—non-tax measure

Control of the use of tax havens may also be achieved though co-operation with non-tax authorities. Since 1974, Australia has dealt with the tax haven problem by means of a tax screening process based on the exchange control mechanism. Under the Banking Act, the Reserve Bank of Australia, which is responsible for administering exchange control, is required not to grant exchange control approval for most agreements, contracts or arrangements of a capital nature (as well as certain current payments with Vanuatu) with residents of 18 countries listed in a notice under the Act unless a tax clearance certificate has been issued by the Commissioner of Taxation. These arrangements are simply an administrative device for preventing tax avoidance and evasion and, if no tax avoidance or evasion is involved with a particular transaction, a tax clearance certificate is normally issued promptly on receipt of an application. Genuine transactions are, therefore, not hindered by the screening process. The Government of Australia decided in December 1983 to remove a major part of the restrictions imposed by means of exchange control. As a result of that decision the Reserve Bank will no longer be directly involved in granting approval for foreign exchange dealings. Instead, foreign exchange dealers and the general public have been authorized to deal in foreign currencies subject to adherence to certain conditions. These conditions form the basis of the revised tax screening arrangements.

V. OPTIONS FOR INTERNATIONAL CO-OPERATION

A. Co-operation through legal instruments

1. Facilitating exchange of information

114. Member countries have an extensive network of tax treaties containing exchange of information provisions, usually on the lines of Article 26 of the OECD Model Convention. These provisions, however, do not always permit the gathering of information from tax havens. In some conventions, Article 26 can be used only for the correct application of the convention, and not for the application of domestic tax laws. Few tax treaties have been signed with tax haven countries, and even where a tax treaty exists, the tax haven treaty partner is obliged to give only such information as is obtainable under local law. Thus, if the jurisdiction has a bank secrecy law, bank account information may not be obtainable; if the jurisdiction has a commercial secrecy law, corporate ownership and business information may not be obtainable and, perhaps, even interviews with residents of the jurisdiction will be prohibited. In many tax havens, not only foreign governments but also the government of the jurisdiction itself is restricted in having access to such information. Even where secrecy laws are not a factor, the effectiveness of exchange of information depends significantly upon the attitude of treaty partners. Some countries take a very restrictive view of the exchange of information provision, and this attitude may affect the quality of information exchanged.

115. Nevertheless, exchanges of information frequently prove useful in enabling treaty partners to collect facts, in so-called "triangular" cases, on transactions with entities situated in a third (frequently tax haven) country.

2. General treaty policy with regard to tax havens

116. Member countries have few tax treaties with tax havens. While the United States had until recently treaties with about 15 jurisdictions generally considered, according to the Gordon Report, to be tax havens to some degree, this was mainly the result of the extension of the old 1945 United States-United Kingdom income tax treaty to the former British colonies. The reasons for the small number of treaties with tax havens are both that benefits granted by treaties are not balanced by corresponding tax in tax haven jurisdictions and that double taxation which may not be dealt with under domestic provisions hardly ever arises. The likelihood of tax haven areas becoming a base for conduit companies is another explanation for this tendency. The use of tax havens for tax treaty shopping could be substantially reduced by refusing to have new treaties with tax havens and by denouncing existing treaties with tax havens, though this may conflict with other policy objectives.

117. However, limited treaties with tax havens focusing on administrative assistance and non-discrimination could be useful instruments for dealing with the problems of abuse of tax havens, if they could be concluded on terms satisfactory to the non-tax haven treaty partner. The conditions to be satisfied would vary from case to case, but to assure both that the benefits of the treaties are received only by persons properly entitled to them (prevention of treaty shopping) and that the tax administration of the treaty partner of the tax haven has the information necessary to enforce its tax laws with respect to any transactions which may take place within its jurisdiction, any such treaty would require comprehensive exchange of information provisions possibly overriding secrecy laws in the tax haven. It has to be added, however, that unless the tax haven jurisdiction were offered some quid pro quo (e. g. economic aid, in particular with former colonies) it seems unlikely that the tax haven country would be willing to conclude such a treaty.

118. The United States took this approach in the Caribbean Basin Initiative (CBI) legislation of 1983, the main purpose of which is to promote economic revitalization and to facilitate expansion of economic opportunities in the Caribbean Basin region. The CBI legislation also makes 27 qualifying jurisdictions eligible for "North American area" status, that is, they can be the

sites of business conventions for which expenses are deductible for the United States tax purposes if these jurisdictions enter into an exchange of information agreement on tax matters with the United States. The exchange of information agreement would apply to both criminal and non-criminal matters and would override local secrecy laws. However, for non-criminal tax purposes, bearer share and bank account information are not a necessary part of the exchange of information agreement if the President of the United States determines that the exception to the standards in the case of a particular agreement is in the security interest of the United States, and it is determined that the modified agreement would assist in the administration and enforcement of United States tax laws. However, as to criminal tax matters, the agreement must include exchanges of bearer share and bank account information. The agreement also would impose on the officials of each country a duty not to disclose information other than to tax administrators. A Model for such exchange of information agreements has now been issued by the U. S. Treasury Department. However, so far there has not been much progress in concluding agreements on the exchange of information, except in the case of Barbados.

3. Multilateral approaches

119. Multilateral efforts are increasingly being made in this field, early examples of which are the Nordic Convention on Mutual Assistance in Tax Matters in 1973 and the EEC-Directive on Mutual Assistance by the Competent Authorities of Member States in the Field of Direct Taxation, dated 19th December 1977. The OECD/Council of Europe draft Multilateral Convention on Mutual Administrative Assistance in tax matters provides some forms of assistance which could be of special use in the tax haven situation. In its comprehensive provisions on exchange of information, the multilateral convention raises the possibility of participation in tax examinations abroad and simultaneous tax examinations.

B. Administrative co-operation

120. Within the present framework of exchange of information under double taxation agreements, tax administrations could improve international co-operation in the following ways to deal with tax avoidance and evasion involving tax havens:

—Spontaneous exchanges of information;

—Exchanges of information on specific industries;

—Regional co-operation schemes;

—Simultaneous examinations;

—Central pooling of relevant information.

121. Some Member countries have been working closely in regional co-operative groups exchanging views and experience on the use of tax havens. The "Group of Four" (the United States, the United Kingdom, France and Germany) and "PATA" (Pacific Association of Tax Administrators: the United Stated, Canada, Japan and Australia) are cases in point. Exchanges of this kind help to detect avoidance schemes and to facilitate the use of exchange of information provisions in tax treaties to improve enforcement activities. As a result of examiners'/inspectors' meetings of the Group of Four and PATA, taxpayers using tax havens have been identified for bilateral simultaneous examinations. These examinations are based on the exchange of information provisions of the income tax treaties between the countries concerned. Industrywide exchanges of information could be extended both by considering additional industries and by more treaty partners taking part.

122. Simultaneous tax examination have proved to be an important tool in auditing multinational companies with intra-group transactions involving tax havens, by enabling the tax authorities of the examining countries to see the transaction from both sides. The development of such procedures is likely to be cost-effective if restricted to major, well-selected cases.

123. At a national level, Germany has organized a central pooling system for information (Informationszentrale Ausland, foreign information centre) from national sources. In the United States a task force on information gathering was set up in May 1983 to identify taxpayers who are using business entities and bank accounts protected by stringent foreign secrecy laws for the purpose of avoidance and evasion.

124. Pooling and sharing of relevant information at an international level does not yet exist but could constitute a new form of co-operation, and should be possible if the problem of secrecy and administration can be overcome.

Improved co-operation may also come from organizing tax inspectors' meetings to consider problems relating to gathering of information on tax havens and tax haven use, as is done from time to time in OECD.

Examples of MNEs' Tax Planning Structures

—selected from OECD Addressing Base Erosion and Profit Shifting

1. E-commerce structure using a two-tiered structure and transfer of intangibles under a cost-contribution arrangement

Company A is a company that is organised in Country A and that initially developed technology and intangibles supporting its business through research conducted primarily in Country A. Company A is the parent of a multinational group of companies.

Under the tax planning structure of the Group, rights to technology developed by the parent, Company A, are licenced or otherwise transferred to Company C under a cost sharing or cost contribution arrangement. Company C is an unlimited liability company organised (i.e. registered) under the laws of Country B but managed and controlled in Country C, and so tax resident in Country C. Under the cost sharing arrangement, Company C agrees to make a "buy in" payment equal to the value of the existing technology transferred under the arrangement and to share the cost of future enhancement of the transferred technology. The buy-in payment would be fully taxable in Country A and could take the form of a single lump-sum payment or a running royalty over time. Ongoing research expense would be shared on the basis of the relative anticipated benefits from the intangibles being developed. The cost sharing arrangement would typically be established early in the life of Company A, before development of a significant track record of sales in the markets allocated to Company C under the agreement. ①

Company C licences all of its rights in the technology to Company D in exchange for a running royalty. Company D is a company organised, managed and controlled in Country D. Company D in turn sub-licences the technology to Company B.

Company B is organised, managed and controlled in Country B. Company B employs several thousand people in its operations in Country B. Country B imposes corporate income tax on taxable profit of Company B. However, the taxable profit of Company B is less than 1 per cent of its gross revenues. This is because in calculating its income in Country B, following the OECD transfer pricing principles Company B deducts the full amount of the royalty it pays to Company D for the search and advertising technology.

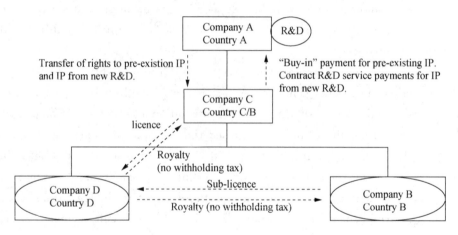

Figure C.1. Group A's tax-planning structure (Scenario 1)
Source: OECD.

The royalty payment made by Company B to Company D is free of withholding tax in Country B. Country B would impose a withholding tax on payments directly to a company tax resident in a country like Country C.

---

① In the case of Company A and Company C, the arm's length nature of the initial buy-in payment and the formula for sharing future technology development costs was confirmed through an Advance Pricing Agreement, although subsequent in Country A law and policy might well make it more difficult to obtain such an APA today.

However, under the law of Country B, applying the EU Interest and Royalties Directive, because the royalty payments are made to a company which is organised and subject to tax in a country that is a member of the European Union, the royalties qualify for exemption from Country B withholding tax.

Country D imposes corporate income tax on the profits of Company D. However, taxable profit is reduced by the deductible royalty payments made by Company D to Company C. Accordingly, corporate income tax is imposed in Country D only on the small amount of royalty "spread" between Company D's royalty receipts from Company B and its royalty payments to Company C. The spread between royalty receipts and royalty payments is very small because Company D engages only in a flow-through transaction. Company D, unlike Company B, performs no functions and holds no assets. It also bears little or no risk with regard to the royalty flows. Under the arm's length principle, it is therefore entitled to very little income. Typically a tax ruling would be obtained in Country D defining the amount of income subject to tax in Country D, thereby providing Group A with certainty regarding the results of its tax planning structure.

Country D does not levy withholding tax on royalty payments under its domestic law. The payments made by Company D to Company C are, therefore, not subject to withholding tax in Country D.

Company C is managed and controlled in Country C. Country C does not impose a corporate income tax. Country B does not impose tax on Company C because it has no presence in Country B, is centrally managed and controlled in Country C and its income arises from sources outside of Country B. Accordingly, the royalty income received by Company C is not subjected to tax in Country D, Country C or Country B.

Under some circumstances, Country A's CFC rules might tax royalty payments received by either Company D or Company C as passive income. However, it is probable that Company A will file a check-the-box election with respect to Company D and Company B. Under such an election, these companies would be disregarded for Country A tax purposes, and the income of Company B and Company D would be treated as having been earned directly by Company C. The royalty transactions between the disregarded entities would similarly be disregarded, meaning that they would be deemed not to exist for Country A tax purposes. For purposes of applying the Country A CFC rules, Company C would therefore be treated as if it had earned the fees and revenues directly through active business operations. Such active business income could be structured in such a way that it would not be subject to tax under the Country A CFC regime.

2. Transfer of manufacturing operations together with a transfer of supporting intangibles under a cost-contribution arrangement

Company A is a publicly-traded company, based in Country A. It is the parent of an MNE group with global operations. The Group invests heavily in research, product design, and development activities (see Figure C. 2).① R&D activities are carried out by the parent company, Company A. Previously, Company A owned all IP resulting from its research and development activities. It also had sole responsibility for and risks associated with the manufacture of products and sold those products through a network of sales and distribution companies in markets around the world. Company A's managers then decided to create a wholly-owned subsidiary, Company B in Country B, and assign to it IP and responsibility for the manufacture and sale of products outside of Country A. Company A retained domestic intangible property rights related to the manufacture and sale of products within Country A, and continued to carry out research and development activities for the Group.

At the same time Company B was organised, the Group organised two additional foreign subsidiaries. Each of these companies was wholly-owned by Company B. Company B serves in a dual capacity. First, it acts as a holding company for the non-Country A IP rights of the Group. Second, it acts as a holding company for the investments in the shares of Company C and Company D. One of these, Company C, was organised in Country C and serves as the principal company responsible for the manufacture and sale of Group products

---

① Figure C. 2 depicts a simplified version of Company A's Group global structure. Company A, for example, refers to the Country A parent company together with its domestic affiliates (filing a consolidated income tax return).

outside Company A. The other, Company D, is a manufacturing entity responsible for the production of Group products outside of Country A.

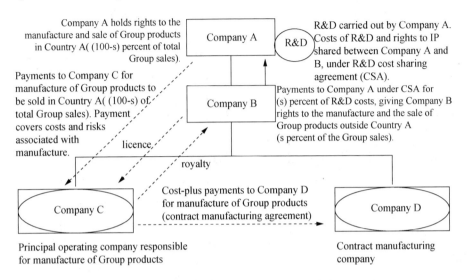

Figure C.2. Group A's tax-planning structure (Scenario 1)

Source: Based on "Present Law and Background Related to Possible Income Shifting and Transfer Pricing", prepared by staff of the Joint Committee on Taxation, submitted to the US House Committee on Ways and Means, 20 July 2010, JCX-37-10, p.93.

While Company C and Company D are treated as corporations under the laws of Country C and Country D, respectively, both are treated as disregarded entities under Country A's check-the-box rules. This treatment carries important implications. Transactions between these disregarded entities and Company B—including royalty and dividend payments to Company B—are disregarded for Country A tax purposes (i.e. they are viewed as transactions occurring within the same entity). Moreover, under the check-the-box election, Company B is viewed for Country A tax purposes as performing the activities in fact performed by Company C and Company D.

The transfer of IP from Company A to Company B is taxable in Country A. Often, but not invariably, in structures of this type the transfer would take place pursuant to a cost-sharing agreement (CSA). Under the CSA, Company C is obliged to make a buy-in payment for pre-existing IP to Company A. The buy-in payment may be structured as either a lumpsum payment or a running royalty. Company C then assumes responsibility going forward to reimburse Company A for a share of ongoing research and development expense reflecting the share of anticipated benefit Company C expects to derive from the ongoing research and development expenditures. For example, if Company C were to be responsible for 45% of global revenues and to derive 45% of global operating income, it would be expected to reimburse Company A for approximately 45% of the product area research and development costs covered under the cost sharing agreement. This effectively eliminates the current Country A tax deduction for that portion of research and development expense reimbursed by Company C under the cost sharing agreement. Despite the fact that Company C reimburses it for a percentage share of its research and development costs, Company A is entitled to an R&D tax credit in Country A for the full amount of its R&D expenditures (including the portion reimbursed by Company B).

By virtue of its buy-in payments and CSA payments, Company B is treated as the owner of the non-Country A IP rights of the Group. Company B licences those IP rights to Company C. Company C contractually assumes responsibility for producing and selling Group products outside Country A and contractually assumes the risks associated with the business. Company C engages Company D to serve as a contract manufacturer. Under the contract manufacturing agreement, Company D manufactures Group products for a fee equal to direct and indirect costs of production plus a 5% mark-up. The manufacturing agreement between Company C and Company D specifies that Company C bears the principal risks associated with the production of the product. Actual production of products may take place in Country D or in a branch of Company D in a low-cost manufacturing country. Company D includes this fee in its taxable income.

The manufactured products are the property of Company C, which sells the products to or through related sales and marketing entities in higher tax jurisdictions around the world. The contractual arrangements between Company C and the marketing companies specify that Company C assumes the principal risks related to the marketing of the products. On this basis, sales and marketing companies are compensated for their efforts on a basis reflecting their limited risk status. Such compensation would usually be computed on the basis of a target return on sales determined for transfer pricing purposes by reference to the returns earned by arguably comparable limited risk marketing and distribution companies. Company C would earn profit equal to its gross sales revenue on foreign sales, less fees paid to Company D for the manufacture of the goods, payments to any related commission-based marketing entities, and less in royalties paid to Company B. This profit is subject to corporate income tax in Country C.

Royalties paid to Company B by Company C for its foreign IP rights are deductible in the computation of the corporate tax base of Company C. The royalty payment to Company B may be determined annually under an advanced pricing agreement (APA) or other ruling between Company C and Country C tax authorities. The APA or ruling may stipulate a certain amount of taxable income in Country C determined on the basis of the activities Company C performs and the production risks it takes in Country C. The royalty amount is the residual computed after such taxable returns. As Country C does not impose withholding tax on royalty payments, and Country B does not impose corporate income tax, the royalty is free of withholding tax upon payment, and free of income tax upon receipt. Moreover, possible Country A taxation of Company A on royalty income received by Company B under Country A CFC rules is avoided with application of check-the-box rules under which Company C can be treated as a disregarded entity. Under check-the-box provisions in the Country A, Company C is treated for Country A tax purposes as a branch of Company B. Thus royalty payments from Country C to Company B are treated as payments within a single corporation, and thus are disregarded (not recognised) for Country A tax purposes. Allowing check-the-box provisions to apply in this way effectively allows the Group to erode the Country C tax base with deductible royalty payments and simultaneously side-step application of the Country A CFC provisions that would otherwise apply to royalty income passively received by Company B.

Similarly, dividends paid to Company B are free of tax at source, Country B does not tax dividend income, and the dividend payments are disregarded for Country A tax purposes.

3. Leveraged acquisition with debt-push down and use of intermediate holding companies

A MNE headquartered in State P and with operations in a number of countries, including State L, plans to acquire a successful manufacturing company resident in State T (Target Co). The acquisition price is EUR 1 billion and about 60% of that will be financed with external bank debt. The remaining 40% will be financed through the MNE's retained earnings.

In order to carry out the acquisition, the MNE sets up a holding company in State L (L Hold Co) which receives an intra-group loan for EUR 400 million. L Hold Co in turn sets up a company in State T (T Hold Co). T Hold Co is financed partly by L Hold Co through a hybrid instrument (EUR 400 million) and partly with the external bank debt (EUR 600 million). T Hold Co acquires Target Co and enters into a tax grouping with the latter for State T tax purposes.

The structure can be depicted as shown in Figure C.3.

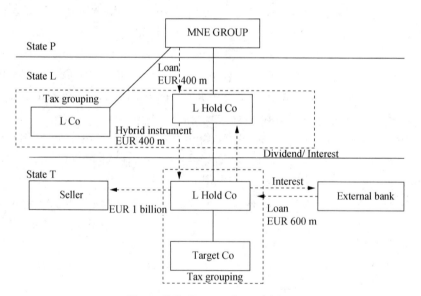

Figure C.3. Leveraged acquisition

Source: OECD.

This structure potentially allows the MNE group to achieve a number of tax benefits.

The debt push-down technique ensures that subject to applicable limitations interest expenses on the external bank loan are deducted from the target company's operating income through the applicable group tax regimes. L Hold Co finances T Hold Co through a hybrid instrument, e. g. redeemable preference shares. This financing is treated as debt in State T while it is treated as equity in State L. As a consequence, and subject to the applicable limitations, additional interest income will be deducted against the income of Target Co for tax purposes. At the same time, the payment will be treated as a dividend and therefore exempt under the domestic law of State L.

Further, the interest L Hold Co pays on the EUR 400 million intra-group loan can also be deducted against the income of other group companies operating in State L (subject to the applicable limitations) via the local tax grouping regime, thus also reducing the tax burden in State L.

The structure also allows the group to claim the benefits of the tax treaty between State T and State L, liminating or reducing State T withholding tax on the payments made by T Hold Co to L Hold Co.

Upon exiting the investment, the shares in T Hold Co can be sold tax-free to the purchaser. State T may in fact be prevented from taxing the income under the relevant double tax treaty, while State L exempts capital gains on shares under its domestic law.

Overview of BEPS Package

—selected from OECD/G20 Base Erosion and Profit Shifting Profit Explanatory Statement 2015 Final Reports

Action 1—Address the Tax Challenges of the Digital Economy

The Action 1 report concludes that the digital economy cannot be ring-fenced as it is increasingly the economy itself. The report analyses BEPS risks exacerbated in the digital economy and shows the expected impact of the measures developed across the BEPS Project. Rules and implementation mechanisms have been developed to help collect value-added tax (VAT) based on the country where the consumer is located in the case of cross-border business-to-consumers transactions. These measures are intended to level the playing field between domestic and foreign suppliers and facilitate the efficient collection of VAT due on these transactions. Technical options to deal with the broader tax challenges raised by the digital economy such as nexus and data have been discussed and analysed. As both the challenges and the potential options raise systemic issues regarding the existing framework for the taxation of cross-border activities that go beyond BEPS issues, OECD and G20 countries have agreed to monitor developments and analyse data that will become available over time. On the basis of the future monitoring work, a determination will also be made as to whether further work on the options discussed and analysed should be carried out. This determination should be based on a broad look at the ability of existing international tax standards to deal with the tax challenges raised by developments in the digital economy.

Action 2—Neutralise the Effects of Hybrid Mismatch Arrangements

A common approach which will facilitate the convergence of national practices through domestic and treaty rules to neutralise such arrangements. This will help to prevent double non-taxation by eliminating the tax benefits of mismatches and to put an end to costly multiple deductions for a single expense, deductions in one country without corresponding taxation in another, and the generation of multiple foreign tax credits for one amount of foreign tax paid. By neutralising the mismatch in tax outcomes, but not otherwise interfering with the use of such instruments or entities, the rules will inhibit the use of these arrangements as a tool for BEPS without adversely impacting cross-border trade and investment.

Action 3—Strengthen CFC Rules

The report sets out recommendations in the form of building blocks of effective Controlled Foreign Company (CFC) rules, while recognising that the policy objectives of these rules vary among jurisdictions. The recommendations are not minimum standards, but they are designed to ensure that jurisdictions that choose to implement them will have rules that effectively prevent taxpayers from shifting income into foreign subsidiaries. It identifies the challenges to existing CFC rules posed by mobile income such as that from intellectual property, services and digital transactions, and allows jurisdictions to reflect on appropriate policies in this regard. The work emphasises that CFC rules have a continuing, important role in tackling BEPS, as a backstop to transfer pricing and other rules.

Action 4—Limit Base Erosion via Interest Deductions and Other Financial Payments

A common approach to facilitate the convergence of national rules in the area of interest deductibility. The influence of tax rules on the location of debt within multinational groups has been established in a number of academic studies and it is well-known that groups can easily multiply the level of debt at the individual group entity level via intra-group financing. At the same time, the ability to achieve excessive interest deductions including those that finance the production of exempt or deferred income is best addressed in a coordinated manner given the importance of addressing competitiveness considerations and of ensuring that appropriate interest expense limitations do not themselves lead to double taxation. The common approach aims at ensuring that an entity's net interest deductions are directly linked to the taxable income generated by its economic activities and fostering increased coordination of national rules in this space.

Action 5—Counter Harmful Tax Practices More Effectively, Taking into Account Transparency and Substance

Current concerns on harmful tax practices are primarily about preferential regimes which can be used for artificial profit shifting and about a lack of transparency in connection with certain rulings. The Action 5 report sets out a minimum standard based on an agreed methodology to assess whether there is substantial activity in a preferential regime. In the context of IP regimes such as patent boxes, consensus was reached on the "nexus" approach. This approach uses expenditures in the country as a proxy for substantial activity and ensures that taxpayers benefiting from these regimes did in fact engage in research and development and incurred actual expenditures on such activities. The same principle can also be applied to other preferential regimes so that such regimes would be found to require substantial activities where they grant benefits to a taxpayer to the extent that the taxpayer undertook the core income-generating activities required to produce the type of income covered by the preferential regime. In the area of transparency, a framework has been agreed for mandatory spontaneous exchange of information on rulings that could give rise to BEPS concerns in the absence of such exchange. The results of the application of the elaborated substantial activity and transparency factors to a number of preferential regimes are included in the report.

Action 6—Prevent Treaty Abuse

The Action 6 report includes a minimum standard on preventing abuse including through treaty shopping and new rules that provide safeguards to prevent treaty abuse and offer a certain degree of flexibility regarding how to do so. The new treaty anti-abuse rules included in the report first address treaty shopping, which involves strategies through which a person who is not a resident of a State attempts to obtain the benefits of a tax treaty concluded by that State. More targeted rules have been designed to address other forms of treaty abuse. Other changes to the OECD Model Tax Convention have been agreed to ensure that treaties do not inadvertently prevent the application of domestic anti-abuse rules. A clarification that tax treaties are not intended to be used to generate double non-taxation is provided through a reformulation of the title and preamble of the Model Tax Convention. Finally, the report contains the policy considerations to be taken into account when entering into tax treaties with certain low or no-tax jurisdictions.

Action 7—Prevent the Artificial Avoidance of PE Status

Tax treaties generally provide that the business profits of a foreign enterprise are taxable in a State only to the extent that the enterprise has in that State a permanent establishment to which the profits are attributable. The definition of permanent establishment included in tax treaties is therefore crucial in determining whether a non-resident enterprise must pay income tax in another State. The report includes changes to the definition of permanent establishment in Article 5 of the OECD Model Tax Convention, which is widely used as the basis for negotiating tax treaties. These changes address techniques used to inappropriately avoid the tax nexus, including via replacement of distributors with commissionaire arrangements or via the artificial fragmentation of business activities.

Actions 8-10—Assure that Transfer Pricing Outcomes are in Line with Value Creation

Transfer pricing rules, which are set out in Article 9 of tax treaties based on the OECD and UN Model Tax Conventions and the Transfer Pricing Guidelines, are used to determine on the basis of the arm's length principle the conditions, including the price, for transactions within an MNE group. The existing standards in this area have been clarified and strengthened, including the guidance on the arm's length principle and an approach to ensure the appropriate pricing of hard-to-value-intangibles has been agreed upon within the arm's length principle. The work has focused on three key areas. Action 8 looked at transfer pricing issues relating to controlled transactions involving intangibles, since intangibles are by definition mobile and they are often hard-to-value. Misallocation of the profits generated by valuable intangibles has heavily contributed to base erosion and profit shifting. Under Action 9, contractual allocations of risk are respected only when they are supported by actual decision-making and thus exercising control over these risks. Action 10 has focused on other high-risk areas, including the scope for addressing profit allocations resulting from controlled transactions which are not commercially rational, the scope for targeting the use of transfer pricing methods in a way which results in diverting profits from the most economically important activities of the MNE group, and the use of certain type of payments between members of the MNE group (such as management fees and head office expenses) to erode the tax base in the absence of alignment with the value-creation. The combined report contains revised guidance which responds to these issues and ensures that transfer pricing rules secure outcomes that better align operational profits with the economic activities which generate them.

The report also contains guidance on transactions involving cross-border commodity transactions as well as on low value-adding intra-group services. As those two areas were identified as of critical importance by developing countries, the guidance will be supplemented with further work mandated by the G20 Development Working Group, which will provide knowledge, best practices, and tools for developing countries to price commodity transactions for transfer pricing purposes and to prevent the erosion of their tax bases through common types of base-eroding payments.

Action 11—Measuring and Monitoring BEPS

There are hundreds of empirical studies finding evidence of tax-motivated profit shifting, using different data sources and estimation strategies. While measuring the scope of BEPS is challenging given the complexity of BEPS and existing data limitations, a number of recent studies suggest that global CIT revenue losses due to BEPS could be significant. Action 11 assesses currently available data and methodologies and concludes that significant limitations severely constrain economic analyses of the scale and economic impact of BEPS and improved data and methodologies are required. Noting these data limitations, a dashboard of six BEPS indicators has been constructed, using different data sources and assessing different BEPS channels. These indicators provide strong signals that BEPS exists and suggest it has been increasing over time. New OECD empirical analyses estimate, while acknowledging the complexity of BEPS as well as methodological and data limitations, that the scale of global corporate income tax revenue losses could be between USD 100 to 240 billion annually. The research also finds significant non-fiscal economic distortions arising from BEPS, and proposes recommendations for taking better advantage of available tax data and improving analyses to support the monitoring of BEPS in the future, including through analytical tools to assist countries to evaluate the fiscal effects of BEPS and impact of BEPS countermeasures for their countries. Going forward, enhancing the economic analysis and monitoring of BEPS will require countries to improve the collection, compilation and analysis of data.

Action 12—Require Taxpayers to Disclose their Aggressive Tax Planning Arrangements

The lack of timely, comprehensive and relevant information on aggressive tax planning strategies is one of the main challenges faced by tax authorities worldwide. Early access to such information provides the opportunity to quickly respond to tax risks through informed risk assessment, audits, or changes to legislation. The Action 12 report provides a modular framework of guidance drawn from best practices for use by countries without mandatory disclosure rules which seeks to design a regime that fits those countries' need to obtain early information on aggressive or abusive tax planning schemes and their users. The recommendations in this report do not represent a minimum standard and countries are free to choose whether or not to introduce mandatory disclosure regimes. The framework is also intended as a reference for countries that already have mandatory disclosure regimes, in order to enhance the effectiveness of those regimes. The recommendations provide the necessary flexibility to balance a country's need for better and more timely information with the compliance burdens for taxpayers. It also sets out specific best practice recommendations for rules targeting international tax schemes, as well as for the development and implementation of more effective information exchange and co-operation between tax administrations.

Action 13—Re-examine Transfer Pricing Documentation

Improved and better-coordinated transfer pricing documentation will increase the quality of information provided to tax administrations and limit the compliance burden on businesses. The Action 13 report contains a three-tiered standardised approach to transfer pricing documentation, including a minimum standard on Country-by-Country Reporting. This minimum standard reflects a commitment to implement the common template for Country-by-Country Reporting in a consistent manner. First, the guidance on transfer pricing documentation requires multinational enterprises (MNEs) to provide tax administrations with high-level information regarding their global business operations and transfer pricing policies in a "master file" that is to be available to all relevant tax administrations. Second, it requires that detailed transactional transfer pricing documentation be provided in a "local file" specific to each country, identifying material related-party transactions, the amounts involved in those transactions, and the company's analysis of the transfer pricing determinations they have made with regard to those transactions. Third, large MNEs are required to file a Country-by-Country Report that will provide annually and for each tax jurisdiction in which they do business the amount of revenue, profit before income tax and income tax paid and accrued and other indicators of economic activities. Country-by-country reports should be filed in the ultimate parent entity's jurisdiction and shared automatically through government-to-government exchange of information. In limited circumstances, secondary mechanisms, including local filing can be used as a backup. An agreed implementation plan will ensure that information is provided to the tax administration in a timely manner, that confidentiality of the reported information is preserved and that the Country-by-Country Reports are used appropriately.

Taken together, these three documentation tiers will require taxpayers to articulate consistent transfer pricing positions, and will provide tax administrations with useful information to assess transfer pricing risks, make determinations about where audit resources can most effectively be deployed, and, in the event audits are called for, provide information to commence and target audit enquiries. By ensuring a consistent approach to transfer pricing documentation across countries, and by limiting the need for multiple filings of Country-by-Country Reports through making use of information exchange among tax administrations, MNEs will also see the benefits in terms of a more limited compliance burden.

Action 14—Make Dispute Resolution Mechanisms More Effective

Countries recognize that the changes introduced by the BEPS Project may lead to some uncertainty, and could, without action, increase double taxation and MAP disputes in the short term. Recognising the importance of removing double taxation as an obstacle to cross-border trade and investment, countries have committed to a minimum standard with respect to the resolution of treaty-related disputes. In particular, this includes a strong political commitment to the effective and timely resolution of disputes through the mutual agreement procedure. The commitment also includes the establishment of an effective monitoring mechanism to ensure the minimum standard is met and countries make further progress to rapidly resolve disputes. In addition, a large group of countries has committed to quickly adopt mandatory and binding arbitration in their bilateral tax treaties.

Action 15—Develop a Multilateral Instrument

Drawing on the expertise of public international law and tax experts, the Action 15 report explores the technical feasibility of a multilateral instrument to implement the BEPS treaty-related measures and amend bilateral tax treaties. It concludes that a multilateral instrument is desirable and feasible, and that negotiations for such an instrument should be convened quickly. Based on this analysis, a mandate has been developed for an ad-hoc group, open to the participation of all countries, to develop the multilateral instrument and open it for signature in 2016. So far, about 90 countries are participating in the work on an equal footing.

第六章 转让定价的法律制度

第一节 转让定价概述

转让定价(transfer pricing)是目前跨国关联企业之间转移利润、逃避税收的最主要手段。由于各国在税制上的差异性,跨国关联企业无不从整体利益出发,通过转让定价方式对跨国的收入和费用在全球范围内作出不合理的分配和调整,将跨国收入尽可能分配到位于低税率国的关联企业,而将费用尽可能分配到位于高税率国的关联企业,从而实现总体税负的最小化。转让定价不仅会对投资东道国,特别是发展中国家的东道国的财政收入带来损害,而且也使跨国投资者的母国政府的税收利益蒙受损失。

一、转让定价的概念及成因

所谓转让定价,是指跨国关联企业根据全球战略目标,在母公司与子公司之间、子公司与子公司之间订立有关商品、资本、技术、劳务等的交易价格,这种内部交易价格亦称作"转让价格"或"划拨价格"。转让定价的特点在于其往往不是根据独立竞争的市场原则决定的,而是人为地故意抬高或压低有关货物、技术、劳务等的价格或费用标准,以实现其整体经营目标或集团利益最大化目的。

国际关联企业之所以在内部交易往来中从事转让定价安排,具体可分为税收和非税收两大原因。基于非税收方面的原因而进行的转让定价安排,是指跨国关联企业基于企业整体经营策略或目标的考虑而非出于规避税负的动机所进行的转让定价行为。从结果的角度讲,跨国关联企业之间的转让定价行为除了可以实现避税目标之外,作为一种重要的全球经营策略,它同时也是实现下述目标的手段:一是转移资金,如利用转让定价,提高从母公司或从其他子公司进口货物的价格,使利润以支付货款的形式汇出,从而达到转移资金的目的;二是调节利润,如通过调整半成品或零部件的进出口价格来影响子公司的产品成本,或通过内部借贷关系及其利率的高低来调节子公司的产品成本和利润等;三是控制市场,如低价供应子公司原料、中间产品和服务,高价买进子公司的产品,使子公司在账务上显示出较高的利润率,从而在当地树立良好的市场信誉。

由此可见,避税并非是转让定价的唯一动因或目的,尽管如此,国际税法领域所提到的转让定价通常特指以避税为目的的转让定价,即跨国关联企业之间基于共同股权或控制关系,彼此在进行交易时从全球战略目标出发,违背独立各方在公平市场上的独立交易定价原则,人为地提高或压低交易价格,使利润从高税国转移到低税国去,从而达到减轻纳税义务的目的。无论是不是基于税收动机而实施的转让定价安排,国际关联企业间内部交易确定的价格如果背离了市场竞争条件下的独立交易价格,客观上都会造成利润在位于不同国家境内的关联企业实体之间的转移,从而影响到利润被转出国家的所得税税基,损害其税收利益。因此,各国从税收上管制关联企业转让定价的侧重点,在于认定转让定价是否与正常的市场交易价格相偏离,并不强调作为纳税人的关联企业在动机上是否存在逃避本国税收的企图。

二、关联企业的界定

跨国关联企业亦称"联属企业"(associated enterprises),是指同一企业集团内存在互相依存关系的公司,多指跨国公司集团中的母公司和子公司或那些处于共同控制下的公司。根据两大范本的定义,联属企业包括下列两种情况:(1)缔约国一方的企业直接或间接参与缔约国另一方企业的管理、控制或资本;或者(2)同一人直接或间接参与缔约国一方企业和缔约国另一方企业的管理、控制或资本。跨国关联企业是转让定价中的一个重要概念,其法律意义在于明确转让定价税制适用的主体范围。只有存在控制关系的关联企业之间的交易行为才受到各国转让定价税法制度的调整规范,而非关联企业之间的交易安排并不适用转让定价税制的规范。[①]

从各国转让定价税收法律制度看,由于各国认定关联控制关系的标准不同,导致据此标准认定的关联企业范围也不完全一致。常见的关联方判定标准有两种:一是股权判定法,即以持有企业股权的比例来判定是否构成关联企业。例如,日本、英国、比利时等国家的税法规定,一个企业直接或间接持有另一个企业50%或以上的资本股份,即可认定彼此为存在控制关系的关联企业;德国、西班牙等国要求直接或间接控股25%以上,就构成税法意义上的关联企业。二是实际控制管理判定法,即依据企业之间事实上的控制关系来判定是否构成关联企业,遵循实质重于形式原则,而不论持有的股权是否达到一定比例。以日本为例,根据日本《租税特别措施法》及国税厅有关规定,除股权控制外,存在下列关

---

① 参见廖益新主编:《国际税法学》,高等教育出版社 2008 年版,第 283 页。

系之一的,也会被认定为关联企业:企业一方至少有一名常务董事以及一半以上管理人员由企业另一方派出;企业一方的经营资金一半以上由企业另一方借入或提供借款担保;企业一方购进销售的商品一半以上是与企业另一方进行的;企业一方的生产经营活动必须依赖企业另一方提供工业产权或专有技术才能正常进行;其他控制与被控制的关系。① 美国联邦所得税法上认定控制关系的标准更为灵活,即两个或两个以上的企业之间如果所得额和费用扣除额被任意转移,便可推断彼此之间存在着控制关系。

我国《企业所得税法实施条例》第109条对关联关系的认定作了规定。根据规定,关联方是指与企业有下列关联关系之一的企业、其他组织或个人:(1)在资金、经营、购销等方面存在直接或间接的控制关系;(2)直接或间接地为第三者控制;(3)在利益上具有相关联的其他关系。在此框架下,国家税务总局在《特别纳税调整实施办法(试行)》(国税发〔2009〕2号文)第9条中提出了更为具体的八条判定标准,只要符合以下八条中的任意一条,便构成了关联关系:(1)25%以上的股权控制:一方直接或间接持有另一方的股份总和达到25%以上,或者双方直接或间接同为第三方所持有的股份达到25%以上。若一方通过中间方对另一方间接持有股份,只要一方对中间方持股比例达到25%以上,则一方对另一方的持股比例按照中间方对另一方的持股比例计算。(2)借贷资金或担保资金达到一定标准:一方与另一方(独立金融机构除外)之间借贷资金占一方实收资本50%以上,或者一方借贷资金总额的10%以上是由另一方(独立金融机构除外)担保。(3)高级管理人员委派:一方半数以上的高级管理人员(包括董事会成员和经理)或至少一名可以控制董事会的董事会高级成员是由另一方委派,或者双方半数以上的高级管理人员(包括董事会成员和经理)或至少一名可以控制董事会的董事会高级成员同为第三方委派。(4)共享高级管理人员:一方半数以上的高级管理人员(包括董事会成员和经理)同时担任另一方的高级管理人员(包括董事会成员和经理),或者一方至少一名可以控制董事会的董事会高级成员同时担任另一方的董事会高级成员。(5)一方的生产经营活动必须由另一方提供工业产权、专有技术等特许权才能正常进行。(6)一方的购买或销售活动主要由另一方控制。(7)一方接受或提供劳务主要由另一方控制。(8)一方对另一方的生产经营、交易具有实质控制,或者双方在利益上具有相关联的其他关系,包括虽未达到本条第1项持股比例,但一方与另一方的主要持股方享受基本相同的经济利益,以及家族、亲属关系等。

---

① 参见尹晓宇:《中日转让定价税收管理制度之比较》,载《涉外税务》2006年第1期。

三、关联企业利用转让定价进行避税的主要方式

关联企业针对不同的交易对象并结合其特定目的,通常采用以下五种方式来实施转让定价进行国际避税:

1. 有形资产的销售

关联企业在对内部交易的有形资产(如半成品、零部件等货物)定价时,可以综合考虑各国税率高低和集团经营战略,制定出背离独立交易价格(即无关联企业之间独立交易决定的市场价格)的转让定价。例如,某联属企业所在国税率较低时,跨国企业可以低于独立交易价格的转让定价向该联属企业销售半成品、零部件,然后再从该企业高价购买其产品,从而将超过独立交易的利润转移到该联属企业账面,达到减轻公司整体税负的目的。反之,当该联属企业所在国税率较高时,跨国公司则可以通过向其高价销售半成品、零部件,低价收购其产品的方法,减少该联属企业的利润,甚至使它处于亏损状态,从而减轻或避免其在高税率国家的纳税,这就是通常见到的某些外商投资企业存在的"高进低出"现象。

2. 有形资产的使用

跨国公司可以通过租赁(leasing)、租用(hire)和租购(hire purchase)等不转移有形资产所有权的方法,将该资产的使用权转移给另一国的联属企业,然后收取一定的租金。这方面惯用的避税手段是位于高税国的一个联属企业购置一项资产,并将其按尽可能达到的最低价格租赁给位于低税国的一个联属企业,再由该联属企业以尽可能高的价格转移给另一联属公司。这样,两种租金之间的差额便转化为低税国联属企业的利润,而且该有形资产的折旧往往可以作为位于高税国的出租方的成本扣除项目,达到削减出租方纳税所得的目的。即使不存在上述复杂的安排,联属企业之间也可以通过支付过高或过低的租金,起到调整利润的作用。

3. 无形资产交易

无形资产交易主要包括转让或许可使用专利、专有技术、商标、著作权等知识产权。跨国公司可以通过向国外联属企业收取高额特许权使用费或转让费,降低该联属企业的利润;也可以通过收取较少的特许权使用费或转让费,一方面减低转让方的利润额,另一方面增加受让方的竞争能力。近年来,转让定价领域的一个突出趋势便是跨国公司越来越多地使用无形资产转让定价的方法调整其位于不同国家的联属企业之间的利润分配。

4. 贷款

贷款是跨国公司联属企业之间进行投资或融资安排的常见形式。由于联属

企业偿还贷款时支付的利息可以作为费用扣除，所以在一定条件下，贷款可以获得纳税上的好处。例如，跨国公司利用本集团内部的金融机构向联属企业提供贷款时，出于加强其产品竞争能力的考虑，可以不收或少收利息，使该企业的产品成本减少；相反，为了造成该联属企业亏损或微利的局面，达到在东道国少纳税的目的，则可以按较高的利息收取，以此提高子公司的产品成本。

随着跨国银行业务的进一步发展，跨国银行总行与分支机构以及分支机构之间在相互贷款利率方面采取转让定价，已成为进行国际避税的重要手段。例如，总行拆借给分行或分行之间相互拆借的款项，可以按照不同于独立交易的利率收取利息，从而调整了它们之间的利润分配。由于银行相互拆借是经营的正常方式，尤其当银行之间拆借的利率计算采用银行同业拆借利率再浮动一定百分比的方法，这种转让定价更具有隐蔽性和灵活性。

5. 服务收费与管理成本分摊

跨国公司作为一个经营整体，经常通过总公司设立的某些职能部门向联属企业提供各类服务，如法律、广告、咨询、培训、管理等方面。此外，总公司为了维持整个集团的运作，也会产生一些管理费用，如制订计划、监督集团运转、财务管理、合并会计报表、审计等方面的费用。各个联属企业对总公司为其提供的服务，或受益于总公司的有关管理活动，均应支付费用或分摊总公司的管理成本。因此，这就产生了总公司不按独立交易价格收取服务费用，或不按正常会计原则以联属企业受益程度向其分摊管理成本的可能。这种类型的转让定价，同样可以达到调整联属企业利润的目的。

通过不合理分摊成本费用的办法进行国际避税，同样可发生在跨国公司总机构与国外分支机构之间。例如，总机构可以把那些与常设机构的经营活动毫无关系的管理费用和一般行政费用大量分摊给常设机构，从而人为地降低常设机构本身的盈利水平；另外，也可以采用不把有关的成本费用分摊给国外分支机构的方法，从而压低总机构利润，提高分支机构的营业利润水平，实现国际避税的目的。[1]

---

[1] 参见廖益新主编：《国际税法学》，高等教育出版社2008年版，第285—287页。

第二节 规制转让定价的基本原则

一、独立交易原则的定义

所谓独立交易原则(arm's length principle),亦称"正常交易原则"或"独立核算原则",是指将跨国关联企业的母公司与子公司、总公司与分公司,以及子公司或分公司相互间的关系,当作独立竞争的企业之间的关系来处理,即按照在同样条件下,从事相同或类似交易的彼此没有关联的独立企业在公开竞争的市场上达成的价格标准,来调整分配跨国关联企业之间发生的收入和费用。

《OECD范本》第9条对此作出了规定:"如果两个企业之间在商业或财务关系中达成或施加的交易条件不同于独立企业之间达成的交易条件,那么,本应由其中一个企业取得,但由于这些条件而没有取得的利润,可以计入该企业的利润,并据以征税。"也就是说,关联企业之间的交易应该按照独立企业之间的交易一样,依据市场条件下的交易原则来处理关联企业之间的收入和费用分配问题,否则,税务机关有权对企业的转让定价进行税务调整。特别值得一提的是,《OECD转让定价指南》也强调了独立交易原则的运用。虽然《OECD转让定价指南》不具有强制约束力,但它已成为各国,特别是经合组织成员国处理转让定价问题的重要参考,在一定程度上指引着各国转让定价法规的发展方向。到目前为止,世界上制定转让定价法规的国家大多都借鉴了该指南中的独立交易原则。

二、独立交易原则的特点

首先,独立交易原则之所以成为各国管制关联企业转让定价的基本原则,一个主要的原因是实行此原则能够在关联企业与独立企业之间实现税收待遇的平等。独立交易原则通过将关联企业与非关联企业置于同等的税收地位,避免了这两类企业之间可能的税收优势和劣势从而扭曲它们的相对竞争地位。其次,采用独立交易原则,实质是以可比的独立企业在相同或类似条件下的市场交易价格标准来衡量判断关联企业内部交易往来的定价是否合理,这符合市场竞争规则和价值规律,容易为作为纳税人的关联企业和各国税务当局接受。再次,对于大多数关联企业间涉及一般商品买卖或金钱借贷的转让定价交易,税务机关可以方便地找到可比的独立企业进行的可比交易从而确定正常的交易价格,所以独立交易原则能够有效地被用来审查判断关联交易定价是否正常合理。最后,适用独立交易原则的经验已经足够丰富,便于在纳税人和各国税务机关之间就该原则的理解与应用达成共识。①

另外,独立交易原则也有其内在的缺陷和问题。首先,这一原则要求将存在着共同的资本拥有和控制关系的关联企业的各个实体,当作彼此间不存在这种关系的各个独立企业看待,按照独立交易价格标准来确定关联企业内部交易的利润分配,没有充分考虑到关联企业一体化经营所带来的规模经济效益和各实体不同经济活动的相互关系。无视关联企业一体化经营和规模经济的优势这样的客观现实,在经济逻辑上显然是不合理的。其次,执行独立交易原则,要求将关联企业的内部交易与公开市场上独立企业之间的相同或类似的交易进行比较,但有时要找到这种可比较的独立企业之间的交易很困难,因为关联企业可能从事的某次交易是独立企业所不可能从事的,并且关联企业之间从事的活动在独立企业之间没有发生这一事实本身并不能说明该交易不符合独立交易原则。最后,由于执行独立交易原则要求关联企业间的交易与独立企业间的交易进行比较,以确定独立交易价格,这就需要收集大量的有关的市场行情和交易数据资料,并进行复杂的可比性分析,从而给纳税人和税务机关造成沉重的守法成本和管理负担,不符合税收效率原则。②

三、总利润原则——全球公式分配法

上述独立交易原则的理论基础是"独立实体论"(separate entity theory),主张对跨国收入和费用的分配实行独立交易原则。与之相对的另外一种学说是"单一实体论"(unitary entity theory),主张对跨国纳税人的收入和费用的调整实行总利润原则。所谓总利润原则,是指将跨国关联企业视为一个整体的经济实体,并将来自全球的利润加以汇总,然后按照某种方法将汇总的利润在总体所属的各个企业之间进行重新分配,各国税务当局根据企业重新分配后的利润进行征税。对跨国收入和费用分配实行总利润原则,主要是从影响企业利润的各个因素中,选定某个关键性的因素来决定总利润在各个企业之间的分配。一般来说,影响关联企业利润的因素主要有:企业组织结构、资本结构、规模;企业的主要经营业务和经营成果;企业经营活动的地域分布状况;企业的雇员数量及素质等。③

---

① See OECD Transfer Pricing Guidelines for Multinational Enterprises and Tax Administrations, July 2010, paragraphs 1.8, 1.9, 1.14, 1.15.
② Ibid., paragraphs 1.10—1.13.
③ 参见曹建明、陈治东主编:《国际经济法专论》(第六卷),法律出版社 2000 年版,第 118 页。

自 20 世纪末期以来备受关注的全球公式分配法(global formulary apportionment)可以看作"单一实体论"的应用。该方法要求按照事先确定的各关联企业的资产、工资和销售额等要素在跨国企业集团内所占的份额,确定每个企业对跨国企业全部所得的贡献率,然后根据贡献率确定每个企业的所得和利润。简言之,公式分配法就是根据企业占有和使用生产要素的比例来确定企业在跨国公司全部所得、利润中分配的比例,从而确定各个企业的应税所得。公式分配法的讨论已经进行了几十年,近年来之所以备受重视,根本原因在于它反映了跨国公司基于全球化生产和全球化经营因而要求全球计税的现实,正视并试图消解适用公平交易原则引发的问题,包括无形资产的计价问题,以及各国税务当局的管理问题等。

但是,用公式法来分配跨国公司各企业的所得和利润,还存在一些问题。首先,国际协调难度大。全球公式分配法使用预先设定的公式进行分配,由于公式中涉及各种因素,如全球税基的确定、统一的会计政策的使用等等,这些方面的统一需要大量的国际协调,十分耗时且极其困难。

其次,各国是否接受通用的公式也不明确。在既定的要素框架内,存在很多代表不同利益和立场的争议,劳动力密集国家强调工资因素,制造业发达国家强调生产地点,高新技术国家强调无形资产所在地,各个不同类型的国家都希望把对自己有利的因素在分配公式中加重、放大,从而得到对自己有利的税收效果,这些争议很可能会带来一些不公平的结果。

再次,个体差异无法体现。全球公式分配法是对跨国集团整体进行征税,实际上不能认识到重要的地域差异、单个公司的效率及跨国集团下某一子公司的特定因素,而这些因素对于不同税收管辖地区的企业利润分配发挥着重要作用。相对而言,独立交易原则是把关联企业看作独立的经济实体,即使当跨国集团整体发生亏损,该企业也有可能盈利。而全球公式分配法则不能合理地解释这种可能性。

又次,预设公式较为武断。全球公式分配法的分配公式是由资产、收入、工资等因素组合而成,意味着各税收管辖区内的每个集团成员按照公式组成要素获得固定的利润率,而不管跨国集团成员在功能、资产、风险、效率上的差异,也不考虑市场状况、单个企业的具体情形以及管理者自身对资源的分配,该方法所考虑到的利润分配与交易的具体事项缺乏联系。[1]

最后,从纳税人与征税国的角度看,由于存在严重的信息不对称,主动权更

---

[1] 参见范坚主编:《国际反避税实务指引》,江苏人民出版社 2012 年版,第 11—12 页。

多地掌握在纳税人手里,所以公式分配法可能更有利于跨国公司纳税人,而不利于征税国。①

到目前为止,独立交易原则仍为绝大多数国家的转让定价立法所采用,但值得注意的是,独立交易原则也受到很多因素的挑战:首先,非经合组织成员国的兴起,它们并不必然将经合组织所推崇的这一原则标准作为最合适的处理转让定价的方法,同时也考虑到独立交易原则的实施成本高等因素。2011年3月,经合组织发布了关于转让定价行政管理方面的报告,其中提到了对独立交易原则进行修订的意见。其次,一些国际组织倡议,如联合国倡议,支持发展中国家通过综合"能力建设"计划(comprehensive "capacity building" programme)实施有效的转让定价立法,强调考虑独立交易原则替代方法的重要性,如全球公式分配法。再次,2011年3月16日的一项欧洲指令建议包括了三种因素的公司税基分配机制,这事实上是在建议欧洲委员会在统一市场内优先选择全球公式分配法。最后,正如2010年《OECD转让定价指南》所指出的,现代公司的组织方式尤其容易受到规模经济、协同作用、集团优势或者"软实力"等因素影响,而适用独立交易原则未能充分考虑到这些因素。② 这些都表明,传统的独立交易原则正日益受到挑战。

第三节 针对转让定价的调整方法

转让定价方法,是指企业向关联方转让有形资产、无形资产、融通资金或提供劳务等确定价格所依据的方法。关联方之间的交易采用何种转让定价方法属于企业的自主权利,不同企业对相同或类似的关联交易可能采用不同的定价方法,但由于关联交易不受市场力量主导,因此并非所有的转让定价方法都符合独立交易原则。如果关联交易采用了不符合独立交易原则的转让定价方法,将会影响到不同国家或同一国家不同地区的税收利益。因此,大部分国家均建立了规范转让定价的法律体系,设定了各具特色但又不乏共性的符合独立交易原则的转让定价方法,主要包括传统交易方法(可比非受控价格法、再销售价格法、成本加成法)、交易利润法(交易净利润法和利润分割法)以及其他符合独立交易原

---

① 参见那力、夏佩天、薛晓波:《无形资产转让定价的国际税法调整:公平交易原则 VS 全球公式法》,载《当代法学》2010年第5期。

② See Antonio Russo, Chapters Ⅰ and Ⅲ of the 2010 OECD Guidelines: Capita Selecta; Dennis Weber & Stef van Weeghel (eds), The 2010 OECD Updates: Model Tax Convention & Transfer Pricing Guidelines—A Critical Review, pp. 170—171.

则的方法。

上述符合独立交易原则的转让定价方法通常有两方面的作用:(1)判断关联交易是否符合独立交易原则。即首先运用符合独立交易的转让定价方法计算出关联交易的应有价格或利润,然后将其与关联交易的实际价格或利润进行比较,以此来判断企业与其关联方之间的业务往来是否符合独立交易原则。(2)调整不符合独立交易原则的关联交易。企业与其关联方之间的业务往来,若不符合独立交易原则而减少企业或者其关联方应纳税收入或者所得额的,税务机关有权按照符合独立交易原则的转让定价方法进行调整,以使关联交易的价格和利润与可比非关联交易的价格和利润一致,从而尽可能消除企业利用转让定价避税导致的应纳税收入在关联方之间的不合理分配,使关联企业和独立企业承担同等的纳税义务,体现税收公平。[①]

一、转让定价调整方法的选择

1995年《OECD转让定价指南》采用优先顺序法作为转让定价方法选择的原则,即传统交易方法优于交易利润方法,交易利润方法被认为是次优的选择,只有在例外情况——"传统交易方法的数据无法获得或者可以获得的数据不足以依赖"时才能适用。2010年《OECD转让定价指南》在一定程度上放弃了优先顺序法,明确以最优法作为选择转让定价方法的原则,即选择对于特定案情最为合适的转让定价方法,这里的考虑因素主要有:各种方法的优势和缺陷、关联交易的性质、可比信息的可获得性,以及受控交易和非受控交易的可比程度。没有任何一种方法是适合所有情形的,也没有必要证明某一种特定方法在某种情形下并不适合。[②]

然而,经合组织仍然肯定了传统交易方法在同等条件下的优先性。传统交易方法被认为是检验关联交易中的商业和财务条件是否符合独立交易的最直接的方法。这是因为任何受控交易与可比非受控交易之间的价格差异都可以直接追踪到企业间的商业和财务关系,采用可比非关联交易的价格直接替换关联交易的价格就可以简单有效地使关联交易符合独立交易原则。所以,当考虑到上述方法选择的因素,传统交易方法和交易利润方法在适用中同样可靠时,传统交易方法优先适用;同时,在可比非受控价格法与其他转让定价方法在适用中同样

---

① 参见范坚主编:《国际反避税实务指引》,江苏人民出版社2012年版,第25页。
② See OECD Transfer Pricing Guidelines for Multinational Enterprises and Tax Administrations, July 2010, paragraph 2.2.

可靠时,可比非受控价格法优先适用。①

根据《OECD 转让定价指南》的规定,跨国公司也可以适用指南中没有列举的转让定价方法来证明其转让定价符合独立交易原则,但在经合组织规定的方法更适合于案情时,不得适用经合组织没有列明的方法。也就是说,在适用经合组织没有列明的方法时,需要证明为什么经合组织规定的方法对于该案来说是不适合的,而其他方法更合适。②

二、传统交易方法

1. 可比非受控价格法

可比非受控价格法(comparable uncontrolled price method)以非关联企业之间进行的与关联交易相同或类似的业务活动所收取的价格作为关联交易的公平成交价格。例如,某企业将某项产品销售给其境外母公司,单位售价为 1000 元,而该企业同时向境外另一家非关联企业销售同样产品,售价为 1300 元,据此,税务当局有权比照该企业与非关联企业的成交价格来调整其把产品售给母公司的价格。

运用该方法的关键是确定关联交易和作为可比参照物的非关联交易的可比性以及两者存在差异时的可调整性。该方法可以适用于所有类型的交易。其优势在于:(1)是运用独立交易原则最直接的方法。即在能够找到可比非关联交易的情况下,采用可比非关联交易的价格直接替代关联交易的价格就可以简单有效地使关联交易符合独立交易原则。(2)同时考虑到了交易双方的情况。独立企业间交易价格的形成是双方协商博弈的结果,成交价格包含了交易双方各自对交易目的和交易条件的考虑。因此,与其他一些仅考虑交易一方的调整方法相比,避免了极端的、不符合经营常规的情况出现。

然而,可比非受控价格法也存在一些问题:(1)可比非关联交易难以找到。因为,可比非受控价格法要求关联交易和可比非关联交易在各个方面均具有高度可比性,特别是在转让标的本身的可比性方面。然而,在实际工作中,要找到与关联交易十分类似的非关联交易,且两项交易间不存在对价格有实质性影响的差异是非常困难的。另外,有些关联交易可能仅在关联企业之间发生,在这种

---

① See OECD Transfer Pricing Guidelines for Multinational Enterprises and Tax Administrations, July 2010, paragraph 2.3.

② Ibid., paragraph 2.9.

情况下,更是无法找到可比的非关联交易。(2)实质性差异调整非常困难。① 实质性差异调整的准确与否将会对可比非受控价格法的可靠性产生重大影响,但实践中,对实质性差异进行准确量化调整通常比较困难,有些实质性差异,如商标、品牌等甚至可能无法作出准确量化调整。②

2. 再销售价格法

再销售价格法(resale price method)以向关联方购进商品再销售给非关联方的价格减去可比非关联交易毛利后的金额作为向关联方购进商品的公平成交价格。例如,境外控股公司的母公司以40万元的价格出售给设在中国境内的子公司一批产品,该子公司又以35万元的价格将产品转售给另一家无关联关系的公司。税务机关可按此转售价减去合理的销售毛利,来调整该跨国母子公司之间的交易价格。假设该子公司正常的销售毛利率为15%,则母子公司间正常价格应是35万元－(35万元×15%)＝29.75万元。税务机关可据此价格来调整该子公司的购货价格。一般的计算公式如下:

公平成交价格＝再销售给非关联方的价格×(1－可比非关联交易毛利率)

可比非关联交易毛利率＝可比非关联交易毛利/可比非关联交易收入净额×100%

该方法适用于再销售者从事未对商品进行外形、性能、结构或更换商标等实质性增值加工的简单加工或单纯购销业务,一般仅针对有形资产购销交易。因为当销售者没有对产品增加显著的价值时,最易于确定适当的再销售价格毛利。该方法的优势在于:(1)受产品差异影响小。因为运用该方法的关键是确定可比毛利,如果关联企业并未使用相对独特的资产(如价值较高的无形资产)为所转让的产品增加明显的价值,则该企业的毛利主要与其发挥的再销售功能等因素有关,而与所转让的产品关系不大。(2)结果确定受较少因素影响。毛利是销售收入扣除直接成本和间接成本,净利则要在毛利的基础上再扣除期间费用。由于存在期间费用,企业的净利润会受更多因素的影响,而这些因素并不会对毛利润和价格产生影响(或很少产生实质性影响或直接影响)。因此,相对于净利,再销售价格法使用毛利指标可能使该转让定价受较少因素影响。

---

① 关联交易与非关联交易之间的差异分为实质性差异和非实质性差异,区别的关键在于该差异是否会对各转让定价方法中的关键指标产生实质性影响,如可比非受控价格法中的价格、再销售价格法中的再销售毛利、成本加成法中的成本加成率及交易利润法中的净利润率。非实质性差异对上述关键指标没有实质性影响,不需要调整;而实质性差异对上述指标有实质性影响,只有经过可靠合理的调整消除该实质性影响,才能使该非关联交易成为关联交易的可比对象。

② See OECD Transfer Pricing Guidelines for Multinational Enterprises and Tax Administrations, July 2010, paragraphs 2.12—2.16.

再销售价格法的不足之处在于:(1) 只考虑了交易一方的情况。因为该方法应用的关键是寻找可比的非关联再销售毛利,这就决定了该方法只能保证关联交易一方的利润,而忽视了交易另一方的利润情况。这种仅对交易一方分析的方法,往往不会出于可比的目的考虑跨国企业在关联交易中的整体获利能力。当税务机关应用该方法对关联交易进行调整后,可能使跨国集团某成员获得相应的利润水平,但却可能暗中造成集团其他成员的利润水平畸高或畸低。(2) 易受会计核算口径差异影响。该方法采用的是毛利指标,这就要求可比的非关联交易与关联交易在成本核算会计口径上保持一致,或者即使在不一致的情况下,该差异仍然能够进行可靠的调整。但是,除非可比交易为同一企业发生的非关联交易,否则运用外部可比非关联交易则往往难以获取足够的财务信息以保证会计口径的一致性,此时再销售价格法的可靠性可能明显降低。①

3. 成本加成法

成本加成法(cost plus method)以关联交易发生的合理成本加上可比非关联交易毛利作为关联交易的公平成交价格。例如,某企业以 20 万元的价格出售某项产品给境外母公司,而该产品的生产成本为 18 万元,销售费用为 2 万元。假设该企业的正常利润率为 20%,则该产品的合理价格应为:(18 万元+2 万元)×(1+20%)=24 万元。税务机关有权依此价格来调整该企业的销售价格。一般的计算公式如下:

公平成交价格=关联交易的合理成本×(1+可比非关联交易加成率)

可比非关联交易加成率=可比非关联交易毛利/可比非关联交易成本×100%

该方法通常适用于有形资产的购销、转让和使用,劳务提供或资金融通的关联交易。由于其采用与再销售价格法相似的毛利指标,其优势也在于,受产品差异影响较小以及结果确定受较少因素影响。不足之处在于:(1) 对成本基础可比性要求高。成本和费用总体上可以分三大类:直接成本、间接成本和期间费用。如果成本基础不可比,将直接影响到方法的可靠性。而由于会计政策和会计处理方法的不同,不同企业间成本基础往往存在很大的差异,这就对成本基础的可比性提出了很高的要求。(2) 无法得到足够的可比信息。包括上市公司在内,企业对成本核算的会计处理信息披露有限,这就使得我们往往无法得到足够的可比信息去对成本基础进行必要的可比性分析,从而难以保证该方法适用的

---

① See OECD Transfer Pricing Guidelines for Multinational Enterprises and Tax Administrations, July 2010, paragraphs 2.21—2.35.

可靠性。(3)与再销售价格法相同,也仅考虑了交易一方的状况。①

三、交易利润方法

1. 交易净利润法

交易净利润法(transaction net margin method)是指按照没有关联关系的交易各方进行相同或类似业务往来取得的净利润水平确定利润的方法,操作与成本加成法和再销售价格法相类似。该方法适用于无重大无形资产企业的有形资产的购销、转让和使用以及劳务提供等关联交易。其优势在于:(1)受产品、功能差异的影响较小。(2)具有实际操作优势。运用交易净利润法时,经营活动的所有参与方一般无须依据相同的准则进行会计核算。

交易净利润法的不足在于:(1)结果易受产品、功能以外的更多因素影响。当使用交易净利润法来确定转让定价时,可能需要考虑更多因素的影响。一是由于企业期间费用的存在,净利润会受某些因素的影响,但这些因素可能并不会对毛利润和价格产生影响(或很少产生实质性影响或直接影响)。这就意味着当使用该方法时,两个企业并不会仅因为产品相似、功能类似就必然会有较高的可比性。因此,可比性分析要特别注意考察关联交易和非关联交易之间在功能风险及经济环境上的差异以及影响营业利润的其他因素。二是影响价格和毛利的因素(如竞争地位)同样也会影响到净利润,并且这些因素的影响往往难以被量化调整,而在传统交易方法中,由于坚持要求在产品和功能上有更多的可比性,这些因素的影响可能会自然消除。(2)结果受更多因素的影响也使相应的调整困难增大。(3)与再销售价格法和成本加成法相同,仅考虑了交易一方的情况。②

在运用该方法时,存在多个利润指标,故应根据被测试企业履行的功能和承担的风险以及关联交易的类型,确定与被测试企业的利润关系密切的因素,选择具体的利润指标。

完全成本加成率=息税前营业利润/(销售成本+销售费用+管理费用),通常适用于测试以关联销售为主的常规制造企业和劳务提供企业取得的利润是否符合独立交易原则,而以关联采购为主的企业以及分销企业通常不适用该指标;销售利润率=息税前营业利润/销售收入,通常适用于测试从关联企业购入材

---

① See OECD Transfer Pricing Guidelines for Multinational Enterprises and Tax Administrations, July 2010, paragraphs 2.39—2.52.

② Ibid., paragraphs 2.62—2.67.

料,进行产品制造并将产品销售给独立第三方时取得的利润是否符合独立交易原则;营运资产回报率＝息税前营业利润/营运资产,通常适用于测试资本密集型企业;贝里利率＝息税前营业利润/营运费用,通常适用于测试分销企业、提供劳务企业获得利润是否符合独立交易原则,而不适用于具有显著无形资产的企业,因为无形资产的存在使得我们难以从利润总额中准确划分出与营业费用对应的利润。

除上述指标外,还可以使用利润与零售企业的占地面积、运输产品的重量、雇员数量、时间、距离等指标的比值作为利润指标,只要它们能够合理客观地反映和衡量受测试方在关联交易中的盈利情况,且能够获得可靠的可比信息,这些指标就可以被采纳使用。[1]

2. 利润分割法

利润分割法（transaction profit split method）是指根据企业与其关联方对关联交易合并利润的贡献计算各自应该分配的利润额的方法。该方法适用于关联交易高度整合且难以单独评估各参与方交易结果的情况,以及交易各方对交易本身都有独特且有价值贡献的情况。该方法的优点在于:(1) 同时考虑了交易双方的情况。(2) 为高度整合交易提供了解决方案。在高度整合交易中,交易各方往往对交易本身都提供了独特且有价值的贡献。由于涉及独占性、有价值的贡献,其他方法往往不能找到足够的可比信息来确定各关联方的相关利润。但利用利润分割法,按照交易各方在整合交易中各自贡献等指标,可以从总体利润中为关联交易各方分割出相对合理的应得利润。

利润分割法的不足之处在于:(1) 分配结果主观性较强。与其他方法相比,该方法中用来评估各关联企业对关联交易贡献大小的外部市场数据与这些关联交易的联系不够紧密,而使用的外部数据性质越空泛越空洞,利润分配的结果就越主观。(2) 获取国外关联公司信息困难。(3) 难以保证会计计量一致性。确定所有关联企业参与关联交易的合并收入和合并成本也是很困难的,因为它要求在共同准则下进行会计处理和记录。此外,在企业的关联交易和其他经济活动之间分配收入、成本及费用也往往非常困难。[2]

利润分割方法又可以区分为两种情形。一种是一般利润分割法,也称"贡献分割法",是根据关联交易各参与方所执行的功能、承担的风险以及使用的资产,

---

[1] See OECD Transfer Pricing Guidelines for Multinational Enterprises and Tax Administrations, July 2010, paragraphs 2.86—2.102.

[2] Ibid., paragraphs 2.109—2.114.

以经济上合理的、按照独立交易原则订立的协议中预期和反映的利润分割方式，在关联企业间分割这些利润，确定各自应取得的利润。该方法应以有效的可比数据作为支撑，如独立企业之间类似的利润分割方法。如果没有有效的可比数据，则以每个关联企业在关联交易中履行功能的相对价值来划分，并考虑其拥有的资产及预期的风险。通常情况下，确定贡献的相对价值是很困难的，其方法往往取决于每一个案的事实和环境，可能需要通过比较参与各方不同贡献类型（如劳务提供、发生的开发费用、资本投入）的性质和程度，并在外部市场数据的基础上，确定各方贡献的相对价值。①

另外一种方法是剩余利润分割法，即将关联交易各参与方在相关交易中的合并利润减去分配给各方常规利润后的余额作为剩余利润，再根据各方对剩余利润的贡献程度进行分配。对该方法的运用分为两步。第一步：基于关联交易各方在相关交易中的常规贡献分配利润，使各方基于其常规贡献获得应有的市场回报。常规贡献的市场回报应根据独立企业从事类似活动获取的市场回报确定。但是，常规贡献回报并不能解决因参与方拥有独特且有价值的无形资产所产生的回报。第二步：应根据关联交易各方无形资产在关联交易中作出的非常规贡献对剩余利润进行分配。关联交易各方无形资产贡献的相对价值需根据反映此无形资产公允市场价值的外部市场数据计量。在无法取得相关外部市场数据的情况下，相关无形资产贡献的相对价值也可以通过开发此无形资产过程中产生的资本化成本，加上相关的改进、更新支出，减去因使用无形资产的合理摊销金额来计量。若关联交易各方的无形资产开发支出在一定时间内保持稳定，且各方无形资产的使用寿命基本一致，则相同年度的实际开发支出可用来计量无形资产贡献的相对价值。如果关联交易参与一方贡献的无形价值在其他交易中也有所使用，则需要采用合适的分配方法，在全部使用该无形资产的交易中进行分摊。②

在运用利润分割法时，分割指标的选择至关重要。利润分割法是通过一个或多个分割指标实现利润分割的，当使用多个分割指标时，必须为每一个分割指标赋予权重。为了使分割指标更有意义，交易中的关联各方都要一致使用该指标。实践中，经常使用资产类、资本类、成本类、费用类等分割指标。考虑到具体个案的事实和环境，其他一些指标可能也是合适的，如职员数量（当产生价值的

---

① See OECD Transfer Pricing Guidelines for Multinational Enterprises and Tax Administrations, July 2010, paragraphs 2.119—2.120.

② Ibid., paragraphs 2.121—2.123.

关键功能设计人员时)、工时数(当人工耗时和合并利润产生有较强的相关性时)、服务的数量、零售点的面积等。①

四、可比性分析

根据独立交易原则,关联企业之间的交易应该与独立企业之间的交易一样,依据市场条件下的交易原则来处理关联企业之间的收入、成本及费用分配问题。应用独立交易原则的核心就是将关联交易与作为参照的非关联交易进行充分的比较,以寻找与被测试关联交易最可比的非关联交易,并最终确定符合独立交易原则的价格(利润)水平,这一过程被称为"可比性分析"。所谓可比,是指关联交易与参照的非关联交易的差异对所考察的因素不产生任何实质性影响,或者实质性影响可以通过合理可靠的调整来消除。

一个可比的非关联交易应该是两个独立企业之间发生的交易。它既可以是关联交易一方与第三方独立企业之间的交易,称为内部可比信息;也可以是两个第三方企业之间的交易,称为外部可比信息。内部可比信息比外部可比信息更接近于被测试的关联交易,财务分析也会更简单和可靠,因为内部可比信息与关联交易的会计标准和处理一般来说是一样的,并且可以更完整、更方便地获得相关信息。但如果找不到内部可比信息,就需要寻找外部可比信息。

《OECD转让定价指南》认为较为重要的影响可比性的要素包括:交易货物或劳务的属性、交易各方履行的功能(同时考虑使用的资产和承担的风险)、合同条款、经济环境以及交易各方的经营策略。这些因素不仅会影响被测试交易,同时也会影响潜在的可比交易,因此要同时考虑这些因素对被测试交易和潜在可比交易两方面的影响。在进行可比性分析时,这些因素的重要程度主要取决于关联交易本身的属性以及所选择的转让定价方法。②

可比性分析的典型程序共有以下九步:第一步,确定分析的调查年度;第二步,广泛分析纳税人的整体情况;第三步,分析被测试的关联交易,特别是以功能分析为基础,以选择被测试方(如需要)、最适于案情的转让定价方法、将测试的财务指标(在运用交易利润方法时),并确定重要的需要考量的可比性因素;第四步,现有的内部可比交易的审核(若有);第五步,考量到外部可比交易的可靠性,需要该外部可比交易时,关于该外部可比交易信息的可获得性;第六步,选择

---

① See OECD Transfer Pricing Guidelines for Multinational Enterprises and Tax Administrations, July 2010, paragraphs 2.134—2.135.
② Ibid., paragraphs 1.33—1.63.

最适于案情的转让定价方法,并基于该方法确定相关的财务指标;第七步,识别潜在的可比交易,即基于第三步确定的可比性因素,确定任何非关联交易成为潜在可比交易需要满足的关键特征;第八步,确定可比性并在需要时进行可比性调整;第九步,根据收集的数据,确定符合独立交易原则的价格(利润)水平。

上述程序被认为是可以接受的方法,但并不具有强制性,任何其他能达到识别可靠可比对象的检索方法都被认为是可以接受的,毕竟结果的可靠性比程序更为重要。实践中,以上九个步骤并不是直线型的,特别是第五步到第七步可能需要反复实施以达到满意的结果。例如,当不可能发现可比交易的信息时(第七步)和/或作出合理准确的调整时(第八步),纳税人可能需要重新选择另外一种转让定价方法,并从第四步重新开始。①

第四节 避免和解决转让定价争议的方法

一、安全港规则

1. 安全港规则的定义

运用独立交易原则需要获得大量信息并加以适当的判断,这给纳税人和税务机关带来了不确定性和沉重的管理负担,并随着税收立法和遵从的复杂化而加剧,这使得各国开始考虑在转让定价领域使用安全港规则(safe harbor rules)的可行性。

就转让定价来说,安全港规则主要是指在规定的情形下,纳税人只要遵从一套简单的规则,其转让定价会自动被一国税务机关接受。一般来说,安全港规则的应用有两种形式:一种是把某些交易排除在适用转让定价规定的范围之外(具体可以通过设立最低标准,如要求纳税人达到一定规模才需要准备涉及关联交易的同期资料),另一种则是将某些特定的关联交易的遵从规定简化(如适用由税务机关规定的简化的转让定价方法,或确定价格及利润必须介于的范围)。②

2. 安全港规则的优势

适用安全港规则的优势主要在于以下三方面:

---

① See OECD Transfer Pricing Guidelines for Multinational Enterprises and Tax Administrations, July 2010, paragraphs 3.4—3.5.

② Ibid., paragraphs 4.94—4.95.

(1) 遵从简化

不管是税务机关还是纳税人,运用独立交易原则都会要求收集和分析各种资料,有的资料可能难以获得,或者可能需要花费极大的代价获得,有的资料可能难以评估。这种过程的复杂性往往会与公司的规模或其关联交易水平不成比例,造成遵从成本较高。使用安全港规则,一方面能够使纳税人免于遵守有关规定,从而大大减轻纳税人的遵从义务;另一方面,在没有相匹配的或可比的独立交易价格时,使用安全港规则便于操作,减轻了税务机关的管理负担。根据安全港规则,纳税人可以预先了解到为了满足安全港规则的要求,公司的价格和利润必须处于的范围。这些条件往往采用的是一个简化的方法,如对获利能力的衡量。因此,纳税人无须再寻找可比对象,从而节省了原本用来确定转让定价的时间和资源。

(2) 确定性

税务机关将向纳税人提供一些参数指标,这些参数指标规定了税务机关认为合适的转让价格或结果。因此,在安全港规则下,符合条件的纳税人将能确保不会受到税务机关针对其转让价格的审计或再评估,从而提供了确定性。

(3) 管理简化

一旦税务机关确定纳税人符合安全港的条件,只需要对这些纳税人在其关联交易的转让价格或结果方面进行最低限度的检查。这样,税务机关可以节省更多的资源用于对其他交易和纳税人的检查。

3. 安全港规则存在的问题

使用安全港规则在带来便利的同时,也存在着一定的问题,如向他国转嫁税收管理负担、双重征税风险、引发新的税收筹划等。这些问题的产生主要是基于以下事实:(1)安全港规则的影响并不局限于采用该规则的国家,同时还会影响关联企业所在其他国家的税收计算;(2)很难确立安全港的理想标准,适用安全港规则的价格或结果可能与独立交易原则不符。[①] 一种情况是,安全港规则的要求较高,超出了独立交易原则所能实现的利润或价格。例如,关联公司 A 和 B 分别是 A 国和 B 国的居民企业,A 公司与 B 公司之间的一项关联交易共产生了 18 个单位的利润,按照独立交易原则计算,A 公司实现的利润为 8 个单位,B 公司实现的利润为 10 个单位。A 国采用安全港规则,如 A 公司在该项关联交易中获得 10 个单位以上的利润,那么可以免于遵从 A 国的转让定价审查。故

---

① See OECD Transfer Pricing Guidelines for Multinational Enterprises and Tax Administrations, July 2010, paragraphs 4.98—4.118.

A 公司为了满足安全港规则，将其利润调增至 10 个单位，B 公司的利润则为 8 个单位。在此情形下，虽然 A 公司满足了其所在国的安全港规则，实现了对于 A 国规定遵从的简化，即 A 国税务管理机关不用审查 A 公司的此项关联交易，但对于 B 国而言，其认为 A 公司与 B 公司之间的利润分配不符合独立交易原则，需要重新按照独立交易原则定价，由此增加了 B 国的税务管理负担，在 B 国将 B 公司实现的利润调增至 10 个单位时，其中的 2 个单位利润遭到了 A 国和 B 国的双重征税。另一种情况是，安全港规则的要求较低，低于独立交易原则所能实现的利润或价格。在上述案例中，若 A 国采用安全港规则，如 A 公司在该项关联交易中获得 5 个单位以上的利润，那么将免于遵从 A 国的转让定价审查。同时，A 国的所得税率高于 B 国，则 A 公司会将其利润调减至 5 个单位，B 公司的利润则调增至 13 个单位，由于 B 国的所得税税率低于 A 国，则 A 公司和 B 公司整体上实现了节税，达到了税收筹划的目的。

此外，安全港规则还会带来公正性和一致性问题。因为，如果实行安全港规则，意味着这个国家在转让定价领域可能存在两套截然不同的规则。在实际经济生活中，很可能会发生这样的情况：类似的纳税人被分成两类，一类纳税人符合安全港规定，可以免于一些遵从义务，而另一些纳税人却只能参照独立交易原则开展业务，并花费更多的时间和成本达到遵从目的。这种不一致的税收处理可能会造成不公平的后果。

虽然一些国家对安全港规则持反对态度，但是近几年来，越来越多的国家在某些转让定价领域进行安全港规则的实践和探索。虽然纳税人和税务机关都能从应用安全港规则中获益，但其固有的缺陷也不可避免，如何在使用安全港规则的利弊之间进行衡量也是各国税务机关需要考虑的问题。

经合组织认为，按照一般的税收法律，对于纳税人而言，确定性并不能保证，因为税务机关应当保留对于纳税人收入进行任何纳税评估的审查权力，包括转让定价。从根本上说，安全港规则的引入是税务机关将其部分裁量权交给自动规则。税务机关可能还没准备好作出这种变化，故仍然认为，保留审查纳税人自己评估的税收责任和税基的准确性的权力是必要的。遵从简化的目标也通常服从于其他的税收政策目标，如合理且充足的档案及报告要求、防止避税。另外，税务机关在管理税收法律方面具有很大的灵活性。它可以选择将更多的资源用于涉及重大纳税人的案子或重大的受控交易，而对小型纳税人则给予更多的容忍。虽然对于小型纳税人的灵活行政管理实践并不是正式的安全港规则的替代,但却可以在较小程度上实现与安全港规则相同的目标。[①]

二、预约定价安排

前面所介绍的转让定价调整方法属于事后调整,实践证明,事后调整不仅会给纳税人和税务机关双方都带来管理上的负担,而且调整结果的不确定性还会影响到企业的正常经营和决策。为了克服事后调整的缺陷,越来越多的国家开始引入预约定价制度(advance pricing arrangement),把对纳税人关联交易的事后调整变成事前防范。

所谓预约定价安排,又称"预先定价协议",《OECD 转让定价指南》对其作了如下定义:它是指税务当局和纳税人在关联交易发生之前作出的一种协议,制定出一套恰当的标准(如定价方法、可比对象和适当的调整、对未来情势的关键性假设等),用以确定未来一定期限内关联交易的转让价格。

各国的预约定价程序大同小异,达成一项预约定价协议通常要经过以下步骤:

(1) 纳税人提出申请。预约定价协议一般由纳税人主动提出申请,税务机关在收到申请后,通常会与纳税人进行初步讨论,探讨预约定价安排的可行性,并对纳税人的关联交易情况进行初步了解。然后,纳税人在初步接触的基础上正式提出申请,并提交申请材料,材料中包括预约定价协议草案建议。

(2) 税务机关审核。税务机关收到纳税人的正式申请和相关材料后,应在一定期限内对这些材料进行审核,重点判断纳税人所建议的转让定价调整方法是否合理,有关假设是否全面可靠。

(3) 签署预约定价协议。税务机关审核以后,会就申请材料中某些问题与纳税人磋商,双方达成一致意见后即正式签署预约定价协议。预约定价协议通常有一定的有效期,一般规定为 3 年,有的国家规定长于或短于 3 年。在有效期内,如果纳税人违背协议,税务机关可能会对安排进行撤销。

预约定价协议最初只是一种单边安排,但由于单边预约定价安排只能为企业提供其在某一国的税收确定性,无法避免国际双重征税的风险,于是双边或多边的预约定价安排逐渐受到业界青睐。应美国著名零售商沃尔玛公司于 2006 年 6 月提出的双边预约定价安排申请,中美两国税务主管当局经过北京及华盛顿两轮磋商,于 2006 年 12 月 22 日最终签署了两国间的首例双边预约定价协

[①] See OECD Transfer Pricing Guidelines for Multinational Enterprises and Tax Administrations, July 2010, paragraphs 4.119—4.122.

议。与单边预约定价协议相比,双边或多边预约定价协议不仅能够解决双重征税问题,而且也是防范转让定价跨国争议的一种有效手段。可以说,双边或多边预约定价安排代表了预约定价制度的发展方向,必将会越来越多地得到各国的重视。[1]

预约定价协议的优势非常明显,它使纳税人的转让定价方法更具有确定性,从而减轻了纳税人的合规成本。但其存在的问题也不容忽视,问题具体表现在两个层面:首先,在预约定价协议的谈签过程中,企业和税务机关都面临诸多的不确定性和制约因素。从企业的角度看,面临最大的一个挑战就是资料的收集和准备。在预约定价协议的谈签过程中,税务机关关注的不仅是申请企业自身的财务数据信息等,还包括企业所在的集团供应链上各环节的所有相关信息和数据,因此会涉及企业的各海外关联方,这在很大程度上要通过集团总部的协调,否则很难完成资料的收集。从税务机关的角度看,尤其是在双边预约定价协议的磋商过程中,由于协商结果通常被解读为所涉相关税务主管当局对某一行业或交易类型的主导立场,并对以后其他相似预约定价安排的谈签或是相关行业的转让定价调查产生重要影响,因此双方税务机关在磋商的过程中往往都持谨慎或保守的立场。同时,不同国家之间由于利益差异或理解分歧,对诸如"市场溢价"等一些核心问题通常立场不一,甚至观点对立,这无疑会增加谈签的难度,拖延谈签的进度。其次,即便在预约定价协议的执行过程中也会遇到一些问题,如果达成预约定价协议的关键假设在执行期间发生重大变化,或是企业的业务状况发生实质性改变等,都可能使已签订的预约定价安排面临终止或取消的风险。[2] 预约定价协议所具备的上述特点,决定了它不可能完全取代传统的转让定价调整方法,但只要国际社会将其合理运用,并在实践中不断完善,预约定价协议一定能在转让定价法律体系中发挥重要作用。

第五节 关于无形资产转让定价的特殊考虑

一、无形资产的定义和分类

根据《OECD转让定价指南》,无形资产(intangible property)包括使用各种工业资产的权利,如专利、商标、商业名称、设计或模型,也包括文学和艺术产权、

---

[1] 参见程永昌主编:《国际税法学》,中国税务出版社2006年版,第197页。
[2] 参见高阳:《中国预约定价安排:谈签技巧与制度完善》,载《涉外税务》2012年第9期。

知识产权。① 这些无形资产在公司的资产负债表上可能不具有账面价值,但仍具有相当大的经济价值及与其相关的风险。

无形资产分为商业性和非商业性两类。商业性无形资产(commercial intangibles)是与商业活动相关的无形资产,包括用于生产商品或提供服务的专利、专有技术、设计和模型,也包括转让给客户或用于商业运作、本身就是商业资产的无形资产(如计算机软件)。商业性无形资产又可分为交易性无形资产和营销型无形资产。

交易性无形资产(trade intangibles)通常产生于高风险和高投入的研发活动,开发者一般试图通过产品销售、服务合约或者许可协议来弥补支出并获得回报。交易性无形资产的开发通常有三种方式:(1) 开发者以自己的名义从事研究活动并试图获得交易性无形资产法律和经济上的所有权;(2) 通过签订开发协议,开发者为一个或多个其他集团成员从事合约研发,并且受益人获得法律和经济上的无形资产所有权;(3) 开发者自身及一个或多个集团成员共同从事研发活动并且共同获得无形资产的经济所有权。此外,互惠许可(又称为"交叉许可")也比较常见,并且可能更为复杂。②

营销性无形资产(marketing intangibles)包括用于产品或服务商业开拓的商标和商业名称、客户名单、分销渠道以及对产品推广有重要价值的独特的名称、符号或图片。一些营销性无形资产(如商标)是受到某些国家法律保护的,并且只能在所有者的授权下才能够用于相关的产品或服务。营销性无形资产的价值取决于多种因素,包括以往通过产品或服务的质量所建立起的商业名称、商标的声誉和信用,质量控制程度和持续的研发活动,营销中的产品和服务的分销程度及可获得性,用于开发潜在客户的宣传支出的程度及是否成功,尤其是用于拓展与分销商、代理商等关系网络的广告和营销行为。其他因素还包括获取市场准入的市场价值,以及该无形资产按法律所产生的权利的性质等。

知识产权是一类比较特殊的无形资产,它既可以是交易性无形资产,也可以是营销性无形资产。知识产权包括专有技术和商业秘密,它们在跨国集团的商业活动中扮演了极其重要的角色。专有技术和商业秘密是能够辅助或促进商业活动开展的专有信息或知识,但是它们并不像专利或者商标那样需要注册而得到一定的法律保护。根据《OECD 范本》的定义,专有技术一般应包括秘密的工

---

① 《OECD 转让定价指南》中所指的知识产权是指除专利、商标、外观设计以外的知识产权,如专有技术和商业秘密。

② See OECD Transfer Pricing Guidelines for Multinational Enterprises and Tax Administrations, July 2010, paragraph 6.3.

艺流程、公式或其他关于工业、商业和科技经验的情报,并且不在专利权的涵盖范围之内。任何专有技术或商业秘密的泄露都会实质性减少该资产的价值。①

二、独立交易原则适用的特殊考虑

独立交易原则的一般性指导原则同样适用于无形资产转让定价,但是由于无形资产的特殊性质,使得这些原则的应用变得困难,在寻找可比对象和评估价值时也更为复杂。一般来说,在对无形资产转让定价运用独立交易原则时,需要考虑的重要因素、角度等与有形资产不完全一致,需要根据无形资产的特殊性质作出一些特殊考虑。

1. 应分别从转让方和受让方角度考虑

无形资产的关联交易在运用独立交易原则时,应分别从资产转让方和受让方的角度来考虑可比性。从资产转让方的角度来说,运用独立交易原则应该考虑可比独立企业愿意转让无形资产的价格。从资产受让方的角度来说,运用独立交易原则应该考虑可比独立企业根据无形资产对其价值的作用,以及是否愿意接受这样的价格。相对于其他实际可能的选择,受让方如果使用该无形资产能够确保带来合理的预期收益,受让方一般会接受许可费用。如果受让方为利用这项许可,还需要进一步的投资或其他支出,那么应该考虑独立企业在衡量许可带来的预期收益和额外的投资支出下,是否还会接受该项许可费用。

之所以需要这样的分析,是出于考虑无形资产的效用对可比性的影响。在确定可比性时,应考虑到关联企业的商业运作和其他相关情形。当无形资产对该企业只有有限效用时,需要确保该关联企业不是被迫购买和使用该无形资产,确保所支付的金额不是基于该无形资产的最高或最具生产能力的效用。②

2. 不同转让方式下的适用

转让无形资产的方式较多,可以是直接出售,也可以是通过许可协议收取特许权使用费;可以是单个无形资产的转让,也可以是多个无形资产的转让,甚至可能与有形资产捆绑转让。所以,需要根据不同的转让方式,适用独立交易原则。

(1) 如果直接出售无形资产,应该在充分的可比性分析的基础上,对出售的无形资产参照独立企业间的交易进行公平估价。

(2) 如果通过签订许可协议并收取特许权使用费的方式转让,应根据无形

---

① See OECD Transfer Pricing Guidelines for Multinational Enterprises and Tax Administrations, July 2010, paragraphs 6.4—6.5.
② Ibid., paragraphs 6.13—6.15.

资产的特点,基于使用者的产量、销售或利润等指标,来收取特许权使用费。当特许权使用费基于被许可的产量和销售额时,可能考虑特许权使用费率是否要随被许可方营业额的变化而变化。

(3) 当无形资产和其他有形商品或劳务被打包转让时,如果该无形资产(如特许权使用费)涉及预提税,则需要对这一揽子定价加以划分,从中单独计算出符合独立交易原则的无形资产定价。

(4) 当多个无形资产被捆绑在一起打包转让时,对这种一揽子合同中的各个部分可能需要单独考虑,以验证这项转让是否具有独立交易的性质。

需要注意的是,不管以何种方式转让无形资产,对与转让无形资产一起提供的类似技术支持、雇员培训等服务,以及被许可人对无形资产实施的可能给许可人带来利益的服务,都必须按照独立交易原则,并结合相关服务的特殊考虑,对这些服务作出评价。在这方面,要注意区分获得专业技术的不同途径。根据《OECD范本》以及有关国家国内法的规定,对专业技术和服务合同可能有不用的处理,如分别适用特许权使用费的预提税规则和营业利润的常设机构规则。[①]

3. 可比性分析的特殊考虑

选择哪种转让定价方法,很大程度上依赖于可比性分析的情况。进行无形资产的可比性分析时,需要结合无形资产的特殊性质,对相关的特殊因素加以考虑,包括:无形资产的预期收益;地域限制;由于权利转移而产生的出口货物限制;排他或非排他性权利;资本投资、启动费用和市场开发;再许可的可能性、被许可方的分销网络,以及被许可方是否有权参与今后许可方关于无形资产的开发活动等。下面着重介绍两种情形的无形资产可比性分析。

如果转让的无形资产是专利权,那么在进行可比性分析时,应考虑该无形资产的特性以及不同国家专利法对专利保护的程度和持久度。例如,如果能在旧专利基础上很快地开发出新专利,则无形资产的有效保护期可能大大延长。不但专利的法定保护期很重要,而且在该期限内保持其经济价值也是至关重要的。一项极具"突破性"的全新专利能使现有专利迅速过时。与对现有专利范围内工艺作一些改善的专利或很容易被替代的专利相比,突破性新专利可以得到更高的价格。对专利进行可比性分析时,还应考虑专利在最终产品中形成的价值。例如,如果一项专利性发明仅涉及设备的一个部件,则参照整个产品的销售价格收取特许权使用费可能并不合理,也许还应该参照该部件相对于产品其他部件的价值。

[①] See OECD Transfer Pricing Guidelines for Multinational Enterprises and Tax Administrations, July 2010, paragraph 6.16—6.18.

对于销售包含无形资产的货物,当涉及营销性无形资产时,可比性分析应当考虑商标等营销性无形资产带来的增值,并结合消费者的可接受度、区位优势、市场份额以及其他相关的因素;当涉及交易性无形资产时,可比性分析应着重考虑归属于无形资产的价值,以及持续性研发功能的重要性。[1]

4. 无形资产价值不确定时的适用

由于无形资产的特殊性质,可能造成在有些情况下难以确定无形资产的价值。当无形资产的价值高度不确定时,应该根据具体事实和情形,参照独立企业的做法,合理适用独立交易原则。独立企业往往采用预期收益作为无形资产定价的基础,并根据预期收益的可预测程度,采取相应的定价安排。一种可能是,独立企业可能会发现能够对预期收益作出非常可靠的预测。在这种情况下,可以在交易开始时,以这些估计为基础确定无形资产交易的价格,而不再需要保留以后进行调整的权利。

另一种可能是,独立企业可能会发现难以对预期收益进行可靠的预测,并会因此造成无形资产价值的高度不确定性。在这种情况下,独立企业可能采用预期较短的协议或在协议条件下加入价格调整条款,以预防不可预期的未来发展。例如,可以将特许权使用费率规定为随着被许可人销售额的增加而提高。独立企业也可能决定,承担一定程度不可预测带来的风险,前提是双方存在共识,即如果不可预见的重大发展改变了定价所基于的假设,将通过双方相互协商的方式,对定价重新安排谈判。例如,A 授权 B 生产一种专利药品,双方根据未来预期确定了特许权使用费,但同时规定,如果出现了预料之外的低成本替代疗法,将进行相互协商,对上述特许权使用费率按照独立交易原则重新进行谈判。[2]

5. 不拥有商标和商业名称的企业进行营销活动时的适用

当进行营销活动的企业(如品牌产品的分销商)并不拥有其正在推广的品牌或商业名称时,在适用独立原则时,应注意:分销商是否有权获得营销性无形资产回报以及归属于营销活动回报的确认问题。

首先,在分销商是否有权获得营销性无形资产回报方面,根据协议双方的权利义务,一般有三种情形:(1) 分销商如仅扮演代理商的角色,其促销支出由营销性无形资产的所有者予以补偿。那么,这个分销商因为其代理行为已经取得了充分的补偿而不应该再分享归属于营销性无形资产的任何回报。(2) 当分销

---

[1] See OECD Transfer Pricing Guidelines for Multinational Enterprises and Tax Administrations, July 2010, paragraphs 6.20—6.24.

[2] Ibid., paragraphs 6.28—6.31.

商实际承担了其营销活动的成本时(即不存在由所有者补偿支出的协议),应根据独立分销商在可比情形下能获得的份额确定其能在什么程度上分享这些活动带来的潜在利益。一般来说,在符合独立交易原则的交易中,非营销性无形资产法定所有者一方,从增加了该无形资产价值的营销活动中获得其未来利益的能力,主要依赖于其权利的实质。例如,当分销商拥有商标产品独家销售权的长期合同时,就能够通过其流转额和市场份额,从其用于提高营销性无形资产价值的投资中获利。(3) 在有些情况下,分销商可能承担超乎寻常的营销支出,这种支出超过了具有类似权利的独立分销商为进行分销活动发生的支出。这时,独立分销商可以从商标所有者那里获得额外回报。这种回报可能是通过降低产品购买价格或是减少特许权使用费率来实现的。

其次,如何确认归属于营销活动的回报。营销活动的价值通常来自于广告和促销。广告和促销支出对于保持商标的价值有重要意义。商标的价值及其变化,在一定程度上取决于市场上对该商标进行推广的有效程度。在许多情况下,从销售商标产品取得的较高回报,有赖于产品的独特特征或其优质品质,也同样有赖于成功的广告以及其他推广支出。然而,实际工作中,往往很难确定这些支出对产品成功作出的贡献程度。[①]

第六节 关于集团内劳务转让定价的特殊考虑

集团内劳务是指集团成员之间相互提供的,独立企业愿意购买或自己提供的,能使劳务接受方受益的劳务。《OECD 转让定价指南》认为每个跨国公司都可能会向其成员提供范围广泛的各种劳务,如行政、技术、财务以及商务方面的劳务,这些劳务还可能包括对整个集团的管理、协调以及控制等。[②]

一、集团内劳务的判定

根据独立交易原则,判断集团内部活动是否构成集团内劳务,不能简单地规定哪些活动属于集团内劳务,哪些活动不属于集团内劳务。但仍可以按照一些标准和指导性原则,根据个案的实际情况来进行判断。[③]

[①] See OECD Transfer Pricing Guidelines for Multinational Enterprises and Tax Administrations, July 2010, paragraphs 6.37—6.39.

[②] Ibid., paragraph 7.2.

[③] Ibid., paragraph 7.7.

1. 构成集团内劳务的标准

集团内部活动是否构成集团内劳务,简单的判断标准就是看受让方是否受益,即劳务的提供是否为劳务接受方带来了利益。当跨国集团内的一个成员为其他成员提供的劳务,为劳务接受方带来了经济或商业上的价值,则可以判断该劳务属于集团内劳务。根据受益性标准判断一项集团内部活动是否属于集团内劳务,还可以参照在可比的情况下,独立企业是否愿意向独立第三方购买该项劳务,或者是否愿意自己从事此项劳务。构成集团内劳务的集团内部活动一般包括:(1) 与集团整体有关的劳务。对于使集团受益的活动,即那些由母公司或集团共享服务中心集中控制并提供给集团内大多数成员的活动,如行政管理、财务服务、员工事项等,一般认为属于集团内劳务,因为独立企业也会愿意为之付费或自己完成。(2) 应特定需求而提供的劳务。当跨国集团的某个成员应集团内其他成员的特定需要而提供劳务时,一般认为该劳务为劳务接受方带来了利益,因此,可以直接认定该项劳务属于集团内劳务。[①]

2. 不构成集团内劳务的几类特殊活动

如果独立企业既不需要为某类活动付费,也不需要自己完成,一般认为该类活动不构成集团内劳务,如股东行为、重复活动、被动关联活动、间接活动。集团母公司或地区性控股公司作为股东,通常会由于其拥有集团内一个或多个成员的股份,而进行一定的管理、控制、监管的活动,如召开股东会议、为集团筹集资金、发行母公司股票等与母公司本身的法律组织相关的活动。一般这些活动与投资管理有关,这类活动被称为股东行为。对于股东行为,即使一些集团成员不需要该活动,也仍然会发生。事实上,当这些集团成员是独立企业时,将不会愿意为此付费,因为这些活动并未使该集团成员受益。因此,股东行为不属于集团内劳务,集团成员不应对此付费,也不得在税前列支。从集团整体看,股东行为可能会给整个集团带来利益,但股东行为的收益应体现在税后利润的分配中,而不是仅因彼此之间的投资和被投资关系就有别于独立第三方在税前直接收取的费用。

如果一个集团成员从事的活动,仅仅是重复其他集团成员正在为自己进行的活动,或是已由第三方提供给该其他集团成员的活动,则属于重复活动。重复活动包括母公司与子公司就同一活动的纵向重复,还包括母公司提供的各类劳务之间或不同关联企业分别提供各类活动之间存在的横向重复。通常来说,重

[①] See OECD Transfer Pricing Guidelines for Multinational Enterprises and Tax Administrations, July 2010, paragraphs 7.6, 7.8, 7.14.

复活动并不能给劳务接受方带来利益,因此重复活动一般不构成集团内劳务。对于接受了重复性活动的集团成员来说,当其为独立企业时,一般不会愿意为此付费。一般认为,如果母公司与子公司都下设某个相同的部门(如人力资源、营销、法律或会计),那么母公司相关部门为子公司提供的劳务可能是重复活动。需要注意的是,有些重复活动,尽管形式上重复,但能给劳务接受方带来利益,因此仍属于应收费的集团内劳务,这类情况包括:(1)临时性重复活动。如某跨国集团正在重组以使其管理功能集中化。重组后,将由母公司 A 集中行使管理功能。在重组阶段,出于工作的衔接以及效率的考虑,A 公司及其子公司同时行使管理职能。重组时期的这些重复性管理活动,保证了子公司的正常运转。子公司受益于这种临时性的重复活动,因此该重复活动属于集团内劳务。(2)为减少错误经营决策的风险而发生的重复活动。

被动关联活动,是指当某企业仅因为它是一个跨国集团的一部分,而不是因为集团成员企业对其进行的某项具体活动而得到了附带利益时,不应认为该企业接受了集团内劳务,因而也不应对此付费。此外,间接活动也不属于集团内劳务。当某一集团成员,如母公司或区域服务中心,提供的劳务只与部分集团成员有关,但附带给其他集团成员带来了利益,不应认为其他受益集团成员接受了集团内劳务,因此也不应对此付费。①

二、适用独立交易原则的特殊考虑

独立交易原则的一般性原则同样适用于集团内劳务转让定价,但是由于集团内劳务的特殊性质,我们在集团内劳务中应用独立交易原则时,需要作出一些特殊考虑。

1. 对劳务双方进行评估

在判断集团内劳务的价格是否符合独立交易原则时,要从劳务提供者和接受者两个角度来考虑。一方面要将劳务接受者支付的对价与可比情形下愿意为该劳务支付的价款进行比较。寻找劳务的独立企业会对其需要的特定劳务进行估值,判断劳务价值,并在此基础上确定愿意支付的价格。如劳务提供者要求的价格与需求者对劳务的估值差距较大时,独立企业一般不会愿意接受此劳务并对此付费。另一方面需要考虑劳务提供者花费的成本。劳务的提供者一般会通过比较提供劳务需要花费的成本与劳务接受方愿意支付的对价,来判断是否愿

---

① See OECD Transfer Pricing Guidelines for Multinational Enterprises and Tax Administrations, July 2010, paragraphs 7.10—7.13.

意提供相应的劳务。除了商业策略等因素考虑,一般独立企业不会以低于成本的价格提供劳务。①

2. 考虑劳务提供方的获利水平

在判断集团内劳务是否符合独立交易原则时,也需要考虑劳务提供者是否必须产生利润。在非关联交易中,独立企业提供劳务所收取的费用一般要保证其获得利润,而不仅仅是弥补成本。但是,符合独立交易原则也并不必然使提供集团内劳务的关联企业一定盈利。例如,存在这样的情况,独立企业提供劳务活动本身并不获利,但是出于拓展劳务范围而增加其未来潜在获利能力的考虑,劳务提供方在其预期成本或实际成本超过其所提供劳务的市场价格时,仍可能同意提供劳务。因此,不能简单地把劳务提供者是否产生利润,作为判断集团内劳务是否符合独立交易原则的标准。不能只为了确保关联企业获利,而使集团内劳务价格高于公平市场价格,这样做,显然有悖于独立交易原则。②

第七节 成本分摊协议

一、成本分摊协议概述

成本分摊协议(Cost Contribution Arrangement,CCA)是指两个以上企业议定的一项框架,用以确定各方在研发、生产或获得资产、劳务和权利等方面承担的成本和风险,并确定各参与方在这些资产、劳务和权利中的利益的性质和范围。③ 无形资产成本分摊协议是最主要的类型,但成本分摊协议并不局限于此,也适用于任何联合投资或分摊成本和风险,开发或获取资产,或取得服务。成本分摊协议最大的特点即"共担成本(分享),共享收益"。对于无形资产类成本分摊协议而言,每一个参与方都被授予独立利用目标无形资产的权利,尽管可能只有某一特定参与方是目标无形资产法定所有者,但从经济角度看,各参与方都拥有该目标无形资产实际的所有者权益,且当其贡献比例与预期收益比例相配比时,参与方无须为使用与其权益相一致的目标无形资产而支付特许权使用费或其他报酬。

《OECD 转让定价指南》关于成本分摊协议应用独立交易原则的内容,为各

---

① See OECD Transfer Pricing Guidelines for Multinational Enterprises and Tax Administrations, July 2010, paragraphs 7.29—7.30.
② Ibid., paragraphs 7.33—7.34.
③ Ibid., paragraph 8.3.

国税务实践提供了很好的指导，多数国家对成本分摊协议的税务处理都遵循指南的精神，故在此主要介绍《OECD 转让定价指南》中对于符合独立交易原则的成本分摊协议的要求和税务处理。

二、成本分摊协议的签订、执行、变更和终止

一项成本分摊协议要满足独立交易原则，参与方的贡献必须与独立企业在可比条件下考虑到能从该成本分摊协议中获取的预期利益而能够同意的成本贡献相一致。① 下面从成本分摊协议的签订执行、变更和终止三个阶段来具体分析如何判断成本分摊协议是否符合独立交易原则。确定一项已签订执行的成本分摊协议是否符合独立交易原则，其标准可归纳为：各参与方的预期收益是前提，各参与方分摊的成本与预期收益的配比是根本原则，当配比原则在实际执行中出现偏差时符合独立交易原则的平衡支付是保证。②

（1）预期收益

成本分摊协议与一般的集团内部资产和劳务转让的差别，在于各参与方愿意接受一项贡献资源和技术但不作另行补偿的协议的基本条件时对共同利益的预期。即各参与方存在预期收益是达成符合独立交易原则的成本分摊协议的前提。这意味着，是先有预期收益，然后根据预期收益的比例来分摊成本或贡献的份额，而不是根据成本或贡献的份额来划分预期收益。实际上，没有合理的预期收益，就不能定义为成本分摊协议的参与方。

（2）配比原则

独立企业会要求分摊的贡献比例与预期收益的份额相符合，因此成本与收益相配比原则是判断成本分摊协议符合独立交易原则的根本原则，即每一参与方根据协议按比例划分实际全部贡献的份额，是否与其根据协议按比例划分预期获得的全部利益的份额相一致。③

（3）平衡支付

当某一参与方实际的贡献份额与其协议中规定的预期收益比例不相一致，且不配比程度超过独立企业可接受范围时，平衡支付就是维持成本分摊协议能够符合独立交易原则的保证措施。平衡支付，是指调整参与方贡献份额的一种

---

① See OECD Transfer Pricing Guidelines for Multinational Enterprises and Tax Administrations, July 2010, paragraphs 8.6—8.8.
② 参见范坚主编：《国际反避税实务指引》，江苏人民出版社 2012 年版，第 277 页。
③ See OECD Transfer Pricing Guidelines for Multinational Enterprises and Tax Administrations, July 2010, paragraphs 8.8—8.9.

支付,通常是由一个或多个参与方向另一个或多个参与方支付,支付者根据其支付款项的额度相应增加其贡献份额,接受者则根据其接受款项的额度相应减少其贡献份额。简单来说,平衡支付就是在成本分摊协议执行过程中,出现各参与方收益与其成本显著不配比的情况时,在各参与方之间进行的补偿性调整。①

在参与方未发生变化条件下,通过平衡支付可以保证已签订执行的成本分摊协议符合独立交易原则,而当成本分摊协议的参与方发生变更时,买进支付(buy-in payment)和买出支付(buy-out payment)则是保证其继续符合独立交易原则的重要举措。买进支付是指新参与方为加入一项已生效的成本分摊协议,并获得以前协议活动产生的利益而进行的一种支付。简单来说,买进支付是成本分摊协议的新参与方与原参与方之间进行的补偿性调整。买出支付是指参与方为退出一项已生效的成本分摊协议,转让其以前协议活动产生的利益而从其他参与方处获得的补偿。即买出支付时成本分摊协议的退出者与剩余参与方间进行的补偿性调整。

成本分摊协议终止时,独立交易原则也要求各参与方根据成本分摊协议按比例划分的贡献份额,与其因成本分摊协议活动而获得的收益相一致。②

三、同期文档要求

《OECD转让定价指南》第五章"证明文件"对转让定价文档管理提出了一般性的指导原则,用以指导税务当局建立与转让定价调查相关的文档管理制度,帮助纳税人准备相关的证明文件,最大限度地表明其关联交易符合独立交易原则,配合税务检查的开展,更好地解决转让定价问题。具体包括如何认识证明文档与举证责任之间的关系、证明文件规章和程序的指导原则、对有效实施转让定价审计有用的信息、对证明文件应当涉及的内容的列举式建议、倡导税务机关与纳税人加强高层次的合作等。

在成本分摊协议中,经合组织建议应准备以下同期文档内容:(1)参与方的名单;(2)成本分摊协议活动可能涉及的或希望利用成本分摊协议结果的其他关联企业名单;(3)成本分摊协议涉及的活动范围和具体项目;(4)协议的期限;(5)衡量参与方按比例划分的预期收益份额的方式,即在确定份额过程中运用的预测;(6)参与方最初贡献的形式和价值,并详细说明如何确定最初和后续

---

① See OECD Transfer Pricing Guidelines for Multinational Enterprises and Tax Administrations, July 2010, paragraph 8.18.
② Ibid., paragraph 8.39.

贡献的价值,以及在确定贡献者的支出和贡献价值时,如何对所有参与方连贯一致地运用会计准则;(7)参与方与其他企业涉及成本分摊协议活动的责任和任务的预期分配;(8)参与方加入或退出成本分摊协议及成本分摊协议终止的程序和后果;(9)平衡支付或协议调整条款的规定,以反映经济环境变化。同时,建议在成本分摊协议执行中准备以下同期文档内容:(1)协议的变化(如条款、参与方、目标行为)及其后果;(2)成本分摊协议预期利益的预测和实际结果的比较;(3)成本分摊协议活动过程中的年度支出,成本分摊协议期限内各参与方贡献的形式和价值,并详细说明如何确定贡献的价值,以及在确定贡献者的支出和贡献价值时,如何对所有参与方连贯一致地运用会计准则。

四、成本分摊协议的税务处理

对于符合独立交易原则的成本分摊协议,其税务处理的方式应与该参与方适用税制一般规则的方式相同,根据成本分摊协议中贡献活动的性质从税收角度进行定性,大部分时候贡献被视为可扣除费用,但同时平衡支付也可能会超过接受者按国内税法允许扣除的支出或成本,超出部分要作为应税利润处理。但是,成本分摊协议下的成本不得被视为使用无形资产的特许权使用费,除非该成本授予支付该成本的参与方使用另一参与方或第三方拥有的且支付方对其没有受益权的无形资产。

对于不符合独立交易原则的成本分摊协议,税务部门有权对参与方的贡献进行调整,甚至参与方在运用平衡支付进行调整后,按比例划分的贡献份额与其按比例划分的预期收益的分割始终存在实质性差异,税务部门可摒弃成本分摊协议的部分或全部条款。[①]

第八节 UN 转让定价指南

前面介绍的内容主要是结合了《OECD 转让定价指南》。2012 年 10 月,联合国也发布了《联合国发展中国家转移定价操作手册》(the United Nations Practical Manual on Transfer Pricing for Developing Countries,简称《UN 转让

---

① See OECD Transfer Pricing Guidelines for Multinational Enterprises and Tax Administrations, July 2010, paragraphs 8.23—8.26.

定价指南》）[①]，为发展中国家应对转移定价提供了更好的政策和管理方面的指导。《UN 转让定价指南》不是对《OECD 转让定价指南》的替代，而是在《OECD 转让定价指南》的基础上提出的一个考虑到发展中国家利益的操作手册。所以，虽然独立交易法备受病垢，但《UN 转让定价指南》还是认为独立交易法的优势大大超过其劣势。《UN 转让定价指南》的创新是在第十章中列出了四个有代表性的发展中国家，即巴西、中国、印度和南非的转让定价经验和立场，其中中国提出的区位优势概念得到许多发展中国家的关注。

中国提出的区位优势（location-specific advantages）概念针对的是因特定地区存在的资产、资源、政府产业政策和激励措施而产生的生产优势。区位优势包括选址节约（location savings）和市场溢价（market premium）两个部分。

选址节约是指跨国企业在低成本地域开展业务时所产生的净成本节约。净成本节约是指对原材料、劳动力、租金、运输和基础设施等方面支出的减少和由于经营迁移所带来的额外支出，如雇用非熟练劳动力所带来的培训支出的增加，相抵后的净节约成本。来自中国的选址节约主要包括较低的劳动力成本、资本成本、环境保护成本以及社会保障成本。

市场溢价是指跨国企业在某一特定区域由于独特的产品或服务质量对当地销售和需求产生影响所带来的额外利润，如市场规模、政府对相关产业的刺激政策、市场准入、消费倾向以及需求弹性等因素。

中国在《UN 转让定价指南》中提出用"四步骤法"来处理区位优势问题：

(1) 识别是否存在区位优势；

(2) 衡量区位优势是否创造了额外利润；

(3) 定量化的计量来自于区位优势而产生的额外利润；

(4) 决定采用合适的转让定价调整方法来分配来自于区位优势而产生的额外利润。

[①] See United Nations，ST/ESA/347，"Practical Manual on Transfer Pricing for Developing Countries"，New York，2013/12/13.

> 本章阅读材料

Examples to Illustrate the Guidance on Special Considerations for Intangible Property

—selected from Discussion Draft Revision of the Special Considerations for Intangibles in Chapter VI of the OECD Transfer Pricing Guidelines and Related Provisions

Examples Illustrating the Provisions of Chapter VI. B.

Example 1

182. Premiere is the parent company of an MNE group. Company S is a wholly owned subsidiary of Premiere and a member of the Premiere group. Premiere performs ongoing R&D functions in support of its business operations. When its R&D functions result in patentable inventions, it is the practice of the Premiere group that all rights in such inventions be assigned to Company S in order to centralise and simplify global patent administration. Company S employs three lawyers to perform its patent administration work. It does not, however, conduct or control any of the R&D activities of the Premiere group. Company S has no technical R&D personnel, nor does it incur any of the Premiere group's R&D expense. At the time of each assignment of rights from Premiere to Company S, Company S makes a 100 Euro payment to Premiere in consideration of the assignment of rights to a patentable invention and simultaneously grants to Premiere an exclusive, royalty free, patent license for the full life of the registered patent. The nominal payments of Company S to Premiere are made purely to satisfy technical contract law requirements related to the assignments and are generally much lower than the arm's length price of the assigned rights to patentable inventions.

183. Under these circumstances Company S is not entitled to intangible related returns for transfer pricing purposes, notwithstanding the fact that it holds patent registrations and other contractual rights to intangibles. Company S neither bears nor controls risks related to intangible development or

enhancement. It does not perform or control any functions related to intangible development or enhancement and does not bear any expense related to the development or enhancement of intangibles. Accordingly, Premiere, and not Company S, is entitled to all intangible related returns attributable to patents developed through Premiere's research and development efforts. Company S should receive arm's length compensation from Premiere for its patent administration services, including amounts to cover its nominal payments to Premiere for patent rights, its other patent administration costs, and an appropriate profit element, but should not receive intangible related returns related to the patents for which it holds registrations.

Example 2

184. Primero is the parent company of an MNE group engaged in the pharmaceutical business. It does business in country M. Primero develops patents and other intangibles relating to Product X and registers those patents in countries around the world.

185. Primero retains its wholly owned country N subsidiary, Company S, to distribute Product X throughout Europe and the Middle East on a limited risk basis. Company S purchases Product X from Primero and resells Product X to unrelated customers in countries throughout its geographical area of operation. In the first three years of operations, Company S earns arm's length returns from its distribution functions, consistent with its limited risk characterisation and the fact that Primero, and not Company S, is entitled to intangible related returns with respect to Product X. After three years of operation, it becomes apparent that Product X causes serious side effects in a significant percentage of those patients that use the product and it becomes necessary to recall the product and remove it from the market. Company S incurs substantial costs in connection with the recall. Primero does not reimburse Company S for these recall related costs or for the resulting product liability claims.

186. Under these circumstances, there is a mismatch between Primero's asserted entitlement to intangible related returns with respect to Product X and the costs associated with the risks supporting that assertion. A transfer pricing adjustment would be appropriate to remedy the mismatch. In all likelihood,

the most appropriate adjustment would be an allocation of the recall and product liability related costs from Company S to Primero, although in some circumstances an appropriate alternative may be to adjust the product pricing for all years between Primero and Company S to reflect the fact that the relationship was not actually a limited risk relationship.

Example 3

187. Primair, a resident of country X, manufactures watches which are marketed in many countries around the world under the R trademark and trade name. Primair is the registered owner of the R trademark and trade name. The R name is widely known in countries where the watches are sold and has obtained considerable economic value in those markets through the efforts of Primair. R watches have never been marketed in country Y, however, and the R name is not known in the country Y market.

188. In Year 1, Primair decides to enter the country Y market and incorporates a wholly owned subsidiary in country Y, Company S, to act as its distributor in country Y. At the same time, Primair enters into a long-term royalty-free marketing and distribution agreement with Company S. Under the agreement, Company S is granted the exclusive right to market and distribute watches bearing the R trademark and using the R trade name in country Y for a period of five years, with an option for a further five years. Company S obtains no other rights relating to the R trademark and trade name from Primair, and in particular is prohibited from re-exporting watches bearing the trademark and trade name. The sole activity of Company S is marketing and distributing watches bearing the R trademark and trade name. It is assumed that the R watches are not part of a portfolio of products distributed by Company S in country Y. Company S undertakes no secondary processing, as it imports packaged watches into country Y ready for sale to the final customer.

189. Under the contract between Primair and Company S, Company S purchases the watches from Primair in country Y currency, takes title to the branded watches and performs the distribution function in country Y, incurs the associated carrying costs (e.g. inventory and receivables financing), and assumes the corresponding risks (e.g. inventory, credit and financing risks). Under the contract between Primair and Company S, Company S is required to

act as a marketing agent to assist in developing the market for R watches in country. Y. Company S consults with Primair in developing the country Y marketing strategy for R watches. Primair develops the overall marketing plan based largely on its experience in other countries, it develops and approves the marketing budgets, and it makes final decisions regarding advertising designs, product positioning and core advertising messages. The costs and risks of developing the market are primarily borne by Primair, which reimburses Company S for the cost of advertising and other marketing efforts that Company S incurs in assisting with market development for R watches in country Y. Company S consults on local market issues related to advertising, assists in executing the marketing strategy under Primair's direction, and provides evaluations of the effectiveness of various elements of the marketing strategy. As compensation for providing these marketing support activities, Company S receives from Primair a fee based on the level of marketing expenditure it incurs and including an appropriate profit element.

190. Assume for the purpose of this example that, based upon a thorough comparability analysis, including a detailed functional analysis, it is possible to conclude that the price Company S pays Primair for the R watches should be analysed separately from the compensation Company S receives for the marketing it undertakes on behalf of Primair. Assume further that based upon identified comparable transactions, the price paid for the watches is arm's length and that this price enables Company S to earn an arm's length level of compensation from selling the watches for the distribution function it performs and the associated risks it assumes.

191. In Years 1 to 3, Company S embarks on a strategy that is consistent with its agreement with Primair to develop the country Y market for R watches. In the process, Company S incurs marketing expenses. Consistent with the contract, Company S is reimbursed by Primair for the marketing expenses it incurs, together with a markup on those expenses. By the end of Year 2, the R trademark and trade name have become well established in country Y. The compensation derived by Company S for the marketing activities it performed on behalf of Primair is determined to be arm's length, based upon comparison to that paid to independent advertising and marketing

agents identified and determined to be comparable as part of the comparability analysis.

192. Under these circumstances, Primair is entitled to the intangible related returns attributable to the R trademark and trade name. While Company S's performance of certain marketing functions contributes to the value of the trademark in country Y, the best measure of Company S's arm's length return for those contributions is determined by reference to the returns earned by identified independent advertising and marketing agents whose functions, risks and assets have been determined to be comparable to those of Company S through the comparability analysis.

Example 4

193. The facts in this example are the same as in Example 3, except as follows:

- Under the contract between Primair and Company S, Company S is now obligated to develop and execute the marketing plan for country Y without detailed control of specific elements of the plan by Primair. Company S bears the costs and assumes certain of the risks associated with the marketing activities. The agreement between Primair and Company S does not specify the amount of marketing expenditure Company S is expected to incur, only that Company S is required to use its best efforts to market the watches. Company S receives no reimbursement from Primair in respect of any expenditure it incurs, nor does it receive any other indirect or implied compensation from Primair, and Company S expects to earn its reward solely from its profit from the sale of R brand watches to third party customers in the country Y market.

- A thorough functional analysis reveals that Primair exercises a lower level of control over the marketing activities of Company S in that it does not review and approve the marketing budget or design details of the marketing plan. Company S bears different risks and is compensated differently than was the case in Example 3. The contractual arrangements between Primair and Company S are very different and the risks assumed by Company S are greater in Example 4 than in Example 3. Company S does not receive cost reimbursements or a separate fee for marketing activities. The only controlled transaction between Primair and Company S in Example 4 is the transfer of the branded watches. As a result, Company S can obtain its reward only through selling R brand watches to third party customers.

• As a result of these differences, Primair and Company S adopt a lower price for watches in Example 4 than the price for watches determined for purposes of Example 3. As a result of the differences identified in the functional analysis, different criteria are used for identifying comparables and for making comparability adjustments than was the case in Example 3.

194. Assume that in Years 1 through 3, Company S embarks on a strategy that is consistent with its agreement with Primair and, in the process, incurs marketing expenses. As a result, Company S has high operating expenditures and slim margins in Years 1 through 3. By the end of Year 2, the R trademark and trade name have become established in country Y because of Company S's efforts. Where the marketer/distributor actually bears the costs and associated risks of its marketing activities, the issue is the extent to which the marketer/distributor can share in the potential benefits from those activities. Assume that the enquiries of the country Y tax authorities conclude that Company S would have been expected to have incurred its actual level of marketing expense if it were unrelated to Primair.

195. Given that Company S bears the costs and associated risks of its marketing activities under a long-term contract of exclusive distribution rights for the R watches, there is an opportunity for Company S to benefit (or suffer a loss) from the marketing and distribution activities it undertakes. Based on an analysis of reasonably reliable comparable data, it is concluded that, for purposes of this example, the benefits obtained by Company S result in profits similar to those made by independent marketers and distributors bearing the same types of risks and costs as Company S in the first few years of comparable long-term marketing and distribution agreements for similarly unknown products.

196. Based on the foregoing assumptions, Company S's return is arm's length and its marketing activities, as illustrated by its marketing expenses, are not significantly different than those performed by independent marketers and distributors in comparable uncontrolled transactions. Under these circumstances, while Primair and Company S may each be entitled to a portion

of the intangible related returns associated with the R trademark and related intangibles, the information on comparable uncontrolled arrangements suggests that the return earned by Company S provides it with the arm's length return for its functions, risks, costs and its resulting entitlement to intangible related returns. No separate or additional compensation is required to Company S.

Example 5

197. The facts in this example are the same as in Example 4, except that the market development functions undertaken by Company S in this Example 5 are far more extensive than those undertaken by Company S in Example 4.

198. Where the marketer/distributor actually bears the costs and risks of its marketing activities, the issue is the extent to which the marketer/distributor can share in the potential benefits from those activities. A thorough comparability analysis identifies several uncontrolled companies engaged in similar marketing and distribution functions under similar long-term marketing and distribution arrangements. Assume, however, that the level of marketing expense Company S incurred in Years 1 through 5 far exceeds that incurred by the identified comparable independent marketers and distributors. Given the extent of the market development activities undertaken by Company S, it is evident that Company S has assumed significantly greater costs and risks than comparable independent enterprises (and substantially higher costs and risks than in Example 4). There is also evidence to support the conclusion that the profits realised by Company S are significantly lower than the profits made by the identified comparable independent marketers and distributors during the corresponding years of similar long-term marketing and distribution agreements.

199. As in Example 4, Company S bears the costs and associated risks of its marketing activities under a long-term contract of exclusive marketing and distribution rights for the R watches, and therefore has an opportunity to benefit (or suffer a loss) from the marketing and distribution activities it undertakes. However, in this case Company S has borne marketing expenditures beyond what independent enterprises in comparable transactions with similar rights incur for their own benefit, resulting in significantly lower

profits for Company S than are made by such enterprises.

200. Based on these facts, it is evident that by incurring marketing expenditure substantially in excess of the levels of such expenditure incurred by independent marketer/distributors in comparable transactions, Company S has acted to increase the value of the intangibles of Primair and has not been adequately compensated for doing so by the margins it earns on the resale of R watches. Under such circumstances it would be appropriate for the country Y tax authority to propose a transfer pricing adjustment based on compensating Company S for the marketing activities performed and expenditure incurred for the benefit of Primair, consistent with what independent enterprises dealing at arm's length in comparable transactions might be expected to have agreed. Depending on the facts and circumstances, such an adjustment could be based on:

• Reducing the price paid by Company S for the R brand watches purchased from Primair. Such an adjustment could be based on applying a resale price method or transactional net margin method using available data about profits made by comparable marketers and distributors with a comparable level of marketing and distribution expenditure.

• An alternative approach might apply a residual profit split method that would split the combined profits from sales of R branded watches in country Y by first giving Company S and Primair a basic return for the functions they perform and then splitting the residual profit on a basis that takes into account the relative entitlements to intangible related returns of Company S and Primair and the relative contributions of both Company S and Primair to the value of the R trademark and trade name.

• Directly compensating Company S for the excess marketing expenditure it has incurred over and above that incurred by comparable independent enterprises including an appropriate profit element for the functions and risks reflected by those expenditures.

201. In this example, the proposed adjustment is based on Company S's having performed functions, incurred risks, and incurred costs that provide it with an entitlement to intangible related returns for which it is not adequately compensated under its arrangement with Primair. If the arrangements between

Company S and Primair were such that Company S could expect to obtain an arm's length return on its additional investment during the remaining term of the distribution agreement, a different outcome could be appropriate.

Example 6

202. The facts in this example are the same as in Example 4, except that Company S now enters into a three-year royalty-free agreement to market and distribute the watches in the country Y market, with no option to renew. At the end of the three-year period, Company S does not enter into a new contract with Primair.

203. Assume that it is demonstrated that independent enterprises do enter into short-term distribution agreements where they incur marketing and distribution expenses, but only where they stand to earn a reward commensurate with the functions performed, assets used and the risks assumed. Evidence derived from comparable independent enterprises shows that they do not invest large sums of money in developing marketing and distribution infrastructure where they obtain only a short-term marketing and distribution agreement, with the attendant risk of non-renewal without compensation. The potential short-term nature of the marketing and distribution agreement is such that Company S could not, or may not be able to, benefit from the marketing and distribution expenditure it incurs at its own risk. The same factors mean that Company S's efforts may well benefit Primair in the future.

204. The risks assumed by Company S are substantially higher than in Example 4 and Company S has not been compensated on an arm's length basis for bearing these additional risks. In this case, Company S has undertaken market development activities and borne marketing expenditures beyond what comparable independent enterprises with similar rights incur for their own benefit, resulting in significantly lower profits for Company S than are made by comparable enterprises. The short term nature of the contract makes it unreasonable to expect that Company S has the opportunity of obtaining appropriate benefits under the contract within the limited term of the agreement with Primair. Under these circumstances, Company S is entitled to intangible related returns in the form of higher compensation for having acted

to increase the value of the R trademark and trade name during the term of its arrangement with Primair.

205. Such compensation could take the form of direct compensation from Primair to Company S for the marketing expenditures and market development functions it has undertaken. Alternatively, such an adjustment could take the form of a reduction in the price paid by Company S to Primair for R watches during Years 1 through 3.

Example 7

206. The facts in this example are the same as in Example 4 with the following additions:

• By the end of Year 3, the R brand is successfully established in the country Y market and Primair and Company S renegotiate their earlier agreement and enter into a new long-term licensing agreement. The new agreement, which is to commence at the beginning of Year 4, is for five years with Company S having an option for a further five years. Under this agreement, Company S agrees to pay a royalty to Primair based on the gross sales of all watches bearing the R trademark. In all other respects, the new agreement has the same terms and conditions as in the previous arrangement between the parties. There is no adjustment made to the price payable by Company S for the branded watches as a result of the introduction of the royalty.

• Company S's sales of R brand watches in Years 4 and 5 are consistent with earlier budget forecasts. However, the introduction of the royalty from the beginning of year 4 results in Company S's profitability declining substantially.

207. Assume that there is no evidence that independent marketers/distributors of similar branded products have agreed to pay royalties. Company S's level of marketing expenditure and activity, from Year 4 on, is consistent with that of independent enterprises, but Company S's profits are consistently lower than the profits made by independent enterprises during the corresponding years of similar long-term marketing and distribution agreements because of the royalty.

208. For transfer pricing purposes, it would not generally be expected

that a royalty would be paid in arm's length dealings where a marketing and distribution entity obtains no rights for transfer pricing purposes in trademarks and similar intangibles other than the right to use such intangibles in distributing a branded product supplied by the entity entitled to the intangible related returns attributable to such intangibles. In this circumstance, the royalty causes Company S's income to be lower than that of independent enterprises with comparable functions, risks and assets. Accordingly, a transfer pricing adjustment disallowing the royalties paid would be appropriate based on the facts of this example.

Example 8

209. The facts in this example are the same as those set out in Example 5 with the following additions:

• At the end of Year 3, Primair stops manufacturing watches and contracts with a third party to manufacture them on its behalf. As a result, Company S will import unbranded watches directly from the manufacturer and undertake secondary processing to apply the R name and logo and package the watches before sale to the final customer. It will then sell and distribute the watches in the manner described in Example 5.

• As a consequence, at the beginning of Year 4, Primair and Company S renegotiate their earlier agreement and enter into a new long term licensing agreement. The new agreement, to start at the beginning of Year 4, is for five years, with Company S having an option for a further five years.

• Under the new agreement, Company S is granted the exclusive right within country Y to process, market and distribute watches bearing the R trademark in consideration for its agreement to pay a royalty to Primair based on the gross sales of all such watches. Company S receives no compensation from Primair in respect of the renegotiation of the original marketing and distribution agreement. It is assumed for purposes of this example that the purchase price Company S pays for the watches from the beginning of Year 4 is arm's length and that no consideration with respect to the R name is embedded in that price.

210. In connection with a tax audit conducted by country Y tax authorities in Year 6, it is determined, based on a proper functional analysis, that the

level of marketing expenses Company S incurred during Years 1 through 3 far exceeded those incurred by independent marketers and distributors with similar long term marketing and distribution agreements. It is also determined that the level of marketing activity undertaken by Company S exceeded that of independent marketers and distributors. Given the extent of the market development activities undertaken by Company S, it is evident from the comparability and functional analysis that Company S has assumed significantly greater costs and risks than comparable independent enterprises. There is also evidence that the profits realised by Company S are significantly lower than the profits made by comparable independent marketers and distributors during the corresponding years of similar long-term marketing and distribution arrangements.

211. The country Y audit also identifies that in Years 4 and 5, Company S bears the costs and associated risks of its marketing activities under the new long-term licensing arrangement with Primair, and because of the long-term nature of the agreement has an opportunity to benefit (or suffer a loss) from those activities. However, Company S has undertaken market development activities and incurred marketing expenditure far beyond what comparable independent licensees with similar long-term licensing agreements undertake and incur for their own benefit, resulting in significantly lower profits for Company S than are made by comparable enterprises.

212. Based on these facts, Company S has become entitled to intangible related returns by virtue of the functions, risks and costs it has assumed. It should be compensated by an additional return for the market development activities undertaken by Company S on Primair's behalf. For Years 1 through 3, the possible bases for such an adjustment would be as described in Example 5. For Years 4 and 5 the bases for an adjustment would be similar, except that the adjustment could reduce the royalty payments from Company S to Primair, rather than the purchase price of the watches. Depending on the facts and circumstances, consideration could also be given to whether Company S should have been compensated for its entitlement to intangible related returns in some manner in connection with the renegotiation of the arrangement at the end of Year 3.

Example 9

213. Shuyona is the parent company of an MNE group. Shuyona is organised in and operates in country X. The Shuyona group is involved in the production and sale of consumer goods. In order to maintain and, if possible, improve its market position, ongoing research is carried out by the Shuyona group to improve existing products and develop new products. The Shuyona group maintains two R&D centres, one operated by Shuyona in country X and the other operated by Company S, a subsidiary of Shuyona operating in country Y. The Shuyona R&D centre is responsible for the overall research programme of Shuyona group. The Shuyona R&D centre designs research programmes, develops and controls budgets, makes decisions as to where R&D activities will be conducted, monitors the progress on all R&D projects and, in general, controls the R&D function for the MNE group, operating under strategic direction of Shuyona group senior management.

214. The Company S R&D centre operates on a separate project by project basis to carry out specific projects assigned by the Shuyona R&D centre. Suggestions of Company S R&D personnel for modifications to the research programme are required to be formally approved by the Shuyona R&D centre. The Company S R&D centre reports on its progress on at least a monthly basis to supervisory personnel at the Shuyona R&D centre. If Company S exceeds budgets established by Shuyona for its work, approval of Shuyona R&D management must be sought for further expenditures. Contracts between the Shuyona R&D centre and the Company S R&D centre specify that Shuyona will bear all risks and costs related to R&D undertaken by Company S. All patents, designs and other intangibles developed by Company S research personnel are registered by Shuyona, pursuant to contracts between the two companies. Shuyona pays Company S a service fee for its research and development activities.

215. Under these circumstances, Shuyona is entitled to intangible related returns that may be derived from intangibles developed through the R&D efforts of Company S. In determining the amount of the service fee payable to Company S, the relative skill and efficiency of the Company S R&D personnel should be considered as a comparability factor. To the extent transfer pricing

adjustments are required to reflect the amount a comparable R&D service provider would be paid for its services, such adjustments should generally relate to the year the service is provided and would not affect the entitlement of Shuyona to future intangible related returns derived from the Company S R&D activities.

Example 10

216. Shuyona is the parent company of an MNE group. Shuyona is organised in and operates exclusively in country X. The Shuyona group is involved in the production and sale of consumer goods. In order to maintain and, if possible, improve its market position, ongoing research is carried out by the Shuyona group to improve existing products and develop new products. The Shuyona group maintains two R&D centres, one operated by Shuyona in country X, and the other operated by Company S, a subsidiary of Shuyona, operating in country Y.

217. The Shuyona group sells two lines of products. All R&D with respect to product line A is conducted by Shuyona. All R&D with respect to product line B is conducted by the R&D centre operated by Company S. Company S also functions as the regional headquarters of the Shuyona group in North America and has global responsibility for the operation of the business relating to product line B. However, all patents developed by Company S research efforts are registered by Shuyona.

218. The Shuyona and Company S R&D centres operate autonomously. Each bears its own operating costs. Under the general policy direction of Shuyona senior management, the Company S R&D centre develops its own research programmes, establishes its own budgets, makes determinations as to when R&D projects should be terminated or modified, and hires its own R&D staff. The R&D centre reports to the product line B management team in Company S, and does not report to the Shuyona R&D centre. Joint meetings between the Shuyona and Company S R&D teams are sometimes held to discuss research methods and common issues.

219. Under these circumstances, Company S is entitled to intangible related returns derived from the research outputs of its own R&D centre related to product line B, notwithstanding Shuyona's registration of Company

S developed patents.

Example 11

220. Shuyona is the parent company of an MNE group. Shuyona is organised in and operates exclusively in Country X. The Shuyona group is involved in the production and sale of consumer goods. In order to maintain and, if possible, improve its market position, ongoing research is carried out by the Shuyona group to improve existing products and develop new products. The Shuyona group maintains two R&D centres, one operated by Shuyona in country X, and the other operated by Company S, a subsidiary of Shuyona, operating in country Y. The relationships between the Shuyona R&D centre and the Company S R&D centre are as described in Example 9.

221. In Year 1, Shuyona transfers patents and other technology related intangibles to a new subsidiary, Company T, organized in country Z. Company T establishes a manufacturing facility in country Z and begins to supply products to members of the Shuyona group around the world. For purposes of this example, it is assumed that the compensation paid by Company T in exchange for the transferred patents and related intangibles reflects the arm's length value of the transferred intangibles.

222. At the same time as the transfer of patents and other technology related intangibles, Company T enters into a contract research agreement with Shuyona and a separate contract research agreement with Company S. Pursuant to these agreements, Company T agrees to bear the risk of future R&D, to assume the cost of all future R&D activity, and to pay Shuyona and Company S a service fee based on the cost of the R&D activities undertaken plus a markup equivalent to the profit markup over cost earned by allegedly comparable companies engaged in providing research services.

223. Company T has no technical personnel capable of conducting or supervising the research activities. Shuyona continues to develop and design its own R&D programme, to establish its own R&D budgets, and to determine its own levels of R&D staffing. Moreover, Shuyona continues to supervise and control the R&D activities in Company S in the manner described in Example 9.

224. Under these circumstances, Shuyona should be treated as the party entitled to intangible related returns with respect to R&D conducted after the date of the transfer of patents and related technology intangibles. It should be entitled to intangible related returns both with respect to its own R&D activities and to the R&D activities conducted by Company S. Company T should not be entitled to intangible related returns related to the ongoing R&D because it does not control risks or perform and control the key R&D functions.

Examples Illustrating the Provisions of Chapter VI. C.

Example 12

225. Primarni is organised in and conducts business in country A. Company S is an associated enterprise of Primarni. Company S is organised in and does business in country B. Primarni develops a patented invention and manufacturing know-how related to Product X. Primarni and Company S enter into a written license agreement pursuant to which Primarni grants Company S the right to use the Product X patents and know-how to manufacture and sell Product X in country B, while Primarni retains the patent and know-how rights to Product X throughout the rest of the world.

226. Assume Company S uses the patents and know-how to manufacture Product X in country B. It sells Product X to unrelated customers in country B and also sells Product X to related distribution entities pursuant to sales agreements that call for title to the products to pass from Company S to the distribution entities at Company S's factory in country B. The distribution entities resell the units of Product X to customers throughout Asia and Africa. The prices paid for Product X by the distribution companies enable those distribution entities to earn an arm's length return for their distribution functions, but no return related to the Product X intangibles. Primarni does not exercise its retained patent rights for Asia and Africa to prevent the resale of Product X by the distribution entities or to demand royalties or other compensation for intangibles from the distribution entities operating in those geographies.

227. Under these circumstances, the conduct of the parties suggests that the transaction between Primarni and Company S should be characterised as a

license of the Product X patent and know-how for country B, plus Asia and Africa. The provision of the agreement limiting Company S's rights to country B should not be respected for purposes of a transfer pricing analysis of the amount of compensation due Primarni from Company S for the licensed intangibles.

Example 13

228. Ilcha is organised in country A. It has for many years manufactured and sold Product Q in country B through a branch or permanent establishment located in that country. Ilcha owns patents related to the design of Product Q and has developed a unique trademark and other brand intangibles. The patents and trademarks are registered by Ilcha in country B.

229. For sound business reasons, Ilcha determines that its business in country B would be enhanced if it were operated through a separate subsidiary in that country. Ilcha therefore organizes Company S in country B as a wholly owned subsidiary. It transfers the tangible manufacturing and marketing assets previously used by the branch to Company S and enters into a long-term license agreement with Company S granting it the exclusive right to use the Product Q patents, trademarks and other intangibles in country B. Company S thereafter conducts the Product Q business in country B.

230. Assume that over the years of its operation in branch form, Ilcha developed substantial goodwill and ongoing concern value in country B. The transfer of the going business to Company S, together with the license of rights to use the patents, trademarks and other intangibles in country B, implicitly conveys the value of that continuing goodwill to Company S. In conducting a transfer pricing analysis related to the amount to be paid by Company S to Ilcha, for the tangible assets transferred and the licensed right to use the intangibles in country B, the goodwill and ongoing concern value of the going business transferred to Company S should be taken into account.

Example 14

231. Första is a consumer goods company organised and operating in country A. Prior to Year 1, Första produces Product Y in country A and sells it through affiliated distribution companies in many countries around the world. The Product Y trademark is well recognised and valuable, and Första is

entitled to intangible related returns with respect to the Product Y trademark.

232. In Year 2, Första organises Company S, a wholly owned subsidiary, in country B. Company S acts as a super distributor and invoicing centre. Första continues to ship Product Y directly to its distribution affiliates, but title to the products passes to Company S, which reinvoices the distribution affiliates for the products.

233. Beginning in Year 2, Company S reimburses the distribution affiliates for a portion of their advertising costs. Prices from Company S to the distribution affiliates are adjusted upward so that the distribution affiliate margins remain constant notwithstanding the shift of advertising cost to Company S. Assume that the margins earned by the distribution affiliates are arm's length both before and after Year 2. Company S performs no functions with regard to advertising nor does it control any risk related to marketing the products.

234. In Year 3, the prices charged by Första to Company S are reduced. Första and Company S claim such a reduction in price is justified because Company S is entitled to intangible related returns associated with goodwill in respect of Product Y created through the advertising costs it has borne.

235. In substance, Company S has no claim to a return to goodwill with respect to Product Y and transfer pricing adjustments to increase the income of Första in Year 3 and thereafter would be appropriate. Company S has not performed or controlled functions and risks related to the creation, enhancement, maintenance and protection of that goodwill. A transfer pricing adjustment would be appropriate to deny any intangible related return to Company S.

Example 15

236. Birincil acquires all of the shares of an unrelated company, Company T for 100. Company T is a company that engages in research and development and has partially developed several promising technologies but has only minimal sales. The purchase price is justified primarily by the value of the promising, but only partly developed, technologies and by the potential of Company T personnel to develop further new technologies in the future. Birincil's purchase price allocation performed for accounting purposes with

respect to the acquisition attributes 20 of the purchase price to tangible property and identified intangibles, including patents, and 80 to goodwill.

237. Immediately following the acquisition, Birincil causes Company T to transfer all of its rights in developed and partially developed technologies, including patents, trade secrets and technical know-how to Company S, a subsidiary of Birincil. Company S simultaneously enters into a contract research agreement with Company T, pursuant to which the Company T workforce will continue to work exclusively on the development of the transferred technologies and on the development of new technologies on behalf of Company S. The agreement provides that Company T will be compensated for its research services by payments equal to its cost plus a mark-up, and that all rights to intangibles developed or enhanced under the research agreement will belong to Company S. As a result, Company S will fund all future research and will assume the financial risk that some or all of the future research will not lead to the development of commercially viable products. Company S has a large research staff, including management personnel responsible for technologies of the type acquired from Company T. Following the transactions in question, the Company S research and management personnel assume full management responsibility for the direction and control of the work of the Company T research staff. Company S approves new projects, develops and plans budgets and in other respects controls the ongoing research work carried on at Company T. All company T research personnel will continue to be employees of Company T and will be devoted exclusively to providing services under the research agreement with Company S.

238. In conducting a transfer pricing analysis of the arm's length price to be paid by Company S for intangibles transferred by Company T, and of the price to be paid for ongoing R&D services to be provided by Company T, it is important to identify the specific intangibles transferred to Company S and those retained by Company T. The definitions and valuations of intangibles contained in the purchase price allocation are irrelevant for transfer pricing purposes. The 100 paid by Birincil for the shares of Company T represents a risk-adjusted arm's length price for the business of Company T. The full value of that business should be reflected either in the value of the tangible and

intangible assets transferred to Company S or in the value of the tangible and intangible assets and workforce retained by Company T. Depending on the facts, a substantial portion of the value described in the purchase price allocation as goodwill of Company T may have been transferred to Company S together with the other Company T intangibles. Depending on the facts, some portion of the value described in the purchase price allocation as goodwill may also have been retained by Company T. Under arm's length transfer pricing principles, Company T should be entitled to compensation for such value, either as part of the price paid by Company S for the transferred rights to technology intangibles, or through the compensation Company T is paid in years following the transaction for the R&D services of its workforce. It should generally be assumed that value does not disappear, nor is it destroyed, as part of an internal business restructuring.

Example 16

239. Zhu is a company engaged in software development consulting. In the past Zhu has developed software supporting ATM transactions for client Bank A. In the process of doing so, Zhu created and retained an interest in proprietary software code that is potentially suitable for use by other similarly situated banking clients, albeit with some revision and customisation.

240. Assume that Company S, an associated enterprise of Zhu, enters into a separate agreement to develop software supporting ATM operations for another bank, Bank B. Zhu agrees to support its associated enterprise by providing employees who worked on the Bank A engagement to work on Company S's Bank B engagement. Those employees have access to software designs and know-how developed in the Bank A engagement, including proprietary software code. That code and the services of the Zhu employees are utilised by Company S in executing its Bank B engagement. Ultimately, Bank B is provided by Company S with a software system for managing its ATM network, including the necessary license to utilise the software developed in the project. Portions of the proprietary code developed by Zhu in its Bank A engagement are embedded in the software provided by Company S to Bank B.

241. A transfer pricing analysis of these transactions should recognise that Company S received two benefits from Zhu which require compensation. First,

it received services from the Zhu employees that were made available to work on the Bank B engagement. Second, it received rights in Zhu's proprietary software which was utilised as the foundation for the software system delivered to Bank B. The compensation to be paid by Company S to Zhu should include compensation for both the services and the rights in the software.

Example 17

242. Prathamika is the parent company of an MNE group. Prathamika has been engaged in several large litigation matters and its internal legal department has become adept at managing large scale litigation on behalf of Prathamika. In the course of working on such litigation, Prathamika has developed proprietary document management software tools unique to its industry.

243. Company S is an associated enterprise of Prathamika. Company S becomes involved in a complex litigation similar to those with which the legal department of Prathamika has experience. Prathamika agrees to make two individuals from its legal team available to Company S to work on the Company S litigation. The individuals from Prathamika assume responsibility for managing documents related to the litigation. In undertaking this responsibility they make use of the document management software of Prathamika. They do not, however, provide Company S the right to use the document management software in other litigation matters or to make it available to Company S customers.

244. Under these circumstances, it would not be appropriate to treat Prathamika as having transferred rights in intangibles to Company S as part of the service arrangement. However, the fact that the Prathamika employees had experience and available software tools that allowed them to more effectively and efficiently perform their services should be considered in a comparability analysis related to the amount of any service fee to be charged for the services of the Prathamika employees.

Examples Illustrating the Provisions of Chapter VI. D.

Example 18

245. Osnovni is the parent company of an MNE Group engaged in the development and sale of software products. Osnovni acquires Company S, a

publicly traded company organised in the same country as Osnovni, for a price equal to 160. At the time of the acquisition, Company S shares had an aggregate trading value of 100. Competitive bidders for the Company S business offered amounts ranging from 120 to 130 for Company S.

246. Company S had only a nominal amount of fixed assets at the time of the acquisition. Its value consisted primarily of rights in developed and partially developed intangibles related to software products and its skilled workforce. The purchase price allocation performed for accounting purposes by Osnovni allocated 10 to tangible assets, 60 to intangibles, and 90 to goodwill. Osnovni justified the 160 purchase price in presentations to its Board of Directors by reference to the complementary nature of the existing products of the Osnovni group and the products and potential products of Company S.

247. Company T is a wholly owned subsidiary of Osnovni. Osnovni and Company T are parties to a research and development cost contribution arrangement. By virtue of that cost contribution arrangement, Company T holds the exclusive right to produce and sell all software products of the Osnovni group in European and Asian markets. For purposes of this example it is assumed that all arrangements related to the cost contribution arrangement as regards products and intangibles in existence in the Osnovni group prior to the acquisition of Company S are arm's length. Historically 50 percent of MNE group sales and profits have been derived from markets allocated to Company T under the cost contribution arrangement.

248. Immediately following the acquisition of Company S, Osnovni liquidates Company S in a transaction that is not taxable in Osnovni's country, and thereafter grants an exclusive and perpetual license to Company T for intangible rights related to the Company S products. The cost contribution arrangement is amended to include the products and potential products acquired in the Company S acquisition, and the developed and partially developed intangibles related to the Company S products.

249. In determining an arm's length price for the Company S intangibles made available to Company T under the foregoing arrangements, the premium over the original trading value of the Company S shares included in the acquisition price should be considered. To the extent that premium reflects the

complementary nature of Osnovni group products with the acquired products in the European and Asian markets allocated to Company T under the cost contribution agreement, Company T should pay an amount for the transferred Company S intangibles and rights in intangibles that includes an appropriate share of the purchase price premium. To the extent the purchase price premium is attributable exclusively to product complementarities outside of Company T's markets, the purchase price premium should not be taken into account in determining the arm's length price paid by Company T for Company S intangibles related to Company T's geographic market. The value attributed to intangibles in the purchase price allocation performed for accounting purposes is irrelevant for transfer pricing purposes.

Example 19

250. Pervichnyi is the parent of an MNE group organised and doing business in country X. Prior to Year 1, Pervichnyi developed patents and trademarks related to Product F. It manufactured Product F in country X and supplied the product to distribution affiliates throughout the world. For purposes of this example assume the prices charged to distribution affiliates were consistently arm's length.

251. At the beginning of Year 1, Pervichnyi organised a wholly owned subsidiary, Company S, in country Y. In order to save costs, Pervichnyi transfers all of its production of Product F to Company S. At the time of the organisation of Company S, Pervichnyi sells the patents and trademarks related to Product F to Company S for a lump sum.

252. Assume the following facts:

• Pervichnyi's distribution affiliates consistently sell 1000 of Product F annually and expect to do so each year for the next five years. However, if production cost savings would support a price reduction, the distribution affiliates believe it would be in their interest to avoid long-term erosion of Pervichnyi's market position to reduce prices by 5 percent so that total sales of the same quantity would generate 950 of revenue.

• Prior to Year 1, Pervichnyi's cost of goods sold for Product F is consistently 600 annually and would be expected to remain at that level if production remains in country X. If production is moved to Company S in country Y, cost of goods sold for the same production volume would fall to 500 annually.

• The selling expenses of the distribution affiliates are consistently 100 annually.

• Country X imposes corporate income tax at a 30 percent rate. Country Y imposes corporate tax at a 10 percent rate.

• The distribution affiliates are subject to tax on their income at a rate of 10%.

• The transferred intangibles have a 5 year useful life.

• An appropriate return for manufacturing activities is 5 percent of COGS. An appropriate return for distribution activities is 2 percent of sales.

• An appropriate discount rate for a DCF type analysis, taking into account the risks of the Product F business, is 14 percent.

253. Under these circumstances, Pervichnyi and Company S seek to identify an arm's length price for the transferred intangibles by utilising a discounted cash flow valuation technique. As shown in Table 1 below, viewed from the point of view of Pervichnyi, and assuming that Pervichnyi itself continues to manufacture Product F, the residual after tax cash flows notionally attributable to the transferred intangibles have a present value of 594.

Table 1　From the Seller's Viewpoint—Pervichnyi owns the intangible
Pervichnyi manufactures and sells to distributors

	Pervichnyi	Year 1	Year 2	Year 3	Year 4	Year 5	Total PV
(1)	Revenues	880	880	880	880	880	
(2)	COGS	600	600	600	600	600	
(3)	Selling Expenses	0	0	0	0	0	
(4)	Operating Income	280	280	280	280	280	
(5)	Tax Rate	30%	30%	30%	30%	30%	

(续表)

	Pervichnyi	Year 1	Year 2	Year 3	Year 4	Year 5	Total PV
(6)	Taxes	84	84	84	84	84	
(7)	Income after tax (14% DR)	196	196	196	196	196	673
(7A)	Value of intangible (14% DR)	173	173	173	173	173	594

	Distributors	Year 1	Year 2	Year 3	Year 4	Year 5	Total PV
(8)	Revenues	1000	1000	1000	1000	1000	
(9)	COGS	880	880	880	880	880	
(10)	Selling Expenses	100	100	100	100	100	
(11)	Operating Income	20	20	20	20	20	
(12)	Tax Rate	10%	10%	10%	10%	10%	
(13)	Taxes	2	2	2	2	2	
(14)	Income after tax	18	18	18	18	18	

Company S			DOES NOT EXIST			

	Global (Consolidated) Results	Year 1	Year 2	Year 3	Year 4	Year 5	Total PV
(15)	Revenues	1000	1000	1000	1000	1000	
(16)	COGS	600	600	600	600	600	
(17)	Selling Expenses	100	100	100	100	100	
(18)	Operating Income	300	300	300	300	300	
(19)	Tax Rate						
(20)	Taxes	86	86	86	86	86	
(21)	Income after tax	214	214	214	214	214	735

254. If the intangibles are transferred to Company S, the residual after tax cash flows notionally attributable to intangibles would have a higher present

value of 941, as reflected in Table 2. This difference results from the lower manufacturing costs at Company S and from the lower tax rate at Company S, partially offset by the lower revenue attributable to a price reduction made possible by the production cost savings.

Table 2 From the Buyer's Viewpoint—Company S owns the intangible Company S manufactures and sells to distributors

Pervichnyi		HAS NO ROLE					

	Distributors	Year 1	Year 2	Year 3	Year 4	Year 5	Total PV
(29)	Revenues	950	950	950	950	950	
(30)	COGS	830	830	830	830	830	
(31)	Selling Expenses	100	100	100	100	100	
(32)	Operating Income	20	20	20	20	20	
(33)	Tax Rate	10%	10%	10%	10%	10%	
(34)	Taxes	2	2	2	2	2	
(35)	Income after tax	18	18	18	18	18	

	Company S	Year 1	Year 2	Year 3	Year 4	Year 5	Total PV
(36)	Revenues	830	830	830	830	830	
(37)	COGS	500	500	500	500	500	
(38)	Selling Expenses	0	0	0	0	0	
(39)	Operating Income	330	330	330	330	330	
(40)	Tax Rate	10%	10%	10%	10%	10%	
(41)	Taxes	33	33	33	33	33	
(42)	Income after tax (14% DR)	297	297	297	297	297	1020
(42A)	Value of Intangible (14% DR)	274	274	274	274	274	941

Global (Consolidated) Results		Year 1	Year 2	Year 3	Year 4	Year 5	Total PV
(43)	Revenues	950	950	950	950	950	
(44)	COGS	500	500	500	500	500	
(45)	Selling Expenses	100	100	100	100	100	
(46)	Operating Income	350	350	350	350	350	
(47)	Tax Rate						
(48)	Taxes	35	35	35	35	35	
(49)	Income after tax	315	315	315	315	315	1081

255. Another option open to Pervichnyi would be for Pervichnyi to retain ownership of the intangible, and to retain Company S or an alternative supplier to manufacture products on its behalf. The consequences of following such an option are reflected in Table 3. In this scenario, Pervichnyi would be able to capture the benefit of manufacturing Product F in a lower cost environment without transferring the intangibles to Company S. As reflected in the Table 3, the cash flows attributable to the intangible would have a present value of 735.

Table 3 From the Seller's Viewpoint—Pervichnyi owns the intangible Pervichnyi contracts manufactures through Company S and sells to distributors

Pervichnyi		Year 1	Year 2	Year 3	Year 4	Year 5	Total PV
(22)	Revenues	830	830	830	830	830	
(23)	COGS	525	525	525	525	525	
(24)	Selling Expenses	0	0	0	0	0	
(25)	Operating Income	305	305	305	305	305	
(26)	Tax Rate	30%	30%	30%	30%	30%	
(27)	Taxes	92	92	92	92	92	
(28)	Income after tax (14% DR)	214	214	214	214	214	735

	Distributors	Year 1	Year 2	Year 3	Year 4	Year 5	Total PV
(29)	Revenues	950	950	950	950	950	
(30)	COGS	830	830	830	830	830	
(31)	Selling Expenses	100	100	100	100	100	
(32)	Operating Income	20	20	20	20	20	
(33)	Tax Rate	10%	10%	10%	10%	10%	
(34)	Taxes	2	2	2	2	2	
(35)	Income after tax	18	18	18	18	18	

	Company S	Year 1	Year 2	Year 3	Year 4	Year 5	Total PV
(36)	Revenues	525	525	525	525	525	
(37)	COGS	500	500	500	500	500	
(38)	Selling Expenses	0	0	0	0	0	
(39)	Operating Income	25	25	25	25	25	
(40)	Tax Rate	10%	10%	10%	10%	10%	
(41)	Taxes	3	3	3	3	3	
(42)	Income after tax	23	23	23	23	23	

	Global (Consolidated) Results	Year 1	Year 2	Year 3	Year 4	Year 5	Total PV
(43)	Revenues	950	950	950	950	950	
(44)	COGS	500	500	500	500	500	
(45)	Selling Expenses	100	100	100	100	100	
(46)	Operating Income	350	350	350	350	350	
(47)	Tax Rate						
(48)	Taxes	96	96	96	96	96	
(49)	Income after tax	254	254	254	254	254	872

256. In defining arm's length compensation for the intangibles it is

important to take into account the perspectives of both parties and the options realistically available to each of them. Pervichnyi would certainly not sell the intangibles at a price that would yield an after tax return lower than 594, the present value of intangible related cash flows reflected in Table 1, because it could generate after tax income with a present value of that amount by continuing to operate the business as it has in the past. Moreover, there is no reason to believe Pervichnyi would sell the intangible for a price that would yield an after tax return lower than the 735 reflected in Table 3, because it could achieve such a value by outsourcing the manufacturing to a lower cost provider on an arm's length basis.

257. Company S would not pay more than 941 for the intangibles, since if it did it would derive no return from the risks associated with intangible ownership, as reflected in Table 2. A higher price would be inconsistent with the reasonably available option to Company S of not entering into the transaction.

258. A transfer pricing analysis utilising a discounted cash flow approach would have to consider how unrelated parties dealing at arm's length would take into account the cost savings and tax rate benefits in setting a price for the intangibles. That price should, however, fall in the range between a price that would yield Pervichnyi an after tax return equivalent to that reflected in Table 3, and a price that would yield Company S a positive return to its investments and risks, which would be a price lower than the present value of the intangible related cash flow calculated in Table 2.

Example 20

259. Manufacturing and distribution rights for an established drug are licensed between associated enterprises under an agreement that fixes the rate of royalty for the three year term of the agreement.

Those terms are found to be in accordance with industry practice and equivalent arm's length agreements for comparable products, and the rate is accepted as being equivalent to that agreed in uncontrolled transactions based on the benefits reasonably anticipated by both parties at the time the agreement is executed.

260. In the third year of the agreement, it is discovered that the drug has

capabilities in another therapeutic category in combination with another drug, and the discovery leads to a considerable increase in sales and profits for the licensee. Had the agreement been negotiated at arm's length in year three with this knowledge, there is no doubt that a higher royalty rate would have been agreed to reflect the increased value of the intangible.

261. There is evidence to support the view (and the evidence is made available to the tax administration) that the new capabilities of the drug were unanticipated at the time the agreement was executed and that the royalty rate established in year one was adequately based on the benefits reasonably anticipated by both parties at that time. The lack of price adjustment clauses or other protection against the risk of uncertainty of valuation also is consistent with the terms of comparable uncontrolled transactions. Based on analysis of the behaviour of independent enterprises in similar circumstances, there is no reason to believe that the development in year three was so fundamental that it would have led at arm's length to a renegotiation of the pricing of the transaction.

262. Taking all these circumstances into account, there is no reason to adjust the royalty rate in year three. Such an adjustment would be contrary to the principles set out in Chapter VI because it would represent an inappropriate use of hindsight in this case. See paragraph 173. There is no reason to consider that the valuation was sufficiently uncertain at the outset and that the parties at arm's length would have required a price adjustment clause, or that the change in value was so fundamental a development that it would have led to a re-negotiation of the transaction. See paragraphs 174 and 175.

Example 21

263. The facts are the same as in the previous example. Assume that at the end of the three-year period the agreement was re-negotiated between the parties. At this stage it is known that the rights to the drug are considerably more valuable than they had at first appeared. However, the unexpected development of the previous year is still recent, and it cannot reliably be predicted whether sales will continue to rise, whether further beneficial effects will be discovered, and what developments in the market may affect sales as competitors piggyback on the discovery. All these considerations make the re-

evaluation of the intangible rights a highly uncertain process. Nevertheless, the associated enterprises enter into a new licensing agreement for a term of ten years that significantly increases the fixed royalty rate based on speculative expectations of continuing and increasing demand.

264. It is not industry practice to enter into long-term agreements with fixed royalty rates when the intangible involved potentially has a high value, but that value has not been established by a track record. Nor is there evidence that, given the uncertainty in valuation, any projections made by the associated enterprises would have been considered adequate by independent enterprises to justify an agreement with a fixed royalty rate. Assume that there is evidence that independent enterprises would have insisted on protection in the form of prospective price adjustment clauses based on reviews undertaken annually.

265. Assume that in year 4 sales increased and the royalty rate established under the ten-year agreement is regarded as appropriate under the arm's length principle. However, at the beginning of year 5, a competitor introduces a drug that has greater benefit than the first drug in the therapeutic category in which the first drug, in combination, unexpectedly had provided benefits, and sales of the first drug for that use rapidly decline. The royalty rate fixed at the outset of the ten-years agreement cannot be regarded as arm's length beyond year 5, and it is justifiable for the tax administration to make a transfer price adjustment from the beginning of year 6. This adjustment is appropriate because of the evidence, mentioned in the preceding paragraph that in comparable circumstances independent enterprises would have provided in the agreement for a price adjustment based on annual review. See paragraph 177.

Example 22

266. Assume that Company X licenses the rights to produce and market a microchip to Company Y, a newly established subsidiary, for a period of five years. The royalty rate is fixed at 2 percent. This royalty rate is based on a projection of benefits to be derived from the exploitation of the intangible, which shows expected product sales of 50 to 100 million in each of the first five years.

267. It is established that contracts between independent enterprises dealing with comparable intangibles in comparable circumstances would not

consider the projections sufficiently reliable to justify a fixed royalty rate, and so would normally agree upon a price adjustment clause to account for differences between actual and projected benefits. An agreement made by Company X with an independent manufacturer for a comparable intangible under comparable circumstances provides for the following adjustments to the rate:

Sales	Royalty
Up to 100 million	2.00%
Next 50 million	2.25%
Next 50 million	2.50%
In excess of 200 million	2.75%

268. In fact, although sales by Y in year 1 are 50 million, in subsequent years sales are three times greater than the projected figures. In accordance with the principles of this section, for these subsequent years the tax administration would be justified in determining the royalty rate on the basis of the adjustment clause that would be provided in a comparable uncontrolled transaction such as that between Company X and the independent manufacturer. See paragraphs 174, 176, and 177.

China Country Practice

—selected from United Nations Practical Manual on Transfer Pricing for Developing Countries

10.3.1. Introduction—Bridging the Gap: Applying the Arm's Length Principle in Developing Countries

10.3.1.1. The OECD Transfer Pricing Guidelines for Multinational Enterprises and Tax Administrations (the OECD Transfer Pricing Guidelines) have been the "gold standard" for tax administrations and taxpayers to apply the "arm's length principle" for the valuation, for tax purposes, of cross-border transactions between related parties for much of the period since the original version of the guidelines was first issued in 1995. As the world economy becomes increasingly globalized, transfer pricing is an issue faced not only by developed countries, but is increasingly a critical matter for developing countries. Such nations face a set of unique issues that have not been addressed, or at least not sufficiently or practically addressed by the OECD Guidelines.

Therefore, while much of the OECD guidelines may still be applicable to developing countries, the UN Transfer Pricing Manual should put aspecial focus on offering practical solutions to issues faced by developing countries.

10. 3. 1. 2. China started looking into transfer pricing issues in the late 1990s. While the early focus of transfer pricing investigations was mostly on tangible goods transactions, it has since been expanded into a range of other transactions, and in particular, those involving intangibles and services. As a developing country, China faces a number of difficult challenges, many of which remain unanswered by the OECD Guidelines. These include a lack of appropriate comparables, quantification and allocation of location-specific advantages, and identification and valuation of intangibles. The UN Transfer Pricing Manual must address these common issues for it to be useful to developing countries.

10. 3. 1. 3. This paper intends to highlight some of the challenging issues faced by developing countries, and to share China's practical experience in dealing with these issues.

10. 3. 2. The Challenge of a Lack of Reliable Comparables

10. 3. 2. 1. The "arm's length principle" is at the core of the OECD Transfer Pricing Guidelines. Under this approach, transactions between group companies are compared with transactions between unrelated companies under comparable circumstances. Where there are no comparable transactions, then an alternative comparison maybe made with unrelated companies that perform similar functions, own similar assets and bear similar risks to the taxpayer whose related party transactions are being examined, and operate under comparable circumstances.

10. 3. 2. 2. Therein lies one of the key challenges for a developing countries—a lack of reliable, public information on comparables. For

developing countries, there are usually only a small number of public companies, while information on domestic private companiesis lacking or inadequate. This limits the amount of publicly available information on domestic companies that can be used for transfer pricing analysis. There would be, in particular, a lack of comparables for companies who are first-movers in an industry not yet fully exploited. In practice, foreign companies are often used as an alternative to domestic comparables. As a result, comparables sets are often dominated by companies in developed countries, simply because there are usually a much larger number of public companies in these countries.

10.3.2.3. While globalization and free capital mobility are the basis for the use of foreign comparables, the existence of foreign exchange controls in many developing countries violates this pre-condition. Accordingly, significant comparability adjustments may be necessary for companies in developed countries to be used as comparables for companies in developing countries. In some cases, it may require adifferent methodology such as profit split as no sufficiently reliable comparability adjustment may be feasible.

10.3.2.4. One of the most common adjustments in China is accounting for differences in geographic comparability when applying profit based transfer pricing methods, such as the Transactional Net Margin Method (TNMM), to determine an arm's length price. For example, when an Asia Pacific set of companies is used to benchmark the transfer prices of a Chinese taxpayer, as often being the case, it often includes companies from both developed countries (such as Japan and Korea), as well as developing countries (such as Indonesia and Vietnam). Generally speaking, the Asia Pacific set is more likely to contain companies from developed countries, due to a greater number of listed companies in those countries and hence there is a greater volume of publicly available financial information.

10.3.2.5. China takes the view that there may be instances where the differences in geographical markets are so material that it warrants comparability adjustments to bridge the differences. By making such comparability adjustments, taxpayers in developing countries can overcome the practical difficulties in applying the arm's length principle to their transfer pricing analysis.

10.3.3. Location-specific Advantages

10.3.3.1. The globalization of trade and economies has given rise to concepts such as "location savings", "market premium," and more generally, "location-specific advantages" (LSAs). LSAs are advantages for production arising from assets, resource endowments, government industry policies and incentives, etc., which exist in specific localities.

For example, household electronics manufacturers invest in China to take advantage of a large pool of well-educated low-cost labour and a well-developed network of suppliers. Likewise, global automotive companies set up joint ventures (JVs) in China to assemble automobiles locally to be close to the market and the customers and to take advantage of lower costs. Limited guidance is available on these concepts in the OECD Guidelines; it has been seen that certain issues such as location savings and market premium arise more frequently in China and other developing economies, rather than in established and developed economies (which comprise the bulk of the membership of the OECD). China outlines its solutions to reconcile the arm's length principle with the lack of reliable comparables in developing countries in the following paragraphs.

10.3.3.2. Location savings are the net cost savings derived by a multinational company when it sets up its operations in a low-cost jurisdiction. Net cost savings are commonly realized through lower expenditure on items such as raw materials, labour, rent, transportation and infrastructure even though additional expenses (so-called dis-savings) may be incurred due to the relocation, such as increased training costs in return for hiring less skilled labour.

10.3.3.3. Market premium relates to the additional profit derived by a multinational company by operating in a jurisdiction with unique qualities impacting on the sale and demand of a service or product.

10.3.3.4. In dealings with Chinese taxpayers, the Chinese tax administration has adopted a four step approach on the issue of LSAs:

1. Identify if an LSA exists;
2. Determine whether the LSA generates additional profit;
3. Quantify and measure the additional profits arising from the LSA; and

4. Determine the transfer pricing method to allocate the profits arising from the LSA.

10.3.3.5. In determining LSAs and their impact on transfer pricing, both industry analysis and quantitative analysis are critical.

10.3.3.6. The automotive industry is a good example where there are many LSAs that have led to extraordinarily high profits that are rightly earned by Chinese taxpayers. The LSAs here include:

✍ The "market-for-technology" industry policy, which requires foreign automotive manufacturers to form joint ventures (JVs) in order to assemble automobiles in China, forcing foreign automotive manufacturers to compete for limited market access opportunities by offering favourable terms including provision of technologies at below market price;

✍ Chinese consumers' general preference for foreign brands and imported products—this general preference, as opposed to loyalty to a specific brand, creates opportunities for MNEs to charge higher prices and earn additional profits on automotive products sold in China;

✍ Huge, inelastic demand for automotive vehicles in China due to the large population and growing wealth of the population;

✍ Capacity constraints on the supply of domestically assembled automotive vehicles;

✍ Duty savings from the lower duty rates on automotive parts (e.g. 10 per cent) compared to imported vehicles (e.g. 25 per cent)—when MNEs manufacture products in China as opposed to importing the products from outside of China, they are able to generate overall savings from the lower duty rates, even if the MNEs incur manufacturing costs and sell their domestically-manufactured products at a lower sales price compared to a foreign-manufactured vehicle; and

✍ A large supply of high quality, low costs parts manufactured by suppliers in China.

10.3.3.7. For a 50/50 JV with partners having conflicting interests in the Chinese automotive industry, the Chinese JV partner generally contributes the local distribution network, intimate knowledge about the local market, and the right market access. However, the Chinese partner does not typically have control over the JV operation, which is usually controlled by the foreign JV partner. The foreign JV partner also controls the supply chain of the parts. To the extent there could still be potential transfer pricing issues, the primary issue involves the JV being over charged for the parts and services that are provided by related parties. In the absence of such overcharging, the JV's results mainly reflect an arm's length outcome, which in turn reflect the contribution of LSAs to the JVs.

10.3.3.8. A further example is that of a Chinese taxpayer performing contract research and development (R&D) services for an offshore affiliate, and the full cost mark-up (FCMU) as the profit level indicator for a comparable set comprising of foreign companies located in developed countries (and hence, incurring higher costs). The following example outlines the steps used to calculate the adjusted FCMU taking into consideration the location savings.

10.3.3.9. It is assumed that the Chinese taxpayer's cost base was 100, the average cost base for the company's R&D centres in developed countries was 150, and the median FCMU of the comparables was 8 per cent. The comparison of the cost base between the Chinese taxpayer and that of the foreign companies is measured on an equal platform, such as the total costs (labour, raw materials, land and rent, etc.) per unit of output.

	Steps	Calculations
1	Calculate the arm's length range of FCMUs based on foreign comparables, mostly in developed countries	Assume the median FCMU is 8%
2	Calculate the difference between the cost base of the Chinese taxpayer (e.g. 100) and the average cost base of the foreign companies (e.g. 150)	$150 - 100 = 50$
3	Multiply the arm's length FCMU (e.g. 8 per cent) with the difference in the cost bases (50)	$0.08 \times 50 = 4$
4	The resulting profit is the additional profit (i.e. 4) attributable to China for location savings	4
5	Determine the total arm's length profit for the Chinese taxpayer	$4 + 0.08 \times 100 = 12$
6	Determine the adjusted arm's length FCMU for the Chinese taxpayer	$12/100 = 12\%$

10.3.3.10. The Chinese tax administration has come across many other cases of market premiums for Chinese taxpayers, particularly in the luxury goods sector.

10.3.4. Intangibles

10.3.4.1. Intangibles are as major an issue for developing countries as they are for developed countries. While MNEs in developed countries often have superior technology intangibles, they need the fast growing market in the developing countries and contribution of the subsidiaries in these countries to develop these markets in order to monetize the value in such intangibles. For developing countries, marketing intangibles and LSAs are often closely integrated, and due consideration is necessary to properly compensate the contribution of the subsidiaries in developing countries.

10.3.4.2. MNEs often provide intangibles to their Chinese affiliates in the initial stages of the local operation to help establish the business in China. These intangibles may take various forms, such as a global brand name, technical know-how or business processes. Overtime, the local Chinese affiliates acquire the skill and experience from operations in China, and may even contribute to the improvement of the MNE's original intangibles. The issue in this scenario is whether the local Chinese affiliates should be entitled to additional profit, and if so, what is the appropriate method to calculate the additional profit?

10.3.4.3. For example, if a Chinese affiliate was charged a 3 per cent royalty for the use of a manufacturing process when the Chinese operations were established ten years ago in 2002, then it may not be reasonable for the Chinese affiliate to continue paying the same royalty in 2012 without revisiting whether the intangible has continued to provide the same value over time. This is particularly the case if the Chinese affiliate has improved upon the manufacturing process provided by its parent company, through a process of trial and error and conducting manufacturing operations over a ten year period. We would question whether the Chinese affiliate should continue to pay a royalty to the parent company for the manufacturing process, or whether the Chinese affiliates should be entitled to a return on the intangibles that they have developed and shared with the group companies.

10.3.5. Practical Issues and Solutions

10.3.5.1. In a globalizing economy, MNEs usually set up operations in developing countries to take advantage of comparative advantages that these countries offer. For example, they set up manufacturing operations to take advantage of the abundant cheap labour or natural resources to supply products for overseas markets, R&D to take advantage of local talent for overseas principals, and distribution of imported products to the local market. These operations often take the form of contract or toll manufacturing, contract R&D, and limited risk distribution to leave little profit to the local country, despite the fact that many such comparative advantages contribute significant profits to the multinational group. The following paragraphs share some of the Chinese experience in dealing with these transfer pricing issues.

10.3.5.2. A holistic view of functions and risks may need to be taken. Many MNEs have set up multiple companies in China with each company performing only a single function, such as manufacturing, distribution, R&D, and services, and with the claim that each of these entities is entitled to a limited return. Others have some or all of manufacturing, distribution, R&D, and services functions in one entity, and still claim that each of these functions is entitled to only a routine return. The Chinese tax administration takes the view that when a group has multiple single function entities, they may have to be taken into consideration as a whole in order to properly determine the return the group companies should earn in China. Similarly, an entity with multiple functions may have to be reviewed in its entirety in order to properly determine its returns.

10.3.5.3. While China generally respects the limited risk characterization of sole function entities;① determining an adequate return for such entities is a challenge, as explained below. Further, China has legislated a specific article in its transfer pricing rules to require that such entities should not bear risks or suffer from losses arising from strategic failures, capacity under-utilization, or hold-up in the sales of products, etc., if they do not perform business strategy

---

① For example toll or contract manufacturing, limited risk distribution, or limited risk service provider.

decision making, product R&D, or sales functions. Simply put, if their upside is limited, their downside should be limited too.

10.3.5.4. Contract R&D is an area where the contribution of developing countries is often under estimated. The transfer pricing method commonly used to reward R&D activities performed by a subsidiary of an MNE in China is the Cost Plus Method. Sometimes, it has been found that the principal entity that is claimed to be responsible for the R&D has neither the technical expertise nor the financial capacity to be responsible. In other instances, the Chinese entity has obtained "high and new technology status" in Chinese law and therefore enjoys tax incentives on the basis of ownership of valuable core technology on the one hand. However, it also claims to be a contract R&D service provider with no valuable intangibles on the other hand. These are only a few examples where a cost plus approach would not be adequate, and a different method such as Profit Split Method would be more appropriate. It is expected that companies claiming high tech status should be performing activities that result in the creation of intellectual property of which they can claim economic or legal ownership. It is not sufficient by itself that the contract R&D entity has shifted the majority of its risks (e.g. unsuccessful research) to its entrepreneurial related party. A proper analysis of the value provided by the contract R&D entity to the overall group operations should be conducted to determine the appropriate arm's length return for the R&D entity.

10.3.5.5. Contract manufacturing is one of the most common forms of manufacturing used by MNEs in China, particularly dealing with manufacturing products for export. In evaluating a contract manufacturer's return, the TNMM is often used as the transfer pricing method with the FCMU being the most commonly used profit level indicator.

10.3.5.6. The arm's length principle involves testing controlled transactions with uncontrolled transactions to determine how independent parties would have acted in broadly comparable situations. This principle becomes challenging to apply where a company relies on its related parties for both input purchase and output sales. If such a company is to be evaluated on a cost plus basis, a low inter-company purchase price results in an undervalued cost base that will ultimately under compensate the contract manufacturer. However, the reasonableness of the purchase price is often difficult to assess. A further issue therefore arises as to how the reasonableness of a taxpayer's inter-company arrangements in this situation should be evaluated.

10.3.5.7. The Chinese approach to evaluating such companies is to start with the general presumption that the related party purchase price of materials is at arm's length, and evaluate the reasonableness of the mark-up earned by the contract manufacturer on its cost base. The rationale for accepting the related party purchase price is that the customs administration can act as a check on the reasonableness of the import price of materials and safeguard against unreasonably low inter-company purchase prices. The next step is to proceed with the transfer pricing analysis by adopting a cost plus methodology and using the FCMU as the profit level indicator. The challenge that follows lies in the search for suitable comparable companies, as discussed earlier in this paper.

10.3.5.8. Toll manufacturing is a common form used by MNEs indeveloping countries, but its proper return is difficult to determine since there are only a few independent listed companies that perform such activities. Some taxpayers simply use the FCMU for contract manufacturers as the mark-up for toll manufacturers. This grossly underestimates the return to toll manufacturers. Others use return on assets as a profit level indicator, using contract manufacturers as comparables, and this may also underestimate the return, particularly for toll manufacturers that are highly labour intensive, as is often the case in developing countries.

10.3.5.9. In practice, the Chinese tax administration has sought to first estimate the total cost of the toll manufacturing operation as if it were a contract manufacturer, usually by adding back the costs of raw materials which may be obtained from the customs administration. It then estimates the appropriate returns (say, FCMU) for contract manufacturing based on contract manufacturing comparables, and applies this to the estimated total cost to arrive at the total contract manufacturing profit, from which it then adjusts for factors such as inventory carrying costs, to arrive at the total profit for the toll manufacturer. This approach works well when reliable customs information on raw materials exists. In cases where customs information on raw materials is not available or not reliable, however, there are unresolved issues as to what should be an appropriate profit level indicator and how it couldbe derived.

10.3.5.10. Sales, marketing and distribution are another set of functions where MNEs often underestimate the contribution of developing countries. Chinese experience shows that many MNEs treat their Chinese distribution entities as a limited risk distributor, and use a set of simple distributors performing limited functions in a mature market such as Japan as the comparables. There are a couple of obvious deficiencies in such an approach. Firstly, there is often a mismatch interms of functional profile, as the Chinese entity may perform significantly more functions than these so-called comparables, which is evident as the Chinese businesses incur significantly more operating expenses relative to sales. Second, it does not account for differences in market differences, with China being a fast-growing economy and having strong demand which requires relatively less selling effort and therefore can achieve higher efficiency and profitability. Other location-specific advantages such as country premium and any marketing intangibles that are created by the Chinese entity are also commonly ignored.

10.3.5.11. In practice, the Chinese tax administration has attempted to correct such deficiencies by using a more appropriate transfer pricing method, such as the Profit Split Method in the cases where the administration identifies significant local marketing intangibles or LSAs. Alternatively, the Chinese tax administration performs comparability adjustments when TNMM is used. For example, if the median operating expense to sales ratio for the comparable set is only 7 per cent, and the same ratio for the taxpayer is 40 per cent. To the extent that there are location savings, cost base is adjusted first. The Chinese tax administration would then calculate the additional return required for the extra efforts made by the Chinese taxpayer to derive the total return for the Chinese taxpayer.

10.3.6. Alternative Methods to the Traditional Transactional Net Margin Method

10.3.6.1. While the TNMM may still be used when there is a lack of adequate local comparables, such as using foreign comparables with proper adjustments, as in the contract R&D example, sometimes a different method such as the Profit Split Method may be more appropriate. An example is the electronic manufacturing services (EMS) sector, where the entire, or nearly the whole manufacturing and assembly activities of a foreign EMS multinational group, have been outsourced to its Chinese affiliate.

10.3.6.2. The typical set up for these manufacturing and assembly operations is such that the majority of the work force and tangible assets of these foreign EMS multinational groups are located in China, including many high-level operational staff. The headquarters of these EMS companies are located outside of China, with the EMS group's revenues supported by significant manufacturing contracts with third party global consumer electronics companies. Often, in such instances, the multinational group's transfer pricing policies have little regard for properly compensating the Chinese manufacturer. The profits of the Chinese manufacturer are stripped away as much as possible on the basis that the manufacturer is a contract manufacturer or a toll manufacturer with a very low risk profile.

10.3.6.3. Under this scenario, China takes the view that a risk-based approach may have insufficient regard for the fact that there are sizeable assets located in China (i.e. the work force and factory plants). In many cases, the majority of the headcount of the EMS group are based in China, with only a few management personnel residing outside of China. Rather than a transactional or profits-based approach, a contribution analysis approach may be more suitable. This means that remuneration to each party involved would be commensurate with its role and contribution to the value chain in the group. In this case, the assets and the people should largely dictate where the group's profits should stay, and a global formulary approach should be a realistic and appropriate option.

10.3.6.4. Alternatively, the Chinese tax administration may determine the property return for the headquarters, with the Chinese manufacturer earning the residual profits. Another potential alternative may be to evaluate the Chinese manufacturer on the return on its assets or capital employed, using the group's results as a comparable for the Chinese manufacturer.

10.3.7. Other Experience and Recommendations

10.3.7.1. One of the key issues faced by developing countries is the lack of experience and knowledge on how MNEs operate and on the characteristics of particular industries. Transfer pricing is commonly acknowledged as one of the most difficult international tax issues, and MNEs as well as tax administrations in developed countries have built up and dedicated substantial resources including human resources to this area. The Chinese experience has been that a dedicated team, with backgrounds in accounting, economics and industry understanding would be very critical, in order for tax administrations in developing countries to effectively administer transfer pricing rules.

10.3.7.2. Issues such as LSAs further raise the stakes. To effectively deal with such issues, solid economic and quantitative analyses are necessary. Compared with MNEs, which have vast resources at their disposal to hire the best professionals, and with tax administrations indeveloped countries which also have developed a large team of economists and quantitative analysts, developing countries such as China have a clear disadvantage, which has to be remedied urgently. China currently has more than 200 officials dedicated to transfer pricing issues, and aims to increase this number to 500 specialists over the next two to three years. This will include a specialist panel to review substantial cases such as national transfer pricing audits. This panel review system, together with the centralized approval system on transfer pricing audit cases and national information system, will ensure that Chinese transfer pricing investigations are carried out consistently and with a high level of quality.

10.3.7.3. One way to address the disadvantages faced by developing countries in transfer pricing administration is to expand the statute of limitations. For example, the statute of limitations for corporate income tax is normally five years in China. However, the statute of limitation for transfer pricing has been extended to ten years, allowing more time for tax administration to examine taxpayers' transfer pricing issues. Another way is to set clear compliance and penalty rules,putting the burden of proof on taxpayers and encouraging taxpayers to be in compliance and to make self-adjustments when needed. It has been found that contemporaneous documentation requirements coupled with penalty rules have been very effective in encouraging taxpayer compliance. An industry-wide or a multinational group-wide audit has also been a very effective and efficient way for the tax administration to best make use of its limited resources.

10.3.7.4. As an emerging market economy, China's priority is to establish a robust system that is based on a balanced approach with three pillars—administration, service, and investigation. Administration includes having the right policies in place, including avoiding loopholes and having effective disclosure requirements. The Service pillar includes reducing the effort and resources businesses have to employ to show their tax compliance. The Advance Pricing Arrangement Programme, for example, exemplifies this focus. For investigation, China does not always have the same technical expertise and resources that developed countries possess. Nevertheless, transfer pricing work in China is developing quickly. The real objective in conducting audits is to raise awareness of the Chinese determination to enforce tax compliance, and the tax administration, the third pillar, has been using an industry based approach to accomplish this. As a testament to its success, the average profit margin in one of the industries focused on has increased from less than 1 to 5.6 per cent between 2004 and 2008.

10.3.8. Conclusion

10.3.8.1. Application of the arm's length principle to MNEs operating in developing countries poses a practical challenge. Once developing countries overcome the issues involved in establishing a sound legal framework for transfer pricing, they often encounter the issue of a lack of sufficient transfer pricing specialists to carry out the analysis, and a lack of reliable comparables for the analysis itself.

10.3.8.2. China, as a developing country, has unique economic and geographic factors which contribute to the profitability of Chinese taxpayers and their foreign parent companies. These factors include, but are not limited to, readily available migrant labour, low labour and infrastructure costs, first-mover advantages in certain industries, foreign exchange controls, growing population and consumer demand for foreign and luxury products. Other developing countries have their own unique features that similarly require special attention from a transfer pricing perspective.

10.3.8.3. In China's experience, MNEs have often implemented group transfer pricing policies that are sensitive to developed countries' transfer pricing regulations and nuances, but neglect to consider whether the arm's length principle has been applied properly in developing countries.

10.3.8.4. China has overcome this challenge by using some practical solutions that are sensitive to unique economic and geographic factors for companies operating in China. These solutions include concepts such as location savings, market premium and alternative methods of analysis besides the traditional transactional and profit-based methods.

10.3.8.5. The Chinese tax administration has shared its insights on applying the arm's length principle for developing countries, and welcomes other perspectives on these issues.

第七章 国际税务合作的法律机制

国际合作是当代国际税收秩序的主旋律,在全球化背景下,国际税务合作不论是在广度还是深度上都已取得了巨大的发展。根据《多边税收征管互助公约》的规定,税务合作包括三种形式,即税收情报交换、税款协助征收和文书送达。实际上,除这三种形式之外,广义的国际税务合作还包括更多内容,所有以双边或多边途径而不是单边途径解决国际税收问题的方式都可以纳入到国际税务合作的范畴。鉴于本书的体系安排,本章介绍国际税收竞争及其协调、国际税收情报交换、税款协助征收、文书送达,以及国际税收争端的解决机制。

第一节 国际税收竞争及其协调

从 20 世纪 80 年代开始,随着经济全球化步伐的加快,资本的跨国流动变得日益便利和频繁。为了更多更好地吸引外资来加快本国的经济发展,各国试图通过各种途径来改善本国的投资环境,税收优惠政策一直是用来吸引资本流向本国的最常用手段之一。不仅是发展中国家,发达国家也开始热衷于改革本国税制,并提供各种各样的税收优惠。[①] 正是在这一背景下,经合组织认识到各国政府之间的税收竞争行为不仅会减少政府的财政收入,影响公共支出能力,而且还会产生一系列的扭曲效应,于是在 1998 年提出了抑制税收竞争的主张,从此在全球范围内掀起了关于税收竞争问题的讨论高潮。

一、税收竞争的概念及有关争论

税收竞争并不是国际税收领域特有的现象,按照竞争主体所属的地域范围

[①] 以欧洲为例,2004 年,国际知名的安永会计师事务所发布了一份报告,报告在对新加入欧盟的成员国的实际税率进行比较后认为,德国公司在国内的税负比新入盟的 10 个成员国的税负要高得多,而且随着 10 个新成员国的减税计划的实施,这一差距进一步扩大了。德国公司在国内的实际所得税税率是 36%,而在马耳他为 34.62%,在立陶宛则为 15.03%。立陶宛、拉脱维亚、匈牙利、斯洛伐克和波兰当年都实行了减税政策,爱沙尼亚、捷克和塞浦路斯也跟着减税。塞浦路斯实行减税后,国内企业所得税实际税率仅为 9.75%。另外,随着荷兰政府宣布要将企业所得税税率由目前的 34.5%逐渐降至 2007 年的 30%后,原欧盟 15 国也进行减税以吸引外来投资的竞争。面对日益加剧的税收竞争,法国和德国政府由于预算紧张,很难效法这些国家,于是要求在欧盟内进行税收协调,阻止欧盟内部的低税竞争。参见杨海涛:《欧洲税收竞争加剧》,载《中国税务报》2004 年 10 月 8 日第 7 版。

不同,税收竞争可以分为国内税收竞争和国际税收竞争,本章所说的税收竞争仅指国际税收竞争。

目前,关于税收竞争还没有一个统一的定义,一般认为,税收竞争是指各国政府为了吸引国际资本流入本国,竞相降低税率或提供税收优惠待遇而形成的一种竞争状态。

有关税收竞争的争论点很多,尤其是关于税收竞争的是与非,以及国际社会到底是否应该对税收竞争实施干预和协调。在税收竞争的是非问题上,以经合组织为代表的观点认为,税收竞争会侵蚀其他国家的税基,影响国家的公共支出能力,扭曲贸易和投资活动,破坏税收中性,影响税收公平等等。而以广大发展中国家和部分发达国家为代表的观点则认为,税收竞争可以提高资源配置的效率,不仅可以促进国际公平,而且有利于经济的发展,更重要的是,通过制定适合本国国情的税收政策来推动本国经济的发展是一国主权范围内的事,不存在有害之说。为了调和这两种观点之间的矛盾,有人对税收竞争进行分类,按照竞争的程度或者竞争的目的或结果,将税收竞争分为适度的税收竞争和恶性税收竞争,适度的税收竞争有利于实现资源在全球范围内优化配置,而恶性税收竞争则会减少国家的财政收入,危及公共产品的供给,不利于实现资源的优化配置。

由于对税收竞争本身的认识存在分歧,理论界对于是否应该限制和协调税收竞争也存在两种截然相反的观点。一种观点认为,经济全球化意味着市场正在打破国家疆域的限制,因此政府的干预程度应该降低到最低限度,以充分发挥市场机制的作用。国际税收竞争本质上不过是自由竞争的延伸,没有必要去限制和协调,市场竞争将会使得各国税制趋同或均等化,这种观点又被称为"自由主义观点"。另一种观点即干预主义观点则认为,经济全球化下,政府将有更大的空间来实施自身职能,经济全球化并未限制政府的作用,相反,政府为了最大化地获取经济全球化所带来的利益,必须加强政府对经济的管理职能。尤其是国际公共产品的增多,使得政府之间需要进行财政合作,因此,对国际税收竞争必须进行限制和协调。[①]

由于税收只是国家调节经济的一种手段,因此对税收竞争的研究和判断不能局限于这一现象本身,应从经济全球化背景下政府与市场的关系的角度来判断其合理性。学者们的上述争论正是反映了对这一关系的不同认识,但有一点是确定的,如果在实践中各国都充分感受到了税收竞争给本国利益和国际经济秩序带来的冲击,国际社会一定会通过寻求合作来协调和限制竞争,到那时候,

---

① 参见邓力平:《经济全球化下的国际税收竞争研究:理论框架》,载《税务研究》2003年第1期。

任何理论上的争论都将没有意义。

二、经合组织的反税收竞争框架

可以说,经合组织是目前国际社会中反税收竞争的主导力量,迄今为止,经合组织已就"有害税收竞争"问题发表了五份报告,[①]这些报告不仅体现了该组织在限制有害税收竞争这一问题上的进展,而且也反映了该组织对税收竞争的认识和态度的变化。

第一份报告是 1998 年发布的,题为《有害税收竞争:一个正在出现的全球性问题》(Harmful Tax Competition: An Emerging Global Issue),该报告规定了有害税收竞争的含义和危害,以及认定"有害税收措施"和"避税港"的标准,并提出了限制有害税收竞争的 19 项措施。

2000 年经合组织发布了题为《走向全球税务合作》(Towards Global Tax Co-operation)的第二份报告,该报告的主要内容包括:提出了抑制有害税收竞争的程序,包括审查、认定、冻结并消除有害税收竞争措施;列举了成员国内存在的 9 类 47 项有害税收措施;列举了 35 个避税港名单;[②]提出了针对有害税收竞争的防御框架,以及下一步的行动计划。

与前两份报告相比,经合组织于 2001 年发布的《2001 年进展报告》(The OECD's Project on Harmful Tax Practices: The 2001 Progress Report)实质内容要少得多,除了回顾和总结一年以来的工作情况以外,主要是修改了有害税收竞争的认定标准,不再坚持"非实质性活动"标准,转向强调税收政策透明度和信息交换标准。另外,这一报告中还将公布不合作避税港名单的时间从原定的 2001 年 7 月 31 日推迟到 2002 年 2 月 28 日,同时还改变了原定从 2001 年 7 月 31 日对不合作避税港适用税收防御措施的计划,提出税收防御措施在没有适用于成员国之前,不会用于不合作的避税港。

《2004 年进展报告》(The OECD's Project on Harmful Tax Practices: The 2004 Progress Report)首先重点提及了有害税收措施认定标准的应用说明(Consolidated Application Note),以及各成员国根据这一说明进行自查的情况;接下来介绍了与非成员国在反税收竞争领域的合作情况,对《税务信息交流示范协议》(Model Agreement on Exchange of Information on Tax Matters)的

[①] 报告原文可从 OECD 官方网站下载:www.oecd.org。
[②] 截至 2007 年 8 月,绝大部分被认定为避税地的国家或地区已向经合组织作出关于透明度和信息交流的承诺,只有安道尔、列支敦士登和摩纳哥仍被认为是"不合作的避税港"。

产生过程和主要内容作了简要说明;报告最后还提出了税收防御措施应遵循的8条原则和8项措施,以及下一步的工作计划。

《2006年进展报告》(The OECD's Project on Harmful Tax Practices:2006 Update on Progress in Member Countries)主要总结了成员国在消除有害税收竞争方面的工作,在2000年认定的47项有害税收措施中,19项已被取消,14项经过修改后不再被认为有害,13项在进一步审核中被认定为不具有有害性,剩下来的只有卢森堡对控股公司的税收措施仍被认定为属于有害税收。[①] 报告最后认为针对成员国的工作目标已经实现,接下来的工作主要是监控成员国新实施的优惠措施。

在2006年之后,虽然税收竞争现象依然存在,经合组织也在多个场合提到税收竞争问题,但随着国际社会关于国际税收的工作重心从抑制竞争转向推动合作,税收竞争问题很少再作为一个专题问题来讨论。

三、国际税收竞争的前景展望

尽管国际社会关于税收竞争还存在诸多争论,就其发展前景下结论还为时过早,但从近年来的国际实践中我们可以得出以下启示:

第一,不论是理论还是实践领域,税收竞争在相当长的时期内仍将是国际社会关注和讨论的重点问题之一。经合组织在最初的报告中可谓措辞强硬,尤其是对于那些被认为"不合作的避税港",俨然摆出一副"不合作即制裁"的架势,但后来经合组织通过修改认定标准、推迟公布"不合作的避税港"、推迟防御措施的实施等,导致其拟定的防御措施并未能真正得到实施。另外,绝大多数被认定为"不合作的避税港"的国家或地区都逐步向经合组织作出了关于透明度和信息交流的承诺。这种局面不宜简单地被解读为一种妥协和合作,它同时说明了包括税收竞争概念和判断标准在内的基础理论问题还处于探索之中,而且不论是实施税收竞争的国家还是反对税收竞争的国家,其实践策略也还远未定型。这两方面的因素决定了税收竞争问题不可能随着经合组织总结报告的出台而结束,它还会在国际税收实践中进一步演进和发展。

第二,不论国际税收竞争的理论和实践发展态势如何,它都必将对未来的国际税收格局和国际税收筹划产生重大影响。国际税收格局是从宏观效应上讲的,而税收策划则是从微观效应上说的。从这个意义上讲,一味讨论税收竞争的

---

① 经合组织《2006年进展报告》公布之后,卢森堡于2006年12月通过立法废除了对控股公司的税收优惠措施,但对于其中的个别条款适用过渡期到2010年12月31日。

是与非已没有多大实际意义,我们应该更多地关注税收竞争的宏观和微观效果,以及更好地参与国际税收竞争,如认识和处理税收竞争与WTO规则的关系等。

第三,加强税收政策的透明度和信息交流将是协调国际税收竞争的主要出路。尽管存在税收竞争行为的国家和地区通常都实施低税率和税收优惠政策,反对者也正是抱怨该低税率和税收优惠措施影响了他国的利益,但问题在于,所谓的低税率和优惠政策都是相对而言的,只要各国的税率不统一,就存在高低之分,只要各国税收政策不一致,就可以通过比较认定某一国的政策较优惠。很难将一国税收政策本身的调整作为税收竞争协调的出路,更何况制定符合本国国情的税率和税收政策是一国主权范围内的事,各国不会轻易放弃。早在2001年,时任法国总理若斯潘表示,欧洲各国税收政策的不同使欧洲各国在贸易中出现了不公平竞争,因此很有必要讨论制定一项协调一致的税收政策。时任英国首相布莱尔随即表示,英国政府不可能接受若斯潘提出的要求欧盟国家执行协调一致的税收政策的建议,尽管欧洲目前的税收政策存在很多问题,使得欧洲统一市场无法顺利运转,但英国政府不会同意在全欧范围内执行统一的税收政策。① 既然税收竞争的协调不可能通过税收政策本身的修改来实现,现实条件下就只能通过加强税收政策的透明度和信息交流来寻求解决办法。经合组织的实践证明,这一办法更有助于解决问题,它能增进国家之间的合作和信任,易为不同立场的国家所接受,代表了国际税收竞争协调的发展方向。

第二节 国际税收情报交换

一、国际税收情报交换的概念与类型

从字面上看,国际税收情报交换是指不同国家的税务主管部门之间就纳税人的相关信息进行交换。按照适用的范围和目的,国际税收情报交换可分为广义和狭义的情报交换。狭义的国际税收情报交换仅指国际税收协定的缔约国之间为了协定的实施而在相互之间开展的情报交换;广义的国际税收情报交换不仅包括为了实施税收协定而开展的情报交换,还包括一国为了实施国内法的有关规定而与他国之间进行的情报交换。

除了广义与狭义的提法之外,经合组织还在1998年《有害税收竞争:一个正在出现的全球性问题》报告中首次引入了"有效税收情报交换"这一称谓,将"缺

---

① 参见张振安:《欧洲税收政策难统一》,载《国际金融报》2001年5月30日第1版。

乏有效税收情报交换"作为识别避税港的关键因素之一,并在2001年的进度报告中对"有效税收情报交换"进行了全面的描述,包括:建立允许将情报提供给另一国税务主管当局的机制,以回应对特定税收情报的请求;采取适当的措施以确保情报的使用只限于被请求的目的;充分保障纳税人的权利;在涉税刑事案件的调查中,取消"双重入罪"要求;在税收案件中,被请求国在提供情报时不应要求存在国内税收利益;各国应有相应的行政惯例保证情报交换法律机制得到有效的实施和监管。

由于全球化背景下跨国纳税人的收入和资产分布在不同国家境内,任何单个国家都不可能全面掌握其本国境内纳税人在全球范围内的收入和资产状况,于是情报交换就成了各国在实施税收征管时都不得不倚仗的手段。《OECD范本》第26条第1款规定,缔约国双方主管当局应交换可预见与本协定规定的实施相关的情报,以及可预见与缔约国、其所属行政区及其地方当局所征收的税收的有关国内法的实施或执行相关的情报。具体而言,税收情报交换具有以下几个方面的重要作用:(1)有助于顺利地实施税收协定的相关条款,促进各国税务机关之间的协作,防止国际税收协定的滥用;(2)有助于各国及时了解与税务合作有关的国内法律的变动情况,便于缔约国之间加深理解与配合;(3)加强对跨国纳税人的征收管理,对纳税人具有很大的劝诫效果,能有效地防止并打击国际逃税和避税行为。

按照适用情形和实施程序的不同,税收情报交换分为应要求交换(on request)、自动/例行交换(automatic)、自发交换(spontaneous)、同时交换(simultaneous)等不同类型。应要求交换是一国的主管机关应另一国主管机关的要求提供特定信息;自动/例行交换则是针对不同纳税人的同类信息,通常包括纳税人在收入来源国的收入状况,如股息、利息、红利等,收入来源国在根据国内例行常规申报系统取得这些信息后自动提供给缔约方;自发交换是指一国税务机关认为其在税务执法过程中获得的信息对协定国的税务执法有用时,在对方没有提出请求的情况下提供给对方;同时交换是指两个或多个国家为了就某一相关或共同事项获得信息,同时独立地在各自境内对纳税人的相关信息进行检查,并在此基础上交换有关信息,通常在转让定价领域应用较广。① 不难看出,不同类型的情报交换适用于不同的情形,而且程序上也有差别。

需要提及的是,境外税务调查(tax examinations abroad)也是情报交换的一

---

① 参见经合组织财政事务委员会2006年1月通过的《税收情报交换实施手册》(Manual on the Implementation of Exchange of Information Provisons for Tax Purposes)。

种方式。按照这种方式,被请求国应允许请求国主管当局派代表到现场获取情报,即被请求国应准许请求国授权代表入境约见个人或检查某个人的账簿和记录,或在被请求国主管当局进行这种约见或检查时,允许请求国授权代表到场参加。由于该种方式涉及允许外国的税务官员到本国约见当事人、检查账簿等行为,出于对本国税收主权的担忧,绝大多数发展中国家对此不能接受。

二、不同国际税收情报交换制度的比较

目前,规定税收情报交换制度的国际性文件较多,其中影响较大的主要有《OECD范本》《UN范本》《税收情报交换协定范本》《多边税收征管互助公约》等,不同文件对于税收情报交换的种类、范围、保密义务、可以拒绝的理由(例外规定)以及不得拒绝的理由等规定各不相同。

1. 关于情报交换种类的规定

不同的国际性文件对于税收情报交换种类的规定各不相同,具体的对比见表7-1:

表7-1 情报交换类型

事项	国际性文件	应要求交换	自动/例行交换	自发交换	同时交换	境外税务调查
情报交换的种类	《税收情报交换协定范本》(2002年)	√				√
		强调缔约国协商一致可以扩展到其他形式的税收情报交换				
	《OECD范本》第26条及其注释(2010年)	√	√	√		
		强调并不限于这三种方式,缔约国可以采取其他方式				
	《UN范本》第26条及其注释(2011年)	√	√	√		
		强调并不限于这三种方式,缔约国可以采取其他方式				
	《多边税收征管互助公约》(2011年)	√	√	√	√	√

从上述对比中可见,随着时间的推移,国际性文件中对情报交换种类的规定有逐步扩展的趋势,2011年修订的《多边税收征管互助公约》更是涵盖了上述五种税收情报交换形式,足见税收情报交换制度的发展之迅猛。

2. 关于情报交换范围的规定

在税收情报交换的范围上,经合组织 2002 年制定的《税收情报交换协定范本》第 1 条原则性地规定了"可预见相关性标准"(foreseeable relevance),即"该情报可预见性地与缔约国国内法上与本协定涵盖的税收的征收管理以及强制执行有关,包括与上述税收的决定、评估、征收、税收请求权的主张、强制执行,或者税务事项的调查或起诉有关"。协定涵盖的税收范围允许双方在协定中列明,并适用于缔约国管辖权范围内的所有人。该协定范本还在第 5 条第 5 款中规定了请求国需要提供的证明这种可预见相关性的材料:(1)涉案人员的身份。(2)关于请求交换情报的声明,包括性质、希望以何种方式得到。(3)请求交换的情报涉及的税收目的。(4)相信请求交换的情报由被请求国掌握或由被请求国境内的人员占有或控制的根据。(5)在已知的范围内,任何占有被请求情报的人员的姓名和地址。(6)关于下列事项的表明:请求符合请求国的法律和行政实践;如果被请求的情报位于请求国境内,请求国主管当局可以依法或在正常的行政实践过程中取得;请求符合协定的规定。(7)关于请求国已在其领土范围内用尽一些可行的方法(除了会造成不成比例的困难的方法)的声明。《OECD 范本》和《UN 范本》均在第 26 条第 1 款原则性地规定了"可预见相关性标准",即"可预见地与执行本公约,或以缔约国或其部门或其当地政府名义征收各种税收的国内法的管理和实施有关,只要该国内税收与本公约不相冲突"。虽然其没有具体说明如何证明这种可预见相关性,但其规定情报交换不受税收协定本身税种范围和人的范围的限制,相比于《税收情报交换协定范本》适用于协定本身列明的税收种类而言,范围更为广泛。具体的对比见表 7-2:

表 7-2 情报交换的范围

事项		《税收情报交换协定范本》(2002 年)	《OECD 范本》第 26 条及其注释(2010 年)	《UN 范本》第 26 条及其注释(2011 年)	《多边税收征管互助公约》(2011 年)
情报交换的范围	可预见的相关性标准	1:原则性规定 5.5:具体的证明材料	26.1:原则性规定		4.1:原则性规定
	税种范围	3:双方在协定中列明的税种	26.1:不限于第 2 条,可以与执行任何国内与公约不冲突的税种有关		4.1:协定中规定的税种
	人的范围	在缔约国管辖权范围内的所有人	26.1:无限制		无规定

3. 关于保密义务的规定

在保密义务上,四大国际性文件的规定大致相同。对于保密方式,均规定"应视同根据被请求国国内法所得到的情报予以保密"①,2011年修订的《多边税收征管互助公约》特别强调还应根据被请求国国内法规定的保护个人数据的必要程度予以保密。② 在披露对象和目的上,应仅限于向与税收情报交换适用的税收的评估、征收、执行、起诉、裁决上诉有关的人员或当局(包括法院和行政机关)或其监督部门披露;并且上述人员或当局应仅为上述目的使用该项情报,但可以在公开法庭程序或法院判决中披露有关情报。③ 值得注意的是,《多边税收征管互助公约》以及2012年7月修订的《OECD范本》中的税收情报交换条款还规定,在缔约国国内法均允许并且提供该情报的缔约国同意的情况下,上述情报可用于其他目的。④

4. 关于拒绝理由的规定

在被请求国可以拒绝交换的理由方面,经合组织《税收情报交换协定范本》第7条规定了6种理由:(1)按照被请求国税收征收管理和强制执行的法律无法得到的情报;(2)提供泄露任何贸易、经营、工业、商业、专业秘密或贸易过程的情报;(3)将泄露律师、代理人或其他认可的法律代表人和其客户间的保密性沟通——这种沟通是为了寻求法律意见或者用于已经存在或预计存在的法律程序;(4)披露将违反公共政策(公共秩序);(5)请求国的税收请求权尚存在争议;(6)与请求国的公民相比,披露该信息构成对被请求国公民的歧视。两大范本第26条第3款均只规定了上述第1、2、4三项例外。《多边税收征管互助公约》第21条在上述第1、4、6项例外之外,还规定了其他两项例外:请求国并未用尽按照其法律或行政惯例视具体情况可以采取的一切合理的征收或保全措施;被请求国因此所承受的行政负担明显超出请求国可获得的利益。

在不得拒绝交换的理由方面,四大国际性文件都规定了被请求国不得以被请求交换的情报与本国利益无关,或者该情报由银行、其他金融机构、被指定人、以代理或受托资格行事的人所持有,或者由于情报与某人的所有权利益有关而

---

① 经合组织《税收情报交换协定范本》(2002年)第1条、第8条,两大范本第26条第2款,《多边税收征管互助公约》第22条第1款。

② 参见《多边税收征管互助公约》第22条第1款。

③ 参见经合组织《税收情报交换协定范本》(2002年)第8条,两大范本第26条第2款,《多边税收征管互助公约》第22条第2款。

④ Update to Article 26 of the OECD Model Tax Convention and Its Commentary(Approved by the OECD Council on 17 July 2012).

拒绝提供情报。① 此外,经合组织《税收情报交换协定范本》还作出了关于上市公司或公众投资的保留规定。②

三、国际税收情报交换中的几个法律问题

1. 国际税收情报交换与银行保密制度

作为情报交换客体的税收情报通常与纳税人的银行账户或资金状况有关,因此银行等金融机构成为税收情报交换中的主要情报来源之一。但纵观各国银行保密法,都无一例外地规定了银行对客户资料的保密义务,除非满足法定的例外情形,否则银行不得对外提供与客户身份及账户有关的任何信息。如此一来,银行就有可能依据这一保密规定,拒绝提供客户资料,从而使得有关信息无法获得,阻碍情报交换的顺利进行。为了清除这一障碍,国际社会开始直指银行保密法,要求对其予以修改甚至取消。首先是经合组织于2005年对其税收协定范本中的情报交换条款进行修订,规定情报交换条款优于各国国内的银行保密法。紧接其后,联合国国际税务合作专家委员会也于2008年对其税收协定范本中的情报交换条款进行了类似修订。2009年《二十国集团伦敦峰会公报》(The Global Plan for Recovery and Reform)甚至宣布"银行保密法的时代已经结束"③,并表示将对那些不能满足税收信息透明度的国家或地区实施反制措施。

在这种高压态势之下,一些国家的国内银行保密法开始出现松动迹象,瑞士银行保密法之严格堪称"世界之最",但迫于压力,瑞士不得不改变姿态,或规定银行保密法的例外,或同意对外提供客户的账户信息;④比利时、奥地利和卢森堡等国家也撤回对《OECD范本》第26条情报交换条款的保留;其他一些国家包括被列为避税港的国家开始接受经合组织税收情报交换标准,与他国签署税收情报交换协定。可见,国际社会的努力在推动税收信息透明度方面取得了相当的成就,为清除银行保密制度对税收情报交换的障碍奠定了基础。但同时我们也应看到,目前所采用的通过在协定中规定情报交换优先于银行保密法这一思

---

① 参见经合组织《税收情报交换协定范本》第5条第4款,两大范本第26条第4、5款,《多边税收征管互助公约》第21条第3、4款。

② 参见经合组织《税收情报交换协定范本》第5条第4款。

③ 参见《二十国集团伦敦峰会公报》第15段,原文为"the era of banking secrecy is over"。资料来源:http://www.g20.org/pub_communiques.aspx,2011年2月9日访问。

④ 瑞士政府迫于美国的压力于1990年通过修订国内法,使得美国可以在反洗钱调查中从瑞士银行取得账户信息及交易资料。See Michele Moser, Switzerland: New Exceptions to Bank Secrecy Laws Aimed at Money Laundering and Organized Crime, Case Western Reserve Journal of International Law, Spring/Summer, 1995. 另外,2009年8月,瑞银迫于美国政府的压力,向美国提供了数千客户的账户资料。参见美国国内税务署网站:www.irs.gov,2009年12月3日访问。

路过于简单,无法从根源上解决问题,因为它实际上是主张在情报交换中不再考虑各国银行保密法的要求,这在实践中势必会遭到有关国家的抵制,[①]而且这一思路还可能被扩大化运用,从而侵蚀银行保密这一基本原则。银行保密法的存在具有客观必然性,无视这一事实的任何途径都不可能取得实质效果。

首先,银行保密法是维护金融市场安全和稳定的重要制度基础。严格完善的银行保密制度是维持现代金融体系稳定的重要前提之一,一旦没有了银行保密制度,公众就会对银行失去信心,这势必会动摇整个金融体系的基础。

其次,银行保密是银行对客户承担的约定或法定义务。银行账户信息以及交易资料属于客户金融隐私权的范畴,基于银行与客户之间的合同关系,银行有义务对客户的金融隐私实行严格保密,这一原则早在1924年英国著名的Tournier案中就得以确认。[②] 此外,公共政策理论也支持银行对客户资料负有法定的保密义务,美国法院在Diowharzadeh案中指出,银行特殊的强势地位以及公众对银行的信赖使银行对客户信息负有法定的保密义务。[③]

最后,从渊源上看,银行保密法在一些国家具有深刻的社会和历史基础。以瑞士为例,其具有三百多年历史的银行保密制度最初是为了保护那些因受宗教或政治迫害而逃离到瑞士的人士而制定的。[④] 虽然这一功能在二战后已不再像当初那么重要,但其悠久的历史积淀使其不仅成了瑞士金融法制的一个分支,而且也构成了瑞士传统文化的重要组成部分。

可见,不论是从历史还是现实的角度分析,银行保密法都有其存在的客观必然性,断言"银行保密法的时代已经结束"是不切实际的,要消除银行保密法的障碍不能靠简单地否定或超越银行保密法,而是应该在承认和接受银行保密法这一事实的前提下探求解决的途径。其实,银行保密与情报交换中信息的可获得性并非水火不容。各国在规定银行保密这一原则的同时,无不规定了特定情形下的例外,如能把情报交换纳入银行保密的例外情形,前述障碍将得到解决。

虽然现行的银行保密法都规定了例外情形,但由于目前的银行保密法都是

---

① 根据《OECD范本》,情报交换义务优先于银行保密法,但在实践中真正要一个国家撇开本国的保密规定对外提供情报并非易事,以美国与瑞士之间的税收情报交换纠纷为例,在瑞士联合银行案中,美国最终以司法程序相威胁,迫使瑞士联合银行与美国国内税务署之间签订了和解协议,后又专门在美国与瑞士两国之间就此签署了协定,才迫使瑞士政府及瑞士联合银行同意提供约四千个客户的账户资料。

② See Tournier v. National Provincial and Union Bank of England, [1924] 1 KB 461 (C. A. 1923).

③ See Diowharzadeh v. City National Bank and Trust Company of Norman, 646 P. 2d 616 (Okla. Ct. App. 1982).

④ See Michele Moser, Switzerland: New Exceptions to Bank Secrecy Law Aimed at Money Laundering and Organized Crime, Case Western Reserve Journal of International Law, Spring/Summer, 1995.

国内法上的规定,很少考虑到国际情形,而情报交换恰好是国际合作的范例,所以这些例外情形无法将情报交换纳入其中。与其通过国际社会强行要求有关国家取消银行保密法,不如在国际社会的协调之下,对银行保密法的例外条款加以调整,作出具体化、统一化的规定,明确将税收情报交换纳入例外情形。在全球化背景下,各国的金融政策和金融法规已远远超出了其对本国的意义,加强各国金融法制的协调已成为包括联合国、欧盟、经合组织在内的多个国际平台讨论的话题,因此,对各国银行保密法例外条款进行统一化调整不仅是必要的,而且也是可行的。具体而言,可考虑在保留传统的法定例外事由的前提下,同时规定出于履行国际条约义务而作的披露并不违反保密义务。由于情报交换通常是以有关国家之间的税收协定或情报交换协定为基础的,这样既兼顾了各国国内对银行保密制度的需求,同时也保证了银行信息的可获得性,从而消除了银行保密制度对情报交换机制的障碍。

2. 国际税收情报交换中的纳税人权益保障

从另一角度讲,银行等机构的保密义务是体现纳税人权益保护的一个重要方面。税收情报通常涉及纳税人的银行账户及财产状况等信息,这些信息属于隐私权的范畴,情报交换过程中银行等机构或部门将此类信息对外提供就有可能与纳税人的隐私权相冲突。作为《世界人权公约》所确定的权利内容之一,隐私权受到各国国内法和国际法的严格保护,绝大多数国家都将其作为基本人权的内容在宪法中加以规定,有些国家或地区还通过了专门的单行法,如美国的《金融隐私权利法案》、我国香港地区的《个人私隐条例》等等。在国际法层面,欧盟和经合组织联合签署的《多边税收征管互助公约》第21条明确规定,税务行政合作中要保证纳税人的权益不受影响;经合组织《税收情报交换协定范本》及税收协定范本中也提到,要保护纳税人在被请求国所享有的各项权利,税收情报交换的范围以不损害纳税人由一般规则和法律规定所保护的权利为前提。①

除了隐私权以外,在情报交换过程中,纳税人的另一重要权利就是在被请求国享有被通知的权利,以及提出异议的权利,即有关机构在对外提供纳税人信息之前应该通知纳税人,纳税人可以依照法定程序提出异议。

不论是隐私权,还是通知和异议权,在实践中都可能成为情报交换的障碍,在 United States v. Davis 一案中,被告就曾利用国内法所规定的异议程序,通过申请当地法院向银行发禁令,禁止银行对外提供他的信息资料。② 由于纳税

---

① 参见《OECD 范本》第26条注释第1段、经合组织《税收情报交换协定范本》第1条。
② See United States v. Davis, 767 F. 2d 1025,1032-33,1036-39(2d Cir. 1985).

人的金融隐私权与银行等机构的保密义务是同一问题的两个方面，前文对此已有论述，所以这里不再赘述，仅讨论纳税人通知和异议权的规范问题。

与隐私权一样，纳税人在情报交换中的通知和异议等程序性权利也体现在国际法和各国国内法中。在国际法层面，根据经合组织《税收情报交换协定范本》的规定，税收情报交换过程中，纳税人在被请求国所享有的权利包括被通知的权利、提出异议的权利以及国际人权公约中所规定的其他权利。在国内法层面，除了前面提到的美国之外，德国法律也规定，如果外国机构向德国的税务部门提出获取纳税人信息的要求，该纳税人有权要求举行听证。[1] 瑞士法律还规定，瑞士政府依据税收协定对外提供银行信息时，将按照其国内法的规定通知纳税人，纳税人如果反对对外提供其信息，将由瑞士法院决定是否提供，瑞士法院只有在有证据表明存在税务欺诈时才会批准对外提供。[2] 不论是国际条约，还是各国国内法，前述规定在保护纳税人权益以及规范纳税人权益保护与促进税收情报交换两者关系方面都还存有不足。首先，虽然国际条约中确认了纳税人通知和异议的权利，但如果被请求国违反了这一义务，由于纳税人通常属于被请求国的国民，且纳税人不是条约的缔约方，纳税人实际上无法获得救济，从而使得条约规定的权利落空。其次，虽然条约也注意到纳税人在行使权利时可能阻碍情报交换的实施，但对此也只是原则性要求"被请求国有义务确保纳税人权利不得不合理地阻碍或延迟信息的提供"[3]。这一规定过于原则，缺乏必要的操作性。最后，各国国内法规定的内容差异很大，在实施过程中所把握的标准也不尽一致，这也会阻碍国际税收情报交换的有效实施。

对此，国外有学者建议制定一个纳税人权利保护公约，对纳税人的权利从程序和实体上予以规范，在保护纳税人权利的同时，也保证税收情报交换的有效实施。[4] 2000年9月，国际财政协会第54届会议讨论纳税人权利保护问题时，有专家提出：随着世界经济的发展，跨国纳税现象越来越普遍，纳税人权利保护问题也日趋国际化，与此同时，各国对纳税人权利保护的立法差别很大，因此确定一个统一的纳税人权利保护最低国际标准非常必要。[5] 应该说，通过公约的形

---

[1] See Alexander F. Peter, U.S. Cross-border Discovery in International Tax Proceedings: An Overview from a European Comparative Law Perspective, Tax Lawyer, Summer, 2005.

[2] See Marnin Michaels and Marie-Thérèse Yates, The Death of Information Exchange Agreements, Part 2, Journal of International Taxation, April, 2009.

[3] 经合组织《税收情报交换协定范本》第1条注释第5段。

[4] See Bruce Zagaris, The Procedural Aspects of U.S. Tax Policy Towards Developing Countries: Too Many Sticks and No Carrots, George Washington International Law Review, 2003.

[5] 参见刘剑文、熊伟：《税法基础理论》，北京大学出版社2004年版，第89页。

式对纳税人权利作出统一规定,并对纳税人权利的行使加以规范这一思路不乏合理性。但我们应该看到,由于与此相关的人权和税收这两个问题对任何国家而言都极具敏感性,要让国际社会在纳税人权利保护上达成一个多边公约的难度是可想而知的。在目前阶段,我们还只能是借助各国之间已经签署的大量的情报交换协定,通过完善情报交换协定中的纳税人权利条款,在确认纳税人享有知情权和异议权的同时,对知情权及异议权的行使期限及程序等问题作出具体统一的规定,并明确规定纳税人的权利救济途径,这样既可保证纳税人权利的可操作性,同时通过协调和统一各国在保障纳税人通知和异议权利问题上的立法与实践,来消除对税收情报交换可能带来的障碍。

3. 国际税收情报交换与司法协助的关系

情报交换有时候是在税务行政稽查过程中进行,有时候是在对涉税案件进行侦查或审判的司法程序中实施,如果是在司法程序中实施情报交换,则属于国际司法协助的范畴。国际司法协助是指一国法院或其他主管机关,根据另一国法院或其他主管机关的请求,代为或协助进行调查取证、送达文书等诉讼行为,或为外国法院的诉讼活动提供其他协助。国际条约是司法协助的主要法律依据,如果一国在涉税案件的侦查或审判中需要他国提供税务信息,则既可以依据司法协助条约提出请求,同时也可以依据税收协定或《税收情报交换协定范本》提出请求,诚如《OECD范本》注释所指出的:涉税刑事案件中的情报交换也可以建立在双边或多边司法协助条约的基础上(只要这些条约同样适用于税务犯罪)。① 如此一来,在司法协助条约的缔约国之间,情报交换就存在司法协助条约和税收情报交换协定双重依据,可这两种依据在适用范围和实施主体等诸多方面都不尽相同,两种不同的途径不仅会在程序上产生差异,甚至可能影响到情报交流的实质效果。因此,厘清二者之间的关系对于情报交换的有效实施具有重要的意义。

司法协助包括民事司法协助和刑事司法协助,与涉税案件相关的主要是后者。纵观目前各国之间刑事司法协助中的适用范围条款,对涉税案件的规定可分为三种情形。第一种情形是,明确将涉税案件纳入到刑事司法协助的适用范围,如中国在与澳大利亚和西班牙签订的刑事司法协助条约中分别规定,"'刑事'包括与触犯涉及税收、关税以及其他财税方面法律的犯罪有关的事项","双方应当根据本条约的规定,就涉及违反有关税收、关税、外汇管制及其他财税法

---

① 参见《OECD范本》(2005年版)第26条注释第1段。

律的犯罪的请求提供协助"。① 此外,美国与英国、波兰、韩国、土耳其等国之间的刑事司法协助条约也有类似的规定。第二种情形是,明确将涉税案件排除在刑事司法协助条约的适用范围之外,这主要是那些被称为"避税港"的国家或地区对外签订的条约,如开曼群岛、巴拿马、维京群岛、瑞士等一些国家或地区在对外签署司法协助条约时,通常排除条约对涉税案件的适用,或者是对条约在涉税案件中的适用规定了诸多限制。第三种情形是,司法协助条约中不明确规定是否适用于涉税案件,如中国与葡萄牙、新西兰、美国、墨西哥、巴西、拉脱维亚等国家之间签署的刑事司法协助条约,没有对适用范围作出明确规定。

在上述第二种情形中,由于司法协助条约明确排除了涉税案件,因此情报交换只能依据《税收情报交换协定范本》或者税收协定中的情报交换条款,不存在重叠的问题。但另外两种情形就比较复杂了,在两种依据并存的情况下,有必要厘清二者之间的关系。考虑到此时的案件主管机关往往是从事案件侦查或审判的司法机关,由司法机关来主导情报交换不仅可以保证情报的针对性,而且还可以提高情报交换的效力,有助于更快更好地对案件作出最终处理。同时,由于例行交换模式下的情报交换是一种常态模式,它可以较全面地提供涉税信息,这些信息可以为司法协助条约下的情报交流提供补充资料,所以在同时存在司法协助条约和情报交换协定时,宜采用以司法协助条约为主、税收情报交换机制为补充的适用机制。当然,如果情报交换不是针对具体案件,而只是例行性的,此时即使有关国家之间存在上述两类条约依据,也不用考虑适用何种依据问题,可以直接按照情报交换协定或税收协定中的情报交换条款规定来实施。

民事司法协助是司法协助的另一领域,关于税收情报交换与民事司法协助的关系问题,目前还存在一些理论上的分歧,争论主要集中在税收案件是否属于民商事案件,或者税法是否属于私法的范畴。国内有学者认为从马克思主义"国家学说"和西方"社会契约论"出发来分析问题,将得出不同的结论,前者认为税法与私法对立,后者认为二者统一。② 另有一些学者也在尝试用私法规则来研究税收法律关系。③ 国内主流学术观点认为,税收法律关系不属于民商事案件的范畴。因此,税收情报交换也就不属于民事司法协助的范围,不存在情报交换

---

① 参见《中华人民共和国和澳大利亚关于刑事司法协助的条约》第 1 条、《中华人民共和国和西班牙王国关于刑事司法协助的条约》第 1 条。
② 参见廖益新、李刚、周刚志:《现代财税法学要论》,科学出版社 2007 年版,第 61—67 页。
③ 参见龙英锋:《试析涉外税收与国际私法的关系》,载《税务研究》2004 年第 7 期;陈延忠:《国际税法上的识别冲突问题及其解决》,载《涉外税务》2006 年第 9 期;李刚:《税收法律行为的私法学分析》,载《税务研究》2008 年第 3 期。

协定与民事司法协助条约交叉的情形。

与此相关的另一个问题是,1970年《关于从国外调取民事或商事证据的公约》(以下简称《海牙取证公约》)在国际税收情报交换过程中的适用性问题。该公约的宗旨是为了加强各国在民商事案件中域外取证的国际合作,其中所规定的请求书制度在程序上与情报交换极其相似,[①]如果认为税收案件属于民商事案件,则缔约国之间就可以该公约为依据实施税收情报交换。尽管英国上议院曾在 In re State of Norway's Application 一案中指出:税收事项属于《海牙取证公约》所说的"民商事"范畴,[②]但这一观点至今仍未得到国际社会的普遍认同,绝大多数国家在实践中仍坚持税收案件不属于民商事案件的范畴,《海牙取证公约》不能作为国际税收情报交换的依据。

第三节 税款协助征收与文书送达

一、税款协助征收

(一)税款协助征收概述

绝大多数情况下,纳税人都能依照法律规定向有关税务当局履行纳税义务,但有时候也可能由于主客观方面的原因,导致纳税人欠缴税款情形的发生。如果欠缴税款的纳税人不在一国境内且在该国境内没有足以支付税款的资产时,就需要通过国际合作途径,请求他国予以协助,保障税款征收到位。税款协助征收是指一国(被请求国)协助另一国(请求国)征收后者根据其征税权有效确定但纳税人欠缴、少缴或拒绝缴纳的税款的一系列程序。

税款协助征收是国际行政协助的重要方式之一,不同于国际司法协助。即便是一国法院针对欠缴税款作出了司法判决,很多国家也拒绝对此类判决的承认与执行提供司法协助,其主要理由在于:(1)税款征收请求权的执行是国家主权的延伸,而在他国领土内主张本国的主权是与独立国家的理念相抵触的;(2)执行外国判决通常需要对外国判决进行审查,而对外国财税法的审查可能侵犯该外国的主权;(3)执行税务判决将产生极大的行政负担。[③] 尽管上述考虑

---

① 请求书制度,又称"代为取证制度",是指一国的主管机关通过提交请求书的方式,委托另一国的主管机关代为调取证据的司法协助行为。参见《海牙取证公约》第1条。

② See James P. Springer, An Overview of International Evidence and Asset Gathering in Civil and Criminal Tax Cases, George Washington Journal of International Law and Economics,1988.

③ See Government of India v. Taylor, [1955] AC 491, 511(Lord Keith of Avonholm).

未必具有合理性,但正是基于各种因素的掣肘,国家间在税务方面的司法协助一直裹足不前,一些关于承认和执行司法判决的国际公约都排除了税款请求权的执行。

在全球化时代,纳税人和资本的流动性日益增强,税款协助征收的必要性日益凸显。1998年,经合组织在其关于有害税收竞争的报告中强调,"如果一国不执行另一国的税收请求权,那么避税将更加严重",因此该报告建议:"各国审查关于执行税收请求权的现行规则,经合组织财政事务委员会将继续在该领域推进工作,以起草可纳入《OECD范本》的税款协助征收条款。"[①] 2003年,在《OECD范本》的修订中,税款协助征收条款作为第27条纳入其中。2007年,经合组织财政事务委员会发布了基于该条款以及《多边税收征管互助公约》而制定的《税款协助征收指南》。[②] 2011年,联合国在修订其协定范本时也加入了与《OECD范本》相同的税款协助征收条款。考虑到这一问题的复杂性,两大范本在引入这一条款时,都在其范本的注释中规定了很多灵活性的解释,提供多种可供缔约国选择的方式。下文将主要结合两大范本、《多边税收征管互助公约》以及《税款协助征收指南》中的规定介绍税款协助征收制度。

(二)税款协助征收的适用范围

各国是否以及在何种程度上向他国提供税款征收协助主要取决于以下几方面的因素:(1)国内法对于为其他国家税款征收提供协助所采取的态度;(2)两国之间税收制度、税收征管和法律标准是否具有相似性以及相似程度,特别是在纳税人基本权利保护(如纳税人得到及时和适当的纳税通知的权利、纳税人信息的保密权、申诉权、纳税人要求主管机关听取其申辩并举证的权利、获得自主选择的辩护律师帮助的权利、受到公平审判的权利等)方面;(3)税款协助征收是否能给缔约国双方带来平等互惠的结果;(4)各个国家的税务机关是否能够有效地提供这样的协助;(5)两国之间的贸易和投资流动是否足以解释这种形式的协助的正当合理性;(6)为了宪法上的原因或其他原因,是否应对所适用的税种有所限制。只有在各国考虑了上述因素并得出结论,其可以同意在其他国家税款的征收过程提供协助时,才能将税款协助征收条款列入税收协定中。[③] 当然,上述因素只是一个框架性的考虑,实践中仍需要从多方面限定其适用范围。

---

① 参见经合组织1998年发布的报告《有害税收竞争:一个正在出现的全球性问题》。

② See Manual on the Implementation of Assistance in Tax Collection, Approved by the OECD Committee on Fiscal Affairs on 26 January 2007.

③ 参见《OECD范本》第27条注释第1段。

1. 对税收事项的适用范围

即使根据上述因素,各国同意提供税款协助征收,还需要考虑提供这种协助所针对的产生税收的事由范围,具体分为全面的协助和有限制的协助两类。全面的征收协助是指,不论请求国税款请求权产生的事由如何,在符合其他条件的情况下,被请求国都需要提供税款协助征收。有限的税款协助征收只在特定的产生税收事项情形下才提供。如一个国家可能将其协助限于纳税人主张其本无权获得的协定提供的优惠待遇(如要求在利息之类所得的来源国享有税收减免)的情况。① 举例来说,当 A 国的 A 公司在 B 国设立了壳公司 B 以收取来源于 C 国的特许权使用费,从而减少在所得来源地 C 国所缴纳的税款。若发现 B 公司不当适用了 B 国和 C 国的税收优惠条款,就其来源于 C 国的所得享受了预提税优惠待遇,C 国可以请求 B 国对 B 公司采取措施以追缴该公司不当少缴的税款。

2. 对人的适用范围

两大范本都规定,税款协助征收条款的适用不受第 1 条(人的范围)的限制。因此,任何个人,无论是不是缔约国的居民,其欠缴缔约国一方的税款,缔约国另一方都必须提供协助。《多边税收征管互助公约》在适用税款协助征收时区分纳税人是不是请求国的居民,若其是请求国的居民,那么提供税款协助征收的条件为在请求国可强制执行以及该税款请求权没有争议;若其不是请求国的居民,那么税款协助征收的条件不包括在请求国可强制执行这一条件。② 这种规定主要是考虑到如果纳税人不是请求国的居民,请求的强制执行可能存在法律和实践中的障碍。

当然,也有一些国家希望将协助限制在缔约国任何一方的居民所欠缴的税款范围内。另外,除了传统意义上的纳税人、由于从事应税行为而产生纳税义务的最终纳税责任人外,对相应税款负有法律义务的其他主体,如代扣代缴义务人、担保人等等,也可能会成为税款协助征收适用的对象,各国可以在签订条约时明确约定。

3. 对税种的适用范围

关于税种的适用范围,两大范本都规定,税款协助征收条款的适用可以不受第 2 条(税种范围)的限制,但缔约国也可以选择将其限制在第 2 条规定的税种范围内。如果选择将其适用范围限制在范本规定的税种范围以内,则在条文上

---

① 参见《OECD 范本》第 27 条注释第 1 段。
② 参见《多边税收征管互助公约》第 11 条第 2 款。

应明确表明,如规定:"本条所说的'税款请求权'是指纳税人欠缴的本协定规定范围内的税收款项,以及与该款项有关的利息、行政罚款和征收或保全费用。"①

根据范本的推荐,如果缔约国希望通过在定义中列举详细的税种清单来澄清这些条款的适用范围,则可以通过双边协商自由选择以下定义方式:"本条使用的'税款请求权'一语是指纳税人欠缴的以下种类的税收款项,以及与该款项有关的利息、行政罚款和征收或保全费用:a)(在 A 国):……b)(在 B 国):……"②

4. 税款的范围

两大范本均采用肯定列举的方式明确了税款协助征收中的"税款请求权"的组成,包括"纳税人欠缴的缔约国一方、所属行政区或地方当局所征收的任何税收(但以该税款的征收不违背本协定或缔约国双方共同加入的其他国际法律文件为限),以及与该欠缴税款相关的利息、行政罚款以及征收或保全费用"③。还有些协定采取否定式排除方法,即列举不能提供征收协助的范围,如 1966 年美国与奥地利签署的双边税收协定就明确排除了刑事性质的税收罚金的征收协助。《多边税收征管互助公约》对此未作规定。

(三) 税款协助征收的方式和法律适用

税款协助征收一般有两种方式:一是征收协助,是指如果根据缔约国一方法律,一项应征税收在该国国内满足有关可予执行的条件,并且根据该国法律,该项应征税收的债务人无权阻止此项征收,那么在缔约国一方主管当局发出协助请求时,缔约国另一方的主管当局应对此项应征税收予以认可,并根据其有关法律规定将此项应征税收视同本国的应征税收予以征收。这里规定了请求征收协助需要满足的条件,即请求国根据国内法拥有征收该项应征税收的权力,而其债务人并不享有能制止这种征收的行政或司法上的权利。在许多国家,往往规定纳税人对税收的合法性或数额存在异议时,有权向行政机构、法院提起复议或者诉讼,但一般同时规定,即使提起复议或者诉讼,也并不影响税收的征收,即"复议(诉讼)不停止执行"原则。二是保全协助,指的是请求国的税款请求权依照其法律可以采取保全措施以确保其征收,应该国主管当局的请求,被请求国的主管当局在采取保全措施上应承认该税款请求权。④ 但上述条件不再符合时,请求国的主管当局应迅速将此项事实告知被请求国的主管当局。在收到这样的通知

---

① 《OECD 范本》第 27 条第 2 款注释第 10—11 段。
② 《OECD 范本》第 27 条第 2 款注释第 12 段。
③ 参见两大范本第 27 条第 2 款。
④ 参见两大范本第 27 条第 3、4 款。

以后,被请求国可选择要求请求国中止或撤回请求。如果请求被中止,则该中止将持续到请求国给予被请求国如下通知为止:作出相关税款请求权的协助请求须符合的条件已经重新满足或是撤回其请求。①

无论是在征管上还是采取保全措施上承认请求国的税款请求权以后,被请求国应将该税款请求权视同本国的税款请求权,按照被请求国法律的规定,对该税款请求权采取征收或保全措施。即根据程序自治原则和属地管辖原则,税款协助征收中适用的法律是被请求国的法律,但涉及税款请求权时限和优先权的除外。

两大范本指出,被请求国的时限不能适用于请求国提出协助请求的税款请求权,而应仅适用请求国的时限。该时限是指超过一段时间就不能再对一项税款请求权进行强制执行或是征收。也就是说,只要一项税款请求权在请求国仍能被强制执行或是采取保全措施,被请求国就不能以其国内法规定的时限为由拒绝对该税款请求权提供征收协助。但缔约国双方也可以对此作出不同的规定。②《多边税收征管互助公约》也规定税款请求权的时限适用请求国的法律,但被请求国根据请求国的要求提供征收协助时,其行为根据被请求国的法律使上述征收期限中止或被打断的,应在请求国法律上发生相同的效果。这是由于征收行为本身适用被请求国的法律。③ 缔约国也可以约定在经过一定期限后,提供税款协助征收的义务不再存在。这一期间必须从授权强制执行的原始文件颁布之日起计算。④ 如《多边税收征管互助公约》第14条第3款规定,在任何情况下,自授权强制执行的原始文件颁布之日起15年后,被请求国无义务再提供税款协助征收。

两大范本以及《多边税收征管互助公约》均指出,即使被请求国一般应将请求国的税款请求权视同本国的税款请求权,但被请求国和请求国给予本国税款请求权以相对于其他债权人的债权优先规则,不适用于税款协助征收中的税款请求权。⑤

(四) 税款协助征收义务的例外

在例外情况下,即使满足了提供税款协助征收的条件,被请求国也无须提供税款协助征收。两大范本规定的例外情况包括,要求被请求国:(1) 采取与该缔

---

① 参见《OECD范本》第27条第7款注释第29段。
② 参见《OECD范本》第27条第5款注释第22—23段。
③ 参见《多边税收征管互助公约》第14条第1、2款。
④ 参见《OECD范本》第27条第5款注释第24段。
⑤ 参见两大范本第27条第5款、《多边税收征管互助公约》第15条。

约国一方或缔约国另一方的法律和行政惯例不相一致的行政措施,如查封资产以偿还税款请求权在被请求国是不允许的,则被请求国在提供税款协助征收时没有义务查封资产;(2) 采取与公共政策(公共秩序)相违背的措施;(3) 提供协助,如果缔约国另一方并未用尽按照其法律或行政惯例视具体情况可以采取的一切合理的征收或保全措施;(4) 提供协助,如果在这些情况下,该缔约国一方因此所承受的行政负担明显超出缔约国另一方可获得的利益。[①] 值得注意的是,这种例外规定并不影响前述关于税款请求权时限适用请求国法律的规定。因此,在被请求国期限届满之后针对一项税款请求权提供征收协助,并不能被认为是与被请求国法律和行政惯例相悖,只要请求国适用于该税款请求权的时限尚未终止。

除上述四项例外之外,《多边税收征管互助公约》第21条还规定了另外两种例外:(1) 请求提供协助的税款征收权与一般认可的税收原则、请求国与被请求国之间缔结的避免双重征税协定或其他任何协定条款不符的;(2) 与在相同情况下的请求国公民相比,构成对被请求国公民的歧视。

二、文书送达

《多边税收征管互助公约》第17条还规定了文书送达这种税务行政互助方式:"在请求国的要求下,被请求国应当向收件人送达文书,包括来源于请求国且与税款征收有关的司法裁决。"同时还规定了协助送达的两种方式:"(1) 根据被请求国国内法上规定的性质实质相似的文书的送达方法;(2) 根据请求国要求的特定方法或者在被请求国国内法上可行的与该方式最接近的方法。"另外,"缔约国一方亦可以直接向在另一方境内的人员邮寄送达。根据本条进行的文书送达,不需附有翻译。但是当收件人不能理解文书上的语言时,被请求国应安排将该文书以本国的官方语言翻译或摘要,被请求国也可以要求请求国这么做"。两大范本中均没有对文书送达协助作出规定。

第四节 国际税收争端的解决

随着人员、资本和货物等要素在国际范围的流动日益频繁,产生国际税收纠纷的可能性也日益增大,仅仅通过一些实体性规则来避免或减少双重征税是远远不够的,制定和完善税收争端解决机制对于规范国际税收秩序具有不可替代

[①] 参见两大范本第27条第8款。

的作用。

相互协商程序(Mutual Agreement Procedure,MAP)是目前国际税收条约中广泛援引的争端解决程序。实践证明,MAP不仅具有独特的灵活性,而且易为各国所接受,不失为一种理想的争端解决方式,但近年来,随着国际税收实践的日益复杂化,MAP的一些缺陷和不足也开始显现出来。正是在这一背景下,包括经合组织(OECD)、国际商会(ICC)、国际财政协会(IFA)在内的国际社会提出了一系列的建议和意见来完善MAP,这些意见和建议已在包括我国在内的各国税收实践中或多或少地得到体现。

一、国际税收争端的概念

国际税收争端有广义和狭义之分,广义的国际税收争端包括国家与涉外纳税人之间的税收争端和国家与国家之间的税收争端;狭义的国际税收争端又称为"税收协定争端",即税收协定的缔约方在履行协定的过程中产生的纠纷,内容上仅指国家与国家之间的税收争端,而不包括国家与涉外纳税人之间的税收争端。由于国家与涉外纳税人之间的税收争端的解决更多的是借助于国内行政复议和行政诉讼制度,非本书所关注的重点,这里仅指狭义的国际税收争端,即税收协定争端。需要指出的是,很多情况下,一国国内的涉外税收争端如果不能很好解决的话,则有可能进一步上升为税收协定争端。

根据争端产生的原因,税收协定争端又可以分为直接的税收协定争端和间接的税收协定争端两类。直接的税收协定争端是指协定缔约方之间就协定条款的解释、执行或适用等问题产生的纠纷,纠纷并不涉及某一特定的纳税人。当一个纳税人认为缔约国一方或双方的措施,导致或将导致对其不符合协定规定的征税,就会向其为居民的缔约国提出申诉,如果该国不能单方面使纳税人得到满意的解决,纳税人就会要求将争议提交缔约方之间处理,这样引起的国际税收争端为间接的税收协定争端。

国际税收争端的解决是目前国际税法领域中的一个热点问题,不论是理论界还是实务界都进行了广泛的讨论,OECD、ICC、IFA等国际组织还专门成立工作组对此问题加以跟踪研究,并出台了一系列的工作报告。国际社会一致认为,目前税收条约中所普遍采用的MAP是经过实践证明行之有效的争端解决方式,但随着国际税收争端数量越来越多,复杂程度越来越大,相互协商程序已不能很好地应对这一挑战,其缺陷和不足日益显现出来。于是,国际社会除了努力对MAP本身加以完善之外,还在探讨运用包括斡旋、咨询建议、仲裁等辅助方式的可能性。从目前的实践发展看,仲裁作为一种重要的辅助方式正日益受到国际社会的重视。

在具体介绍争端解决方式之前,有必要先就以下两个问题加以说明:首先,关于 MAP 与仲裁程序的关系问题,目前国内大部分学者都将二者视为平行关系,认为仲裁是国际社会跳出 MAP 找到的解决国际税收协定争议的又一种方法。而从目前国际主流观点看,均认为税收争议仲裁尚未形成一种独立的争端解决方式,它只是 MAP 的一种辅助(supplementary)方式。应该说,国际税收协定仲裁目前还处于探索阶段,OECD、ICC 等组织出台的仲裁方案差异也很大,税收仲裁的诸多理论和实践问题都还未定型,此时将其作为一种独立的争端解决方式不仅不成熟,而且还不利于较好地解决税收协定争议。这也正是为什么国际社会强调仲裁只是 MAP 的辅助方式,而不是与相互协商程序平行的一种选择性(alternative)方式。

其次,目前国内有些学者在探讨通过 WTO 争端解决机制来解决国际税收争议的可能性。[1] 虽然作为一种理论探讨未尝不可,但我们必须看到,根据 WTO《关于争端解决规则与程序的谅解》(DSU)第 1 条,WTO 争端解决机构只解决成员方在履行 WTO 协定中产生的争议,而目前 WTO 协定显然还没有涉及成员方之间的税收管辖权划分等问题,因此我们这里所说的国际税收争端是不可能通过 WTO 争端解决机构来解决的。[2] 实践中,WTO 的很多案例都会涉及某一成员方的税收政策,[3]但分析不难发现,这主要是两种情况:一是关税政策,二是对产品或投资的税收待遇。这两种情况实质上都是属于贸易问题,与税收管辖权等问题具有本质的区别,这些问题都已为 WTO 协定所涵盖,所以会在 WTO 的案例中找到。另外,有人认为《服务贸易总协定》第 22 条为通过 WTO 争端解决机制解决税收争端提供了可能,其实这是一种误读。《服务贸易总协定》第 22 条规定,对于其他成员方就影响本协定运作的任何事项所提出的主张,成员方应予正面考虑并提供适当的磋商机会,该磋商应适用 DSU 的有关规定;对于其他成员方之措施,若系属彼此间为避免双重课税而订定之国际协议的范畴内时,成员方不得依据本条或第 23 条规定(争端解决及执行)引用第 17 条(国

---

[1] 参见王国璋、徐建华、孙文博、潘贤掌:《国际税收争端解决机制分析》,载《福建税务》2003 年第 12 期。

[2] 根据 DSU 第 1 条第 1 款,本谅解的规则和程序应适用于按照本谅解附录 1 所列各项协定的磋商和争端解决规定所提出的争端,以及各成员间有关它们在《建立世界贸易组织协定》规定和本谅解规定下的权利和义务的磋商和争端解决。税收协定争端不在适用范围之内。

[3] 例如,2004 年 3 月,美国政府向 WTO 提起申诉,指控中国对半导体产品实行的出口退税政策违反了 WTO 协定;2007 年 8 月,美国、墨西哥等国家就中国的税收返还和减免等政策要求 WTO 成立专家组进行调查。

民待遇),对于措施是否属于此类协议范围发生分歧的,任一成员方均可将其提交服务贸易理事会,理事会应将该争议交付仲裁。可见,这里提到的分歧是"成员方措施是否属于双重征税协定的范围",而不涉及税收协定争议本身,税收协定本身执行中的纠纷不得通过 WTO 争端解决机制来解决。

二、国际税收争端解决的基本方式——相互协商程序

目前,各国签订的双边税收协定中的 MAP 大多是以《OECD 范本》和《UN 范本》中的 MAP 条款为基础的,两大范本所规定的 MAP 基本一致,只不过《UN 范本》在最后一款还对一些程序性问题提出了要求和建议。根据两大范本的规定,MAP 是指:当一个人认为缔约国一方或双方的措施,导致或将导致对其不符合协定规定的征税时,可以不考虑国内法律所规定的补救方法,将案情提交其本人为居民的缔约国一方主管当局,或者如果其案情属于第 24 条(无差别待遇)第 1 款,可以提交其本人为国民的缔约国主管当局。该案情必须在不符合协定规定的征税行为第一次通知起 3 年内提出。如果前述主管当局认为所提意见合理,又不能单方面解决时,应与缔约国另一方主管当局协商解决。对于协定解释和实施过程中的困难和疑义,缔约国双方主管当局也应设法协商解决。①

如前所述,MAP 已在国际税收协定中得到广泛的援引,是解决国际税收协定争端的一种有效方式。但近年来,随着国际税收实践的深入发展,MAP 的缺陷日益显现,OECD 在谈到 MAP 的不足时,将其比作一个"暗箱"(black box),MAP 启动之后,要么没有任何结果,要么需要经过漫长的等待,要么是一个未经任何解释或说明的结果,让纳税人无法理解。② OECD 的这一评价说明该程序在透明度和有效性等方面都还有明显的不足。具体而言,这种不足体现在以下几个方面:

第一,主管机关受理案件、启动 MAP 的条件缺乏必要的透明度。

MAP 案件可以分为由纳税人启动的案件和非由纳税人启动的案件。纳税人启动的案件主要是指纳税人认为缔约国一方或双方的措施导致或将导致对其与协定内容不符的征税,缔约国单方面又不能圆满地解决这一问题时启动的双方协商程序。非由纳税人启动的案件则是指缔约双方因协定的解释和实施过程中发生的困难和疑义而启动的双方协商程序,以及缔约国双方主管当局为避

---

① 参见两大范本第 25 条。
② See OECD:Improving the Process for Resolving International Tax Disputes,version released for public comments on 27 July 2004,paragraph 9.

免协定未规定的双重征税而进行的协商程序。备受质疑的是第一种情形,纳税人在实践中很难启动MAP。

首先,纳税人启动MAP的条件不够明确,构成纳税人运用MAP的障碍。

纳税人启动MAP通常需要满足一定的条件,这种条件在大多数情况下对于保障协定的正常运作而言是合理和必要的,但如果实施不当的话,它将成为纳税人运用MAP的障碍。在以两大范本为基础的协定中,以下两方面的条件有待进一步明确:一个是当事人提交案情的时间要求。这些税收协定一般都规定,纳税人须在不符合协定规定的征税措施第一次通知之日起3年内向主管当局提交案情。但对于何谓这里所说的"通知"却未作明确的规定,如收入来源地国对纳税人的某项收入征了预提税,后来其居住国拒绝对该项预提税予以抵免,从而产生了双重征税,违背了两国之间关于消除双重征税的协定。这里到底是以来源地国的征税行为为"通知",还是以居住国的拒绝抵免行为为"通知"?两种情况下的后果显然是不一样的,因为来源地国的征税行为在先,而居住国的拒绝抵免行为在后,以后者为起算点将使纳税人有更多的时间向主管当局提交案情。另一个需要明确的问题就是如何判断缔约国的征税行为是否与协定相符。纳税人提起MAP的前提条件是缔约国的措施"导致或将导致对其不符合协定规定的征税",也就是说,缔约国不合规定的征税可能已经发生,也可能还没有发生,如何认定尚没有发生的征税行为是否与协定相符存在一定的主观性。尽管对这一问题很难有一个一般性规则,但考虑到协定本身以通过协调分歧消除双重征税为目的,在认定缔约方的行为是否会导致与协定不符的征税时,要更多地站在纳税人的角度,当然,纳税人的认定也应该是合理的,而且是以事实为根据的。总之,主管机关不应该以纳税人未能证明将发生不合协定的税收为由拒绝接受纳税人提交案情以及启动MAP的申请。①

其次,主管机关受理案件的自由裁量权过大,也不利于当事人启动MAP。

尽管协定条款规定主管机关应该受理案件,但从大多数国家的实践看,如果案件涉及纳税人避税或者需对纳税人施以处罚(penalties)的情形,主管机关将不受理纳税人的MAP申请,这实际上是有关国家在坚持对特定案件行使专属管辖权。一国对与本国公共秩序密切相关的案件主张专属管辖在国际法上是允许的,这里关键要处理好两个问题,一个问题是对当事人施以处罚的范围,也就

---

① 例如,某一缔约国的国内税法改变,根据修改后的税法,将会对某一纳税人的某项特定收入征收与协定不符的税收,那么这里应该在国内税法修改通过,以及在纳税人已经或将要取得该特定收入之时认定"将导致对其不符合协定规定的征税",不应该等到实际征税行为发生时才确认。

是说什么样的处罚措施可以排除当事人的 MAP 申请,如纳税人因为坚持 MAP 而在国内审计过程中不予合作,被施以处罚,是否可以被认为涉及处罚而不得通过 MAP? 如果这种情形也被作为拒绝受理的理由,显然范围太宽,不尽合理。另一个问题就是要考虑国内反避税法与税收协定义务的冲突问题。有些协定本身明确将缔约国国内法规定的反避税条款作为协定的例外情形。即便这样,也不能简单地以适用国内反避税法条款为由拒绝接受纳税人 MAP 的申请,因为纳税人的申请可能是要认定是否存在与协定不符的征税。另外一些协定没有明确的例外条款,这时就需要判断国内的反避税法是否与协定相一致,以及是否存在滥用协定的情形。如果能认定国内反避税法条款将导致对纳税人征收与协定内容不符的税收,而且协定中又没有例外规定时,则应优先适用协定,允许纳税人根据协定条款运用 MAP。

第二,MAP 的实施效力有待加强。

由于协定中的 MAP 条款过于原则性和概括性,对下述一系列重要问题都没有作出详细规定,只能依赖于各国国内法,而各国国内法的规定和实践又很不一致,这种状况影响了 MAP 实际效用的发挥。

首先,主管机关缺乏实施 MAP 的必要权限和独立性。MAP 是以条约为基础的争端解决程序,缔约国必须确保主管当局有足够的权限来负责 MAP 的实施。各国通常都指定本国的税务主管部门为协定中所说的主管机关(competent authority),然而由于 MAP 实施中的很多问题已超出了国内法范畴,该主管机关便无权作出解释和决定。以我国为例,我国对外签订的税收协定中都指定国家税务总局为协定主管机关,虽然税务总局可以根据国内授权处理协定本身所规定的事项,但对于协定的解释、协定与国内法的关系等问题显然无权作决定,而这些问题往往是解决税收协定纠纷的关键所在,可见,主管机关缺乏必要的权限是影响 MAP 发挥实际效用的重要因素之一。

与权限相关的另外一个问题就是独立性。优化主管机关的组织结构,保障其应有的独立性也是确保 MAP 发挥积极效用的条件之一。各国主管机关的组织结构并不一致,有些国家的主管机关同时负责与协定有关的所有事项,包括协定的谈判、签订和执行等,有些国家的主管机关与负责协定谈判和签订的机构是独立的,还有的国家规定 MAP 的启动由税务行政部门负责,但经过协商最终达成的协定则需另一部门批准。不论主管机关的组织结构如何,保证主管机关的独立性以及内部协调性至关重要,否则,就有可能因为内部意见不一致而阻碍 MAP 的运行。另外,主管机关的独立性还有一个含义常常被忽视,那就是主管机关在 MAP 中并不仅仅是本国财政利益的维护者,更重要的它是作为协定的执行者,这一角色要求它保持独立性,客观地对条约解释等问题作出判断,从而保障 MAP 的顺利实施。

其次,MAP 的运作受到国内法的限制和制约,影响其作用的发挥。MAP 与国内法的关系非常复杂,同时又非常重要,但遗憾的是,大多数协定都未对此问题作出明确的规定,各国的实践做法很不一致。例如,有些国家规定,如果某一纠纷正处于国内争端解决程序中,则不得在 MAP 中达成协议,有些国家规定,如果法院已对同一案件作出了裁决,则不得再执行与该裁决相违背的任何协议。此外,还有些国家在条约与国内法的关系问题上坚持国内法优先,这样就使得主管机关不可能背离国内法而通过 MAP 达成协议。① 显而易见,这些国家的立法和实践都是 MAP 运作中的极大障碍。这里还有一个需要注意的问题就是 MAP 与国内法救济措施的关系。虽然协定中的 MAP 条款一般都表明纳税人可以不考虑国内法律所规定的补救方法,但如果纳税人在向主管机关提交案情之前已经启动了国内法救济措施,那么是否需要中止国内法救济措施才能提交案情以启动 MAP？如果需要先中止国内法救济措施,那么万一 MAP 无果而终且又错过了国内法救济措施的时效,此时该如何保证纳税人的权益？对此各国的做法也不统一,在美国,纳税人须中止国内法救济措施,然后再进入 MAP,但如果纳税人最终对 MAP 结果不满意,只要他采取了适当的保全措施,仍可以提起国内法救济。② 而其他一些国家则对中止后能否重新恢复国内法救济措施未作明确规定。

最后,MAP 中纳税人参与的缺失也影响了其有效性。从两大范本的规定看,纳税人除了通过向主管机关提交案情以外,几乎不参与 MAP 的任何阶段。之所以如此规定,主要是考虑到税收协定是国家和国家之间的一种安排,纳税人并不是协定的一方主体,因而无权参与作为协定重要条款之一的 MAP。当然,考虑到纳税人是重要的利益相关方,于是有的国家在协定中赋予纳税人某些权利来加以平衡,例如,规定纳税人可以在 MAP 的任何阶段撤回 MAP 申请,或者规定纳税人可以不接受通过 MAP 达成的协议等。其实,离开了纳税人的积极参与和配合,MAP 是不可能有效发挥作用的。一方面,MAP 过程中常常需要纳税人提交相关证据和资料,或对案情作必要的陈述,没有纳税人的参与将不利于主管机关之间澄清案情;另一方面,通过 MAP 达成的协议最终还要通过纳税

---

① See OECD:Improving the Process for Resolving International Tax Disputes, version released for public comments on 27 July 2004, paragraph. 45.

② See Hugh J. Ault,Improving the Resolution of International Tax Disputes,7 Fla. Tax Rev. 137, 2005.

人来执行,如果纳税人的立场未能得到尊重和考虑,他就有可能不接受甚至抵制协议的执行。可见,纳税人在 MAP 进程中的知情权和参与权对于 MAP 的顺利进行和协议的最终执行具有重要意义。

第三,MAP 不能很好地解决三方或多方之间的案件。

虽然条约可以是双边的,也可以是多边的,但在税收领域,目前几乎所有税收协定都是双边的,多边税收协定更多的还只是一种理论上的探讨。按照"条约只对缔约国有效"的原理,只有双边税收协定的缔约国才能通过 MAP 来解决彼此之间的税收协定纠纷,第三国则无权参与 MAP,也就是说,MAP 很难解决涉及三方或多方的案件。例如,A 国公民在 B 国注册公司后到 C 国去开展业务,B 国与 C 国之间的税务调整必然会影响到 A 国公民的利益,但 B、C 国之间的 MAP 程序不能考虑到对 A 国的影响,如果 A 国要保护其本国居民的利益,则只能根据其与 B 国和 C 国的协定分别启动 MAP 程序。考虑到 MAP 花费时间长、受国内法限制过多等缺陷,A 国分别与 B 国和 C 国进行 MAP 是不现实的。

除了以上几个方面的不足之外,没有确定的时间限制也一直被认为是 MAP 的缺陷之一,由于没有时间限制,加上 MAP 条款只是要求主管机关"努力通过协议来解决纠纷"(endeavor to solve the case by mutual agreement),而不是"必须"达成协议,导致很多提交到 MAP 的案件久拖不决,甚至无果而终。由于不能确定最终是否会达成一个解决方案,纳税人往往不愿意花费时间和精力去启动 MAP。当然,我们也必须看到,要规定一个适合于所有案情的时间限制是不可能的,因为每个阶段所需花费的时间取决于很多因素,如案情的复杂程度、纳税人的合作程度等等。作为一种方案,可以考虑在协定中规定一个指导性的时间框架,然后在个案中确定具体的时间限制,从而来提高 MAP 的实际运用效果。

三、国际税收争端解决的补充方式——仲裁

尽管 MAP 是迄今为止解决国际税收争端的最有效方式,而且国际社会也为进一步完善 MAP 机制付出了巨大的努力,但 MAP 的前述缺陷和不足决定了它在某些案件中仍不能使得双方就争议事项达成协议,尤其是在涉及协定解释和适用的问题上。[①] 为了确保所有纠纷都能得到解决,最大限度地消除双重征

---

① OECD 负责税收协定的专家 Mary Bennett 在解释 OECD 为何支持税收协定争议仲裁时曾指出:美英两国之间一直都是通过 MAP 来解决纠纷,但在 GlaxoSmithKline 一案中,双方却未能最终达成协议,这说明,MAP 不能解决所有类型的案件。See Why the OECD Supports Arbitration, International Tax Review, February 1, 2007.

税，实现协定宗旨，有必要在 MAP 之外采用一些补充方式。从 OECD、ICC 等国际组织提出的方案以及国际实践看，解决国际税收争端的补充方式包括斡旋、咨询意见、仲裁等，其中最受关注的便是仲裁。

仲裁作为一种争端解决方式并不为我们所陌生，但要注意的是，税收协定争端仲裁与我们通常所说的商事仲裁不完全一样。迄今为止，OECD、ICC、IFA 等国际组织都制定了税收仲裁的示范条款，欧共体于 1990 年制定的《关于避免因调整关联企业利润引起的双重征税的公约》(以下简称《仲裁公约》)也规定了争议的仲裁解决方式，这些现有的仲裁条款之间差异很大，有些差异甚至涉及仲裁的基本特征问题，如仲裁裁决的效力、仲裁庭的独立性等。这种差异表明目前还很难归纳出税收争议仲裁的一般特点，只能结合特定的仲裁方案来研究税收争议仲裁问题。这里仅以 OECD 制定的仲裁方案为例，来探讨税收争议仲裁的特点，重点是将其与商事仲裁区别开来。

OECD 在早期并不赞同国际税收协定争议仲裁，1984 年其所公布的《转让定价与跨国公司：三个税收问题》认为，"尚无明显的迹象表明有必要采取这种强制性仲裁程序，而且采用这种程序将意味着对国家财政主权的放弃，这是不可接受的"[①]。但是，随着实践的发展，OECD 对国际税收协定争议仲裁的态度也在不断变化，1995 年出台的《转让定价指导准则》中指出，"应该重视国际税收协定争议仲裁方式"[②]。2004 年公布的《完善国际税收争端解决程序》报告中开始讨论将仲裁作为补充方式的可行性，但至此仍未对仲裁方式作过多的阐述。[③] 时隔三年，2007 年公布的《完善国际税收争端解决程序》报告中却将税收争议仲裁作为一个独立部分重点加以介绍。尤其值得注意的是，2007 年的报告还提出在现行的《OECD 范本》第 25 条 (MAP) 中增加一款内容，明确将仲裁方式作为 MAP 的补充方式。这一提案在 2010 年范本修订时正式被采纳，鉴于《OECD 范本》已在国际范围内得到广泛援引，这一方案的实施，必将对现行的国际税收争端解决机制产生深远的影响。

增加到《OECD 范本》第 25 条的仲裁方案包括如下内容：

如果：a：一个人认为缔约国一方或双方的措施导致或将导致对其不符合协定规定的征税时，根据第 1 款规定向主管当局提出，以及 b：主管机关未能在向

[①] OECD：Transfer Pricing and Multinational Enterprises——Three Taxation Issues，paragraph 63.

[②] OECD Transfer Pricing Guidelines for Multinational Enterprises and Tax Administration, paragraphs 4.167-4.171，1995.

[③] See OECD：Improving the Process for Resolving International Tax Disputes，version released for public comments on 27 July 2004，paragraph 124.

另一缔约国主管机关提交案件之日起两年内按照第 2 款的规定就纠纷的解决达成协议,与纠纷相关的任何未决事项都应该根据当事人的请求提交仲裁。但是,如果任何一个缔约国的法院或行政机关已就有关事宜作出了裁决,则这些事项不得再提交仲裁。除非受案件直接影响的人不接受根据仲裁裁决达成的协议,否则仲裁裁决对双方缔约国均具有约束力,并得以执行,而且裁决的执行不受国内法有关期限的限制。主管机关应该通过相互协商来决定具体实施模式。

从上述内容看,OECD 所规定的税收争议仲裁具有以下几个方面的特点:

第一,仲裁具有强制性。税收争议仲裁分为自愿仲裁和强制仲裁,自愿仲裁是指必须经过缔约国双方主管当局的同意才能启动仲裁;强制仲裁则是指经过一段时间的协商后如果仍然存在未决事项,就必须启动仲裁程序来对这些事项进行裁决,而无须取得缔约国主管当局的同意。由于各国担心强制仲裁会损害国家的税收主权,因此早期的税收协定中所规定的仲裁都是自愿仲裁。实践证明,自愿仲裁更多的只是纸上谈兵,尽管许多协定中都规定了这一机制,但迄今为止尚无利用自愿仲裁来解决纠纷的实例。其实,仲裁作为补充方式的一种,其目的就是要保证能对争议事项最终产生一个解决方案,如果缺乏这种确定性,补充方式的意义也就大打折扣了,显然,自愿仲裁无法保证这种确定性。与之相比,强制仲裁则弥补了自愿仲裁的这一缺陷,对于协商不能解决的纠纷,则可以保证通过仲裁来找到解决方案。欧共体《仲裁公约》中所采用的就是强制仲裁,实践证明,强制仲裁能真正改善 MAP 的实际效果,保证所有的争议都能得到解决。强制仲裁的这一优势已为国际社会所认可,2006 年 6 月,美国和德国对双方于 1989 年签订的税收协定作出修订,将自愿仲裁改为强制仲裁,规定当缔约国双方主管当局不能对税收争议协商一致时即可实施强制仲裁解决。[①]可见,OECD 在仲裁方案中采用强制仲裁,也正是借鉴了国际社会的经验,顺应了税收争端解决机制的发展趋势。

第二,仲裁裁决不具有终局性。一裁终局常常被认为是仲裁的基本特征之一,但 OECD 规定的上述仲裁方案却对此作出了不一致的规定,将直接利害关系人的接受作为仲裁裁决生效和产生约束力的条件,也就是说,仲裁只是产生一种解决纠纷的方案,但该方案是否产生约束力还得依直接利害关系人的态度而定。由于目前还没有实施的先例,很难断言这一方案的实际效果,但从欧盟的经验看,税收争议仲裁自身的特性决定了没有必要强调裁决的终局性,根据欧共体

---

① 在税收协定中规定强制仲裁将是美国的重要政策之一。See US to Arbitrate Tax Disputes, International Tax Review, March 1, 2007.

《仲裁公约》第 12 条,尽管有了仲裁裁决,缔约国主管机关之间仍然可以达成与仲裁裁决不一致的协议。①

第三,仲裁裁决的执行离不开 MAP。诚如前面所强调的,税收协定争议仲裁并不是一个选择性或 MAP 之外的争端解决途径。如果主管机关之间就争议已达成了协议,没有任何未决事项,那么即使受影响的当事人认为 MAP 没能很好地解决争议,也不得再提起仲裁程序。仲裁实际上只是 MAP 的延续,通过确保所有的争议事项都能得到解决来强化 MAP 的有效性。因此,尽管争议中的某些事项是通过仲裁方式解决的,但争议本身还是在 MAP 框架下解决,仲裁裁决作出后,主管机关还得以裁决为依据就纠纷的解决达成协议。这一点也是税收协定争议仲裁与一般商事仲裁的重要区别之一。

第四,对仲裁裁决的过程和结果缺乏监督机制。OECD 的仲裁条款中既没有规定撤销仲裁裁决的理由,也没有规定撤销仲裁裁决的机构,如果出现仲裁庭越权仲裁或者违反仲裁程序规则等情形,将缺乏有效的控制和监督机制,这被有些学者认为是税收仲裁制度的缺陷。② 其实,考虑到税收仲裁的裁决不具有终局性,它只是在 MAP 框架下确保能产生一个解决争议的方案,税收仲裁在仲裁庭的组成、仲裁程序等很多方面都与一般商事仲裁具有明显的区别,因此也没有必要规定监督和撤销机制,以免问题复杂化,使税收仲裁丧失其本来的灵活性。

需要指出的是,上述内容只是作为范本的条款之一,本身并没有强制约束力,有关国家在采用该范本时,可以在双方协商的基础上根据实际情况对范本的任何内容加以增减或变更。就该款规定而言,根据 OECD 对该款的注释,仲裁条款只有在有关缔约国的国内法律和政策都能确保得到有效执行时才应用,如果有些国家不接受该款的解决方案,或者只愿意跟部分国家在双边税收协定中规定该方案,那么可以不规定这一款。另外,如果缔约国允许主管机关对纠纷中的某个特定事项作出与国内法院判决不一致的认定时,缔约国之间还可以协商变更示范条款的内容,规定即使任何一个缔约国的法院或行政机关已就有关事宜作出了裁决,这些事项仍然可以提交仲裁。③

另外,这里介绍的只是 OECD 的仲裁方案,除了 OECD 之外,IFA 和 ICC 也提出了仲裁范本,后两个范本给予仲裁机构更多的独立作用,更接近于传统意

---

① See EC Convention on the Elimination of Double Taxation in Connection with the Adjustment of Profits of Associated Enterprises,Art. 12,90/436/EEC.

② 参见孙文博:《国际税收仲裁为何停留于"纸上谈兵"》,载《涉外税务》2003 年第 4 期。

③ See OECD:Improving the Process for Resolving International Tax Disputes,version released for public comments on 30 January 2007,paragraph 15.

上的仲裁。不过有一点是共同的,所有这些方案目前都只是一种探讨和摸索,还很难对不同方案进行优劣比较。但有一点可以确定的是,税收争议仲裁已经成为完善 MAP 的一种现实选择,它必将成为税收协定争端解决机制的一个重要组成部分。

本章阅读材料

Tax Competition: A Global Phenomenon

—selected from OECD report: Harmful Tax
Competition, an Emerging Global Issue

20. Historically, tax policies have been developed primarily to address domestic economic and social concerns. The forms and levels of taxation were established on the basis of the desired level of publicly provided goods and transfers, with regard also taken to the allocative, stabilising and redistributive aims thought appropriate for a country. Whilst domestic tax systems of essentially closed economies also had an international dimension in that they potentially affected the amount of tax imposed on foreign source income of domestic residents and typically included in the tax base the domestic income of non-residents, the interaction of domestic tax systems was relatively unimportant, given the limited mobility of capital. The decision to have a high rate of tax and a high level of government spending or low taxes and limited public outlays, the mix of direct and indirect taxes, and the use of tax incentives, were all matters which were decided primarily on the basis of domestic concerns and had principally domestic effects. While there were some international spillover effects on other economies, those effects were generally limited.

21. The accelerating process of globalisation of trade and investment has fundamentally changed the relationship among domestic tax systems. As noted in paragraph 8 above, the removal of non-tax barriers to international commerce and investment and the resulting integration of national economies have greatly increased the potential impact that domestic tax policies can have

on other economies. Globalisation has also been one of the driving forces behind tax reforms, which have focused on base broadening and rate reductions, thereby minimising tax induced distortions. Globalisation has also encouraged countries to assess continually their tax systems and public expenditures with a view to making adjustments where appropriate to improve the "fiscal climate" or investment. Globalisation and the increased mobility of capital has also promoted the development of capital and financial markets and has encouraged countries to reduce tax barriers to capital flows and to modernise their tax systems to reflect these developments. Many of these reforms have also addressed the need to adapt tax systems to this new global environment.

22. The process of globalisation has led to increased competition among businesses in the global market place. Multinational enterprises (MNEs) are increasingly developing global strategies and their links with any one country are becoming more tenuous. In addition, technological innovation has affected the way in which MNEs are managed and made the physical location of management and other service activities much less important to the MNE. International financial markets continue to expand, a development that facilitates global welfare-enhancing cross-border capital flows. This process has improved welfare and living standards around the world by creating a more efficient allocation and utilisation of resources.

23. As indicated in paragraphs 8 and 21 above, globalisation has had a positive effect on the development of tax systems. Globalisation has, however, also had the negative effects of opening up new ways by which companies and individuals can minimise and avoid taxes and in which countries can exploit these new opportunities by developing tax policies aimed primarily at diverting financial and other geographically mobile capital. These actions induce potential distortions in the patterns of trade and investment and reduce global welfare. As discussed in detail below, these schemes can erode national tax bases of other countries, may alter the structure of taxation (by shifting part of the tax burden from mobile to relatively immobile factors and from income to consumption) and may hamper the application of progressive tax rates and the achievement of redistributive goals. Pressure of this sort can result in

changes in tax structures in which all countries may be forced by spillover effects to modify their tax bases, even though a more desirable result could have been achieved through intensifying international co-operation. More generally, tax policies in one economy are now more likely to have repercussions on other economies. These new pressures on tax systems apply to both business income in the corporate sector and to personal investment income.

24. Countries face public spending obligations and constraints because they have to finance outlays on, for example, national defence, education, social security, and other public services. Investors in tax havens, imposing zero or nominal taxation, who are residents of non-haven countries may be able to utilise in various ways those tax haven jurisdictions to reduce their domestic tax liability. Such taxpayers are in effect "free riders" who benefit from public spending in their home country and yet avoid contributing to its financing.

25. In a still broader sense, governments and residents of tax havens can be "free riders" of general public goods created by the non-haven country. Thus on the spending side, as well, there are potential negative spillover effects from increased globalisation and the interaction between tax systems.

26. The Committee recognises that there are no particular reasons why any two countries should have the same level and structure of taxation. Although differences in tax levels and structures may have implications for other countries, these are essentially political decisions for national governments. Depending on the decisions taken, levels of tax may be high or low relative to other states and the composition of the tax burden may vary. The fact that a country has modernised its fiscal infrastructure earlier than other countries, for example by lowering the rates and broadening the base to promote greater neutrality, is principally a matter of domestic policy. Countries should remain free to design their own tax systems as long as they abide by internationally accepted standards in doing so. This study is designed, in part, to assist in that regard.

27. Tax competition and the interaction of tax systems can have effects that some countries may view as negative or harmful but others may not. For example, one country may view investment incentives as a policy instrument to

stimulate new investment, while another may view investment incentives as diverting real investment from one country to another. In the context of this last effect, countries with specific structural disadvantages, such as poor geographical location, lack of natural resources, etc., frequently consider that special tax incentives or tax regimes are necessary to offset non-tax disadvantages, including any additional cost from locating in such areas. Similarly, within countries, peripheral regions often experience difficulties in promoting their development and may, at certain stages in this development, benefit from more attractive tax regimes or tax incentives for certain activities. This outcome, in itself, recognises that many factors affect the overall competitive position of a country. Although the international community may have concerns about potential spillover effects, these decisions may be justifiable from the point of view of the country in question.

28. Harmful effects may also occur because of unintentional mismatches between existing tax systems, which do not involve a country deliberately exploiting the interaction of tax systems to erode the tax base of another country. Such unintentional mismatches may be exploited by taxpayers to the detriment of either or both countries. The undesirable effects of such mismatches may be dealt with by unilateral or bilateral measures. If, however, an issue cannot be resolved at this level it may be examined on the basis of the criteria set out in Chapter 2.

29. Unlike the situation of mismatching, where the interaction of tax systems is exploited by the enactment of special tax provisions which principally erode the tax base of other countries, the spillover effects on the other countries is not a mere side effect, incidental to the implementation of a domestic tax policy. Here the effect is for one country to redirect capital and financial flows and the corresponding revenue from the other jurisdictions by bidding aggressively for the tax base of other countries. Some have described this effect as "poaching" as the tax base "rightly" belongs to the other country. Practices of this sort can appropriately be labelled harmful tax competition as they do not reflect different judgements about the appropriate level of taxes and public outlays or the appropriate mix of taxes in a particular economy, which are aspects of every country's sovereignty in fiscal matters,

but are, in effect, tailored to attract investment or savings originating elsewhere or to facilitate the avoidance of other countries' taxes.

30. Tax havens or harmful preferential tax regimes that drive the effective tax rate levied on income from the mobile activities significantly below rates in other countries have the potential to cause harm by:

—distorting financial and, indirectly, real investment flows;

—undermining the integrity and fairness of tax structures;

—discouraging compliance by all taxpayers;

—re-shaping the desired level and mix of taxes and public spending;

—causing undesired shifts of part of the tax burden to less mobile tax bases, such as labour, property and consumption; and

—increasing the administrative costs and compliance burdens on tax authorities and taxpayers.

31. Clearly, where such practices have all of these negative effects they are harmful. However, in other cases, for example where only some of these effects are present, the degree of harm will range along a spectrum and thus the process of identifying harmful tax practices involves a balancing of factors. If the spillover effects of particular tax practices are so substantial that they are concluded to be poaching other countries' tax bases, such practices would be doubtlessly labelled "harmful tax competition".

32. The Committee is aware that many of the preferential tax regimes referred to in this Report have been put in place in response to pressures by the business community on those parts of government that have the responsibility for economic development. It is hoped that the analyses set out in this Report will assist tax policy makers in their discussions with their colleagues in these other government departments and with the business community.

33. While the focus of the analysis so far has been on source country taxation, the interaction between source and residence taxation is also involved. To some extent, the residence country can protect itself against the negative effects and economic behaviour caused by harmful tax practices in other countries by modifying its own tax rules. For example, certain modifications and adjustments of the currently applicable regimes for taxing foreign income may be possible as a targeted response to some of these

problems. These matters are discussed in more detail in Chapter 3.

34. The Committee recognises that some investors may seek to invest in a location with lower rates (and greater after tax return) even if only low public services are available, while others may seek to invest in a location with higher public services even if they have to endure a higher tax burden to finance them. Investors will favour different locations for these reasons but these genuine location decisions have to be distinguished from the type of behaviour which is the focus of this Report.

35. The available data do not permit a detailed comparative analysis of the economic and revenue effects involving low-tax jurisdictions. It has also proven difficult to obtain data on activities involving preferential tax regimes, given the problems in separating their effects from aggregate data in countries with otherwise normal tax systems, and the fact that such regimes often are non-transparent. However, the available data do suggest that the current use of tax havens is large, and that participation in such schemes is expanding at an exponential rate. For example, foreign direct investment by G7 countries in a number of jurisdictions in the Caribbean and in the South Pacific island states, which are generally considered to be low-tax jurisdictions, increased more than five-fold over the period 1985-1994, to more than $200 billion, a rate of increase well in excess of the growth of total outbound Foreign Direct Investment. The Committee continues to attach importance to collecting additional data on developments in tax havens and in the use of preferential tax regimes.

36. A regime can be harmful even where it is difficult to quantify the adverse economic impact it imposes. For example, the absence of a requirement to provide annual accounts may preclude access to the data required for an analysis of the economic effects of a regime. Yet, despite the inability to measure the economic damage, countries would agree that such regimes are harmful and should be discouraged.

37. Globalisation and the intensified competition among firms in the global market place has had and continues to have many positive effects. However, the fact that tax competition may lead to the proliferation of harmful tax

practices and the adverse consequences that result, as discussed here, shows that governments must take measures, including intensifying their international co-operation, to protect their tax bases and to avoid the worldwide reduction in welfare caused by tax-induced distortions in capital and financial flows.

附录一　联合国税收协定范本(2011年版本)

United Nations Model Double Taxation Convention between Developed and Developing Countries

SUMMARY OF THE CONVENTION
Title and Preamble

Chapter I
Scope of the Convention
  Article 1 Persons covered
  Article 2 Taxes covered

Chapter II
Definitions
  Article 3 General definitions
  Article 4 Resident
  Article 5 Permanent establishment

Chapter III
Taxation of income
  Article 6 Income from immovable property
  Article 7 Business profits
  Article 8 Shipping, inland waterways transport and air transport (alternatives A and B)
  Article 9 Associated enterprises
  Article 10 Dividends
  Article 11 Interest
  Article 12 Royalties

Article 13 Capital gains

Article 14 Independent personal services

Article 15 Dependent personal services

Article 16 Directors' fees and remuneration of top-level managerial officials

Article 17 Artistes and sportspersons

Article 18 Pensions and social security payments (alternatives A and B)

Article 19 Government service

Article 20 Students

Article 21 Other income

Chapter IV
Taxation of capital

Article 22 Capital

Chapter V
Methods for elimination of double taxation

Article 23 A Exemption method

Article 23 B Credit method

Chapter VI
Special provisions

Article 24 Non-discrimination

Article 25 Mutual agreement procedure (alternatives A and B)

Article 26 Exchange of information

Article 27 Assistance in the collection of taxes

Article 28 Members of diplomatic missions and consular posts

Chapter VII
Final provisions

Article 29 Entry into force

Article 30 Termination

TITLE OF THE CONVENTION

Convention between (State A) and (State B) with respect to taxes on income and capital[①]

PREAMBLE OF THE CONVENTION[②]

Chapter I
SCOPE OF THE CONVENTION

Article 1

PERSONS COVERED

This Convention shall apply to persons who are residents of one or both of the Contracting States.

Article 2

TAXES COVERED

1. This Convention shall apply to taxes on income and on capital imposed on behalf of a Contracting State or of its political subdivisions or local authorities, irrespective of the manner in which they are levied.

2. There shall be regarded as taxes on income and on capital all taxes imposed on total income, on total capital, or on elements of income or of capital, including taxes on gains from the alienation of movable or immovable property, taxes on the total amounts of wages or salaries paid by enterprises, as well as taxes on capital appreciation.

3. The existing taxes to which the Convention shall apply are in particular:

(a) (in State A): ....

(b) (in State B): ....

---

① States wishing to do so may follow the widespread practice of including in the title a reference to either the avoidance of double taxation or to both the avoidance of double taxation and the prevention of fiscal evasion.

② The Preamble of the Convention shall be drafted in accordance with the constitutional procedures of the Contracting States.

4. The Convention shall apply also to any identical or substantially similar taxes which are imposed after the date of signature of the Convention in addition to, or in place of, the existing taxes. The competent authorities of the Contracting States shall notify each other of significant changes made to their tax law.

Chapter II
DEFINITIONS

Article 3

GENERAL DEFINITIONS

1. For the purposes of this Convention, unless the context otherwise requires:

(a) The term "person" includes an individual, a company and any other body of persons;

(b) The term "company" means any body corporate or any entity that is treated as a body corporate for tax purposes;

(c) The terms "enterprise of a Contracting State" and "enterprise of the other Contracting State" mean respectively an enterprise carried on by a resident of a Contracting State and an enterprise carried on by a resident of the other Contracting State;

(d) The term "international traffic" means any transport by a ship or aircraft operated by an enterprise that has its place of effective management in a Contracting State, except when the ship or aircraft is operated solely between places in the other Contracting State;

(e) The term "competent authority" means:

(i) (In State A): _____

(ii) (In State B): _____

(f) The term "national" means:

(i) any individual possessing the nationality of a Contracting State

(ii) any legal person, partnership or association deriving its status as such from the laws in force in a Contracting State.

2. As regards the application of the Convention at any time by a Contracting State, any term not defined therein shall, unless the context

otherwise requires, have the meaning that it has at that time under the law of that State for the purposes of the taxes to which the Convention applies, any meaning under the applicable tax laws of that State prevailing over a meaning given to the term under other laws of that State.

Article 4

RESIDENT

1. For the purposes of this Convention, the term "resident of a Contracting State" means any person who, under the laws of that State, is liable to tax therein by reason of his domicile, residence, place of incorporation, place of management or any other criterion of a similar nature, and also includes that State and any political subdivision or local authority thereof. This term, however, does not include any person who is liable to tax in that State in respect only of income from sources in that State or capital situated therein.

2. Where by reason of the provisions of paragraph 1 an individual is a resident of both Contracting States, then his status shall be determined as follows:

(a) He shall be deemed to be a resident only of the State in which he has a permanent home available to him; if he has a permanent home available to him in both States, he shall be deemed to be a resident only of the State with which his personal and economic relations are closer(centre of vital interests);

(b) If the State in which he has his centre of vital interests cannot be determined, or if he has not a permanent home available to him in either State, he shall be deemed to be a resident only of the State in which he has an habitual abode;

(c) If he has an habitual abode in both States or in neither of them, he shall be deemed to be a resident only of the State of which he is a national;

(d) If he is a national of both States or of neither of them, the competent authorities of the Contracting States shall settle the question by mutual agreement.

3. Where by reason of the provisions of paragraph 1 a person other than an individual is a resident of both Contracting States, then it shall be deemed to be a resident only of the State in which its place of effective management is

situated.

Article 5

PERMANENT ESTABLISHMENT

1. For the purposes of this Convention, the term "permanent establishment" means a fixed place of business through which the business of an enterprise is wholly or partly carried on.

2. The term "permanent establishment" includes especially:

(a) A place of management;

(b) A branch;

(c) An office;

(d) A factory;

(e) A workshop;

(f) A mine, an oil or gas well, a quarry or any other place of extraction of natural resources.

3. The term "permanent establishment" also encompasses:

(a) A building site, a construction, assembly or installation project or supervisory activities in connection therewith, but only if such site, project or activities last more than six months;

(b) The furnishing of services, including consultancy services, by an enterprise through employees or other personnel engaged by the enterprise for such purpose, but only if activities of that nature continue (for the same or a connected project) within a Contracting State for a period or periods aggregating more than 183 days in any 12-month period commencing or ending in the fiscal year concerned.

4. Notwithstanding the preceding provisions of this Article, the term "permanent establishment" shall be deemed not to include:

(a) The use of facilities solely for the purpose of storage or display of goods or merchandise belonging to the enterprise;

(b) The maintenance of a stock of goods or merchandise belonging to the enterprise solely for the purpose of storage or display;

(c) The maintenance of a stock of goods or merchandise belonging to the enterprise solely for the purpose of processing by another enterprise;

(d) The maintenance of a fixed place of business solely for the purpose of purchasing goods or merchandise or of collecting information, for the enterprise;

(e) The maintenance of a fixed place of business solely for the purpose of carrying on, for the enterprise, any other activity of a preparatory or auxiliary character;

(f) The maintenance of a fixed place of business solely for any combination of activities mentioned in subparagraphs (a) to (e), provided that the overall activity of the fixed place of business resulting from this combination is of a preparatory or auxiliary character.

5. Notwithstanding the provisions of paragraphs 1 and 2, where a person—other than an agent of an independent status to whom paragraph 7 applies—is acting in a Contracting State on behalf of an enterprise of the other Contracting State, that enterprise shall be deemed to have a permanent establishment in the first-mentioned Contracting State in respect of any activities which that person undertakes for the enterprise, if such a person:

(a) Has and habitually exercises in that State an authority to conclude contracts in the name of the enterprise, unless the activities of such person are limited to those mentioned in paragraph 4 which, if exercised through a fixed place of business, would not make this fixed place of business a permanent establishment under the provisions of that paragraph; or

(b) Has no such authority, but habitually maintains in the first-mentioned State a stock of goods or merchandise from which he regularly delivers goods or merchandise on behalf of the enterprise.

6. Notwithstanding the preceding provisions of this Article, an insurance enterprise of a Contracting State shall, except in regard to re-insurance, be deemed to have a permanent establishment in the other Contracting State if it collects premiums in the territory of that other State or insures risks situated therein through a person other than an agent of an independent status to whom paragraph 7 applies.

7. An enterprise of a Contracting State shall not be deemed to have a permanent establishment in the other Contracting State merely because it carries on business in that other State through a broker, general commission agent or any other agent of an independent status, provided that such persons

are acting in the ordinary course of their business. However, when the activities of such an agent are devoted wholly or almost wholly on behalf of that enterprise, and conditions are made or imposed between that enterprise and the agent in their commercial and financial relations which differ from those which would have been made between independent enterprises, he will not be considered an agent of an independent status within the meaning of this paragraph.

8. The fact that a company which is a resident of a Contracting State controls or is controlled by a company which is a resident of the other Contracting State, or which carries on business in that other State (whether through a permanent establishment or otherwise), shall not of itself constitute either company a permanent establishment of the other.

Chapter III
TAXATION OF INCOME

Article 6

INCOME FROM IMMOVABLE PROPERTY

1. Income derived by a resident of a Contracting State from immovable property (including income from agriculture or forestry) situated in the other Contracting State may be taxed in that other State.

2. The term "immovable property" shall have the meaning which it has under the law of the Contracting State in which the property in question is situated. The term shall in any case include property accessory to immovable property, livestock and equipment used in agriculture and forestry, rights to which the provisions of general law respecting landed property apply, usufruct of immovable property and rights to variable or fixed payments as consideration for the working of, or the right to work, mineral deposits, sources and other natural resources; ships, boats and aircraft shall not be regarded as immovable property.

3. The provisions of paragraph 1 shall also apply to income derived from the direct use, letting or use in any other form of immovable property.

4. The provisions of paragraphs 1 and 3 shall also apply to the income from immovable property of an enterprise and to income from immovable

property used for the performance of independent personal services.

Article 7
BUSINESS PROFITS

1. The profits of an enterprise of a Contracting State shall be taxable only in that State unless the enterprise carries on business in the other Contracting State through a permanent establishment situated therein. If the enterprise carries on business as aforesaid, the profits of the enterprise may be taxed in the other State but only so much of them as is attributable to (a) that permanent establishment; (b) sales in that other State of goods or merchandise of the same or similar kind as those sold through that permanent establishment; or (c) other business activities carried on in that other State of the same or similar kind as those effected through that permanent establishment.

2. Subject to the provisions of paragraph 3, where an enterprise of a Contracting State carries on business in the other Contracting State through a permanent establishment situated therein, there shall in each Contracting State be attributed to that permanent establishment the profits which it might be expected to make if it were a distinct and separate enterprise engaged in the same or similar activities under the same or similar conditions and dealing wholly independently with the enterprise of which it is a permanent establishment.

3. In the determination of the profits of a permanent establishment, there shall be allowed as deductions expenses which are incurred for the purposes of the business of the permanent establishment including executive and general administrative expenses so incurred, whether in the State in which the permanent establishment is situated or elsewhere. However, no such deduction shall be allowed in respect of amounts, if any, paid (otherwise than towards reimbursement of actual expenses) by the permanent establishment to the head office of the enterprise or any of its other offices, by way of royalties, fees or other similar payments in return for the use of patents or other rights, or by way of commission, for specific services performed or for management, or, except in the case of a banking enterprise, by way of interest on moneys lent to the permanent establishment. Likewise, no account shall be taken, in

the determination of the profits of a permanent establishment, for amounts charged (otherwise than towards reimbursement of actual expenses), by the permanent establishment to the head office of the enterprise or any of its other offices, by way of royalties, fees or other similar payments in return for the use of patents or other rights, or by way of commission for specific services performed or for management, or, except in the case of a banking enterprise, by way of interest on moneys lent to the head office of the enterprise or any of its other offices.

4. In so far as it has been customary in a Contracting State to determine the profits to be attributed to a permanent establishment on the basis of an apportionment of the total profits of the enterprise to its various parts, nothing in paragraph 2 shall preclude that Contracting State from determining the profits to be taxed by such an apportionment as may be customary; the method of apportionment adopted shall, however, be such that the result shall be in accordance with the principles contained in this Article.

5. For the purposes of the preceding paragraphs, the profits to be attributed to the permanent establishment shall be determined by the same method year by year unless there is good and sufficient reason to the contrary.

6. Where profits include items of income which are dealt with separately in other Articles of this Convention, then the provisions of those Articles shall not be affected by the provisions of this Article.

(NOTE: The question of whether profits should be attributed to a permanent establishment by reason of the mere purchase by that permanent establishment of goods and merchandise for the enterprise was not resolved. It should therefore be settled in bilateral negotiations.)

Article 8

SHIPPING, INLAND WATERWAYS TRANSPORT AND AIR TRANSPORT

Article 8 (alternative A)

1. Profits from the operation of ships or aircraft in international traffic shall be taxable only in the Contracting State in which the place of effective management of the enterprise is situated.

2. Profits from the operation of boats engaged in inland waterways

transport shall be taxable only in the Contracting State in which the place of effective management of the enterprise is situated.

3. If the place of effective management of a shipping enterprise or of an inland waterways transport enterprise is aboard a ship or a boat, then it shall be deemed to be situated in the Contracting State in which the home harbor of the ship or boat is situated, or, if there is no such home harbour, in the Contracting State of which the operator of the ship or boat is a resident.

4. The provisions of paragraph 1 shall also apply to profits from the participation in a pool, a joint business or an international operating agency.

Article 8 (alternative B)

1. Profits from the operation of aircraft in international traffic shall be taxable only in the Contracting State in which the place of effective management of the enterprise is situated.

2. Profits from the operation of ships in international traffic shall be taxable only in the Contracting State in which the place of effective management of the enterprise is situated unless the shipping activities arising from such operation in the other Contracting State are more than casual. If such activities are more than casual, such profits may be taxed in that other State. The profits to be taxed in that other State shall be determined on the basis of an appropriate allocation of the overall net profits derived by the enterprise from its shipping operations. The tax computed in accordance with such allocation shall then be reduced by __ per cent. (The percentage is to be established through bilateral negotiations.)

3. Profits from the operation of boats engaged in inland waterways transport shall be taxable only in the Contracting State in which the place of effective management of the enterprise is situated.

4. If the place of effective management of a shipping enterprise or of an inland waterways transport enterprise is aboard a ship or boat, then it shall be deemed to be situated in the Contracting State in which the home harbour of the ship or boat is situated, or if there is no such home harbour, in the Contracting State of which the operator of the ship or boat is a resident.

5. The provisions of paragraphs 1 and 2 shall also apply to profits from the participation in a pool, a joint business or an international operating

agency.

Article 9

ASSOCIATED ENTERPRISES

1. Where:

(a) an enterprise of a Contracting State participates directly or indirectly in the management, control or capital of an enterprise of the other Contracting State, or

(b) the same persons participate directly or indirectly in the management, control or capital of an enterprise of a Contracting State and an enterprise of the other Contracting State,

and in either case conditions are made or imposed between the two enterprises in their commercial or financial relations which differ from those which would be made between independent enterprises, then any profits which would, but for those conditions, have accrued to one of the enterprises, but, by reason of those conditions, have not so accrued, may be included in the profits of that enterprise and taxed accordingly.

2. Where a Contracting State includes in the profits of an enterprise of that State—and taxes accordingly—profits on which an enterprise of the other Contracting State has been charged to tax in that other State and the profits so included are profits which would have accrued to the enterprise of the first-mentioned State if the conditions made between the two enterprises had been those which would have been made between independent enterprises, then that other State shall make an appropriate adjustment to the amount of the tax charged therein on those profits. In determining such adjustment, due regard shall be had to the other provisions of the Convention and the competent authorities of the Contracting States shall, if necessary, consult each other.

3. The provisions of paragraph 2 shall not apply where judicial, administrative or other legal proceedings have resulted in a final ruling that by actions giving rise to an adjustment of profits under paragraph 1, one of the enterprises concerned is liable to penalty with respect to fraud, gross negligence or wilful default.

Article 10

DIVIDENDS

1. Dividends paid by a company which is a resident of a Contracting State to a resident of the other Contracting State may be taxed in that other State.

2. However, such dividends may also be taxed in the Contracting State of which the company paying the dividends is a resident and according to the laws of that State, but if the beneficial owner of the dividends is a resident of the other Contracting State, the tax so charged shall not exceed:

(a) __ per cent (the percentage is to be established through bilateral negotiations) of the gross amount of the dividends if the beneficial owner is a company (other than a partnership) which holds directly at least 10 per cent of the capital of the company paying the dividends;

(b) __ per cent (the percentage is to be established through bilateral negotiations) of the gross amount of the dividends in all other cases.

The competent authorities of the Contracting States shall by mutual agreement settle the mode of application of these limitations.

This paragraph shall not affect the taxation of the company in respect of the profits out of which the dividends are paid.

3. The term "dividends" as used in this Article means income from shares, "jouissance" shares or "jouissance" rights, mining shares, founders' shares or other rights, not being debt claims, participating in profits, as well as income from other corporate rights which is subjected to the same taxation treatment as income from shares by the laws of the State of which the company making the distribution is a resident.

4. The provisions of paragraphs 1 and 2 shall not apply if the beneficial owner of the dividends, being a resident of a Contracting State, carries on business in the other Contracting State of which the company paying the dividends is a resident, through a permanent establishment situated therein, or performs in that other State independent personal services from a fixed base situated therein, and the holding in respect of which the dividends are paid is effectively connected with such permanent establishment or fixed base. In such case the provisions of Article 7 or Article 14, as the case may be, shall apply.

5. Where a company which is a resident of a Contracting State derives

profits or income from the other Contracting State, that other State may not impose any tax on the dividends paid by the company, except in so far as such dividends are paid to a resident of that other State or in so far as the holding in respect of which the dividends are paid is effectively connected with a permanent establishment or a fixed base situated in that other State, nor subject the company's undistributed profits to a tax on the company's undistributed profits, even if the dividends paid or the undistributed profits consist wholly or partly of profits or income arising in such other State.

Article 11

INTEREST

1. Interest arising in a Contracting State and paid to a resident of the other Contracting State may be taxed in that other State.

2. However, such interest may also be taxed in the Contracting State in which it arises and according to the laws of that State, but if the beneficial owner of the interest is a resident of the other Contracting State, the tax so charged shall not exceed __ per cent (the percentage is to be established through bilateral negotiations) of the gross amount of the interest. The competent authorities of the Contracting States shall by mutual agreement settle the mode of application of this limitation.

3. The term "interest" as used in this Article means income from debt claims of every kind, whether or not secured by mortgage and whether or not carrying a right to participate in the debtor's profits, and in particular, income from government securities and income from bonds or debentures, including premiums and prizes attaching to such securities, bonds or debentures. Penalty charges for late payment shall not be regarded as interest for the purpose of this Article.

4. The provisions of paragraphs 1 and 2 shall not apply if the beneficial owner of the interest, being a resident of a Contracting State, carries on business in the other Contracting State in which the interest arises, through a permanent establishment situated therein, or performs in that other State independent personal services from a fixed base situated therein, and the debt claim in respect of which the interest is paid is effectively connected with (a) such permanent establishment or fixed base, or with (b) business activities

referred to in (c) of paragraph 1 of Article 7. In such cases the provisions of Article 7 or Article 14, as the case may be, shall apply.

5. Interest shall be deemed to arise in a Contracting State when the payer is a resident of that State. Where, however, the person paying the interest, whether he is a resident of a Contracting State or not, has in a Contracting State a permanent establishment or a fixed base in connection with which the indebtedness on which the interest is paid was incurred, and such interest is borne by such permanent establishment or fixed base, then such interest shall be deemed to arise in the State in which the permanent establishment or fixed base is situated.

6. Where, by reason of a special relationship between the payer and the beneficial owner or between both of them and some other person, the amount of the interest, having regard to the debt claim for which it is paid, exceeds the amount which would have been agreed upon by the payer and the beneficial owner in the absence of such relationship, the provisions of this Article shall apply only to the last-mentioned amount. In such case, the excess part of the payments shall remain taxable according to the laws of each Contracting State, due regard being had to the other provisions of this Convention.

Article 12

ROYALTIES

1. Royalties arising in a Contracting State and paid to a resident of the other Contracting State may be taxed in that other State.

2. However, such royalties may also be taxed in the Contracting State in which they arise and according to the laws of that State, but if the beneficial owner of the royalties is a resident of the other Contracting State, the tax so charged shall not exceed __ per cent (the percentage is to be established through bilateral negotiations) of the gross amount of the royalties. The competent authorities of the Contracting States shall by mutual agreement settle the mode of application of this limitation.

3. The term "royalties" as used in this Article means payments of any kind received as a consideration for the use of, or the right to use, any copyright of literary, artistic or scientific work including cinematograph films, or films or tapes used for radio or television broadcasting, any patent,

trademark, design or model, plan, secret formula or process, or for the use of, or the right to use, industrial, commercial or scientific equipment or for information concerning industrial, commercial or scientific experience.

4. The provisions of paragraphs 1 and 2 shall not apply if the beneficial owner of the royalties, being a resident of a Contracting State, carries on business in the other Contracting State in which the royalties arise, through a permanent establishment situated therein, or performs in that other State independent personal services from a fixed base situated therein, and the right or property in respect of which the royalties are paid is effectively connected with (a) such permanent establishment or fixed base, or with (b) business activities referred to in (c) of paragraph 1 of Article 7. In such cases the provisions of Article 7 or Article 14, as the case may be, shall apply.

5. Royalties shall be deemed to arise in a Contracting State when the payer is a resident of that State. Where, however, the person paying the royalties, whether he is a resident of a Contracting State or not, has in a Contracting State a permanent establishment or a fixed base in connection with which the liability to pay the royalties was incurred, and such royalties are borne by such permanent establishment or fixed base, then such royalties shall be deemed to arise in the State in which the permanent establishment or fixed base is situated.

6. Where by reason of a special relationship between the payer and the beneficial owner or between both of them and some other person, the amount of the royalties, having regard to the use, right or information for which they are paid, exceeds the amount which would have been agreed upon by the payer and the beneficial owner in the absence of such relationship, the provisions of this Article shall apply only to the last-mentioned amount. In such case, the excess part of the payments shall remain taxable according to the laws of each Contracting State, due regard being had to the other provisions of this Convention.

Article 13

CAPITAL GAINS

1. Gains derived by a resident of a Contracting State from the alienation of immovable property referred to in Article 6 and situated in the other may be

taxed in that other State.

2. Gains from the alienation of movable property forming part of the business property of a permanent establishment which an enterprise of a Contracting State has in the other Contracting State or of movable property pertaining to a fixed base available to a resident of a Contracting State in the other Contracting State for the purpose of performing independent personal services, including such gains from the alienation of such a permanent establishment(alone or with the whole enterprise) or of such fixed base, may be taxed in that other State.

3. Gains from the alienation of ships or aircraft operated in international traffic, boats engaged in inland waterways transport or movable property pertaining to the operation of such ships, aircraft or boats, shall be taxable only in the Contracting State in which the place of effective management of the enterprise is situated.

4. Gains from the alienation of shares of the capital stock of a company, or of an interest in a partnership, trust or estate, the property of which consists directly or indirectly principally of immovable property situated in a Contracting State may be taxed in that State. In particular:

(a) Nothing contained in this paragraph shall apply to a company, partnership, trust or estate, other than a company, partnership, trust or estate engaged in the business of management of immovable properties, the property of which consists directly or indirectly principally of immovable property used by such company, partnership, trust or estate in its business activities.

(b) For the purposes of this paragraph, "principally" in relation to ownership of immovable property means the value of such immovable property exceeding 50 per cent of the aggregate value of all assets owned by the company, partnership, trust or estate.

5. Gains, other than those to which paragraph 4 applies, derived by a resident of a Contracting State from the alienation of shares of a company which is a resident of the other Contracting State, may be taxed in that other State if the alienator, at any time during the 12-month period preceding such alienation, held directly or indirectly at least __ per cent (the percentage is to

be established through bilateral negotiations) of the capital of that company.

6. Gains from the alienation of any property other than that referred to in paragraphs 1, 2, 3, 4 and 5 shall be taxable only in the Contracting State of which the alienator is a resident.

Article 14

INDEPENDENT PERSONAL SERVICES

1. Income derived by a resident of a Contracting State in respect of professional services or other activities of an independent character shall be taxable only in that State except in the following circumstances, when such income may also be taxed in the other Contracting State:

(a) If he has a fixed base regularly available to him in the other Contracting State for the purpose of performing his activities; in that case, only so much of the income as is attributable to that fixed base may be taxed in that other Contracting State; or

(b) If his stay in the other Contracting State is for a period or periods amounting to or exceeding in the aggregate 183 days in any twelve-month period commencing or ending in the fiscal year concerned; in that case, only so much of the income as is derived from his activities performed in that other State may be taxed in that other State.

2. The term "professional services" includes especially independent scientific, literary, artistic, educational or teaching activities as well as the independent activities of physicians, lawyers, engineers, architects, dentists and accountants.

Article 15

DEPENDENT PERSONAL SERVICES

1. Subject to the provisions of Articles 16, 18 and 19, salaries, wages and other similar remuneration derived by a resident of a Contracting State in respect of an employment shall be taxable only in that State unless the employment is exercised in the other Contracting State. If the employment is so exercised, such remuneration as is derived therefrom may be taxed in that other State.

2. Notwithstanding the provisions of paragraph 1, remuneration derived by a resident of a Contracting State in respect of an employment exercised in

the other Contracting State shall be taxable only in the first-mentioned State if:

(a) The recipient is present in the other State for a period or periods not exceeding in the aggregate 183 days in any twelve-month period commencing or ending in the fiscal year concerned; and

(b) The remuneration is paid by, or on behalf of, an employer who is not a resident of the other State; and

(c) The remuneration is not borne by a permanent establishment or a fixed base which the employer has in the other State.

3. Notwithstanding the preceding provisions of this Article, remuneration derived in respect of an employment exercised aboard a ship or aircraft operated in international traffic, or aboard a boat engaged in inland waterways transport, may be taxed in the Contracting State in which the place of effective management of the enterprise is situated.

Article 16

DIRECTORS' FEES AND REMUNERATION OF TOP-LEVEL MANAGERIAL OFFICIALS

1. Directors' fees and other similar payments derived by a resident of a Contracting State in his capacity as a member of the Board of Directors of a company which is a resident of the other Contracting State may be taxed in that other State.

2. Salaries, wages and other similar remuneration derived by a resident of a Contracting State in his capacity as an official in a top-level managerial position of a company which is a resident of the other Contracting State may be taxed in that other State.

Article 17

ARTISTES AND SPORTSPERSONS

1. Notwithstanding the provisions of Articles 14 and 15, income derived by a resident of a Contracting State as an entertainer, such as a theatre, motion picture, radio or television artiste, or a musician, or as a sportsperson, from his personal activities as such exercised in the other Contracting State, maybe taxed in that other State.

2. Where income in respect of personal activities exercised by an

entertainer or a sportsperson in his capacity as such accrues not to the entertainer or sportsperson himself but to another person, that income may, notwithstanding the provisions of Articles 7, 14 and 15, be taxed in the Contracting State in which the activities of the entertainer or sportsperson are exercised.

Article 18

PENSIONS AND SOCIAL SECURITY PAYMENTS

Article 18 (alternative A)

1. Subject to the provisions of paragraph 2 of Article 19, pensions and other similar remuneration paid to a resident of a Contracting State in consideration of past employment shall be taxable only in that State.

2. Notwithstanding the provisions of paragraph 1, pensions paid and other payments made under a public scheme which is part of the social security system of a Contracting State or a political subdivision or a local authority thereof shall be taxable only in that State.

Article 18 (alternative B)

1. Subject to the provisions of paragraph 2 of Article 19, pensions and other similar remuneration paid to a resident of a Contracting State in consideration of past employment may be taxed in that State.

2. However, such pensions and other similar remuneration may also be taxed in the other Contracting State if the payment is made by a resident of that other State or a permanent establishment situated therein.

3. Notwithstanding the provisions of paragraphs 1 and 2, pensions paid and other payments made under a public scheme which is part of the social security system of a Contracting State or a political subdivision or a local authority thereof shall be taxable only in that State.

Article 19

GOVERNMENT SERVICE

1. (a) Salaries, wages and other similar remuneration paid by a Contracting State or a political subdivision or a local authority thereof to an individual in respect of services rendered to that State or subdivision or authority shall be taxable only in that State.

(b) However, such salaries, wages and other similar remuneration shall be taxable only in the other Contracting State if the services are rendered in that other State and the individual is a resident of that State who:

(i) is a national of that State; or

(ii) did not become a resident of that State solely for the purpose of rendering the services.

2. (a) Notwithstanding the provisions of paragraph 1, pensions and other similar remuneration paid by, or out of funds created by, a Contracting State or a political subdivision or a local authority thereof to an individual in respect of services rendered to that State or subdivision or authority shall be taxable only in that State.

(b) However, such pensions and other similar remuneration shall be taxable only in the other Contracting State if the individual is a resident of, and a national of, that other State.

3. The provisions of Articles 15, 16, 17 and 18 shall apply to salaries, wages, pensions, and other similar remuneration in respect of services rendered in connection with a business carried on by a Contracting State or a political subdivision or a local authority thereof.

Article 20

STUDENTS

Payments which a student or business trainee or apprentice who is or was immediately before visiting a Contracting State a resident of the other Contracting State and who is present in the first-mentioned State solely for the purpose of his education or training receives for the purpose of his maintenance, education or training shall not be taxed in that State, provided that such payments arise from sources outside that State.

Article 21

OTHER INCOME

1. Items of income of a resident of a Contracting State, wherever arising, not dealt with in the foregoing Articles of this Convention shall be taxable only in that State.

2. The provisions of paragraph 1 shall not apply to income, other than income from immovable property as defined in paragraph 2 of Article 6, if the recipient of such income, being a resident of a Contracting State, carries on

business in the other Contracting State through a permanent establishment situated therein, or performs in that other State independent personal services from a fixed base situated therein, and the right or property in respect of which the income is paid is effectively connected with such permanent establishment or fixed base. In such case the provisions of Article 7 or Article 14, as the case may be, shall apply.

3. Notwithstanding the provisions of paragraphs 1 and 2, items of income of a resident of a Contracting State not dealt with in the foregoing Articles of this Convention and arising in the other Contracting State may also be taxed in that other State.

Chapter IV
TAXATION OF CAPITAL

Article 22

CAPITAL

1. Capital represented by immovable property referred to in Article 6, owned by a resident of a Contracting State and situated in the other Contracting State, may be taxed in that other State.

2. Capital represented by movable property forming part of the business property of a permanent establishment which an enterprise of a Contracting State has in the other Contracting State or by movable property pertaining to a fixed base available to a resident of a Contracting State in the other Contracting State for the purpose of performing independent personal services may be taxed in that other State.

3. Capital represented by ships and aircraft operated in international traffic and by boats engaged in inland waterways transport, and by movable property pertaining to the operation of such ships, aircraft and boats, shall be taxable only in the Contracting State in which the place of effective management of the enterprise is situated.

[4. All other elements of capital of a resident of a Contracting State shall be taxable only in that State.]

(The question of the taxation of all other elements of capital of a resident of a Contracting State is left to bilateral negotiations. Should the negotiating parties decide to include in the Convention an article on the taxation of capital, they will have to determine whether to use the wording of paragraph 4 as shown or wording that leaves taxation to the State in which the capital is located.)

Chapter V
METHODS FOR THE ELIMINATION OF DOUBLE TAXATION

Article 23 A

EXEMPTION METHOD

1. Where a resident of a Contracting State derives income or owns capital which, in accordance with the provisions of this Convention, may be taxed in the other Contracting State, the first-mentioned State shall, subject to the provisions of paragraphs 2 and 3, exempt such income or capital from tax.

2. Where a resident of a Contracting State derives items of income which, in accordance with the provisions of Articles 10, 11 and 12, may be taxed in the other Contracting State, the first-mentioned State shall allow as a deduction from the tax on the income of that resident an amount equal to the tax paid in that other State. Such deduction shall not, however, exceed that part of the tax, as computed before the deduction is given, which is attributable to such items of income derived from that other State.

3. Where in accordance with any provision of this Convention income derived or capital owned by a resident of a Contracting State is exempt from tax in that State, such State may nevertheless, in calculating the amount of tax on the remaining income or capital of such resident, take into account the exempted income or capital.

Article 23 B

CREDIT METHOD

1. Where a resident of a Contracting State derives income or owns capital which, in accordance with the provisions of this Convention, may be taxed in the other Contracting State, the first-mentioned State shall allow as a deduction from the tax on the income of that resident an amount equal to the income tax paid in that other State; and as a deduction from the tax on the capital of that resident, an amount equal to the capital tax paid in that other

State. Such deduction in either case shall not, however, exceed that part of the income tax or capital tax, as computed before the deduction is given, which is attributable, as the case may be, to the income or the capital which may be taxed in that other State.

2. Where, in accordance with any provision of this Convention, income derived or capital owned by a resident of a Contracting State is exempt from tax in that State, such State may nevertheless, in calculating the amount of tax on the remaining income or capital of such resident, take into account the exempted income or capital.

Chapter VI
SPECIAL PROVISIONS

Article 24

NON-DISCRIMINATION

1. Nationals of a Contracting State shall not be subjected in the other Contracting State to any taxation or any requirements connected therewith which is other or more burdensome than the taxation and connected requirements to which nationals of that other State in the same circumstances, in particular with respect to residence, are or may be subjected. This provision shall, notwithstanding the provisions of Article 1, also apply to persons who are not residents of one or both of the Contracting States.

2. Stateless persons who are residents of a Contracting State shall not be subjected in either Contracting State to any taxation or any requirement connected therewith which is other or more burdensome than the taxation and connected requirements to which nationals of the State concerned in the same circumstances, in particular with respect to residence, are or may be subjected.

3. The taxation on a permanent establishment which an enterprise of a Contracting State has in the other Contracting State shall not be less favourably levied in that other State than the taxation levied on enterprises of that other State carrying on the same activities. This provision shall not be construed as obliging a Contracting State to grant to residents of the other Contracting State any personal allowances, reliefs and reductions for taxation

purposes on account of civil status or family responsibilities which it grants to its own residents.

4. Except where the provisions of paragraph 1 of Article 9, paragraph 6 of Article 11, or paragraph 6 of Article 12 apply, interest, royalties and other disbursements paid by an enterprise of a Contracting State to a resident of the other Contracting State shall, for the purpose of determining the taxable profits of such enterprise, be deductible under the same conditions as if they had been paid to a resident of the first-mentioned State. Similarly, any debts of an enterprise of a Contracting State to a resident of the other Contracting State shall, for the purpose of determining the taxable capital of such enterprise, be deductible under the same conditions as if they had been contracted to a resident of the first-mentioned State.

5. Enterprises of a Contracting State, the capital of which is wholly or partly owned or controlled, directly or indirectly, by one or more residents of the other Contracting State, shall not be subjected in the first-mentioned State to any taxation or any requirement connected therewith which is other or more burdensome than the taxation and connected requirements to which other similar enterprises of the first-mentioned State are or may be subjected.

6. The provisions of this Article shall, notwithstanding the provisions of Article 2, apply to taxes of every kind and description.

Article 25

MUTUAL AGREEMENT PROCEDURE

Article 25 (alternative A)

1. Where a person considers that the actions of one or both of the Contracting States result or will result for him in taxation not in accordance with the provisions of this Convention, he may, irrespective of the remedies provided by the domestic law of those States, present his case to the competent authority of the Contracting State of which he is a resident or, if his case comes under paragraph 1 of Article 24, to that of the Contracting State of which he is a national. The case must be presented within three years from the first notification of the action resulting in taxation not in accordance with the provisions of the Convention.

2. The competent authority shall endeavour, if the objection appears to it

to be justified and if it is not itself able to arrive at a satisfactory solution, to resolve the case by mutual agreement with the competent authority of the other Contracting State, with a view to the avoidance of taxation which is not in accordance with this Convention. Any agreement reached shall be implemented notwithstanding any time limits in the domestic law of the Contracting States.

3. The competent authorities of the Contracting States shall endeavour to resolve by mutual agreement any difficulties or doubts arising as to the interpretation or application of the Convention. They may also consult together for the elimination of double taxation in cases not provided for in the Convention.

4. The competent authorities of the Contracting States may communicate with each other directly, including through a joint commission consisting of themselves or their representatives, for the purpose of reaching an agreement in the sense of the preceding paragraphs. The competent authorities, through consultations, may develop appropriate bilateral procedures, conditions, methods and techniques for the implementation of the mutual agreement procedure provided for in this Article.

Article 25 (alternative B)

1. Where a person considers that the actions of one or both of the Contracting States result or will result for him in taxation not in accordance with the provisions of this Convention, he may, irrespective of the remedies provided by the domestic law of those States, present his case to the competent authority of the Contracting State of which he is a resident or, if his case comes under paragraph 1 of Article 24, to that of the Contracting State of which he is a national. The case must be presented within three years from the first notification of the action resulting in taxation not in accordance with the provisions of the Convention.

2. The competent authority shall endeavour, if the objection appears to it to be justified and if it is not itself able to arrive at a satisfactory solution, to resolve the case by mutual agreement with the competent authority of the other Contracting State, with a view to the avoidance of taxation which is not in accordance with this Convention. Any agreement reached shall be implemented notwithstanding any time limits in the domestic law of the Contracting States.

3. The competent authorities of the Contracting States shall endeavour to resolve by mutual agreement any difficulties or doubts arising as to the interpretation or application of the Convention. They may also consult together for the elimination of double taxation in cases not provided for in the Convention.

4. The competent authorities of the Contracting States may communicate with each other directly, including through a joint commission consisting of themselves or their representatives, for the purpose of reaching an agreement in the sense of the preceding paragraphs. The competent authorities, through consultations, may develop appropriate bilateral procedures, conditions, methods and techniques for the implementation of the mutual agreement procedure provided for in this Article.

5. Where,

(a) under paragraph 1, a person has presented a case to the competent authority of a Contracting State on the basis that the actions of one or both of the Contracting States have resulted for that person in taxation not in accordance with the provisions of this Convention, and

(b) the competent authorities are unable to reach an agreement to resolve that case pursuant to paragraph 2 within three years from the presentation of the case to the competent authority of the other Contracting State,

any unresolved issues arising from the case shall be submitted to arbitration if either competent authority so requests. The person who has presented the case shall be notified of the request. These unresolved issues shall not, however, be submitted to arbitration if a decision on these issues has already been rendered by a court or administrative tribunal of either State. The arbitration decision shall be binding on both States and shall be implemented notwithstanding any time limits in the domestic laws of these States unless both competent authorities agree on a different solution within six months after the decision has been communicated to them or unless a person directly affected by the case does not accept the mutual agreement that implements the arbitration decision. The competent authorities of the Contracting States shall by mutual agreement settle the mode of application of this paragraph.

Article 26

EXCHANGE OF INFORMATION

1. The competent authorities of the Contracting States shall exchange such information as is foreseeably relevant for carrying out the provisions of this Convention or to the administration or enforcement of the domestic laws of the Contracting States concerning taxes of every kind and description imposed on behalf of the Contracting States, or of their political subdivisions or local authorities, insofar as the taxation thereunder is not contrary to the Convention. In particular, information shall be exchanged that would be helpful to a Contracting State in preventing avoidance or evasion of such taxes. The exchange of information is not restricted by Articles 1 and 2.

2. Any information received under paragraph 1 by a Contracting State shall be treated as secret in the same manner as information obtained under the domestic laws of that State and it shall be disclosed only to persons or authorities (including courts and administrative bodies) concerned with the assessment or collection of, the enforcement or prosecution in respect of, or the determination of appeals in relation to, the taxes referred to in paragraph 1, or the oversight of the above. Such persons or authorities shall use the information only for such purposes. They may disclose the information in public court proceedings or in judicial decisions.

3. In no case shall the provisions of paragraphs 1 and 2 be construed so as to impose on a Contracting State the obligation:

(a) To carry out administrative measures at variance with the laws and administrative practice of that or of the other Contracting State;

(b) To supply information which is not obtainable under the laws or in the normal course of the administration of that or of the other Contracting State;

(c) To supply information which would disclose any trade, business, industrial, commercial or professional secret or trade process, or information, the disclosure of which would be contrary to public policy (ordre public).

4. If information is requested by a Contracting State in accordance with this Article, the other Contracting State shall use its information gathering measures to obtain the requested information, even though that other State may not need such information for its own tax purposes. The obligation

contained in the preceding sentence is subject to the limitations of paragraph 3 but in no case shall such limitations be construed to permit a Contracting State to decline to supply information solely because it has no domestic interest in such information.

5. In no case shall the provisions of paragraph 3 be construed to permit a Contracting State to decline to supply information solely because the information is held by a bank, other financial institution, nominee or person acting in an agency or a fiduciary capacity or because it relates to ownership interests in a person.

6. The competent authorities shall, through consultation, develop appropriate methods and techniques concerning the matters in respect of which exchanges of information under paragraph 1 shall be made.

Article 27

ASSISTANCE IN THE COLLECTION OF TAXES[①]

1. The Contracting States shall lend assistance to each other in the collection of revenue claims. This assistance is not restricted by Articles 1 and 2. The competent authorities of the Contracting States may by mutual agreement settle the mode of application of this Article.

2. The term "revenue claim" as used in this Article means an amount owed in respect of taxes of every kind and description imposed on behalf of the Contracting States, or of their political subdivisions or local authorities, insofar as the taxation thereunder is not contrary to this Convention or any other instrument to which the Contracting States are parties, as well as interest, administrative penalties and costs of collection or conservancy related to such amount.

3. When a revenue claim of a Contracting State is enforceable under the laws of that State and is owed by a person who, at that time, cannot, under

---

① In some countries, national law, policy or administrative considerations may not allow or justify the type of assistance envisaged under this Article or may require that this type of assistance be restricted, e.g. to countries that have similar tax systems or tax administrations or as to the taxes covered. For that reason, the Article should only be included in the Convention where each State concludes that, based on the factors described in paragraph 1 of the Commentary on the Article, they can agree to provide assistance in the collection of taxes levied by the other State.

the laws of that State, prevent its collection, that revenue claim shall, at the request of the competent authority of that State, be accepted for purposes of collection by the competent authority of the other Contracting State. That revenue claim shall be collected by that other State in accordance with the provisions of its laws applicable to the enforcement and collection of its own taxes as if the revenue claim were a revenue claim of that other State.

4. When a revenue claim of a Contracting State is a claim in respect of which that State may, under its law, take measures of conservancy with a view to ensure its collection, that revenue claim shall, at the request of the competent authority of that State, be accepted for purposes of taking measures of conservancy by the competent authority of the other Contracting State. That other State shall take measures of conservancy in respect of that revenue claim in accordance with the provisions of its laws as if the revenue claim were a revenue claim of that other State even if, at the time when such measures are applied, the revenue claim is not enforceable in the first-mentioned State or is owed by a person who has a right to prevent its collection.

5. Notwithstanding the provisions of paragraphs 3 and 4, a revenue claim accepted by a Contracting State for purposes of paragraph 3 or 4 shall not, in that State, be subject to the time limits or accorded any priority applicable to a revenue claim under the laws of that State by reason of its nature as such. In addition, a revenue claim accepted by a Contracting State for the purposes of paragraph 3 or 4 shall not, in that State, have any priority applicable to that revenue claim under the laws of the other Contracting State.

6. Proceedings with respect to the existence, validity or the amount of a revenue claim of a Contracting State shall not be brought before the courts or administrative bodies of the other Contracting State.

7. Where, at any time after a request has been made by a Contracting State under paragraph 3 or 4 and before the other Contracting State has collected and remitted the relevant revenue claim to the first-mentioned State, the relevant revenue claim ceases to be:

(a) in the case of a request under paragraph 3, a revenue claim of the first-mentioned State that is enforceable under the laws of that State and is owed by a person who, at that time, cannot, under the laws of that State, prevent its collection, or

(b) in the case of a request under paragraph 4, a revenue claim of the first-mentioned State in respect of which that State may, under its laws, take measures of conservancy with a view to ensure its collection, the competent authority of the first-mentioned State shall promptly notify the competent authority of the other State of that fact and, at the option of the other State, the first-mentioned State shall either suspend or withdraw its request.

8. In no case shall the provisions of this Article be construed so as to impose on a Contracting State the obligation:

(a) to carry out administrative measures at variance with the laws and administrative practice of that or of the other Contracting State;

(b) to carry out measures which would be contrary to public policy (ordre public);

(c) to provide assistance if the other Contracting State has not pursued all reasonable measures of collection or conservancy, as the case maybe, available under its laws or administrative practice;

(d) to provide assistance in those cases where the administrative burden for that State is clearly disproportionate to the benefit to be derived by the other Contracting State.

Article 28

MEMBERS OF DIPLOMATIC MISSIONS AND CONSULAR POSTS

Nothing in this Convention shall affect the fiscal privileges of members of diplomatic missions or consular posts under the general rules of international law or under the provisions of special agreements.

Chapter VII
FINAL PROVISIONS

Article 29

ENTRY INTO FORCE

1. This Convention shall be ratified and the instruments of ratification shall be exchanged at __ as soon as possible.

2. The Convention shall enter into force upon the exchange of instruments of ratification and its provisions shall have effect:

(a) (In State A): _____
(b) (In State B): _____

Article 30

TERMINATION

This Convention shall remain in force until terminated by a Contracting State. Either Contracting State may terminate the Convention, through diplomatic channels, by giving notice of termination at least six months before the end of any calendar year after the year __. In such event, the Convention shall cease to have effect:

(a) (In State A): _____
(b) (In State B): _____

TERMINAL CLAUSE

NOTE: The provisions relating to the entry into force and termination and the terminal clause concerning the signing of the Convention shall be drafted in accordance with the constitutional procedure of both Contracting States.

附录二　经合组织税收协定范本(2014年版本)

OECD Model Convention with Respect to Taxes on Income and on Capital

SUMMARY OF THE CONVENTION
Title and Preamble

Chapter I
SCOPE OF THE CONVENTION
　　Article 1　Persons covered
　　Article 2　Taxes covered

Chapter II
DEFINITIONS
　　Article 3　General definitions
　　Article 4　Resident
　　Article 5　Permanent establishment

Chapter III
TAXATION OF INCOME
　　Article 6　Income from immovable property
　　Article 7　Business profits
　　Article 8　Shipping, inland waterways transport and air transport
　　Article 9　Associated enterprises
　　Article 10　Dividends
　　Article 11　Interest
　　Article 12　Royalties
　　Article 13　Capital gains

Article 14 [Deleted]
Article 15 Income from employment
Article 16 Directors' fees
Article 17 Entertainers and sportspersons
Article 18 Pensions
Article 19 Government service
Article 20 Students
Article 21 Other income

Chapter IV
TAXATION OF CAPITAL

Article 22 Capital

Chapter V
METHODS FOR ELIMINATION OF DOUBLE TAXATION

Article 23 A Exemption method
Article 23 B Credit method

Chapter VI
SPECIAL PROVISIONS

Article 24 Non-discrimination
Article 25 Mutual agreement procedure
Article 26 Exchange of information
Article 27 Assistance in the collection of taxes
Article 28 Members of diplomatic missions and consular posts
Article 29 Territorial extension

Chapter VII
FINAL PROVISIONS

Article 30 Entry into force
Article 31 Termination

TITLE OF THE CONVENTION

Convention between (State A) and (State B) with respect to taxes on income and capital[①]

PREAMBLE TO THE CONVENTION[②]

Chapter I
SCOPE OF THE CONVENTION

ARTICLE 1

PERSONS COVERED

This Convention shall apply to persons who are residents of one or both of the Contracting States.

ARTICLE 2

TAXES COVERED

1. This Convention shall apply to taxes on income and on capital imposed on behalf of a Contracting State or of its political subdivisions or local authorities, irrespective of the manner in which they are levied.

2. There shall be regarded as taxes on income and on capital all taxes imposed on total income, on total capital, or on elements of income or of capital, including taxes on gains from the alienation of movable or immovable property, taxes on the total amounts of wages or salaries paid by enterprises, as well as taxes on capital appreciation.

3. The existing taxes to which the Convention shall apply are in particular:

 a) (in State A): ....

 b) (in State B): ....

4. The Convention shall apply also to any identical or substantially similar

---

 ① States wishing to do so may follow the widespread practice of including in the title a reference to either the avoidance of double taxation or to both the avoidance of double taxation and the prevention of fiscal evasion.

 ② The Preamble of the Convention shall be drafted in accordance with the constitutional procedure of both Contracting States.

taxes that are imposed after the date of signature of the Convention in addition to, or in place of, the existing taxes. The competent authorities of the Contracting States shall notify each other of any significant changes that have been made in their taxation laws.

Chapter II
DEFINITIONS

ARTICLE 3
GENERAL DEFINITIONS

1. For the purposes of this Convention, unless the context otherwise requires:

a) the term "person" includes an individual, a company and any other body of persons;

b) the term "company" means any body corporate or any entity that is treated as a body corporate for tax purposes;

c) the term "enterprise" applies to the carrying on of any business;

d) the terms "enterprise of a Contracting State" and "enterprise of the other Contracting State" mean respectively an enterprise carried on by a resident of a Contracting State and an enterprise carried on by a resident of the other Contracting State;

e) the term "international traffic" means any transport by a ship or aircraft operated by an enterprise that has its place of effective management in a Contracting State, except when the ship or aircraft is operated solely between places in the other Contracting State;

f) the term "competent authority" means:
(i) (in State A): ....
(ii) (in State B): ....

g) the term "national", in relation to a Contracting State, means:
(i) any individual possessing the nationality or citizenship of that Contracting State; and
(ii) any legal person, partnership or association deriving its status as such from the laws in force in that Contracting State;

h) the term "business" includes the performance of professional services and of other activities of an independent character.

2. As regards the application of the Convention at any time by a Contracting State, any term not defined therein shall, unless the context otherwise requires, have the meaning that it has at that time under the law of that State for the purposes of the taxes to which the Convention applies, any meaning under the applicable tax laws of that State prevailing over a meaning given to the term under other laws of that State.

ARTICLE 4

RESIDENT

1. For the purposes of this Convention, the term "resident of a Contracting State" means any person who, under the laws of that State, is liable to tax therein by reason of his domicile, residence, place of management or any other criterion of a similar nature, and also includes that State and any political subdivision or local authority thereof. This term, however, does not include any person who is liable to tax in that State in respect only of income from sources in that State or capital situated therein.

2. Where by reason of the provisions of paragraph 1 an individual is a resident of both Contracting States, then his status shall be determined as follows:

a) he shall be deemed to be a resident only of the State in which he has a permanent home available to him; if he has a permanent home available to him in both States, he shall be deemed to be a resident only of the State with which his personal and economic relations are closer (centre of vital interests);

b) if the State in which he has his centre of vital interests cannot be determined, or if he has not a permanent home available to him in either State, he shall be deemed to be a resident only of the State in which he has an habitual abode;

c) if he has an habitual abode in both States or in neither of them, he shall be deemed to be a resident only of the State of which he is a national;

d) if he is a national of both States or of neither of them, the competent authorities of the Contracting States shall settle the question by mutual agreement.

3. Where by reason of the provisions of paragraph 1 a person other than

an individual is a resident of both Contracting States, then it shall be deemed to be a resident only of the State in which its place of effective management is situated.

ARTICLE 5

PERMANENT ESTABLISHMENT

1. For the purposes of this Convention, the term "permanent establishment" means a fixed place of business through which the business of an enterprise is wholly or partly carried on.

2. The term "permanent establishment" includes especially:

a) a place of management;

b) a branch;

c) an office;

d) a factory;

e) a workshop, and

f) a mine, an oil or gas well, a quarry or any other place of extraction of natural resources.

3. A building site or construction or installation project constitutes a permanent establishment only if it lasts more than twelve months.

4. Notwithstanding the preceding provisions of this Article, the term "permanent establishment" shall be deemed not to include:

a) the use of facilities solely for the purpose of storage, display or delivery of goods or merchandise belonging to the enterprise;

b) the maintenance of a stock of goods or merchandise belonging to the enterprise solely for the purpose of storage, display or delivery;

c) the maintenance of a stock of goods or merchandise belonging to the enterprise solely for the purpose of processing by another enterprise;

d) the maintenance of a fixed place of business solely for the purpose of purchasing goods or merchandise or of collecting information, for the enterprise;

e) the maintenance of a fixed place of business solely for the purpose of carrying on, for the enterprise, any other activity of a preparatory or auxiliary character;

f) the maintenance of a fixed place of business solely for any combination of activities mentioned in subparagraphs a) to e), provided that the overall activity of the fixed place of business resulting from this combination is of a preparatory or auxiliary character.

5. Notwithstanding the provisions of paragraphs 1 and 2, where a person — other than an agent of an independent status to whom paragraph 6 applies — is acting on behalf of an enterprise and has, and habitually exercises, in a Contracting State an authority to conclude contracts in the name of the enterprise, that enterprise shall be deemed to have a permanent establishment in that State in respect of any activities which that person undertakes for the enterprise, unless the activities of such person are limited to those mentioned in paragraph 4 which, if exercised through a fixed place of business, would not make this fixed place of business a permanent establishment under the provisions of that paragraph.

6. An enterprise shall not be deemed to have a permanent establishment in a Contracting State merely because it carries on business in that State through a broker, general commission agent or any other agent of an independent status, provided that such persons are acting in the ordinary course of their business.

7. The fact that a company which is a resident of a Contracting State controls or is controlled by a company which is a resident of the other Contracting State, or which carries on business in that other State (whether through a permanent establishment or otherwise), shall not of itself constitute either company a permanent establishment of the other.

Chapter III
TAXATION OF INCOME
ARTICLE 6
INCOME FROM IMMOVABLE PROPERTY

1. Income derived by a resident of a Contracting State from immovable property(including income from agriculture or forestry) situated in the other Contracting State may be taxed in that other State.

2. The term "immovable property" shall have the meaning which it has under the law of the Contracting State in which the property in question is

situated. The term shall in any case include property accessory to immovable property, livestock and equipment used in agriculture and forestry, rights to which the provisions of general law respecting landed property apply, usufruct of immovable property and rights to variable or fixed payments as consideration for the working of, or the right to work, mineral deposits, sources and other natural resources; ships, boats and aircraft shall not be regarded as immovable property.

3. The provisions of paragraph 1 shall apply to income derived from the direct use, letting, or use in any other form of immovable property.

4. The provisions of paragraphs 1 and 3 shall also apply to the income from immovable property of an enterprise.

ARTICLE 7

BUSINESS PROFITS

1. Profits of an enterprise of a Contracting State shall be taxable only in that State unless the enterprise carries on business in the other Contracting State through a permanent establishment situated therein. If the enterprise carries on business as aforesaid, the profits that are attributable to the permanent establishment in accordance with the provisions of paragraph 2 may be taxed in that other State.

2. For the purposes of this Article and Article [23 A] [23 B], the profits that are attributable in each Contracting State to the permanent establishment referred to in paragraph 1 are the profits it might be expected to make, in particular in its dealings with other parts of the enterprise, if it were a separate and independent enterprise engaged in the same or similar activities under the same or similar conditions, taking into account the functions performed, assets used and risks assumed by the enterprise through the permanent establishment and through the other parts of the enterprise.

3. Where, in accordance with paragraph 2, a Contracting State adjusts the profits that are attributable to a permanent establishment of an enterprise of one of the Contracting States and taxes accordingly profits of the enterprise that have been charged to tax in the other State, the other State shall, to the extent necessary to eliminate double taxation on these profits, make an appropriate adjustment to the amount of the tax charged on those profits. In

determining such adjustment, the competent authorities of the Contracting States shall if necessary consult each other.

4. Where profits include items of income which are dealt with separately in other Articles of this Convention, then the provisions of those Articles shall not be affected by the provisions of this Article.

ARTICLE 8

SHIPPING, INLAND WATERWAYS TRANSPORT AND AIR TRANSPORT

1. Profits from the operation of ships or aircraft in international traffic shall be taxable only in the Contracting State in which the place of effective management of the enterprise is situated.

2. Profits from the operation of boats engaged in inland waterways transport shall be taxable only in the Contracting State in which the place of effective management of the enterprise is situated.

3. If the place of effective management of a shipping enterprise or of an inland waterways transport enterprise is aboard a ship or boat, then it shall be deemed to be situated in the Contracting State in which the home harbour of the ship or boat is situated, or, if there is no such home harbour, in the Contracting State of which the operator of the ship or boat is a resident.

4. The provisions of paragraph 1 shall also apply to profits from the participation in a pool, a joint business or an international operating agency.

ARTICLE 9

ASSOCIATED ENTERPRISES

1. Where

a) an enterprise of a Contracting State participates directly or indirectly in the management, control or capital of an enterprise of the other Contracting State, or

b) the same persons participate directly or indirectly in the management, control or capital of an enterprise of a Contracting State and an enterprise of the other Contracting State,

and in either case conditions are made or imposed between the two enterprises in their commercial or financial relations which differ from those which would be made between independent enterprises, then any profits which would, but for those conditions, have accrued to one of the enterprises, but, by reason of those conditions, have not so accrued, may be included in the profits of that enterprise and taxed accordingly.

2. Where a Contracting State includes in the profits of an enterprise of that State — and taxes accordingly — profits on which an enterprise of the other Contracting State has been charged to tax in that other State and the profits so included are profits which would have accrued to the enterprise of the first-mentioned State if the conditions made between the two enterprises had been those which would have been made between independent enterprises, then that other State shall make an appropriate adjustment to the amount of the tax charged therein on those profits. In determining such adjustment, due regard shall be had to the other provisions of this Convention and the competent authorities of the Contracting States shall if necessary consult each other.

ARTICLE 10

DIVIDENDS

1. Dividends paid by a company which is a resident of a Contracting State to a resident of the other Contracting State may be taxed in that other State.

2. However, dividends paid by a company which is a resident of a Contracting State may also be taxed in that State according to the laws of that State, but if the beneficial owner of the dividends is a resident of the other Contracting State, the tax so charged shall not exceed:

a) 5 per cent of the gross amount of the dividends if the beneficial owner is a company (other than a partnership) which holds directly at least 25 per cent of the capital of the company paying the dividends;

b) 15 per cent of the gross amount of the dividends in all other cases.

The competent authorities of the Contracting States shall by mutual agreement settle the mode of application of these limitations. This paragraph shall not affect the taxation of the company in respect of the profits out of which the dividends are paid.

3. The term "dividends" as used in this Article means income from shares, "jouissance" shares or "jouissance" rights, mining shares, founders' shares or other rights, not being debt-claims, participating in profits, as well as income from other corporate rights which is subjected to the same taxation

treatment as income from shares by the laws of the State of which the company making the distribution is a resident.

4. The provisions of paragraphs 1 and 2 shall not apply if the beneficial owner of the dividends, being a resident of a Contracting State, carries on business in the other Contracting State of which the company paying the dividends is a resident through a permanent establishment situated therein and the holding in respect of which the dividends are paid is effectively connected with such permanent establishment. In such case the provisions of Article 7 shall apply.

5. Where a company which is a resident of a Contracting State derives profits or income from the other Contracting State, that other State may not impose any tax on the dividends paid by the company, except insofar as such dividends are paid to a resident of that other State or insofar as the holding in respect of which the dividends are paid is effectively connected with a permanent establishment situated in that other State, nor subject the company's undistributed profits to a tax on the company's undistributed profits, even if the dividends paid or the undistributed profits consist wholly or partly of profits or income arising in such other State.

ARTICLE 11

INTEREST

1. Interest arising in a Contracting State and paid to a resident of the other Contracting State may be taxed in that other State.

2. However, interest arising in a Contracting State may also be taxed in that State according to the laws of that State, but if the beneficial owner of the interest is a resident of the other Contracting State, the tax so charged shall not exceed 10 per cent of the gross amount of the interest. The competent authorities of the Contracting States shall by mutual agreement settle the mode of application of this limitation.

3. The term "interest" as used in this Article means income from debt-claims of every kind, whether or not secured by mortgage and whether or not carrying a right to participate in the debtor's profits, and in particular, income from government securities and income from bonds or debentures, including premiums and prizes attaching to such securities, bonds or debentures. Penalty

charges for late payment shall not be regarded as interest for the purpose of this Article.

4. The provisions of paragraphs 1 and 2 shall not apply if the beneficial owner of the interest, being a resident of a Contracting State, carries on business in the other Contracting State in which the interest arises through a permanent establishment situated therein and the debt-claim in respect of which the interest is paid is effectively connected with such permanent establishment. In such case the provisions of Article 7 shall apply.

5. Interest shall be deemed to arise in a Contracting State when the payer is a resident of that State. Where, however, the person paying the interest, whether he is a resident of a Contracting State or not, has in a Contracting State a permanent establishment in connection with which the indebtedness on which the interest is paid was incurred, and such interest is borne by such permanent establishment, then such interest shall be deemed to arise in the State in which the permanent establishment is situated.

6. Where, by reason of a special relationship between the payer and the beneficial owner or between both of them and some other person, the amount of the interest, having regard to the debt-claim for which it is paid, exceeds the amount which would have been agreed upon by the payer and the beneficial owner in the absence of such relationship, the provisions of this Article shall apply only to the last-mentioned amount. In such case, the excess part of the payments shall remain taxable according to the laws of each Contracting State, due regard being had to the other provisions of this Convention.

ARTICLE 12

ROYALTIES

1. Royalties arising in a Contracting State and beneficially owned by a resident of the other Contracting State shall be taxable only in that other State.

2. The term "royalties" as used in this Article means payments of any kind received as a consideration for the use of, or the right to use, any copyright of literary, artistic or scientific work including cinematograph films, any patent, trade mark, design or model, plan, secret formula or process, or for information concerning industrial, commercial or scientific experience.

3. The provisions of paragraph 1 shall not apply if the beneficial owner of the royalties, being a resident of a Contracting State, carries on business in the other Contracting State in which the royalties arise through a permanent establishment situated therein and the right or property in respect of which the royalties are paid is effectively connected with such permanent establishment. In such case the provisions of Article 7 shall apply.

4. Where, by reason of a special relationship between the payer and the beneficial owner or between both of them and some other person, the amount of the royalties, having regard to the use, right or information for which they are paid, exceeds the amount which would have been agreed upon by the payer and the beneficial owner in the absence of such relationship, the provisions of this Article shall apply only to the last-mentioned amount. In such case, the excess part of the payments shall remain taxable according to the laws of each Contracting State, due regard being had to the other provisions of this Convention.

ARTICLE 13
CAPITAL GAINS

1. Gains derived by a resident of a Contracting State from the alienation of immovable property referred to in Article 6 and situated in the other Contracting State may be taxed in that other State.

2. Gains from the alienation of movable property forming part of the business property of a permanent establishment which an enterprise of a Contracting State has in the other Contracting State, including such gains from the alienation of such a permanent establishment (alone or with the whole enterprise), may be taxed in that other State.

3. Gains from the alienation of ships or aircraft operated in international traffic, boats engaged in inland waterways transport or movable property pertaining to the operation of such ships, aircraft or boats, shall be taxable only in the Contracting State in which the place of effective management of the enterprise is situated.

4. Gains derived by a resident of a Contracting State from the alienation of shares deriving more than 50 per cent of their value directly or indirectly from immovable property situated in the other Contracting State may be taxed in

that other State.

5. Gains from the alienation of any property, other than that referred to in paragraphs 1, 2, 3 and 4, shall be taxable only in the Contracting State of which the alienator is a resident.

[Article 14 - INDEPENDENT PERSONAL SERVICES]
[Deleted]

ARTICLE 15
INCOME FROM EMPLOYMENT

1. Subject to the provisions of Articles 16, 18 and 19, salaries, wages and other similar remuneration derived by a resident of a Contracting State in respect of an employment shall be taxable only in that State unless the employment is exercised in the other Contracting State. If the employment is so exercised, such remuneration as is derived there from may be taxed in that other State.

2. Notwithstanding the provisions of paragraph 1, remuneration derived by a resident of a Contracting State in respect of an employment exercised in the other Contracting State shall be taxable only in the first-mentioned State if:

a) the recipient is present in the other State for a period or periods not exceeding in the aggregate 183 days in any twelve month period commencing or ending in the fiscal year concerned, and

b) the remuneration is paid by, or on behalf of, an employer who is not a resident of the other State, and

c) the remuneration is not borne by a permanent establishment which the employer has in the other State.

3. Notwithstanding the preceding provisions of this Article, remuneration derived in respect of an employment exercised aboard a ship or aircraft operated in international traffic, or aboard a boat engaged in inland waterways transport, may be taxed in the Contracting State in which the place of effective management of the enterprise is situated.

ARTICLE 16
DIRECTORS' FEES

Directors' fees and other similar payments derived by a resident of a

Contracting State in his capacity as a member of the board of directors of a company which is a resident of the other Contracting State may be taxed in that other State.

ARTICLE 17

ENTERTAINERS AND SPORTSPERSONS

1. Notwithstanding the provisions of Article 15, income derived by a resident of a Contracting State as an entertainer, such as a theatre, motion picture, radio or television artiste, or a musician, or as a sportsperson, from that resident's personal activities as such exercised in the other Contracting State, may be taxed in that other State.

2. Where income in respect of personal activities exercised by an entertainer or a sportsperson acting as such accrues not to the entertainer or sportsperson but to another person, that income may, notwithstanding the provisions of Article 15, be taxed in the Contracting State in which the activities of the entertainer or sportsperson are exercised.

ARTICLE 18

PENSIONS

Subject to the provisions of paragraph 2 of Article 19, pensions and other similar remuneration paid to a resident of a Contracting State in consideration of past employment shall be taxable only in that State.

ARTICLE 19

GOVERNMENT SERVICE

1. a) Salaries, wages and other similar remuneration paid by a Contracting State or a political subdivision or a local authority thereof to an individual in respect of services rendered to that State or subdivision or authority shall be taxable only in that State.

b) However, such salaries, wages and other similar remuneration shall be taxable only in the other Contracting State if the services are rendered in that State and the individual is a resident of that State who:

(i) is a national of that State; or

(ii) did not become a resident of that State solely for the purpose of rendering the services.

2. a) Notwithstanding the provisions of paragraph 1, pensions and other

similar remuneration paid by, or out of funds created by, a Contracting State or a political subdivision or a local authority thereof to an individual in respect of services rendered to that State or subdivision or authority shall be taxable only in that State.

b) However, such pensions and other similar remuneration shall be taxable only in the other Contracting State if the individual is a resident of, and a national of, that State.

3. The provisions of Articles 15, 16, 17, and 18 shall apply to salaries, wages, pensions, and other similar remuneration in respect of services rendered in connection with a business carried on by a Contracting State or a political subdivision or a local authority thereof.

ARTICLE 20

STUDENTS

Payments which a student or business apprentice who is or was immediately before visiting a Contracting State a resident of the other Contracting State and who is present in the first-mentioned State solely for the purpose of his education or training receives for the purpose of his maintenance, education or training shall not be taxed in that State, provided that such payments arise from sources outside that State.

ARTICLE 21

OTHER INCOME

1. Items of income of a resident of a Contracting State, wherever arising, not dealt with in the foregoing Articles of this Convention shall be taxable only in that State.

2. The provisions of paragraph 1 shall not apply to income, other than income from immovable property as defined in paragraph 2 of Article 6, if the recipient of such income, being a resident of a Contracting State, carries on business in the other Contracting State through a permanent establishment situated therein and the right or property in respect of which the income is paid is effectively connected with such permanent establishment. In such case the provisions of Article 7 shall apply.

Chapter IV
TAXATION OF CAPITAL

ARTICLE 22

CAPITAL

1. Capital represented by immovable property referred to in Article 6, owned by a resident of a Contracting State and situated in the other Contracting State, may be taxed in that other State.

2. Capital represented by movable property forming part of the business property of a permanent establishment which an enterprise of a Contracting State has in the other Contracting State may be taxed in that other State.

3. Capital represented by ships and aircraft operated in international traffic and by boats engaged in inland waterways transport, and by movable property pertaining to the operation of such ships, aircraft and boats, shall be taxable only in the Contracting State in which the place of effective management of the enterprise is situated.

4. All other elements of capital of a resident of a Contracting State shall be taxable only in that State.

Chapter V
METHODS FOR ELIMINATION OF DOUBLE TAXATION

ARTICLE 23 A

EXEMPTION METHOD

1. Where a resident of a Contracting State derives income or owns capital which, in accordance with the provisions of this Convention, may be taxed in the other Contracting State, the first-mentioned State shall, subject to the provisions of paragraphs 2 and 3, exempt such income or capital from tax.

2. Where a resident of a Contracting State derives items of income which, in accordance with the provisions of Articles 10 and 11, may be taxed in the other Contracting State, the first-mentioned State shall allow as a deduction from the tax on the income of that resident an amount equal to the tax paid in that other State. Such deduction shall not, however, exceed that part of the tax, as computed before the deduction is given, which is attributable to such items of income derived from that other State.

3. Where in accordance with any provision of the Convention income derived or capital owned by a resident of a Contracting State is exempt from tax in that State, such State may nevertheless, in calculating the amount of tax on the remaining income or capital of such resident, take into account the exempted income or capital.

4. The provisions of paragraph 1 shall not apply to income derived or capital owned by a resident of a Contracting State where the other Contracting State applies the provisions of this Convention to exempt such income or capital from tax or applies the provisions of paragraph 2 of Article 10 or 11 to such income.

ARTICLE 23 B
CREDIT METHOD

1. Where a resident of a Contracting State derives income or owns capital which, in accordance with the provisions of this Convention, may be taxed in the other Contracting State, the first-mentioned State shall allow:

a) as a deduction from the tax on the income of that resident, an amount equal to the income tax paid in that other State;

b) as a deduction from the tax on the capital of that resident, an amount equal to the capital tax paid in that other State.

Such deduction in either case shall not, however, exceed that part of the income tax or capital tax, as computed before the deduction is given, which is attributable, as the case may be, to the income or the capital which may be taxed in that other State.

2. Where in accordance with any provision of the Convention income derived or capital owned by a resident of a Contracting State is exempt from tax in that State, such State may nevertheless, in calculating the amount of tax on the remaining income or capital of such resident, take into account the exempted income or capital.

Chapter VI
SPECIAL PROVISIONS

ARTICLE 24
NON-DISCRIMINATION

1. Nationals of a Contracting State shall not be subjected in the other

Contracting State to any taxation or any requirement connected therewith, which is other or more burdensome than the taxation and connected requirements to which nationals of that other State in the same circumstances, in particular with respect to residence, are or may be subjected. This provision shall, notwithstanding the provisions of Article 1, also apply to persons who are not residents of one or both of the Contracting States.

2. Stateless persons who are residents of a Contracting State shall not be subjected in either Contracting State to any taxation or any requirement connected therewith, which is other or more burdensome than the taxation and connected requirements to which nationals of the State concerned in the same circumstances, in particular with respect to residence, are or may be subjected.

3. The taxation on a permanent establishment which an enterprise of a Contracting State has in the other Contracting State shall not be less favourably levied in that other State than the taxation levied on enterprises of that other State carrying on the same activities. This provision shall not be construed as obliging a Contracting State to grant to residents of the other Contracting State any personal allowances, reliefs and reductions for taxation purposes on account of civil status or family responsibilities which it grants to its own residents.

4. Except where the provisions of paragraph 1 of Article 9, paragraph 6 of Article 11, or paragraph 4 of Article 12, apply, interest, royalties and other disbursements paid by an enterprise of a Contracting State to a resident of the other Contracting State shall, for the purpose of determining the taxable profits of such enterprise, be deductible under the same conditions as if they had been paid to a resident of the first-mentioned State. Similarly, any debts of an enterprise of a Contracting State to a resident of the other Contracting State shall, for the purpose of determining the taxable capital of such enterprise, be deductible under the same conditions as if they had been contracted to a resident of the first-mentioned State.

5. Enterprises of a Contracting State, the capital of which is wholly or partly owned or controlled, directly or indirectly, by one or more residents of the other Contracting State, shall not be subjected in the first-mentioned State

to any taxation or any requirement connected therewith which is other or more burdensome than the taxation and connected requirements to which other similar enterprises of the first-mentioned State are or may be subjected.

6. The provisions of this Article shall, notwithstanding the provisions of Article 2, apply to taxes of every kind and description.

ARTICLE 25

MUTUAL AGREEMENT PROCEDURE

1. Where a person considers that the actions of one or both of the Contracting States result or will result for him in taxation not in accordance with the provisions of this Convention, he may, irrespective of the remedies provided by the domestic law of those States, present his case to the competent authority of the Contracting State of which he is a resident or, if his case comes under paragraph 1 of Article 24, to that of the Contracting State of which he is a national. The case must be presented within three years from the first notification of the action resulting in taxation not in accordance with the provisions of the Convention.

2. The competent authority shall endeavour, if the objection appears to it to be justified and if it is not itself able to arrive at a satisfactory solution, to resolve the case by mutual agreement with the competent authority of the other Contracting State, with a view to the avoidance of taxation which is not in accordance with the Convention. Any agreement reached shall be implemented notwithstanding any time limits in the domestic law of the Contracting States.

3. The competent authorities of the Contracting States shall endeavour to resolve by mutual agreement any difficulties or doubts arising as to the interpretation or application of the Convention. They may also consult together for the elimination of double taxation in cases not provided for in the Convention.

4. The competent authorities of the Contracting States may communicate with each other directly, including through a joint commission consisting of themselves or their representatives, for the purpose of reaching an agreement in the sense of the preceding paragraphs.

5. Where,

a) under paragraph 1, a person has presented a case to the competent authority of a Contracting State on the basis that the actions of one or both of the Contracting States have resulted for that person in taxation not in accordance with the provisions of this Convention, and

b) the competent authorities are unable to reach an agreement to resolve that case pursuant to paragraph 2 within two years from the presentation of the case to the competent authority of the other Contracting State,

any unresolved issues arising from the case shall be submitted to arbitration if the person so requests. These unresolved issues shall not, however, be submitted to arbitration if a decision on these issues has already been rendered by a court or administrative tribunal of either State. Unless a person directly affected by the case does not accept the mutual agreement that implements the arbitration decision, that decision shall be binding on both Contracting States and shall be implemented notwithstanding any time limits in the domestic laws of these States. The competent authorities of the Contracting States shall by mutual agreement settle the mode of application of this paragraph. ①

ARTICLE 26
EXCHANGE OF INFORMATION

1. The competent authorities of the Contracting States shall exchange such information as is foreseeably relevant for carrying out the provisions of this Convention or to the administration or enforcement of the domestic laws concerning taxes of every kind and description imposed on behalf of the Contracting States, or of their political subdivisions or local authorities, insofar as the taxation thereunder is not contrary to the Convention. The exchange of information is not restricted by Articles 1 and 2.

2. Any information received under paragraph 1 by a Contracting State shall be treated as secret in the same manner as information obtained under the

---

① In some States, national law, policy or administrative considerations may not allow or justify the type of dispute resolution envisaged under this paragraph. In addition, some States may only wish to include this paragraph in treaties with certain States. For these reasons, the paragraph should only be included in the Convention where each State concludes that it would be appropriate to do so based on the factors described in paragraph 65 of the Commentary on the paragraph. As mentioned in paragraph 74 of that Commentary, however, other States may be able to agree to remove from the paragraph the condition that issues may not be submitted to arbitration if a decision on these issues has already been rendered by one of their courts or administrative tribunals.

domestic laws of that State and shall be disclosed only to persons or authorities (including courts and administrative bodies) concerned with the assessment or collection of, the enforcement or prosecution in respect of, the determination of appeals in relation to the taxes referred to in paragraph 1, or the oversight of the above. Such persons or authorities shall use the information only for such purposes. They may disclose the information in public court proceedings or in judicial decisions. Notwithstanding the foregoing, information received by a Contracting State may be used for other purposes when such information may be used for such other purposes under the laws of both States and the competent authority of the supplying State authorises such use.

3. In no case shall the provisions of paragraphs 1 and 2 be construed so as to impose on a Contracting State the obligation:

a) to carry out administrative measures at variance with the laws and administrative practice of that or of the other Contracting State;

b) to supply information which is not obtainable under the laws or in the normal course of the administration of that or of the other Contracting State;

c) to supply information which would disclose any trade, business, industrial, commercial or professional secret or trade process, or information the disclosure of which would be contrary to public policy (ordre public).

4. If information is requested by a Contracting State in accordance with this Article, the other Contracting State shall use its information gathering measures to obtain the requested information, even though that other State may not need such information for its own tax purposes. The obligation contained in the preceding sentence is subject to the limitations of paragraph 3 but in no case shall such limitations be construed to permit a Contracting State to decline to supply information solely because it has no domestic interest in such information.

5. In no case shall the provisions of paragraph 3 be construed to permit a Contracting State to decline to supply information solely because the information is held by a bank, other financial institution, nominee or person acting in an agency or a fiduciary capacity or because it relates to ownership interests in a person.

ARTICLE 27
ASSISTANCE IN THE COLLECTION OF TAXES[①]

1. The Contracting States shall lend assistance to each other in the collection of revenue claims. This assistance is not restricted by Articles 1 and 2. The competent authorities of the Contracting States may by mutual agreement settle the mode of application of this Article.

2. The term "revenue claim" as used in this Article means an amount owed in respect of taxes of every kind and description imposed on behalf of the Contracting States, or of their political subdivisions or local authorities, insofar as the taxation thereunder is not contrary to this Convention or any other instrument to which the Contracting States are parties, as well as interest, administrative penalties and costs of collection or conservancy related to such amount.

3. When a revenue claim of a Contracting State is enforceable under the laws of that State and is owed by a person who, at that time, cannot, under the laws of that State, prevent its collection, that revenue claim shall, at the request of the competent authority of that State, be accepted for purposes of collection by the competent authority of the other Contracting State. That revenue claim shall be collected by that other State in accordance with the provisions of its laws applicable to the enforcement and collection of its own taxes as if the revenue claim were a revenue claim of that other State.

4. When a revenue claim of a Contracting State is a claim in respect of which that State may, under its law, take measures of conservancy with a view to ensure its collection, that revenue claim shall, at the request of the competent authority of that State, be accepted for purposes of taking measures of conservancy by the competent authority of the other Contracting State. That other State shall take measures of conservancy in respect of that revenue claim in accordance with the provisions of its laws as if the revenue claim were a

---

[①] In some countries, national law, policy or administrative considerations may not allow or justify the type of assistance envisaged under this Article or may require that this type of assistance be restricted, e. g. to countries that have similar tax systems or tax administrations or as to the taxes covered. For that reason, the Article should only be included in the Convention where each State concludes that, based on the factors described in paragraph 1 of the Commentary on the Article, they can agree to provide assistance in the collection of taxes levied by the other State.

revenue claim of that other State even if, at the time when such measures are applied, the revenue claim is not enforceable in the first-mentioned State or is owed by a person who has a right to prevent its collection.

5. Notwithstanding the provisions of paragraphs 3 and 4, a revenue claim accepted by a Contracting State for purposes of paragraph 3 or 4 shall not, in that State, be subject to the time limits or accorded any priority applicable to a revenue claim under the laws of that State by reason of its nature as such. In addition, a revenue claim accepted by a Contracting State for the purposes of paragraph 3 or 4 shall not, in that State, have any priority applicable to that revenue claim under the laws of the other Contracting State.

6. Proceedings with respect to the existence, validity or the amount of a revenue claim of a Contracting State shall not be brought before the courts or administrative bodies of the other Contracting State.

7. Where, at any time after a request has been made by a Contracting State under paragraph 3 or 4 and before the other Contracting State has collected and remitted the relevant revenue claim to the first-mentioned State, the relevant revenue claim ceases to be

a) in the case of a request under paragraph 3, a revenue claim of the first-mentioned State that is enforceable under the laws of that State and is owed by a person who, at that time, cannot, under the laws of that State, prevent its collection, or

b) in the case of a request under paragraph 4, a revenue claim of the first-mentioned State in respect of which that State may, under its laws, take measures of conservancy with a view to ensure its collection

the competent authority of the first-mentioned State shall promptly notify the competent authority of the other State of that fact and, at the option of the other State, the first-mentioned State shall either suspend or withdraw its request.

8. In no case shall the provisions of this Article be construed so as to impose on a Contracting State the obligation:

a) to carry out administrative measures at variance with the laws and administrative practice of that or of the other Contracting State;

b) to carry out measures which would be contrary to public policy (ordre public);

c) to provide assistance if the other Contracting State has not pursued all reasonable measures of collection or conservancy, as the case may be, available under its laws or administrative practice;

d) to provide assistance in those cases where the administrative burden for that State is clearly disproportionate to the benefit to be derived by the other Contracting State.

ARTICLE 28

MEMBERS OF DIPLOMATIC MISSIONS AND CONSULAR POSTS

Nothing in this Convention shall affect the fiscal privileges of members of diplomatic missions or consular posts under the general rules of international law or under the provisions of special agreements.

ARTICLE 29

TERRITORIAL EXTENSION①

1. This Convention may be extended, either in its entirety or with any necessary modifications [to any part of the territory of (State A) or of (State B) which is specifically excluded from the application of the Convention or], to any State or territory for whose international relations (State A) or (State B) is responsible, which imposes taxes substantially similar in character to those to which the Convention applies. Any such extension shall take effect from such date and subject to such modifications and conditions, including conditions as to termination, as may be specified and agreed between the Contracting States in notes to be exchanged through diplomatic channels or in any other manner in accordance with their constitutional procedures.

2. Unless otherwise agreed by both Contracting States, the termination of the Convention by one of them under Article 30 shall also terminate, in the manner provided for in that Article, the application of the Convention [to any part of the territory of (State A) or of (State B) or] to any State or territory to which it has been extended under this Article.

---

① The words between brackets are of relevance when, by special provision, a part of the territory of a Contracting State is excluded from the application of the Convention.

Chapter VII
FINAL PROVISIONS

ARTICLE 30

ENTRY INTO FORCE

1. This Convention shall be ratified and the instruments of ratification shall be exchanged at .... as soon as possible.

2. The Convention shall enter into force upon the exchange of instruments of ratification and its provisions shall have effect:

a) (in State A): ....

c) (in State B): ....

ARTICLE 31

TERMINATION

This Convention shall remain in force until terminated by a Contracting State. Either Contracting State may terminate the Convention, through diplomatic channels, by giving notice of termination at least six months before the end of any calendar year after the year .... In such event, the Convention shall cease to have effect:

a) (in State A): ....

b) (in State B): ....

TERMINAL CLAUSE[①]

[①] The terminal clause concerning the signing shall be drafted in accordance with the constitutional procedure of both Contracting States.